T0313955

THE **PPLI** SOLUTION

THE PPLI SOLUTION

Delivering Wealth Accumulation,
Tax Efficiency, and Asset Protection
Through Private Placement Life Insurance

EDITED BY KIRK LOURY

Bloomberg Press

PRINCETON

This publication contains the authors' opinions and is designed to provide accurate and authoritative infor-mation. It is sold with the understanding that the authors, publisher, and Bloomberg L.P. are not engaged in rendering legal, accounting, investment planning, business management, or other professional advice. The reader should seek the services of a qualified professional for such advice; the authors, publisher, and Bloomberg L.P. cannot be held responsible for any loss incurred as a result of specific investments or plan-ning decisions made by the reader.

First edition published 2005
1 3 5 7 9 10 8 6 4 2

Library of Congress Cataloging-in-Publication Data

The PPLI solution : delivering wealth accumulation, tax efficiency, and asset protection through private placement life insurance / edited by Kirk Loury. -- 1st ed.
    p. cm.
    Includes index.
    ISBN 1-57660-173-0 (alk. paper)
1. Insurance, Life--Variable policies--United States. 2. Variable annuities--United States. 3. Privately placed securities--United States. 4. Estate planning--United States. 5. Investments--United States. I. Title: Private placement life insurance solution. II. Loury, Kirk.
    HG8850.5.P657 2005
    368.32'5--dc22

                                                                        2004023756

Acquired by Jared Kieling

Edited by Mary Ann McGuigan

To my wife, Brenda, whose faith inspires me
and whose support fuels me

CONTENTS

Is it any surprise that a product weighed down with a moniker like private placement variable universal life (PPVUL)—otherwise known as private placement variable life insurance (PPVLI) and private placement life insurance (PPLI)—has yet to be embraced by wealth advisers? Of course, a snappy name hardly ensures that a product will be considered a vital investment tool, but PPLI's forbidding handle certainly mirrors the complexities that have plagued this investment from its earliest days.

Since 2000, however, the affluent market's need for more sophisticated tax-management, wealth-transfer planning, and asset-protection solutions has converged with an unprecedented demand for alternative investments. It is at this juncture that PPLI stands tall as a maturing, flexible platform able to address an array of complex needs cost-effectively.

Given the dramatic advancements in policy structure and investment options as well as validation by the Internal Revenue Service, it's now clear that the time and effort an adviser expends to learn about PPLI's applications will be fruitful. Toward that end, this book has a simple purpose: to be a reference and guidebook for any wealth adviser seeking the knowledge required to identify and articulate the difference PPLI can make in executing a wealth-management plan.

The contributors gathered here to share that knowledge offer not only their skills and understanding but their collective experience as well. This experience is born from the tough and grinding work of pioneers who have pursued PPLI with a fundamental belief that this platform holds great promise in its capacity to deliver the kind of value sought by sophisticated investors and their advisory teams. Indeed, the current policy designs arose as a result of the efforts to minimize unnecessary impediments to effective execution, and the insights reflected in each chapter were gained from handling tough questions and demanding situations. Now the entire wealth-management industry can benefit from the answers, because these pioneering efforts have culminated in a product that's ready for the challenging task of simultaneously preserving and growing wealth.

Each contributor integrates the needed grounding on terminology, concepts, and approaches so that each chapter—whether it's about tax deferral or policy structure or legal compliance—can convey an understanding of PPLI that's accessible even to the novice. The book speaks frankly about past misconceptions, missteps, and misgivings that early adopters have had to overcome. To be sure, each contributor is a proponent of PPLI and its status as a powerful investment tool; nevertheless, important "best practice" boundaries are identified to prevent avoidable failure. PPLI may not fit into every wealth-management plan, but the benefits it can deliver are so substantial and have such broad applications that it's clearly worth the trouble to find out if it does. These contributors believe—as do I—that PPLI will add substantially to the plan's overall effectiveness.

Acknowledgments

I would like to acknowledge my colleagues at Spencer Trask, particularly our chairman, Kevin Kimberlin, all of whom have been tremendous supporters, giving me the freedom to help lead the charge in bringing PPLI into its own as a core wealth-planning tool. Next, it would be difficult to find another industry so widely populated with the kind of professionals I've found in PPLI. Not only are they sophisticated thinkers motivated by a drive to "serve the client"; they're also willing to help neophytes achieve the understanding needed to be successful. The contributors herein exemplify the personal and professional characteristics that make involvement in the PPLI industry so rewarding.

Paul F. Berlin, CLU, is president of Executive Planning, a Chicago firm that specializes in sophisticated uses of life insurance, and he has more than 22 years of experience in the life insurance industry. In 2001, Berlin developed the product chassis—an intellectual property he later sold to MONY—that's now used by hedge fund managers as well as banks in the private placement market. Over the years, he has been featured in numerous trade journals, including a February 1992 article in *Life Association News* titled "Ten Future Legends," which predicted that Berlin's expertise would eventually make him a legend in the industry. Berlin earned his BS degree in finance from Indiana University and his chartered life underwriter degree from the American College. Berlin may be contacted at exec.planning@prodigy.net; the firm's website address is www.executive planning.com.

Jeffrey S. Bortnick, Esq., is a tax partner of the general practice law firm of Kleinberg, Kaplan, Wolff & Cohen, in New York, and has more than 22 years of experience in a broad range of tax and estates matters. Bortnick frequently advises hedge funds, private-equity funds, and fund managers on tax issues related to fund formation, operations, and investments. He has written articles for industry publications and lectured on many tax issues related to hedge fund and private placement variable insurance. Bortnick earned his JD and LLM degrees in taxation from NYU School of Law and is a member of the Association of the Bar of the City of New York. He may be contacted at JBortnick@kkwc.com.

Richard Brindisi is an expert in the field of private placement life insurance and other structured insurance programs for wealthy individuals. He was the managing director of marketing for the private placement group at Sun Life Financial before leaving to pursue other interests in the insurance and wealth-management industries. Brindisi has been involved in all aspects of putting together privately placed insurance and annuity contracts for wealthy investors and institutions. Before joining Sun Life, Brindisi was a trust officer at Raymond James Trust and later a senior tax and estate-planning consultant for Raymond James Financial, where he built the private placement insurance program in his role as a consultant to financial advisers for their high-net-worth clients. Brindisi is a graduate of the T.C. Williams School of Law at the University of Richmond.

Leslie N. Brockhurst is president of Clark Consulting's Executive Benefits Practice and has been with the firm since 1995. He specializes in the design of executive benefit programs and the funding of benefit-related corporate liabilities. He was previously managing director of the Northwest Region, responsible for the firm's executive compensation and benefit consulting for the region. Brockhurst has more than 20 years of experience in public and private business sectors. Before joining Clark Consulting, he held senior executive positions in human resources at McDonnell Douglas and Arizona Public Service, the state's largest investor-owned utility. Brockhurst's experience includes the design and implementation of executive and employee benefits, installation of strategically driven compensation and performance enhancement systems, and restructuring and subsequent redeployment of human resources. Brockhurst received his BS degree in physics and mathematics from Bishop's University in Lennoxville, Quebec, and received postgraduate degrees in education and business from McGill University in Montreal and Webster University in St. Louis.

Susan Bruno is a principal of Beacon Wealth Consulting, LLC. She specializes in providing tax-, estate-, and financial-planning counseling to high-net-worth individuals. She is a certified financial planner, CPA, and personal financial specialist (PFS). Bruno has developed and delivered seminars on topics such as managing stock options for maximum value, wealth-transfer techniques, and private placement life insurance for individuals of ultra high net worth. Bruno was appointed to the faculty for the American Banking Association Private Wealth Management School to speak on life insurance topics, and was also selected as speaker for the Private Wealth Management MBA program at Columbia University. Bruno is also the finance chair and an executive board member of the Lance Armstrong Foundation as well as a board member of the Lance Armstrong Foundation Endowment. Before forming Beacon Wealth Consulting, LLC, Bruno was a principal of Winged Keel Financial

Advisors and a senior tax manager at Price Waterhouse in Stamford, Connecticut. She graduated magna cum laude from Fairfield University in 1984, where she received a BS in accounting. Bruno may be contacted at sbruno@beacon-wealth.com.

Mike Chong leads the Law Practice Group for MassMutual's Private Client Group and Large Corporate Markets business. He has been with MassMutual since 1994 and has 20 years of experience in the areas of securities, tax, and insurance law. Before joining MassMutual, Chong served as counsel to Travelers Insurance Company, Home Life Insurance Company, and CIGNA. Admitted to the Pennsylvania Bar in 1983 and the Connecticut Bar in 1984, Chong is a 1980 graduate of Fairleigh Dickinson University and a 1983 graduate of Pennsylvania State University Law School.

Keven de la Cruz is vice president of ICMG, the private placement division of Hartford Life, the sixth-largest life insurance group in the nation based on assets and a subsidiary of the Hartford Financial Services Group. As an innovator in this field, ICMG has become one of the leaders in the private placement insurance market, with more $20 billion in separate-account assets. De la Cruz is responsible for high-net-worth private placement sales and has guided both the implementation of alternative assets within the PPVUL product structure and the development of distribution relationships. Before joining Hartford Life/ICMG, de la Cruz worked as a consulting actuary for Navisys, a systems-development subsidiary of Met Life, and at Transamerica Occidental Life in Los Angeles, where he was responsible for illustration software development and Internet marketing support. He began his career at MCG Northwest in Portland, Oregon, as an associate actuary providing funding and benefit analysis in support of large COLI transactions. A fellow of the Society of Actuaries and a member of the American Academy of Actuaries, de la Cruz holds a BA in mathematics/philosophy from Reed College.

Anne Melissa Dowling joined MassMutual in 1996 as head of its Large Corporate Markets group, a collection of several insurance businesses serving the corporate, banking, law firm, and ultra-high-net-worth markets. At MassMutual, Dowling created a stand-alone business entity with its own product-development, legal, sales-support, client-service, and systems-development and support units, as well as investment-strategy, operations, and due diligence units. Her division's revenue grew from $85 million in 1996 to more than $1 billion, becoming one of MassMutual Financial Group's most profitable units. The division is known in the marketplace for the creativity of its product design balanced by strict underwriting guidelines. In 2002, Dowling spearheaded the MMFG Wealth Management strategy as a new business focus and created the Women's Markets Initiative to capitalize on the enormous opportunities to market to and recruit from a largely underserved market in financial services. She came to MassMutual from Connecticut Mutual, where she was chief investment officer, and from Travelers and Aetna, where she focused on securities, derivatives, and currency management. She serves as a trustee on a number of not-for-profit boards, including Amherst College, the University of Connecticut Foundation, Metro Hartford Chamber of Commerce, Wadsworth Athenaeum (Board of Electors), and First Book-Hartford (literacy program), and is a senior fellow of the American Leadership Forum. Dowling is a chartered financial analyst and received her BA in fine arts and French literature from Amherst College and her MBA from Columbia University.

Daniel T. Hayden is managing director of the Client Advisory Group at Van Hedge Fund Advisors International (VAN) and portfolio manager for certain VAN managed fund of funds. VAN, a research-focused hedge fund advisory firm specializing in institutional and retail clients, offers customized portfolio consulting and manages a range of in-house products. Hayden joined VAN in 2001 as a member of the sales and consulting team and subsequently served as the firm's director of research. Hayden had been senior vice president and manager of portfolio services in the Capital Markets Division of a large regional bank. Before entering the investment-banking business, he spent 10 years in public accounting and was a senior manager with KPMG. A certified public accountant, Hayden holds Series 7, Series 3, and Series 63 licenses and earned a BBA from the University of Notre Dame. He may be contacted at dhayden@vanhedge.com.

Brent Kinetz has been providing design and implementation services to private and corporate clients for more than 15 years. He joined Winged Keel Group as director of design services in January 1997 and became a principal in January 1999. Kinetz holds a chartered life underwriter (CLU) designation and is a graduate of New York University.

Al W. King III is co-founder, co-chairman, and co-chief executive officer of South Dakota Trust Company, a state-chartered trust boutique and financial-advisory company for the wealthy, doing business in all 50 states. King was managing director and national director of estate planning for Citigroup and was co-founder and vice chairman of Citicorp Trust, South Dakota. He is a member of the editorial board of *Trusts and*

Estates magazine, and his articles on estate planning have been published by several industry publications. King frequently addresses professional organizations, special interest groups, and general audiences on estate and financial planning. He received a BA cum laude from Holy Cross College, a JD from Syracuse University Law School, and an LLM in tax law from Boston University School of Law. King may be contacted at www.sdtrustco.com.

John B. Lawson has amassed a broad range of experience in financial, estate, business, insurance, and investment planning. He is a certified financial planner licensee and a chartered life underwriter (CLU); holds licenses for Group I Individual Life, Variable Life, NASD Series 6, 7, and 63; and is a member of the Association for Advanced Life Underwriting (AALU). Lawson has a life insurance brokerage license in Bermuda and carries a Bermuda work permit during the facilitation of offshore transactions. He has lectured on the subject of private placement variable life insurance planning and products to various groups, including the Thirty-Seventh Annual Philip E. Heckerling Institute on Estate Planning (2003), M Financial Group (2003), and American Bankers Association (2004). Lawson also participates in private briefings with asset managers and brokerage firms, and addresses numerous insurance conferences on the subject of private placement life insurance.

Kirk Loury is president and chief investment officer for Spencer Trask Asset Management, a wholly owned registered investment adviser of Spencer Trask & Co. Spencer Trask is a venture capital firm catering to the private-equity needs of high-net-worth individuals and investment advisers. As chief investment officer, Loury directs the investment analysis of hedge funds and venture capital as asset classes, sets investment policy and practices, oversees portfolio administration, manages due diligence activities, and maintains the firm's external investment and distribution relationships. As a champion of private placement life insurance, Loury has taken on a broad industry role as an educator and portfolio adviser. He received his BS from the University of Colorado, Boulder, and his MBA from the Harvard Graduate School of Business Administration. Loury may be contacted at kloury@comcast.net.

Pierce H. McDowell III is the co-founder, co-chairman, and co-chief executive officer of South Dakota Trust Company, a state-chartered trust boutique and financial-advisory firm for the wealthy, doing business in all 50 states. McDowell is a member of the South Dakota Bar Association's Real Property, Probate & Trust Law section and serves on its

Probate and Trust Committee. He has been quoted by *Forbes* and other publications and has been published on the advantages of South Dakota trust law. McDowell received a BS from Arizona State University and a JD degree from the University of South Dakota. He may be contacted at www.sdtrustco.com.

Maureen Nelson is an attorney with the international law firm Skadden, Arps, Slate, Meagher & Flom, in Washington, D.C., where she advises insurance companies, fund managers, insurance brokers, investment advisers, and their clients on a variety of federal and state tax issues relating to the structure, sale, acquisition, management, and ownership of insurance products, including variable insurance and annuity policies and corporate-owned life insurance. She also assists clients in developing alternative risk-management solutions and financial structures incorporating insurance products and advises insurance companies on tax planning and controversy issues arising from routine business operations, mergers, demutualizations, privatizations, and restructurings. Nelson regularly represents taxpayers before the Internal Revenue Service on a variety of compliance and controversy matters affecting corporations, partnerships, and individuals. Before joining Skadden, Arps, she was with the National Office of the Office of Chief Counsel, Internal Revenue Service, where she worked primarily on audit and tax litigation matters affecting life insurance and property-and-casualty insurance companies and their products and served as the coordinator for both the Life Insurance Industry Specialization Program and the Property and Casualty Insurance Industry Specialization Program. Nelson also served as National Office counsel to the Corporate Owned Life Insurance issue specialist. She is a speaker and panelist at many conferences for private bar, industry, and government professionals, including the American Bar Association, Section of Taxation (Committee on Insurance Companies and Products); Federal Bar Association Insurance Tax Seminar; Hartford Institute on Insurance Taxation; and National Association of Independent Insurers. Nelson is admitted to the bar in the District of Columbia and Maryland.

Jeremiah Riddle is an independent consultant specializing in advice and product solutions for affluent clients and their advisers both international and domestic. These solutions often involve private placement life and annuity policies. Riddle was managing director in the Life Practice of Marsh Private Client Services, a unit of Marsh & McLennan Companies. He was partner in charge of Deloitte & Touche's Actuarial, Benefits and Compensation Consulting group's New York office before joining Marsh. Riddle received his BBA from Baruch College (CUNY) and is an associate of the Society of Actuaries, a member of the Society of Pension Actuaries, and an enrolled actuary under ERISA. He may be contacted at JRiddle127@aol.com.

Gideon Rothschild is a partner with the New York law firm Moses & Singer, where he is co-head of the Private Client Services Group. He is a fellow of the American College of Trust and Estates Counsel and a member of the editorial advisory boards of the Bureau of National Affairs's *Tax Management, Trusts & Estates,* and *Practical Accountant.* Rothschild is the co-author of the BNA Tax Management portfolio on Asset Protection Planning, published by Tax Management, and the chair of the American Bar Association's International Estate Planning Committee and past chair of the ABA's Committee on Asset Protection Planning of the Section of Real Property, Probate and Trust Law. Rothschild is an adjunct professor at New York Law School and the University of Miami Law School Graduate Program and is licensed as a certified public accountant. He may be contacted at grothschild@mosessinger.com.

Daniel S. Rubin is a partner with the New York law firm Moses & Singer and a member of the firm's Private Client Services Group. He earned a bachelor's degree from the Elliott School of International Affairs of the George Washington University; a JD degree, cum laude, from Brooklyn Law School; and an LLM, in taxation, from the New York University School of Law. Rubin concentrates his practice in domestic and international estate and asset-protection planning for high-net-worth families. He is also a frequent lecturer to professional groups and is the author of numerous articles on estate and asset-protection planning matters for various professional and scholarly publications. He may be contacted at drubin@mosessinger.com.

Ronald J. Surz is president of PPCA, an investment-technology firm in San Clemente, California, specializing in performance evaluation and attribution. He serves on various boards and councils, including the Investment Management Consultants Association (IMCA) Board of Directors; the IMCA Monitor Editorial Board; IMCA Standards of Practice Board Chair; FinanceWare.com Advisory Board; AIMR Investment Performance Council; AIMR After-Tax Performance Subcommittee; Risk Controlled Growth (RCG) Absolute Return Fund LLP Advisory Board; Capital Markets Consultants Advisory Board; Optivisor Advisory Board; President of the Southern California Financial Consultants Society. Surz is published regularly in *Pensions and Investments, Senior Consultant, HorsesMouth,* and the *IMCA Monitor.* He earned an MBA in finance at the University of

Chicago and an MS in applied mathematics at the University of Illinois and holds a CIMA (certified investment management analyst) designation. His firm's web address is www.PPCA-Inc.com.

George Van is chairman and founder of Van Hedge Fund Advisors International, LLC, and its affiliates (VAN). VAN is a research-focused hedge fund advisory firm focusing on institutional and retail clients. The firm offers customized portfolio consulting and manages a range of in-house products. Since 1992, Van and his associates have been involved in portfolio construction and research on alternative investments, and he directed the first research on reward/risk characteristics of hedge funds, using a large statistical sample. Van is internationally recognized as an authority on hedge funds, has been interviewed frequently by the international media, and has published numerous articles on hedge funds. Van is frequently asked to speak to professional investors at hedge fund symposiums. Before he began working on alternative investments, Van managed his family's portfolio, following a career as founder and manager of large health-care companies. Over the years, Van has served as a director of various national and international organizations and held teaching appointments at the University of Alberta. He received a BA degree from McGill University, Montreal, Canada, in 1961; a DHA degree from the University of Toronto in 1963; and various academic honors. He may be contacted at gvan@vanhedge.com.

Mark Watson is a vice president with Asset Management Advisors (AMA), a multifamily office that provides customized, objective wealth-management solutions for high-net-worth individuals and their families. AMA, an affiliate of SunTrust Banks, is headquartered in Palm Beach, Florida, and maintains local offices in Atlanta, Charlotte, Greenwich, Miami, Orlando, and Washington, D.C. Before joining AMA, Watson was a tax partner with KPMG, where he specialized in estate planning. He is a certified public accountant, a certified financial planner, and a personal financial specialist. Watson received an undergraduate degree in finance and a master's degree in taxation from Texas A&M University. He is based in AMA's Orlando office and may be contacted at mark.watson@amaglobal.com.

Peter M. Williams is founder and president of Peter M. Williams and Company, a member firm of M Financial Group. With more than 25 years of experience, Williams has become a recognized leader in the design and marketing of sophisticated wealth-transfer strategies for individuals of ultra high net worth. He has considerable expertise in offshore/onshore private placement life insurance, premium financing design, and loan negotiation. Williams has participated in numerous forums, assisting insurance companies in private placement product design and product pricing. He is a frequent lecturer on private placement life insurance and premium financing to advisers of ultra-high-net-worth individuals. He has earned chartered life underwriter and chartered financial consultant designations from the American College, is a member of the American Association for Life Underwriters, and is a licensed securities principal. He earned his BBA from Stetson University. He may be contacted at peterwilliamsco@cfl.rr.com.

THE PPLI SOLUTION

PART ONE

The Multipurpose Policy

In wealth management—as in any professional-services business —there's really only one performance standard: Do the solutions executed truly meet client needs? If so, business grows; if not, business shrinks.

That's why the chapters in this section don't merely address how private placement life insurance (PPLI) works; they describe the wide range of benefits it can deliver. As John Lawson explains in the opening chapter, PPLI's initial success arose from a problem-solving approach to a client's needs for tax management and asset protection.

It's safe to say that *every* affluent client is likely to have financial concerns that require personalized solutions for risk management, tax management, asset protection, estate planning, and trust management. PPLI can play a role in all of those areas. And for corporate executives, an extremely valuable PPLI application has emerged in executive benefits. The chapters in this section map the territory and provide clear direction on how PPLI functions to address critical wealth-management needs.

CHAPTER 1

An Introduction to PPLI

JOHN B. LAWSON

The road private placement life insurance (PPLI) has traveled to come into its own has been a bumpy one and hardly straight. But what was once a shadowy side business is now a legitimate market, with a foundation solid enough for growth. PPLI is the most recent innovation within the life insurance industry for superaffluent investors (individuals with $10 million or more in liquid net worth). It is a variable universal life (VUL) insurance transaction that occurs within a private placement offering. Private placement adds the flexibility to VUL's product construction, pricing, and asset-management offerings. Because the product is sold through a private placement memorandum (PPM), every transaction can be individually negotiated and custom designed for the investor. The tax benefits it offers to policy owners are available from few other investment vehicles, particularly since they accrue without the need for complex trust structures.

To fully understand PPLI policies and the advantages they make possible, we must look to the basics of life insurance itself.

Life Insurance: Where It Starts

Of the two basic types of life insurance available—term and permanent coverage—term is considered the most cost-effective way to purchase a life insurance death benefit for a relatively short period. But it's the permanent contract that provides buyers with the unique tax benefits that have helped create the PPLI market.

The key distinguishing factor of permanent coverage is that it has a cash value that accumulates on a tax-favored basis inside the product. The policy is funded over one or more years and is intended to last the entire lifetime of the insured. The premiums are typically much higher than they are for a term policy for the same death benefit, but the value of the product is to front load or level the premium amount so that the coverage lasts at least until the insured reaches age 100. This difference is important because it lays the foundation for the tax benefits that come with permanent life insurance products. These benefits help the policy owner grow the cash value that covers the higher costs of insurance charged as an insured ages, without a corresponding increase in premium payments.

The larger early premiums combined with tax-free growth make it possible to pay lower total premiums over the lifetime of the insured. This is especially important considering what cumulative term costs would be over an insured's lifetime. If term were the only option available to buyers, there would be very little coverage purchased that lasts through life expectancy.

Permanent life insurance has a long history in the United States as a tax-advantaged long-term wealth-creation, savings, and investment vehicle. As long as a permanent contract complies with U.S. tax rules, it's entitled to preferential tax treatment. The Internal Revenue Code (IRC) sets forth the testing required for a permanent policy to ensure that it qualifies and remains compliant as a life insurance contract under U.S. tax law.

With a properly designed and legally compliant contract, which is typically assumed as a given when working with the larger, more highly respected U.S. life insurance companies, a policy owner can accumulate tax-deferred investments by paying premiums into a policy. The ultimate death benefit on that policy will one day be paid to the beneficiary free of all income taxes. Once the premiums are paid (often referred to as the investment amount in a policy), these investment benefits accrue under decades-old tax laws as follows:

- ❑ The cash value of the policy can grow free of current taxation, and investment income credited under a life insurance contract is not subject to current taxation.
- ❑ The policy owner retains tax-free access to the cash value through the use of withdrawals up to basis (basis being the amount of paid-in premium) and/or low-cost loans from the carrier, which uses the appreciated cash value as collateral. This tax-preferred access to liquidity is available only from a nonmodified endowment contract (see chapter 2).
- ❑ The death benefit amounts, including any accumulated investment income, received by a beneficiary of a life insurance contract are not subject to income tax.

As a planning tool, life insurance in some states offers an additional benefit in that the cash value (and in some instances, the death benefit) of a life policy is considered an "exempt asset," which means it is statutorily protected in the event of bankruptcy and cannot be claimed by creditors if a judgment is awarded against the owner or beneficiaries (see chapter 4). This unique feature varies by state but is an additional benefit of owning a life insurance policy in about 20 states.

Finally, permanent policies can be written on more than one life, which is the so-called second-to-die or joint-and-survivor contract. With this design, the investment horizon is substantially extended because the contract will not pay a death benefit until the death of the second insured under the contract.

Private placement deferred annuities (PPDA) have been more popular than PPLI to date mainly because they are so simple to implement. They typically involve only a one- or two-page application, and no physical or financial underwriting is required. PPDA tax benefits and asset-protection issues are similar to the benefits of life insurance in that the investment amount grows free of current income taxation. At some point, however, assuming the contract has an investment gain, either the annuity contract owner or the beneficiary will be required to pay income taxes on the gain at the short-term capital gains rate. That makes PPDA an attractive mechanism for deferring current taxation, but it does not have the preferred lifetime access to cash value on a tax-deferred basis or an income tax–free death benefit as do life insurance contracts. For this reason, informed investors typically prefer the PPLI transaction when the ultimate goal is current tax deferral with future access to cash value during the investor's lifetime.

Whole Life and Universal Life Insurance

The architecture of a permanent life policy, often referred to as the *chassis,* typically takes one of two forms. The first is a whole life contract; the second is a universal life contract. The whole life chassis is the older of the two and is somewhat antiquated for today's market. It has a fixed death benefit, a fixed premium amount that must be paid each year, and stated guarantees with respect to the coverage and a portion of the cash value. With whole life, if the stated premium is paid every year, the policy owner is guaranteed to have the stated death benefit to contract maturity (often defined as age 94 to 100).

One problem with whole life coverage is that it is extremely inflexible. But the more important drawback of whole life policies when considered for purchase by sophisticated investors is the lack of disclosure to the buyer of the underlying costs of the policy—a problem often referred to as the "black box." Basically, it's impossible for anyone to break out the costs of the policy, making it hard to determine whether the insurance company is pricing the product fairly. The insurance company declares an annual dividend, and the policy performs based on this unilateral declaration by the insurance company. Although whole life does include guarantees that might be important to some buyers, there are newer products that make the whole life chassis obsolete for the affluent buyer (people with a liquid net worth exceeding $5 million).

The second type of permanent contract, universal life (UL), was created to address many of the complaints buyers and insurance agents expressed regarding the black box. UL products were not widely available until it became possible to arm the agent with point-of-sale computing power. Older whole life products were designed so that an agent could simply consult a rate book to determine an annual premium amount. But with UL, which was built to have flexible premium payments and simplified death-benefit changes, premiums could not be illustrated or modeled without the use of a personal computer. This new and updated product provides much more flexibility and allows the purchaser to see the explicit charges in the contract.

This kind of transparency provides the buyer clarity regarding the amount the company is charging, as well as full disclosure regarding the guaranteed maximum the company can charge at any future time. The sophisticated investor gains the ability to analyze all elements in the contract and make informed cost comparisons. Although UL products do offer many levels of guarantees, they are not the rigid guarantees that whole life products provide. Therefore, the product is more flexible and requires more knowledge to understand, transact, and service after the sale. Despite the increased complexity, most clients quickly understand the economics of a UL product, whereas they never understood the black box associated with a whole life policy. The greatest benefit to working with UL products is the flexibility and the transparency of costs associated with the policy.

Most illustrations represented as computer printouts for UL contracts include a ledger of all costs and the assumed earnings on cash value in the contract, typically shown on a year-to-year basis. This makes it easy to explain and illustrate what happens to the money in the contract, and showing how different assumptions affect the performance of the policy over time is a simple matter (see chapter 11). UL performance depends heavily on a factor called the *crediting rate,* or the earnings rate attributable to the cash value within the product. This rate tends to track long-term corporate bond yields.

Often, when UL contracts are sold, insurance agents illustrate what happens to the contract at the current crediting rate, at the minimum guaranteed rate, and also at a midpoint on the scale. This is done through a sophisticated software program that produces a policy illustration and shows what can happen if certain assumptions occur after the policy is purchased. But there is no way to predict exactly what will happen to interest rates, mortality experience, or carrier profitability after a contract is sold, so the illustration is simply an assumption (see chapter 11).

Within a universal life illustration, it's common to look at different premium streams as well as changes in the death benefit. Premium payments can be increased, decreased, or left unpaid based on the policy owner's discretion with no prior consent from the insurance company. For this reason, a universal life product is often referred to as a flexible premium chassis because it provides the maximum flexibility to investors. The policy owner may determine the frequency and amount of premium payments, subject to minimum policy requirements that there be enough in the cash value account to pay the policy charges and the maximum premium guidelines to keep the contract within the definition of life insurance under IRC § 7702.

The maximum premium guidelines are driven by one of two tests under IRC § 7702—either the guideline premium test (GPT) or the cash value accumulation test (CVAT). Under both tests, there is a maximum amount of premium that can be paid into a contract without creating a modified endowment contract (MEC). Although slightly different, both tests are based on factors such as the age, sex, and health status of the insured and the amount of death benefit in the contract.

The transparency inherent in a UL policy requires the insurance company to closely monitor the disclosed charges in order to remain competitive in the marketplace. If a company's charges become uncompetitive, the policy owner can exchange the policy for a new one with another company, using a tax-free exchange under IRC § 1035. (The caveat for a 1035 exchange is that the insured person must remain in good health.) This factor is important in the process of keeping consumers informed and in keeping companies honest about future charges in a contract. Generally, sophisticated life insurance buyers tend to be much more comfortable with a universal life contract rather than a whole life contract.

In both whole life and UL products, the cash values are invested in conservative fixed-income investments within the insurance company's "general account." General accounts of life insurance companies are heavily regulated, which limits the types of investments that can be made within them. In addition to the investment restrictions, a key disadvantage of general-account investments is that the cash values are subject to the company's creditors. Essentially, the policy owner is a general creditor of the insurance company, and in the event of bankruptcy, the policy owners could lose their cash values to other secured creditors. Therefore, company creditworthiness over a long projected period can be important. For most policy owners, this risk is not a practical concern, but with large, multimillion-dollar contracts, these issues become very important to prospective purchasers.

Variable Life Insurance

In response to the shortcomings of whole and universal life, insurance companies created a new product called a *variable universal life contract,* or VUL. These variable policies include a unique feature called a *separate account,* which is an actual account where the cash values are held. The separate account segregates the cash values of the policy from the general account of the insurance company for protection from the company's creditors in the event of insolvency.

State law dictates the separate-account protection applicable to the company's VUL cash values, but most states and many foreign jurisdictions have laws providing statutory protection of the cash values invested in separate accounts. Separate accounts also enable the policy owner to invest the cash values outside the restricted limits of the general account and take on the investment performance risk of the policy.

A separate account can be invested in anything from fixed-income funds to emerging-market funds and everything in between. Potentially higher long-term rates of return from equity investments can directly benefit the policy owner through superior contract performance. Conversely, if the equity investment experience is less than the crediting rates of UL policies, the policy could underperform a similar UL policy with cash values invested in the general account. Although these separate accounts provide an opportunity for quality professional investment management, diversification and investor-control rules for variable policies under IRC § 817 (see chapter 12) must be observed.

The basic cost difference between a variable policy and a UL policy is the added expense of a professional manager who will be responsible for the investments within each separate account. Many sophisticated investors welcome the equity exposure and understand that the purchase of a life insurance policy is a long-term investment that should be appropriately matched with long-term needs and objectives (see chapter 8).

VUL policies typically are registered products and their sale is highly regulated, requiring a prospectus as the offering document with each policy. Agents selling these VUL products are required to be licensed to sell both insurance and securities.

Private Placement Life Insurance

PPLI was first used more than 10 years ago in the U.S. corporate-owned life insurance (COLI) market as a tool to fund deferred-compensation obligations through extremely large institutional transactions (see chapter 7). The original products were essentially primitive versions of registered products with a single purpose: to lower the insurance agent's commission in order to make the product more attractive to the large corporate buyer. Early COLI contracts were geared specifically toward the cost structure of the policy and were not expected to expand investment options for the corporate buyer.

The market for individual policies, which got started in the offshore markets less than 10 years ago, took the basic COLI policy structure and kept its cost benefits, but shifted the primary focus to the investment options within the contract. The change of emphasis was an effort to appeal to the superaffluent investor. This new emphasis enabled the use of hedge funds, hedge fund of funds, structured products, private equity, and other unique tax-inefficient investments inside the policy, which themselves are typically distributed through private placement offerings. Now, a large investor can access the same type of sophisticated and exclusive investments found in his taxable portfolio, but can do so within the context of a life insurance policy. Superaffluent buyers can grow their tax-inefficient assets tax deferred, gain access to these assets during their lifetime, gain asset protection, and receive an income tax–free death benefit for the estate.

The overriding question, of course, is what do these benefits cost? A competitive PPLI policy from a reputable U.S. or offshore insurance company should cost less than 100 basis points of cash value annually once all of the premiums are paid into the policy. All insurance company expenses, structuring, and servicing compensation are included in the 1 percent charge. Such a low fee represents a drastic departure from a typical retail expense-and-compensation structure. The 1 percent does not include the asset-management fee for the selected investment managers; however, the same management fees would be paid whether the investment was held inside or outside an insurance policy.

History of the Market

Today, a number of companies, both onshore and offshore, offer PPLI contracts. Until a few years ago, there was substantially more activity in offshore jurisdictions than within the United States. The profusion of offshore activity resulted directly from regulatory pressure and undue bureaucracy. Within the United States, we've elected to regulate insurance products state by state. There are 50 regulatory bodies and 50 different sets of laws. As one might imagine, it's difficult for a U.S. carrier to provide cutting-edge innovation and achieve multistate distribution in a short period. It's also very expensive and time consuming for insurance companies to introduce and sell products nationwide.

This regulatory albatross gave the offshore market a definite advantage because the laws and regulations of insurance in many offshore jurisdictions such as Bermuda, Cayman Islands, Ireland, and Liechtenstein are clear and straightforward. This clarity provided the ultimate flexibility for insurance companies domiciled in these jurisdictions, but it also meant the buyer had to be wary. Most of these jurisdictions have few consumer protection mechanisms outside of a brilliant bankruptcy process. Therefore, many companies reaped the benefit of moving offshore by teaming up with or creating insurance companies domiciled in these business-friendly non-U.S. jurisdictions. Interestingly, these companies achieve no tax benefits by being offshore when their focus is on the U.S. customer; the only real advantage is the absence of bureaucratic regulations and, some would say, excessive consumer protections that are not aimed to protect superaffluent buyers. Again, these jurisdictions assume the buyers are sophisticated and able to negotiate their own transactions with the help of educated and experienced legal, tax, and insurance advisers.

Offshore PPLI

The offshore PPLI market is split into two distinct categories. The history of the market explains why this bifurcation exists. The first segment of the market is the oldest group. It started when a few creative tax advisers came up with the idea to push the envelope defining life insurance and created products and companies that participated in questionable transactions for U.S. tax avoidance. Many of these transactions and the offering companies that issued policies incorporating them are in danger of collapsing because of their alleged lack of compliance with U.S. tax law.

The envelope pushing and consequent U.S. and offshore regulatory scrutiny have cast a dark shadow on PPLI's legitimate use, which frankly has slowed the market's acceptance to date. But these aggressive companies will likely disappear quietly into the night as regulators continue to tighten the noose on their activities and their clients. The real question is what will happen to the U.S. investors who entered into these transactions, investors who anticipated a very different tax benefit than they're going to enjoy. PPLI professionals must be prepared to address the fallout by understanding and pointing out the fringe nature of these rogue offshore PPLI transactions.

The newer group of players that moved into the offshore market included legitimate insurance companies looking to take advantage of the reduced regulatory oversight in order to offer unique products to South Americans, Asians, and Europeans. Most of these companies assumed that foreigners would break down their doors to acquire a tax-preferred product denominated in U.S. dollars since life insurance is a tax-favored investment vehicle in many countries, even at a premium when compared to U.S.-domiciled products. Although these companies proceeded to build such a product, the non-U.S. customers didn't come.

The companies involved were eventually left with three choices for their offshore entities: close down or sell their offshore operations altogether, join the first group of pioneers and enter into the questionable side of the market through the use of potentially noncompliant U.S. transactions, or change their focus and concentrate on appealing to superaffluent U.S. taxpayers seeking to ease the overall tax burden on tax-inefficient investments and improve estate planning through the use of products that comply with U.S. insurance regulations.

Because of seemingly insurmountable obstacles for entering the legitimate market, most of the companies took one of the first two paths. Now that truly viable and compliant U.S. and offshore markets are developing, those decisions have damaged reputations and prevented some companies from re-entering a legitimate business. Given the gross malfeasance that has occurred in the investment research, mutual fund, and hedge fund industries, informed advisers would not want any client to risk entanglement with these aggressive companies.

The Case for Compliance

The third choice of creating a more traditional and compliant transaction brought with it tremendous hurdles and hardships for large U.S. carriers. The greatest barrier—trying to sell a nonadmitted product (a product not available for purchase in a U.S. state jurisdiction) to U.S. taxpayers —seemed almost impossible to overcome. After all, only products that are admitted can be sold and discussed with potential policy owners while the agent or the prospective purchaser is within the state.

Realistically, how would a U.S. investor learn about a company's product when, as a nonadmitted product, it could be sold, underwritten, and serviced only in the offshore jurisdiction? Who was capable of introducing such a complex financial tool to these target customers? And most important, what were the rules and regulations related to providing these products to U.S. taxpayers? After all, a broker that sells this type of investment to U.S. superaffluent individuals should be a licensed broker in an offshore jurisdiction, have a real operation in that offshore jurisdiction, and be well informed of the potential pitfalls of the market.

The insurance companies knew they couldn't sell, solicit, or negotiate these transactions while any party was still in the United States. Doing so would violate insurance laws in most U.S. states. Therefore, the brokers and the companies themselves needed to tap into third-party legal advisers who had access to superaffluent clients, the expertise to understand the offshore PPLI products and their potential applications, the legal right and/or obligation to inform their clients about offshore life insurance, and the ability to convince their clients to go outside the United States to procure such a product.

To further complicate matters, most of these sophisticated tax and legal advisers were not comfortable working directly with an insurance carrier because the carrier's interests might conflict with the client's, especially in a lightly regulated market, where pitfalls were surely present but seldom known. In addition, purchasers of life insurance generally prefer to work with an independent and experienced third-party broker who is paid to protect their interests during the acquisition process and who will provide continuing advice and support during the life of the insurance contract. For their part, the life insurance companies were not accustomed to direct marketing and sales of their products; nor did they have a reputation for understanding the unique needs and goals of the superaffluent client.

What's more, executing an offshore PPLI policy is not a simple matter. To do so, an interested investor must complete the following steps:

- ❑ Travel to the offshore marketplace.
- ❑ Undergo a physical examination offshore.
- ❑ Complete all required paperwork offshore.
- ❑ Set up a non-U.S. entity to own the offshore contract.
- ❑ Have the non-U.S. entity pay the premiums to the insurance company.
- ❑ Interact with the broker in follow-up service issues.
- ❑ Take receipt of the policy outside the United States.

Clearly, only the most motivated and sophisticated investors were willing to move forward and establish PPLI's viability. As a result, very few carriers were willing to move forward with them. But there were insurance companies willing to face the opposition and change an entire marketplace by creating a U.S. tax-compliant product that was more flexible than anything available within the United States. Some companies recognized the unique opportunity and knew that the challenge was to appeal to the upper echelon legal, tax, estate, financial, insurance, and asset-management professionals in the United States. That's what it would take to successfully enter the otherwise untapped market of superaffluent U.S. investors in search of tax-advantaged investments that were safe, secure, and protected from creditors.

Clearly, such a marketplace did not exist, but a few forward-thinking insurance executives were willing to risk their own reputations and company brands to enter this untapped field. Mindful of U.S. rules related to life insurance policies for superaffluent American citizens, these carriers obtained the appropriate talent, built an infrastructure, and initiated the necessary marketing programs. Fortunately, these pioneering companies had sound motives, strong compliance standards, and a clear vision of PPLI's strength. Industry leadership, market knowledge, and a large deal flow were the rewards for taking early risks.

Trudging Through the Early Days

Just before the offshore insurance companies needed to select their preferred business course, my firm, WaxmanCavnerLawson, was investigating whether a foreign asset-protection trust could invest in a U.S. life insurance policy for income tax benefits. We also had a few prospects looking for offshore solutions involving the use of life insurance, and we had U.S. lawyers asking about life insurance on behalf of a number of superaffluent clients seeking asset protection offshore.

As a firm, we decided to take on the opportunity presented to tap the superaffluent marketplace with a unique life insurance product. In the process, we learned from attorneys in the asset-protection field that repatriating assets already moved offshore for foreign investment and asset protection was to be avoided. Repatriation would occur as soon as premium payments were sent back to U.S. life insurance companies as premium payments. Our firm embarked on a journey in 1998 that educated us on this otherwise untapped market of offshore life insurance companies.

We determined very early that many pricing changes, contract provisions, controls, and other protections would need to be put in place to protect the policy owners from poorly constructed and unilaterally written contracts that could exploit foreigners looking for U.S. dollar–denominated contracts. These contracts were obviously never intended to appeal to nor had any foresight built in for the preferences of the superaffluent U.S. buyer. This lack was made more problematic given that superaffluent U.S. taxpayers generally avoided life insurance as a planning tool mainly because of the perceived overpricing in the industry.

If these superaffluent individuals could see the real benefits of PPLI and gain a measure of comfort with the protections within the contract provided by the offshore jurisdiction, then a real market would emerge. As a broker with potential deal flow, our firm brought life insurance expertise to the process, but we were prohibited from soliciting buyers while they were in the United States. Therefore, the process of attracting clients turned our efforts to educating legal advisers on the benefits of offshore

PPLI transactions. These marketing efforts were directed to legal advisers who weren't selling the product but who were seeking solutions to clients' needs that PPLI could easily satisfy. Despite PPLI's obvious benefits, we still had to satisfy the lawyers' concern that any perceived risk to the client relationship would be managed through a well-executed transaction. The key was to establish relationships with highly capable and solid insurance companies while building a library of sales materials for the legal community to use in educating clients.

At the outset, we thought the sales process would be the most difficult. We quickly learned that the insurance companies, despite their tremendous investment in the marketplace, represented a much greater hurdle because of their complete lack of practical experience and a general uneasiness regarding new business ventures. We had raw material but no design for product creation, management, and delivery. The good news was that we became central to the policy-design process in building a suitable market. It was tough going, but it became a wonderful opportunity to shape a market to meet the needs of a highly attractive prospect base. We all knew the process would be long but the end result could be a tremendous success if the interests of each of the parties remained priorities throughout the design process.

We moved from creation to application by bringing live opportunities to the insurance companies. Fortunately, we had the foresight to work with advisers and clients who knew the market was immature but who were willing to suffer bumps in the road. Our first client came in early 1999—a 40-year-old male looking to invest approximately $5 million per year over a five-year period. He was patient, extremely intelligent, wealthy, had good legal counsel, an actuarial consultant, and most important, a tolerance for being a guinea pig. What followed was surprising to even the most seasoned and pessimistic insurance professional.

I met with the client in Bermuda to provide a complete explanation of the costs, benefits, and steps involved in the transaction. We took the client to the King Edward VII Memorial Hospital for the physical exam. The problems started there and didn't end for more than six months. Local hospital rules compelled us to check the client into the hospital for the routine medical exam. We met with three insurance companies and signed applications for each company since this was the only time the insured would be offshore to complete his paperwork. Although no implicit commitment was made in taking the medical exam or signing applications, the client was prepared to go forward with the transaction. Our brokerage firm paid for the medical examinations in an effort to keep the three companies at arm's length until a final decision was reached about where to go in the reinsurance market to have the case underwritten.

As underwriting got under way, all three companies admitted that they were unable to put the product or risk together for this case. Each company gave a very different reason for backing out. One said its corporate counsel was uncomfortable with a U.S. citizen as the insured, a detail that was quite obvious when we introduced the case to their representatives and counsel. Another said it was unable to set up a new investment account that would appeal to the needs of the client. A third simply gave up three months later, after failing to secure $115 million of death benefit coverage from its carrier's reinsurers. The reinsurance snafu was extremely puzzling at the time, but the size of this first transaction proved to be such that the reinsurers balked at an exposure that was new to them, hard to quantify, and fit into none of the traditional boxes. Despite the client's excellent health, the reinsurers hadn't contemplated these types of cases offshore and eventually admitted they were uncomfortable with so many unknowns. Neither the insurance companies nor the reinsurers were ready for the types of clients that would want to purchase PPLI offshore.

These were tough lessons, but they've served us well as knowledgeable and experienced advisers.

Finally, we approached a large U.S. company with a Bermuda subsidiary. The company was honest about its capabilities, saying it would not be a good candidate to underwrite the case. However, with more structure, understanding, and realistic expectations in place, the company became willing to move forward and redesign its product in an attempt to attract superaffluent U.S. taxpayers. Indeed, the relationship with this carrier quickly solidified, and we were once again ready to have our first client travel offshore, this time to the Bahamas, to execute documents. Despite the winding process, the client's patience paid off, and he maintains to this day that this was the best financial investment he has made.

We continued to work with our new lead carrier to cut a clear path for the underwriting process and to determine the policy elements necessary to make the chassis attractive to the superaffluent market looking for offshore life insurance solutions. As the typical offshore transaction evolved, it had these components:

- ❑ Average total premiums of $20 million, usually paid over a four- or five-year period
- ❑ Multiple investment accounts
- ❑ Flexibility for adding future managers
- ❑ Separate-account protection for the accumulation of policy values
- ❑ Segregated premium receptacle and reinsurance receipt accounts (something we were unable to provide in the United States)

❑ A non-MEC structure permitting full access to cash values through the withdrawal of basis and access to appreciation through low- or no-cost policy loans

The offshore PPLI industry has made tremendous progress since 1999, and many investors benefit from the early hard work and resulting expertise developed during that period. And although I believe the market will stay strong, it isn't for everybody. Who is the best prospect for an offshore PPLI policy? A superaffluent individual who will pay a total premium of $20 million or more. At these premium levels, the benefits of an offshore policy are very difficult to replicate with one executed onshore. However, the process is complex and expensive to implement, and many people simply aren't comfortable going offshore for their business transactions.

Onshore Migration

Our offshore success made us true believers in PPLI and the many ways it assists the superaffluent in meeting investment objectives. But as U.S.-based life insurance advisers, we saw two major hurdles in limiting our activities to the sole use of offshore companies. First, because an adviser is not allowed to solicit or sell an offshore product within the United States, our success in getting the transaction in front of potential buyers is completely dependent on the work of legal advisers.

Second, the offshore market carries a stigma that's often hard to overcome. Over the years, we've learned that for every one transaction that ends up offshore, a number of investors would have completed a similar transaction if it were available onshore. So using the lessons we learned offshore, we initiated a U.S.-based strategy and pushed onshore U.S. life insurance companies to create products that would appeal to the superaffluent market. Our proven track record offshore helped persuade U.S. carriers to embark on efforts to bring large pools of assets to the life insurance industry. Again, these pools are from people who otherwise would never consider participating in a traditional life insurance transaction.

Since 2002, the domestic market of PPLI offerings from U.S.-domiciled life insurance companies has grown and matured dramatically. Six years ago, the market amounted to one small entrepreneurial company that was quietly building a book of PPLI and PPDA transactions. By 2002, only a dozen or so companies had PPLI products to offer the superaffluent market, but most of them were still confused and stagnant in the face of regulatory issues. Recent IRS rulings, proposed regulations, and significant changes in the law in a few states looking to attract PPLI business have finally cleared a path for these products (see chapter 12). Today, most of the major U.S. life insurance companies are either in the PPLI market or contemplating new PPLI product offerings.

The Future of PPLI

The U.S. PPLI market is now mature enough to earn the confidence of buyers, insurance companies, regulators, brokers, and the asset-management community. But a number of issues will likely continue to thwart the full potential of PPLI over the next few years:

❏ PPLI does not offer insurance agents the traditional upfront commissions they've come to expect. Agents in this market are compensated through asset-based fees, which are not a good fit for many high-end producers, whose practices need large cash inflows from every transaction. Moreover, a PPLI transaction may seem like a more traditional investment transaction, but a number of emotional issues are involved in the sale of a life insurance policy and they are not well understood in the investment community. When an insurance professional starts asking an investor not only for financial information but also for a full review of his medical history and avocations, the sale becomes one that only a handful can negotiate. The successful distribution channels will likely be a limited number of insurance professionals who can afford to change the economics of their practice and work in tandem with investment, tax, and legal advisers.

❏ The PPLI product will become more like a commodity, putting tremendous pressure on insurance carrier margins. The good news is that current market pricing provides only minimal return on earnings for insurers, making this a wonderful screen to bar all but the most serious players from the market.

❏ The life insurance industry as a whole will undergo new pricing algorithms based on new mortality tables reflecting Americans' increasingly longer life spans. These tables, to be adopted by insurance companies sometime in the next few years, will set new guaranteed mortality ceilings within the contracts and will dampen the overall economics of a PPLI policy. A policy owner will have to purchase more death benefit for every dollar of premium invested, without a corresponding decrease in the actual cost of the risk within the policy. A general consensus is that the new mortality tables will drop the maximum amount of premium that can go into a PPLI transaction by as much as 20 percent, with no corresponding drop in costs.

❏ Revenue sharing between the asset managers and the insurance companies in the U.S. market could taint the product by making it seem to the superaffluent buyer more like a retail product. This is a common technique used by life insurance companies in the registered marketplace. They do it to supplement their so-called illustration competitiveness by lowering the charges reflected on the illustration printout. The end result is that the insurance company is able to move charges off the insurance illustration and onto the investment's separate account, where they aren't apparent to the buyer, improving the insurance company's perceived competitive edge. For example, if life insurance company A requires a 25-basis-point revenue-sharing amount and life insurance company B does not, company A could reduce the fees shown in its illustrations by 25 basis points and still have the same perceived level of profitability as company B, thus distorting the comparison. But superaffluent buyers demand full transparency, and this form of revenue sharing will likely be viewed as an under-the-table pricing scheme used to shield costs.

More important, if a PPLI carrier depends on revenue sharing from each of its underlying insurance-dedicated funds, and a certain fund is unwilling to pay such a fee, that fund will find itself excluded from the carrier's platform. Although not terribly negative for the insurance company, this will come as a shock to existing policy owners when they discover that the number of investment choices has been reduced. If this practice were to take hold in the PPLI marketplace, superaffluent investors would not receive it well. Fortunately, the insurance advisers successfully serving this market are on the side of the investor and will put carriers hiding such fees on notice that the practice won't be tolerated.

❑ Because the U.S. life insurance industry made the mistake of attempting to sell PPLI before it was ready for the marketplace, many superaffluent buyers remain confused. The process of educating these buyers is critical. Delivering solid information on what can and can't be done within these contracts is of critical importance for credibility within the industry.

❑ Because the average death benefit amounts associated with PPLI transactions are so large, the shrinking reinsurance market, particularly since 9/11, imposes an effective cap of $125 million on the death benefit. For the many superaffluent families for which this cap will be limiting, advisers must employ creative planning ideas, issuing policies on multiple family members.

The U.S.-domiciled PPLI market is poised for tremendous growth and acceptance as a mainstream transaction for both affluent and superaffluent U.S. investors. The reasons are straightforward:

❑ Product, administrative, and service structures are now in place.
❑ IRS rulings provide clear guidance on acceptable transactions.
❑ Market expertise exists to effectively place large PPLI transactions.

❑ A number of satisfied buyers are now on the books.

❑ Life insurance companies are getting comfortable with the PPLI concept and its marketing challenges.

❑ Fund managers have begun allocating resources to the PPLI market, in which more than 80 insurance-dedicated funds now exist.

THE ENTIRE PRIVATE placement global market is estimated at about $4 billion of total cash values in both PPLI and PPDA products. I would be surprised—and disappointed—if that number is less than $10 billion by 2008 and if PPLI is not a $100 billion industry by 2015.

CHAPTER 2

Risk Management
Redefining Safe Harbors

JEREMIAH RIDDLE

D eciding to purchase insurance is a natural outcome of a risk-management review, but the decision to purchase a private placement life insurance (PPLI) contract is typically based on a focused financial analysis rather than a broader risk assessment. Excluding the PPLI option from the broader review is a mistake and a lost opportunity as well. PPLI is primarily purchased by the affluent, who often face a diverse range of risks, and as with any private placement program, PPLI is available only to accredited investors and qualified purchasers under the federal securities laws. Considering PPLI from a risk-management perspective can benefit the purchaser and his or her advisers as well.

The Risk-Management Process

What is risk management? In general, it's the process of identifying exposures to the risk of loss, evaluating methods of preventing and protecting against loss, and ongoing monitoring of both risks and solutions. In the corporate world, risk management is a full-time function, often with large staffs dedicated to it. But risk management should also be employed in personal finance.

A personal risk-management program focuses on risks to property, life, health, and finances. It assesses the risks faced by one's family and dependents. By identifying and quantifying possible losses, the family gains a better understanding of the risks they face and the critical role of prevention. Preventive measures can minimize risks to property—whether homes, vehicles, or collectibles. Homeowners, for example, can install smoke and carbon monoxide detectors, have heating systems and chimneys maintained, and trim shrubbery to minimize possible wind losses (and to minimize cover for potential burglars). Prevention can also reduce risks to life, health, and safety, with measures such as diet and exercise, medical checkups, and driver training.

The most familiar types of preventive measures for individuals are those taken to mitigate financial risks, such as portfolio diversification. Financial risk management is a cornerstone of personal risk management, and the affluent generally have a number of advisers who focus on these risks. Unfortunately, as with the protection of property, life, and health, it's impossible to eliminate financial risks entirely. But once risks have been minimized, the individual still must determine how to deal with those that remain. Although organizations have a range of available techniques, for individuals the question boils down to deciding which risks to insure and which to self-insure.

Self-insurance occurs when clients purchase no insurance or when they choose insurance with a high deductible. In such cases, available assets are sufficient to cover losses. Typically, the more resources an individual or organization has, the greater the tendency to self-insure. The risk-management review will consider the coverages already in force and identify any gaps or overlaps. The aim is to leverage the total package to produce the best coverage at the best price.

The final element in a personal risk-management program is ongoing monitoring of risks and the decisions made about how to deal with them. A variety of situations exist that can lead to changes in a risk profile or necessitate new solutions to deal with risks. Regular monitoring keeps the personal risk-management program in tune with the individual's needs and helps avoid costly errors. Since life changes are less frequent than purchases or dispositions of tangible assets, a two- or three-year review schedule is not unreasonable.

Risk Assessment

How does PPLI fit into the personal risk-management process? Because of PPLI's powerful tax and investment advantages, it's often viewed solely as a financial instrument, and the purchase decision evaluated only in that light. But the individual's personal risk-management profile should be taken into account, because a PPLI policy has implications for both estate and financial planning.

PPLI offers the most transparent life insurance structure and the widest range of investment options of any permanent (cash value) life insurance policy. Moreover, it is designed to qualify for the tax benefits of other permanent policies, including the following:

❑ No taxes on investment gains in the contract (see chapter 3)
❑ No taxes when investments are redeployed within the contract
❑ No income taxes when a death benefit is paid
❑ Potential to exclude the policy from the insured's estate (see chapters 5 and 6)
❑ Potential for favorable tax treatment on loans and withdrawals (see chapter 3)

Like any life insurance policy, PPLI involves significant death benefits. Under IRC § 7702, a life policy must provide a substantial "net amount at risk," or NAR. The NAR is the portion of the death benefit in excess of the cash value. The amount of NAR required diminishes with age and reaches zero at age 95 (see chapter 11). At younger ages, NAR is much greater than the cash value. A 60-year-old making a $10 million premium payment, for example, would be obliged to purchase an initial death benefit of about $38 million to satisfy the requirements.

This commitment cost has obvious planning implications. First, and most important, the purchase must be integrated with the individual's estate plan. Estate planning for the affluent is a complex undertaking, and the range of potential approaches and solutions is broad and diverse (see chapter 5). An affluent family may have multiple trusts, a family limited partnership, and other structures, most of which hold insurance or investment products (see chapter 6). The aim of the estate plan is to achieve, in a unified way, all of the individual's objectives for wealth transfer, charitable giving, and control over certain assets (for example, a closely owned business). Simply dropping a large life insurance policy into such a complex situation would be ill advised.

Proper planning also involves determining if the individual's financial obligation or risk profile has changed since the last update. Reviews are sometimes infrequent, and the evaluation of PPLI may lead to revisions in the plan, the structures created to support it, and/or other insurance or investments. Does it make sense to add a significant new death benefit to existing coverage? If not, should the idea be dropped, or should other coverage be terminated? If the latter, one must consider the need to satisfy new two-year "incontestable" and "suicide" provisions. (The incontestable provision prevents the insurance company from denying a claim based on misinformation in the insurance application after two years have passed; the suicide provision simply permits the insurer to deny a claim based on the insured's suicide within two years of the policy's issue.)

Many U.S. estate plans are structured to take advantage of the unlimited marital deduction, so estate taxes are not due until both spouses have died. That makes it desirable to purchase "survivorship" or "second-to-die" coverage. A single-life PPLI contract would not match the timing of the obligation, and, depending on ownership structure, could create its own estate tax implications.

Second, the amount of death-benefit coverage available from the world reinsurance market has been shrinking. The amount available on a single life at this time is little more than $100 million, including existing coverage. So for individuals with significant existing life insurance portfolios, capacity could be an issue, potentially leading to questions about terminating existing policies to permit the placement of the PPLI.

When an individual wishes to add PPLI to his or her portfolio without increasing the total insurance in force, a tax-free exchange can be attractive. Under § 1035 of the code, a life insurance policy can be exchanged for another without taxation of the investment gains in the contract. To qualify, the code requires that the insured, the applicant, and the amount of insurance be the same as the policy exchanged. Also, any outstanding policy loans must be duplicated or the amount of loan reduction will be taxed. And the insured is subject to medical underwriting, whether the PPLI is purchased from the insurer that issued the policy to be exchanged or from a new insurer.

Last, the individual's health status must lead to a reasonable underwriting offer, or the benefits will be diluted by the increased costs. Medical conditions that are controlled by medications or that were cured years earlier generally do not lead to a substantial rating (extra premium). The affluent in general receive more frequent and better medical care. With increasing age, however, any number of medical conditions can arise or worsen. It is very helpful for the adviser to form a preliminary estimate of the likely underwriting offer before building up a client's expectation that coverage can be obtained at a reasonable price.

The individual who is offered highly rated coverage, or who cannot secure additional coverage because of capacity constraints, might also consider a private placement deferred annuity (PPDA). Individually owned annuities qualify for favorable tax treatment while the policy is in force. No taxes apply to investment gains or the shifting of cash value among investment options available under the contract. Unlike life insurance, however, the proceeds payable at death are taxed as income to the recipient. If the individual wished to make substantial charitable gifts, then the PPDA approach might be preferable, and the absence of medical underwriting certainly simplifies the process.

Risk Protection

By virtue of its powerful financial and tax attributes, PPLI can help an individual protect against numerous risks. The wide range of sophisticated investment options and the absence of taxes on investment gains combine to make it an outstanding tool to deal with individual financial risks. PPLI excels in the following areas:

❑ *Wealth preservation.* Life insurance is first and foremost a means of creating estate liquidity and passing wealth to future generations. The tax benefits provided by Congress are intended to help individuals protect their families from the financial hardships brought on by death. The policy death benefit is, until one is very old, significantly larger than the cash value. If death occurs prematurely, the gains are enormous. Federal and state estate taxes can drain more than 50 percent of one's estate, so purchasing life insurance to help meet this obligation is a very important means of maximizing the transfer of assets to one's heirs.

❑ *Wealth creation.* PPLI offers an array of sophisticated investment options, many of which are available only to the affluent as defined by the accredited investor and qualified purchaser thresholds under federal securities laws. Hedge funds, private equity, and venture capital funds are among the choices with the highest potential for returns. Combine those investment categories with a nontaxable platform and wealth creation can be dramatic. For example, earning 10 percent annually over 20 years on a $10 million deposit produces a portfolio value of $67 million; if taxes are due annually, the portfolio would grow to just $32 million, assuming a tax rate of 40 percent. The long-term frictional cost of the PPLI policy—that is, the drag or friction that occurs compared to gross returns—should average 1 percent or less annually if the policy is properly structured and priced. In that case, the hypothetical investment would grow to $56 million, 86 percent more than the fully taxable alternative.

Another wealth-creating advantage of PPLI is the elimination of tax obligations on reinvestment. When a particular investment matures or is liquidated, no tax is due since the proceeds remain within the policy. This advantage can also simplify a decision to drop certain investment funds or sectors, since tax considerations play no role in the decision.

❑ *Asset protection.* PPLI is a separate-account insurance product and the cash value is not commingled with the insurer's other (general-account) assets. Fundamentally, this separation protects the insured person's assets against any creditor's claims if the insurance company encounters financial difficulties. Despite that, some purchasers will use more than one insurer in order to diversify their insurance portfolio. Depending on the size and complexity of the transaction and subject to the availability of investment choices attractive to the insured at multiple insurers, this type of diversification can help reduce risk. For example, a diversified insurance portfolio minimizes the impact should an insurer raise its costs because of future financial strain.

Personal assets held in insurance policies and related estate-planning structures are generally protected from creditors or litigants of the insured and the owner, providing an additional level of asset protection to these individuals (see chapter 4).

❑ *Liquidity.* The purchase of life insurance should always be viewed as a long-term proposition. Initial costs, including premium taxes, are higher early on in life than in later years, so the policy's financial performance improves with time. A properly structured policy permits the owner to remove cash value from the policy tax-free until the amount of the entire premium has been withdrawn. Plus, the owner may borrow from the policy at a low net cost, or pledge the policy as collateral to a lending institution.

Risk Factors in Purchasing PPLI

Risks must be considered not only in assessing an individual's particular financial situation but also in evaluating the appropriateness of a PPLI purchase. One risk inherent in the purchase is the possibility of the individual's having a greater need for liquidity in future years than anticipated.

Gaining access to the policy's value is a function of structure. An important consideration here is the modified endowment contract (MEC) rules. A policy becomes a MEC, with no tax-free liquidity, if the premiums are paid in too quickly relative to a benchmark model set forth in the Internal Revenue Code. The model is based on the amount of death benefit the policy provides. Funding a policy with a single premium will most likely force it into MEC status. Four or more premium payments may be necessary to avoid MEC status.

Allowing a policy to become a MEC is not uncommon; MECs make it possible to minimize the total insurance purchase, which often means a lower cost of insurance and improved long-term financial performance. The drawback of MEC status is that withdrawals from the policy are treated as taxable until all of the investment gains have been withdrawn. Only at that point are further withdrawals treated as return of premium. And there is a 10 percent tax penalty if the taxpayer is under age 59½ at the time of the withdrawal. Loans from the policy, or secured by the policy, are treated similarly. And MEC status, once achieved, cannot be undone. So PPLI can provide a reserve for liquidity, but availability of liquidity is only one factor in the decision. And there are constraints as well.

Although a PPLI policy performs best when the cash value is left undisturbed by loans and/or withdrawals, the fact that liquidity is available not only gives comfort in making the decision to move forward and execute a policy in the first place, but also provides important flexibility in future risk reviews. Here, a solution to address a new risk or an existing one that has increased in scope may be to use a non-MEC policy's liquidity to fund added protection. Therefore, giving up the policy's tax-free liquidity initially by establishing a MEC policy should be carefully considered.

Another very important issue is policy ownership, which can determine whether the contract is included in the individual's estate. Frequently, irrevocable life insurance trusts (ILITs) (see chapter 6) are used to buy and hold policies. If properly structured, the ILIT will cause the policy to be excluded, producing potentially huge estate tax savings. However, purchasers of PPLI are motivated in large part by the range of investment options. By placing the policy in an ILIT, one cedes responsibility for investment decisions to the trustee, who may not evaluate investments, especially sophisticated alternative investments, in the same way as the insured, particularly with the passage of time. So the question of asset allocation must be given careful consideration. Frequently, purchasers decide to retain control of the allocation process for the policy despite the eventual estate tax obligation.

These purchasers may find the premium finance option attractive. Premium finance involves purchase of a policy using borrowed funds, pledging the policy and, if necessary, other collateral. The financed policy would be placed in an ILIT and would be designed to provide the funds to meet the estate tax obligation created by including the PPLI policy in the estate. The premium finance structure is intended to: (1) provide life insurance without having to draw down other investments to pay the premiums; (2) preserve the purchaser's investment portfolio; and (3) provide a balance between investments inside and outside of insurance policies. This option is a logical outgrowth of the risk evaluation, which suggested consideration of PPLI, since the use of a financed-premium program is intended to offset the additional estate tax liability produced by the decision to own the PPLI policy directly.

Another risk issue is related to lifetime liquidity. Considering the purchase of life insurance is time-consuming, especially when the work is embedded in the risk-management and planning process. As noted earlier, the costs in the early years are higher than they are later on. That's why it's best to think of buying life insurance as a long-term, even a permanent decision. The planning process should consider how much of an individual's investment portfolio should be held in life insurance, no matter how tax-effective it is, to avoid early withdrawals.

Various studies show that high-net-worth investors use 70 percent of their portfolios to meet working and retirement lifestyle needs; 30 percent is not dedicated to a specific purpose. A long-term commitment of a portion of the portfolio should clearly target that 30 percent. Beyond that, the portion of an individual's investment portfolio that's invested in highly taxed instruments is the logical source of funding for PPLI (see chapter 8). The PPLI purchase usually represents 20 percent or less of an individual's portfolio.

PPLI is a form of permanent life insurance and, therefore, presumably relatively safe from challenge. That said, with government budget deficits expected to run high for some time, it's possible that Congress may limit the tax benefits, perhaps by limiting the amount of cash value that could produce nontaxable gains. The Internal Revenue Service can act administratively even without congressional activity. However, compared with other permanent life insurance, the distinctive feature of PPLI is the investment options it makes available. The IRS took action in 2003 to limit what was perceived as excessive investor control, especially with hedge funds (see chapter 12). Two revenue rulings expressed the view that investment options may be accessed only through the purchase of a life or annuity contract. This forced investment firms to offer purely "insurance dedicated" portfolios if they wanted to serve the PPLI/PPDA market.

Some firms found the cost and effort to create insurance-dedicated versions of their existing funds—which by definition cannot be mirror images of the noninsurance-dedicated funds—unacceptable, and they are no longer available through PPLI contracts (see chapter 14). It appears that the IRS is satisfied that the new rules address the issues it perceived in the selection of investment options under PPLI.

A final risk-management decision in purchasing PPLI is the selection of an insurance adviser or broker. This is an important part of the process, since unlike other financial professionals, these advisers are trained to think in terms of risk management and are able to provide guidance and expertise across a range of issues. They will be key players on the planning team and will guide the carrier selection activity and pricing review, as well as participating in the negotiation of the representations and warranties in the private placement memorandum issued by the insurer.

The adviser must be experienced with this particular market and with the limited number of insurers who offer competitive products in it. The adviser can model alternative policy structures and funding strategies under a range of investment-return assumptions and levels of death benefits (see chapter 11). The adviser must be experienced in the unique underwriting requirements of the affluent market (see chapter 15), including securing jumbo coverage amounts. Finally, the adviser will be needed for ongoing policy monitoring, periodic reviews of policy performance and competitiveness, and a range of service matters in the years that follow (see chapter 11). All of these factors put a premium on the adviser's permanence, since the policy will most likely be in force for decades and will always be among the most complex insurance programs to administer.

The purchase of PPLI or deferred annuities is often handled like the purchase of any other financial instrument. But far better results are achieved when the selection is evaluated from a personal risk-management perspective. In addition to providing an overriding rationale for the purchase and ensuring a proper fit with the planning structure and any other insurance policies, the personal risk-management process will identify gaps and overlaps in the client's risk protection and permit them to be addressed comprehensively.

CHAPTER 3

Tax Management
Building Wealth, Reducing Taxes

JEFFREY S. BORTNICK

I t's not what you make; it's what you keep. And investors and their advisers realize that it's not enough to achieve good gross returns. They want to know what they've earned after fees and taxes have been extracted. Of course, taxes have long put a dent in how much gets kept, but private placement life insurance (PPLI) has the potential to eliminate income tax on investment earnings and, with proper estate planning, eliminate the estate tax as well. Indeed, it can provide a large tax-free death benefit for a cost that comes to much less than the tax savings gained.[1]

This chapter takes a closer look at the income tax savings benefits of PPLI, the estate tax savings benefits of such policies, and questions surrounding how the insurance can be used as part of an overall long-term investment strategy. This chapter simplifies what can otherwise be an area with many tax risks and perils, but PPLI should not be undertaken without the help of qualified tax advisers.

Tax-Efficient Investing

U.S. federal income tax law taxes different types of investment returns very differently. Long-term capital gains and qualified dividends, for example, are taxed at 15 percent. Short-term capital gains and most interest income are taxed at 35 percent. Unrealized appreciation in the value of securities is generally not taxed until the securities are sold. Interest on certain municipal bonds is never taxed. Depending on the investment, the same before-tax return can result in very different after-tax returns, as seen in examples 1 and 2.

Example 1. Lauren invests in a portfolio of growth stocks, which pays no dividends. She holds on to her stocks until her death. Her gross return averages 12 percent per year. Because Lauren received no dividends and sold none of the stocks, she owes no income tax, so her before-tax and after-tax returns are the same—12 percent per year.

Example 2. Allison also invests in a portfolio of stocks. Some of her stocks pay qualified dividends (taxed at the 15 percent federal rate). Allison often sells some of her stocks with gains after she has held the stock for over one year so that her gains are long-term capital gains, and she frequently sells stocks with losses whether or not she held the stock more than a year. Her net long-term capital gains and qualified dividends are taxed at 15 percent. Therefore, if her before-tax yearly return were 12 percent and all of her income were taxed at 15 percent, her tax would be about 1.8 percent of her portfolio (15 percent of 12 percent) and her after-tax return would be 10.2 percent (12 percent - 1.8 percent). In fact, since Allison defers some of the tax until the sale of the securities, her after-tax yearly return would be higher than 10.2 percent. Because of state and local income taxes, however, Allison's overall after-tax return may be less.

Example 3. Jenna is an active trader of securities, who rarely receives qualified dividends or long-term capital gains. She achieves an average yearly return of 12 percent, but that return is almost all taxed each year as short-term capital gains, so that approximately 35 percent of the return must be paid to the federal government. If Jenna lived in a state with personal income taxes, her return would be further reduced by state and local income taxes. Since she is an active trader, all of Jenna's gains are generally realized for tax purposes, so none of the tax is deferred. If Jenna's combined tax rate were 40 percent, her after-tax yearly return would be only 7.2 percent (12 percent - 4.8 percent). And Jenna's after-tax return would be only 60 percent of her before-tax return.

Clearly, after-tax returns can differ greatly, depending on investment strategies. Some funds provide tax-efficient returns. Private-equity funds, for example, often produce long-term capital gains, and some hedge funds are very tax-efficient. But many are not. They produce short-term capital gains and ordinary income, taxed at rates (including state and local tax) exceeding 40 percent.

Despite their tax inefficiency, the allocation of portfolio assets to hedge funds has been rapidly increasing. Many investment professionals recommend significant portions of a portfolio be invested in them. For investors who are interested in investing a portion of their portfolios in hedge funds or any other potentially tax-inefficient strategy, PPLI provides a way to greatly increase the tax efficiency and thereby greatly increase the after-tax return.

What Is PPLI?

PPLI's tax efficiency hinges on the product's key features:

❑ PPLI is life insurance with a separately invested account for that policy's cash value, which may be invested in a hedge fund, a group of hedge funds, or a separately professionally managed account for the insurance company. The separate account can be invested in any diverse portfolio of liquid assets (not necessarily a hedge fund) or any portfolio that has been engineered to support the policy's required liquidity—death benefits, lapses, surrenders, loans, or withdrawals.

❑ The pure insurance portion is essentially low-cost term life insurance, which allows the entire investment, including the cash, to qualify as life insurance. The costs of setting up and maintaining the policy are charged to the account, and the account grows (or shrinks) depending on the success of the investment.

❑ The life insurance is placed on someone's life (the insured), and at that person's death, the policy pays to the beneficiary the amount of pure (term) insurance then in place, as required by the policy, plus whatever is in the cash account—free of income tax.

❑ The entire death benefit (including all the earnings from the hedge funds and/or separate accounts) is received by the beneficiary free of all income tax.

❑ If the owner surrenders the policy before the death of the insured, the income generally is taxed at ordinary rates (plus an excise tax of 10 percent of the gain, if he or she is under age 59½). Under certain policies (that is, a nonmodified endowment contract), as long as the contract is not terminated, a substantial portion of the cash can be withdrawn as a loan, income tax–free.

Income Tax Savings

Placing the investment within a life insurance policy eliminates current taxation, and the payment of the appreciation through a death benefit is tax-free. Therefore, the appreciation can be free of all income taxes. Within such a framework, a tax-inefficient investment can become a tax-efficient one. For Jenna, instead of reducing the return from 12 percent to 7.2 percent for the 40 percent income tax paid—a reduction in the internal rate of return by 4.8 percent—the reduced internal rate of return under the policy may be less than 1 percent, thereby increasing the internal rate of return from 7.2 percent to more than 11 percent. The reduction of less than 1 percent in the internal rate of return is based on the insurance costs rather than the federal tax rate and will vary depending on the policy.

FIGURE 3.1

AGE	SINGLE PREMIUM	END-OF-YEAR CASH VALUE	DEATH BENEFIT (INCLUDING CASH VALUE)	TAXABLE ACCOUNT (AT 35% TAX)
50	$5,000,000	$5,398,996	$17,782,027	$5,390,000
53		6,561,573	7,782,027	6,263,632
60		13,594,803	18,217,036	10,596,382
70		39,928,676	46,317,264	22,456,663
80		117,942,390	123,839,720	47,591,877
90		343,582,426	360,761,548	100,860,340

Although the underlying investment can be any investment that conforms to the insurance company's standards and complies with the various insurance and tax regulations, let's assume here that the investment will be a hedge fund or group of hedge funds—an investment that would be tax-inefficient outside of an insurance policy.

FIGURE 3.1 compares the return on a sample hedge fund life insurance policy purchased at age 50 for $5 million against a taxable investment of $5 million. The chart assumes a 12 percent return per year on the hedge fund investment and uses the costs of an actual policy. The taxable account column assumes a 35 percent tax rate. Of course, the chart simply shows illustrated results. The final results will depend on, among other things, the charges imposed by the insurance company, the actual investment performance achieved by the hedge funds selected, and the investor's marginal income tax rate.

The death benefit greatly exceeds the taxable account value at all ages. Obviously, the after-tax benefit of the insurance policy would be substantially higher if the average returns on the hedge fund investment substantially exceeded 12 percent and would be much lower if the average returns were much less than 12 percent. The tax benefit would also be substantially higher if the investor's assumed tax rate were more than 35 percent. (Many hedge fund investors' marginal tax rates are between 40 percent and 50 percent when state and local taxes are included.)

Estate Tax Savings

A key element of effective estate planning is to make gifts of assets in trust, so that the assets in the trust will not be subject to estate tax for the person who makes the gift (the donor). The beneficiaries of the trust are often the donor's spouse, children, and/or grandchildren. As long as the donor's spouse is living and friendly with the donor, the assets in the trust can be recaptured by distribution to the spouse if they're really needed. A Treasury ruling in 1995 made it possible for the donor to keep substantial control over the trust by retaining the right to fire and replace the trustee. The replacement trustee can be anyone the donor selects except a close relative or subordinate employee.

The best assets to place in such a trust are assets that will grow substantially over time, such as hedge funds and private equity. For example, suppose a donor creates a trust in December 2003, when he or she is 50 years old, and puts $2 million into it. If the donor and the donor's spouse have not used any of their gift tax exemption, this gift would be exempt from U.S. gift tax. Then the donor loans the trust $3 million at the lowest interest rate allowed for a long-term loan (to prevent the loan from being taxed as a gift). These rates, which are set by the IRS, change monthly. Assume that the loan is kept in place for 40 years, until the donor dies at age 90. At that point—at an interest rate of, say, 5.12 percent—the trust owes the donor's estate about $21.1 million on the loan.

The trust invests the $5 million in a PPLI hedge fund portfolio. At the donor's death (see figure 3.1), assuming a 12 percent return, the trust (or donor's beneficiaries) would receive an insurance death benefit of about $360.8 million, which comes to about $350 million after paying the estate tax on the loan. This trust benefit would be free of income, estate, and generation-skipping taxes. In a number of states including Delaware and New Jersey, which have repealed the rule against perpetuities, the trust could continue forever, free of estate and generation-skipping taxes.

Compare this result to three much-less-favorable alternatives. Let's assume that the donor dies at age 90 (in the year 2043) and that the donor's estate will be subject to a 50 percent estate tax. Of course, the rate of the estate tax that far into the future—if the tax is still in place at all—is speculative, but most tax advisers believe it's very likely that there will continue to be an estate tax of 50 percent or more on very large estates. The first alternative is a direct investment in the hedge fund (not through an insurance policy) without a trust. If the donor invested the $5 million in the hedge fund directly, he or she would end up with about $100 million (see figure 3.1, Taxable Account) and the investor's beneficiaries would end up with about $50 million after the 50 percent estate tax—about a seventh of what they end up with under the optimal planning (that is, using a trust as the owner of a PPLI policy).

Under the second alternative, the donor sets up the trust, the trust invests in the hedge fund directly, and the beneficiaries end up with about $100 million. Under the third alternative, the donor buys hedge fund insurance but not in a trust. Under this alternative, the beneficiaries end up with about $180 million (the $360 million death benefit less a 50 percent estate tax). With these assumptions, all three alternatives are much worse than the optimal PPLI planning. Clearly, PPLI invested in a hedge fund can add value in estate planning. It can result in considerable income and estate tax savings, substantially increasing the amount the investor gets to keep.

Domestic versus Offshore Policies

PPLI can be purchased from U.S. or offshore insurance companies (see chapter 17). For U.S. policy owners, the same rules concerning tax deferral or elimination apply to domestic and offshore policies. But an annuity or life insurance policy issued by an offshore foreign company is generally subject to a 1 percent U.S. excise tax. Such foreign companies generally do not pay the state premium taxes or federal deferred acquisition cost (DAC) tax to which domestic policies are subject. The DAC tax for domestic policies usually results in a charge by the insurance company of approximately 1 percent, so that the effective cost of a policy from a domestic insurance company is similar to that of an offshore insurance policy once the excise tax is added. The state premium tax is additional—often 2 percent of the premium—but varies by state and is de minimis in some states.

U.S. insurance companies provide the protection of U.S. regulation and U.S. law. Although foreign laws protecting the cash value from insurance companies' creditors may be similar to U.S. laws, most U.S. investors feel more comfortable with an insurance company that is subject to U.S. law and regulation. Most investors do not have as much confidence in tax-haven countries' laws, courts, legal systems, or political stability as they do in U.S. jurisdictions. Furthermore, many offshore insurance companies have insignificant assets or business, are recently formed, and, in some instances, may ignore U.S. securities law and/or state insurance law requirements. In addition, domestic policies can legally be sold and marketed only in the United States. Foreign insurance companies' policies must be applied for and solicited outside the United States.

Some investors have a concern—unrealistic as it may be—that these small offshore insurance companies will run off with their money. Although the money will generally be under the control of an asset allocator in whom the investor has confidence, and possibly a custodian as well, the investments will be in the name of the insurance company's separate account. Legal protections can be imposed, but the protections often increase the tax risks, and they can never eliminate the risk that the principals or employees of the offshore insurance company may take the money. Although embezzlement is also possible in the United States, U.S. insurance companies are highly regulated and the risk is significantly reduced.

Offshore insurance companies marketing in the United States or otherwise subjecting themselves to U.S. jurisdiction may be violating U.S. securities or insurance laws. Although this is primarily a concern for the insurance companies and not policy owners, it's obviously preferable not to place substantial assets with a company that may be violating U.S. law. It may also be more likely that the IRS would disallow the advantages of a policy issued by an insurance company that is not "real" or substantial, resulting in the policy losing its tax status.

On the other hand, offshore insurance companies may be less likely to catch the attention of the IRS, may be more suitable for asset protection, may allow investment in offshore investments not open to a U.S. insurance company (or those available only with higher minimum investment or with less favorable liquidity rights than those available in the United States).[2] Offshore insurance policies may give investors greater control of their own investments, but this benefit may carry additional tax risks. The income tax and estate-planning benefits generally apply equally to domestic and offshore policies.

Appropriate Investors

PPLI is not for everyone. Insurance companies often require minimum premiums—sometimes as high as $5 million—to open a separate account or $1 million in premiums for each policy, requiring, for example, five $1 million policies or one $5 million policy to get started. Investments of this size are appropriate only for wealthy individuals or families.

The biggest problem for a potential investor, other than the high minimum, is the loss of investor control. Although the investment manager of the insurance company's separate account can generally change investments or reallocate among hedge funds when desired, the policy owner cannot direct the investment manager in any way other than to make broad allocation decisions from one investment option to another. The insurance company ultimately has the power to hire or fire the investment manager. Indeed, the insurance company, not the policy owner, is the investment manager's client. Of course, the policy owner can always surrender the policy and accept the accompanying negative tax consequences or move the policy to a different insurance company and incur brokerage commissions and other costs. Investor control is a critical issue, given that the IRS may find that the policy owner's involvement in the portfolio's management invalidates the policy's insurance status and claim that the investor should be taxed on the earnings currently (see chapter 12).

Recent Developments

In 2003, the IRS released a proposed regulation[3] and two revenue rulings[4] that place some restrictions on the tax advantages of PPLI invested in hedge funds (see chapter 12). The proposed regulation does not prevent such policies from investing in hedge funds; nor does it change the income tax deferral and elimination or estate tax–planning benefits of such policies. To meet the diversification requirement so that the policy owner will not be taxed on hedge fund earnings, the regulation requires that the insurance policies either invest in a hedge fund that is open only to insurance companies (see chapter 14) or invest in a diversified portfolio of at least five hedge funds, when those funds are open to noninsurance investors. Although the rulings permit some flexibility, most insurance companies have taken the conservative route and permit only insurance-dedicated hedge funds and private-equity funds. The revenue rulings also restrict the insurance policy owner's ability to choose the underlying hedge fund investments (especially if the hedge funds allow noninsurance investors).

These developments have prompted many hedge funds or funds of funds to form insurance-dedicated funds, open only to insurance companies (see chapter 14). The investments in an insurance-dedicated fund (sometimes called a cloned fund) often mirror the investments of the manager's existing hedge fund or fund of funds and therefore have the same or similar investment returns. Some insurance companies are issuing policies that allow investors to choose from many such insurance-dedicated funds. Properly structured, the IRS guidelines allow such investments, including the investor's right to periodically reallocate the investment among a number of cloned funds. The policy owner can also allow an independent manager appointed by the insurance company to allocate the insurance account among five or more hedge funds open to investors who are not insurance companies.

The lack of investor control and other limitations may be a problem for some, but the degree of control permitted varies from policy to policy. In any case, the tax-free earnings with successful hedge fund managers as well as the income tax–deferred or income tax–free—and possibly estate tax–free—payout at death make these policies worthwhile for certain wealthy investors.

PPLI in the Overall Portfolio

The greatest tax benefits from PPLI result when the policy is held until the death of the insured, because the death benefit is received free of income tax and possibly estate tax. That's why PPLI is often purchased with only a portion of a wealthy investor's assets—the portion not expected to be needed before the death of the insured (see chapter 8).

Most wealthy investors have a diversified portfolio of investments consisting of different investment strategies. In deciding the investment strategy for PPLI, the policy owner's overall investment mix should be considered. Diversifying a portfolio with high-yield, short-term trading, or other tax-inefficient strategies is often considered beneficial for minimizing risk and increasing after-tax returns. PPLI often allows high-yield and short-term trading strategies to be added to one's investment mix without adding tax inefficiency.

Because a tax deduction to the policy owner is not available for losses on returns inside the policy, assets expected to produce high, consistent, absolute returns are good candidates for PPLI. Investments that are either highly tax efficient or so speculative that losses are contemplated are generally not the best candidates for PPLI investments—unless, of course, the investments produce large returns. That means PPLI is an attractive option even at 15 percent capital gains rate (see chapter 8). Generally, the policy owner can choose the type of investment strategy for the PPLI policy.

Chapter Notes

1. Portions of this chapter were adapted from or originally appeared in the *Journal of Private Portfolio Management* 2, no. 3 (winter 1999): 27, published by Institutional Investor and the *Journal of Wealth Management* 7, no. 2 (fall 2004). To view the original articles, visit www.iijournals.com.

2. The offshore company may be subject to U.S. withholding tax on certain U.S. source income (such as the 30 percent tax on U.S. dividends) and would not be entitled to U.S. tax treaty benefits, both of which might significantly reduce investment returns.

3. Proposed Regulation revoking Reg. Section 1.817-5(f)(2)(ii) [68 FR 44689; July 30, 2003].

4. Revenue Ruling 2003-91 and Revenue Ruling 2003-92.

CHAPTER 4

Asset Protection
Riches Out of Reach

GIDEON ROTHSCHILD AND DANIEL S. RUBIN

L ife insurance policies have long played a significant role in reducing taxes. They're favored under the Internal Revenue Code in several significant ways, as discussed in chapter 12. Specifically, (1) earnings within the life insurance policy are not taxable as they accumulate; (2) accumulated income generally can be withdrawn from the policy as loans without income tax effect; and (3) the policy's death benefit is generally not subject to income taxation. In addition, through the use of a properly drafted irrevocable "insurance" trust, the death benefit may also be made to pass to or for the benefit of the owner's intended beneficiaries without the imposition of estate or generation-skipping transfer taxes.

Tax savings are not, however, the only benefit that can be gained by owning life insurance. Potentially even more significant, at least to certain individuals, is that life insurance is one of a very few forms of investment that's often inherently protected from creditor claims. Private placement life insurance (PPLI), in particular, lends itself to so-called asset protection planning and for many individuals will be a principal motivation for the investment. But it is important to understand the broader asset-protection planning benefits of life insurance before considering the particular benefits that might be afforded by private placement life insurance policies.

Public Policy

Certain classes of assets are favored by statute so as to provide their owner, or debtor, a greater level of protection from the claims of creditors than would other classes of assets. Usually this heightened creditor protection is provided because the asset class is a type that's considered essential for the debtor and/or the debtor's family to maintain at least a minimum level of financial well-being and thereby avoid becoming a burden to the state. In all cases, the extent of such creditor protection is, of course, tempered by society's proper concern for the creditor's competing rights to access the debtor's property toward satisfaction of the creditor's legitimate claims.

Exemption statutes frequently name life insurance as one such favored asset class. Life insurance is favored with an exemption from creditor attachment because it can help to ensure the financial subsistence of the debtor's spouse and/or dependents following the death of the "breadwinning" debtor. However, the statutory exemption afforded to life insurance varies (sometime extensively) by jurisdiction and is also likely subject to some lesser or greater extent to the vagaries of judge-made law.[1] Notwithstanding these differences, the potential value of such an exemption to a debtor or potential debtor means that the exemption for life insurance warrants a careful and considered review by estate and asset-protection planners.

Consideration of the potential creditor protection afforded to life insurance is, however, complicated by the several capacities in which the debtor may be interested in the policy—that is, whether the debtor is the owner of the policy, the insured, or both. Alternatively, the debtor may be the beneficiary of the policy, or the debtor may be the owner of a policy that names his or her estate as the beneficiary of the policy. Since the exemptions afforded to life insurance are intended to further particular public policy goals (that is, protecting the debtor's dependents from financial destitution in the event of the debtor's untimely demise), the relationships between the owner and the insured and between the owner and the beneficiary are often key to determining whether and to what extent the particular life insurance policy at issue may be protected from creditor claims.

The Federal Exemption

The federal bankruptcy exemption for life insurance policies owned by the debtor can be found at Section 522(d)(8) of the U.S. Bankruptcy Code.[2] The federal bankruptcy exemption for life insurance shields unmatured policies owned by the debtor (other than a credit life insurance contract) and up to $8,000[3] of the debtor's aggregate interest in any accrued dividend or interest under, or loan value of, an unmatured life insurance contract, provided that the insured is either the debtor or an individual of whom the debtor is a dependent. Since federal bankruptcy law broadly defines a "dependent" as including a spouse, whether or not the debtor's spouse is actually dependent upon the debtor, the exemption will apply without further inquiry as long as either the debtor or the debtor's spouse is the insured.[4]

The effect of the foregoing exemption is obviously to protect the actual insurance element of the life insurance policy and little else, since only a minimal amount of the cash surrender value of the policy is afforded any exemption. That the primary intent of the Bankruptcy Code as it relates to the exemption of life insurance is to protect a dependent's interest in the life insurance policy, rather than the owner's own interest, is further supported by Section 522(d)(11)(C) of the Bankruptcy Code.[5] That section concerns the beneficiary of the policy as the debtor (rather than the owner of the policy as the debtor) and exempts the debtor's entitlement to the proceeds of a life insurance contract, without any specific dollar limitation, to the extent that such proceeds are "reasonably necessary" for the support of the debtor and any dependent of the debtor. Although the federal bankruptcy exemption of an unmatured life insurance contract without the exemption of any significant portion of the cash surrender value may prove invaluable in certain limited circumstances (for example, if the debtor has become uninsurable since the life insurance policy was originally purchased), it obviously does not provide significant opportunities for asset protection or prebankruptcy planning for the insured.

The State Exemptions

Since the federal exemption scheme for life insurance owned by the debtor is so parsimonious, alternative state exemptions have become the primary focus in asset-protection planning with life insurance. **FIGURE 4.1**, page 50, contains a tabulation of the statutory exemptions afforded by each of the 50 states and the District of Columbia.

As can be seen in figure 4.1, some states follow the model of the federal exemption scheme and provide very limited exemptions for the cash surrender value of life insurance. For example, South Carolina offers an exemption of only $4,000 for the cash surrender value of life insurance (provided that the insured is either the debtor or an individual upon whom the debtor is dependent).[6] Proceeds payable to the insured's spouse, children, or dependents are, however, generally fully exempt from the creditors of the insured.[7] Wisconsin also exempts only $4,000 (and only provided that the insured is either the debtor, a dependent of the debtor, or an individual upon whom the debtor is dependent).[8] If the debtor is the beneficiary of the life insurance policy, however, and provided that the debtor was dependent upon the insured, Wisconsin law exempts payments to the extent reasonably necessary for the support of the debtor and the debtor's dependents.[9]

Most states, however, have exemption schemes that provide for far greater protection of the cash surrender value of life insurance policies than does the federal exemption scheme. For example, in keeping with its generally pro-debtor stance, the state of Florida specifically exempts the entire cash surrender value of life insurance policies from the reach of creditors[10] and the entire death benefit from the creditors of the insured unless the proceeds are payable to the insured's estate.[11] Hawaii similarly specifically exempts the entire death benefit and cash surrender value of life insurance policies from the reach of creditors of the owner of the life insurance policy, provided that the policy is payable to a spouse of the insured or to a child, parent, or other person dependent upon the insured, except (of course) as to premiums paid in fraud to creditors.[12] Louisiana also specifically exempts the entire proceeds (including the full cash surrender value) of life insurance policies from the reach of creditors, provided that the exemption is limited to $35,000 of the cash surrender value if the life insurance policy was issued within nine months of a bankruptcy filing.[13]

New York's scheme for the exemption of life insurance[14] is worth noting because it clearly distinguishes between the several permutations that can result depending on whether the debtor is the owner of the policy (referred to under the New York statute as the person "effecting the policy"),[15] the insured, or the beneficiary, or some combination thereof. More specifically, the New York statutory exemption scheme for life insurance provides that:

> (a) If the owner of a life insurance policy insures his or her own life for the benefit of another (that is, a beneficiary other than the owner's estate), that other person shall be entitled to the proceeds and avails of the policy as against the creditors of the owner.[16] (In other words, the beneficiary's interest in a life insurance policy that is owned by another is protected from claims of the policy owner's creditors.)[17]
>
> (b) If the owner of a life insurance policy insures the life of another for the owner's own benefit, the owner shall be entitled to the proceeds and avails of the policy as against the creditors of the insured.[18] (In other words, the interest of an owner of life insurance in the policy is protected from the creditors of the insured.)
>
> (c) If the owner of a life insurance policy insures the life of his or her spouse for the owner's own benefit, the owner shall also be entitled to the proceeds and avails of the policy as against his or her own creditors.[19] (In

other words, the interest of an owner/beneficiary of life insurance in the policy is protected from the owner/beneficiary's own creditors if the insured is the owner's spouse.)

(d) If the owner of a life insurance policy insures the life of another person for the benefit of a third party, the third party shall be entitled to the proceeds and avails of the policy as against the creditors of both the owner and the insured.[20] (In other words, the beneficiary's interest in a life insurance policy is protected from claims of the creditors of both the owner of the policy and the insured.)

(e) The owner of a life insurance policy, regardless of the identity of the insured, shall be entitled to accelerated payments of the death benefit or accelerated payment of a special surrender value permitted under such policy as against the creditors of the owner.[21] (In other words, the owner's interest in the cash surrender value of a life insurance policy is protected from claims of the owner's own creditors.)

Interestingly, even the extensive New York statutory exemption scheme does not cover all possible permutations. For example, in *Dellefield v. Block,*[22] a husband took out two paid-up life insurance policies on his own life in favor of his wife. Thereafter, both the husband effecting the policy and his wife, the beneficiary of the policy, became debtors of the same judgment creditor. Since §166 of the New York Insurance Law (precursor to the current New York statute) provided that a life insurance policy insuring the owner's own life for the benefit of another is protected from a debtor owner's creditors but did not then expressly provide that the same life insurance policy is protected from a debtor beneficiary's creditors, the novel issue arose as to whether a joint judgment creditor could enforce its judgment against the life insurance policies. Based on a liberal interpretation of legislative intent to the effect that the statutory exemption of the debtor/owner's interest was intended to protect all cases in which a person by investment of his own money insured his or her own life for the benefit of another, the *Dellefield* court held that the life insurance policies could not be reached by the parties' joint judgment creditor.

As shall be seen, the liberal application of statutory creditor exemptions for life insurance policies appears to be the prevailing practice among our nation's judiciary. One example of this phenomenon exists in connection with the court's interpretation of the phrase "proceeds and avails" of an insurance policy pursuant to a statutory exemption. As a baseline, it might be noted that the phrase "proceeds and avails" as used in the New York statute, for example, is defined to include "death benefits, cash surrender and loan values, premiums waived, and dividends, whether used in reduction of premiums or in whatever manner used or applied, except where the debtor has, after issuance of the policy, elected to receive the dividends in cash."[23] Unlike New York, however, not all state statutes expressly define which incidents of value of a life insurance policy (that is, specifically, the debtor's ability to shield the cash surrender value of a life insurance policy versus the debtor's entitlement to the proceeds of a matured policy which insured the life of another) are covered by the exemption scheme at issue. Therefore, the issue has frequently arisen as to whether and to what extent the cash surrender value should be exempted when the statute refers only to "monies paid out of a life insurance policy" or similarly ambiguous language.

In the matter of *In re Worthington*,[24] the Bankruptcy Court, interpreting a Kentucky exemption statute which provided simply that "any money or other benefit to be paid or rendered by any assessment or cooperative life or casualty insurance company is exempt from execution or other process,"[25] determined that an unlimited exemption was provided for the cash surrender value of life insurance policies. The *Worthington* court stated that:

> This statute does not restrict "any money or other benefit to be paid" as exemptible only upon death, but rather it denotes an exemption extending to the debtor on any monetary value or benefits accruing by virtue of ownership. Thus, the loan values or the cash surrender values by virtue of the enactment of the Kentucky legislature have been deemed exempt since the term "any money . . . to be paid" is not restricted as to time of election and offers no alternative but to include the cash surrender value within its definition. The Kentucky legislature has, after due deliberation and in its wisdom, determined that any monetary value in life insurance policies owned by its citizens is exempt without monetary limitation.[26]

Similarly, it has generally been held that when reference is made to the "proceeds and avails" of a life insurance policy, such reference comprehends the protection of cash surrender values and other values built up during the life of the policy as well as the protection of its death benefit even if not expressly so provided by statute. The rationale behind such holdings is made clear in the matter of *In re Beckman*,[27] in which the court stated:

> The legislature well knew that an insured would probably have creditors during his lifetime and no doubt fully realized that if the cash surrender value could be reached by creditors of the insured while he was living, there would not be in many cases any "proceeds and avails" to exempt or safeguard after death. Nowhere in the statute do we find a single word or expression indicating that the exemption is only to be effective after the death of the insured.[28]

Moreover, the unlimited exemption for the cash surrender value of life insurance that exists in some state can be roundly abused by dishonest debtors and has been considered by the courts and disregarded as a basis for judicially recasting the liberally interpreted import of the exemption statutes. For example, in the matter of *In re White*,[29] the court rejected the bankruptcy trustee's objection to an unlimited exemption for the "proceeds and avails" of life insurance. The bankruptcy trustee's objection, rejected by the court, was that to exempt the cash surrender value of the debtor's life insurance policy would

> provide a debtor with an avenue for depositing his funds in unlimited amounts in a species of property that would place it beyond the reach of his creditors but not beyond his own reach after his discharge in bankruptcy.[30]

Similarly, the court in *In re Beckman*[31] was not compelled by the bankruptcy trustee's argument that to hold the cash surrender value of the debtor's life insurance policy exempt would be to make an insurance policy "a refuge for fraud."[32] In each case, the court responded to the creditor's argument by stating that such argument overlooks the fact that the exemption statute expressly provides that premiums paid in fraud of creditors would, nevertheless, inure to the benefit of creditors. Finally, it has been said that in any event "if abuses to enacted exemptions are deemed to exist, the remedy is by other than judicial legislation."[33]

Therefore, for the residents of certain states, at least, valuable asset protection and prebankruptcy planning opportunities exist using life insurance policies, provided, as always, that the conversion of nonexempt assets into exempt assets (be they cash surrender value life insurance policies or otherwise) is not made with the intent to hinder, delay, or defraud creditors.[34]

Insurance Trusts

Whether or not there exists in any particular jurisdiction a significant creditor exemption for life insurance policies, however, the greatest creditor protection will always be achieved through the use of trusts. For example, a policy may be transferred to an irrevocable spendthrift trust (or even better, an irrevocable spendthrift trust can acquire the life insurance policy in the first instance), thereby protecting the value of the life insurance policy not only from future creditors of the settlor and creditors of the trust beneficiaries but from taxation in the settlor's estate as well.[35] At the same time, there is little doubt that Section 541(c)(2) of the Bankruptcy Code would also exclude the trust property from the settlor/debtor's bankruptcy estate as a spendthrift trust enforceable under applicable nonbankruptcy law. The use of a trust also avoids a potential creditor argument that, notwithstanding the existence of a statutory exemption, such exemption was never intended to extend to PPLI policies with cash value and a death benefit far in excess of what might be required for the subsistence of the debtor and/or his or her dependents.

Furthermore, the transfer of life insurance policies to an irrevocable life insurance trust need not have the effect of placing the potential use and enjoyment of the cash value beyond the settlor's reach. Provided that the settlor is married, the spouse may be named as a discretionary beneficiary of the trust. Therefore, to the extent that the trustees are amenable to making a distribution of property out of the trust to the settlor's spouse, the settlor can have an indirect benefit from the trust property for as long as the settlor's spouse is living and the parties have not separated or divorced. Where the settlor is concerned with the possibility of the spouse predeceasing or, alternatively, where the settlor is concerned with the possibility of a divorce, a so-called floating spouse clause may be appropriate. A floating spouse clause would define the spouse of the settlor as the person to whom the settlor is married at the time in question; therefore, if the settlor and the settlor's current spouse should divorce, or the settlor's spouse should predecease the settlor, the settlor could again have access to the trust fund provided only that the settlor remarry.

A less traditional alternative would have the settlor establish the trust under the laws of Alaska, Delaware, Missouri, Nevada, Oklahoma, Rhode Island, or Utah, since the law in each of those states provides that the owner of property (including the owner of a life insurance policy) may create a discretionary trust for his or her own benefit without leaving the transferred property subject to the claims of his or her future creditors (a so-called self-settled trust). Such trusts are frequently also called *domestic asset protection trusts.* A number of foreign jurisdictions, including Bermuda, the Bahamas, the Cayman Islands, and the Cook Islands, have similar laws regarding the use of self-settled trusts to protect against potential future creditor claims. Such trusts are frequently called *foreign asset protection trusts* and are generally considered to be more protective because they are not subject to potential "full faith and credit" and "federalism" attacks under U.S. constitutional law.[36]

A transfer to an *asset-protection trust* settled under the law of one of the aforementioned jurisdictions, wherein the settler retains no rights (other than those of a discretionary beneficiary), would be deemed a completed gift for U.S. gift-tax purposes because of the interplay between the Internal Revenue Code and the applicable law governing creditors' rights.

Furthermore, such a trust should cause the proceeds payable on death to be excluded from the settlor's estate for transfer-tax purposes, irrespective of the fact that the settlor may benefit from the cash value of the policy (albeit at the trustee's discretion) during the settlor's lifetime.[37]

The use of PPLI policies can actually enhance the asset protection afforded by such trusts. This is so because the tax benefits that are expected to inure from the PPLI policy provide a rationale other than the hindrance, delay, or fraud of creditors (a so-called fraudulent transfer) in connection with the settlor's transfer of property to the trust in connection with its funding. As has been discussed in other chapters, the relatively large premium commitment required in connection with PPLI policies frequently warrants that the insurance trust crafted to hold them be established in a jurisdiction like Alaska, which imposes no state premium tax (generally 2 to 3 percent of each premium payment) or, at a minimum, a relatively low state premium tax.[38] An offshore asset-protection trust might be further justified by the fact that an offshore PPLI policy, which may be owned only by a non-U.S. person (such as a foreign asset-protection trust), can invest in foreign securities, which are not otherwise open for investment to U.S. persons because of Securities and Exchange Commission regulation. Moreover, offshore investment opportunities may provide greater flexibility and, perhaps, economies, again because of the absence of regulation over such investments by the SEC.

It's also important to note that similar to the state statutory exemptions discussed earlier, certain foreign jurisdictions with substantial life insurance industries have statutory law exempting life insurance from the reach of creditors. For example, Bermuda's Insurance Act of 1978 provides that:

1 Where a beneficiary is designated, the insurance money, from the time of the happening of the event upon which the insurance money becomes payable, is not part of the estate of the insured and is not subject to the claims of the creditors of the insured.

2 While a designation in favor of a child or grandchild . . . or a spouse or parent of a person whose life is insured, or any of them, is in effect, the rights and interests of the insured in the insurance money and in the contract are exempt from execution or seizure.[39]

In a similar vein, in Barbados the interest of a policyholder is not liable to be applied to or made available in payment of the debts of the policyholder by any judgment, order, or process of any court.[40] The Bahamas has similarly protective legislation.[41]

In contrast to Bermuda, Barbados, and the Bahamas, however, the governing insurance law in the Cayman Islands (which is another relatively substantial offshore insurance jurisdiction) does not specifically address whether there are any special creditor protections for policy values. The law of the Cayman Islands does, however, require that insurers keep separate accounts on behalf of its clients from which no payment can be made "directly or indirectly for any purpose other than those of the insurer's long-term business."[42] This obviously presents a potentially powerful argument that the claims of creditors of a policy owner, insured, or beneficiary cannot be paid out of the cash value of a life insurance policy held with a Cayman insurer.[43]

Therefore, the investment in a PPLI policy, whether domestic or foreign, might provide a concerned individual not only with the potential for tax-free income, but also with an asset that will be protected against even the most aggressive creditor claims. For many individuals, the exemption from creditor claim that is generally afforded to life insurance policies will provide a compelling argument in favor of life insurance as an investment. Even in jurisdictions that have generous exemptions for the cash surrender value of life insurance, however, the use of a properly structured "life insurance" trust to hold the policy remains important. This is especially true in light of the fact that through advanced planning, the use of an irrevocable life insurance trust need not have the effect of placing the potential use and enjoyment of the cash surrender value beyond the settlor's reach.

FIGURE 4.1 *State Regulations on PPLI*

ALABAMA

Life Insurance Proceeds

Beneficiary's interest in proceeds and avails wholly protected from creditors of owner and insured.

Owner's interest in proceeds and avails wholly protected from creditors of insured if owner (or owner's spouse) is insured, and spouse and/or children (or owner and/or children) are beneficiaries.

Applicable Section(s)

Ala. Code § 6-10-8

ALASKA

Life Insurance Proceeds

Owner's interest in up to $12,500 of value of unmatured policy is exempt.

Maximum interest of $438 per week of spouse or dependent beneficiary is exempt.

Applicable Section(s)

Alaska Stat. §§ 09.38.025 and 09.38.030

Alaska Admin. Code Tit. 8 § 95.030

ARIZONA

Life Insurance Proceeds

Cash value and proceeds wholly exempt from creditors of insured and beneficiaries.

Applicable Section(s)

Ariz. Rev. Stat. §§ 20-1131, 20-1131.01, and 33-1126(A)(1) and (6), and (C)

ARKANSAS

Note:

In re Hudspeth, 92 Bankr. 827 (1988), the court held that the state exemption contained in Ark. Code Ann. § 16-66-209 of the value of all insurance benefits without limitation was unconstitutional since Article 9 § 2 of Arkansas's Constitution imposes a $500 limited exemption from creditor claims. In *Federal Sav. & Loan Ins. Co. v. Holt,* 894 F.2d 1005 (8th Cir. 1990), the Court imposed a $500 exemption ceiling on life insurance benefits and policies' cash surrender value.

CALIFORNIA

Life Insurance Proceeds

Unmatured policy wholly exempt from creditors; provided, however, that loan value of only $9,700 ($19,400 if debtor married) is exempt.

Death benefits exempt to extent reasonably necessary for support of debtor, and spouse and dependents of debtor.

Applicable Section(s)

Cal. Code Civ. Proc. § 704.100

COLORADO

Life Insurance Proceeds

Interest in up to $50,000 of cash surrender value (except for increase attributable to previous 48 months' contributions) exempt from creditors of insured except where beneficiary is estate of insured.

Death benefit payable to beneficiary (other than estate of insured) wholly exempt from creditors of insured.

Applicable Section(s)

Colo. Rev. Stat. §§ 13-54-102(1)(l) and (s)

CONNECTICUT

Life Insurance Proceeds

Interest of beneficiary (other than insured) in proceeds wholly protected from creditors of insured.

Applicable Section(s)

Conn. Gen. Stat. § 38a-453

DELAWARE

Life Insurance Proceeds

Beneficiary's interest in "proceeds and avails" wholly protected from all creditors.

Applicable Section(s)

Del. Code Ann. Tit. 18 § 2725

DISTRICT OF COLUMBIA

Life Insurance Proceeds

Maximum exemption of $200 per month for a beneficiary providing principal support of a family or $60 per month for a beneficiary not providing principal support of a family.

Applicable Section(s)

D.C. Code Ann. § 15-503

FLORIDA

Life Insurance Proceeds

Beneficiary's interest in proceeds wholly protected from insured's creditors unless policy payable to insured or his estate.

Owner's interest in cash surrender value wholly exempt.

Applicable Section(s)

Fla. Stat. §§ 222.13 and 222.14

GEORGIA

Life Insurance Proceeds

Owner's interest in unmatured policy (except credit life insurance) wholly exempt; provided that only $2,000 maximum accrued dividend or interest, or loan or cash value, exempt (provided insured is debtor or individual upon whom debtor is dependent).

Beneficiary's interest in death benefit exempt to extent reasonably necessary for support or debtor and dependent if insured was individual of whom debtor was a dependent.

Applicable Section(s)

Ga. Code Ann. §§ 44-13-100(a)(2)(E), 44-13-100(a)(8), 44-13-100(a)(9) and 44-13-100(a)(11)(C)

HAWAII

Life Insurance Proceeds

Proceeds and cash value payable to insured's spouse, child, parent, or other dependent is wholly exempt from insured's creditors.

Applicable Section(s)

Haw. Rev. Stat. § 431:10-232

IDAHO

Life Insurance Proceeds

Beneficiary's interest in "proceeds and avails" wholly protected from all creditors.

Applicable Section(s)

Idaho Code § 41-1833

ILLINOIS

Life Insurance Proceeds

Proceeds and cash value payable to insured's spouse, child, parent, or other dependent is wholly exempt from insured's creditors.

Beneficiary's interest in payment under policy insuring individual of whom beneficiary was a dependent is exempt to extent necessary for support of beneficiary and dependents.

Applicable Section(s)

215 Ill. Comp. Stat. § 5/238(a), 735. Ill. Comp. Stat. § 5/12-1001(f) and (h)(3)

INDIANA

Life Insurance Proceeds

If contract so provides, benefits payable to person other than person effecting policy are wholly exempt from creditors.

Applicable Section(s)

Ind. Code § 27-2-5-1

IOWA

Life Insurance Proceeds

Interest in accrued dividend or interest, or loan or cash surrender value, wholly exempt if beneficiary is spouse, child, or dependent, provided that increases attributable to prior two years limited to $10,000.

Maximum $15,000 of death benefit exempt if payable to spouse, child, or dependent.

Applicable Section(s)

Iowa Code § 627.6(6)

KANSAS

Life Insurance Proceeds
Policy and its reserves, or their present value, wholly exempt from claims of all creditors unless purchased within past year.

Applicable Section(s)
Kan. Stat. Ann. §§ 40-414(a) and (f)

KENTUCKY

Life Insurance Proceeds
Beneficiary's interest in "proceeds and avails" wholly protected from all creditors.

Owner's interest in policy wholly exempt.

Applicable Section(s)
Ky. Rev. Stat. Ann. §§ 427.110(1) and 304.14-300

LOUISIANA

Life Insurance Proceeds
Interest of beneficiary (including estate of insured) in "proceeds and avails" wholly protected from all creditors.

Applicable Section(s)
La. Rev. Stat. Ann. § 22:647

MAINE

Life Insurance Proceeds
Beneficiary's interest in "proceeds and avails" wholly protected from all creditors.

Owner's interest in unmatured policy (except credit life insurance) wholly exempt; provided that only $4,000 maximum accrued dividend or interest, or loan value, exempt (provided insured is debtor or individual upon whom debtor dependent).

Applicable Section(s)
Me. Rev. Stat. Ann. Tit. 24-A, § 2428. Tit. 14 §§ 4422(10) and (11)

MARYLAND

Life Insurance Proceeds
Proceeds wholly exempt if payable to the spouse, child, or dependent relative of the insured.

Applicable Section(s)
Md. Code Ann., Ins. § 16-111

MASSACHUSETTS

Life Insurance Proceeds

Beneficiary's interest in "proceeds" wholly protected from creditors of owner.

Applicable Section(s)

Mass. Gen. Laws ch. 175 § 125

MICHIGAN

Life Insurance Proceeds

Proceeds (including cash value) wholly exempt from creditors.

Applicable Section(s)

Mich. Comp. Laws § 500.2207

MINNESOTA

Life Insurance Proceeds

Proceeds wholly exempt from creditors of person effecting the policy.

Maximum $20,000 of proceeds payable to a spouse or child is exempt from other creditors (increased by $5,000 for each dependent of the spouse or child).

Maximum $4,000 interest in any accrued dividend or interest, or loan value, exempt (provided insured is debtor or individual upon whom debtor dependent).

Applicable Section(s)

Minn. Stat. §§ 61A.12 and 550.37(10) and (23)

MISSISSIPPI

Life Insurance Proceeds

Proceeds (including cash surrender and loan value) wholly protected from creditors of insured; provided maximum $50,000 cash surrender or loan value exempt if from premiums paid in past 12 months.

Applicable Section(s)

Miss. Code Ann. §§ 85-3-1 and 85-3-11

MISSOURI

Life Insurance Proceeds

Owner's interest in unmatured policy (except credit life insurance) wholly exempt; provided that only $150,000 maximum accrued dividend or interest, or loan value, exempt (and provided insured is debtor or individual upon whom debtor is dependent).

Applicable Section(s)

Mo. Rev. Stat. §§ 513.430(7) and (8)

MONTANA

Life Insurance Proceeds

Beneficiary's interest in "proceeds and avails" wholly protected from creditors of owner and insured.

Maximum $4,000 in value of unmatured life insurance contract is exempt.

Applicable Section(s)

Mont. Code Ann. §§ 33-15-511 and 25-13-609(4)

NEBRASKA

Life Insurance Proceeds

Maximum $10,000 of proceeds, cash value, and benefits exempt from insured's creditors (unless beneficiary is estate of insured); also exempt from beneficiary's creditors if beneficiary related by blood or marriage to insured.

Applicable Section(s)

Neb. Rev. Stat. § 44-371

NEVADA

Life Insurance Proceeds

Beneficiary's interest in "proceeds and avails" wholly protected from all creditors.

Owner's interest in all money, benefits, privileges, or immunities, exempt to extent premium not in excess of $1,000 per year.

Applicable Section(s)

Nev. Rev. Stat. §§ 21.090(1)(k) and 687B.260

NEW HAMPSHIRE

Life Insurance Proceeds

Beneficiary's interest in proceeds wholly protected from creditors of person effecting policy unless policy payable to insured's estate.

Applicable Section(s)

N.H. Rev. Stat. Ann. § 408:2

NEW JERSEY

Beneficiary's interest in proceeds and avails wholly protected from all creditors provided beneficiary is not owner or insured.

Applicable Section(s)

N.J. Stat. Ann. § 17B:24-6

NEW MEXICO

Life Insurance Proceeds

Cash surrender value and withdrawal value wholly exempt from all creditors.

Applicable Section(s)

N.M. Stat. Ann. §§ 42-10-3 and 42-10-5

NEW YORK

Life Insurance Proceeds

Beneficiary's interest in proceeds and avails wholly protected from all creditors provided beneficiary is not owner or insured.

Owner's interest in proceeds and avails of policy insuring another is exempt as against creditors of insured (and owner's own creditors if insured is owner's spouse).

Applicable Section(s)

N.Y. Ins. Law § 3212

NORTH CAROLINA

Life Insurance Proceeds

Beneficiary's interest in proceeds wholly protected from creditors of insured provided beneficiary is not owner or insured.

Applicable Section(s)

N.C. Const. Art. X § 5; N.C. Gen. Stat. §§ 1C-1601 and 58-58-115

NORTH DAKOTA

Life Insurance Proceeds

Maximum exemption of proceeds or cash surrender value of $100,000 per policy and $200,000 aggregate (unless more is reasonably necessary for the support of insured and dependents), provided payable to spouse, children, or any dependent relative. Proceeds payable to the deceased, his representatives, heirs, or estate wholly exempt from creditors of owner and insured.

Applicable Section(s)

N.D. Cent. Code §§ 26.1-33-40 and 28-22-03.1

OHIO

Life Insurance Proceeds

Proceeds and avails wholly protected from creditors of insured provided beneficiary is spouse, child, or dependent.

Applicable Section(s)

Ohio Rev. Code Ann. § 3911.10

OKLAHOMA

Life Insurance Proceeds

Policy proceeds and cash values wholly protected from all creditors.

Applicable Section(s)

Okla. Stat. Tit. 36 § 3631.1(A)

OREGON

Life Insurance Proceeds

Beneficiary's interest in proceeds wholly protected from creditors of insured provided beneficiary is not owner or insured.

Owner/insured's interest in cash value wholly exempt provided beneficiary is not owner/insured's estate.

Applicable Section(s)

Or. Rev. Stat. § 743.046

PENNSYLVANIA

Life Insurance Proceeds

Proceeds payable to spouse, child, or dependent relative of insured wholly exempt from creditors of insured.

Proceeds exempt from own creditors to extent necessary to provide for maximum income or return of $100 per month.

Applicable Section(s)

42 Pa. Cons. Stat. § 8124(C)

RHODE ISLAND

Life Insurance Proceeds

Beneficiary's interest in proceeds and avails wholly protected from creditors of insured, provided beneficiary is not owner or insured.

Applicable Section(s)

R.I. Gen. Laws § 27-4-11

SOUTH CAROLINA

Life Insurance Proceeds

Beneficiary's interest in proceeds and cash surrender values wholly protected from creditors of insured provided beneficiary is spouse, child, or dependent of insured.

Maximum $4,000 exemption for owner's interest in accrued dividend or interest under, or loan value of, unmatured policy under which insured is debtor or individual of whom debtor is dependent.

Applicable Section(s)

S.C. Code Ann. §§ 15-41-30(8) and 38-63-40(A)

SOUTH DAKOTA

Life Insurance Proceeds

Maximum $10,000 exemption for proceeds payable to estate or maximum $20,000 exemption for proceeds payable to spouse or children.

Applicable Section(s)

S.D. Codified Laws §§ 43-45-6 and 58-12-4

TENNESSEE

Life Insurance Proceeds

Beneficiary's interest in amounts payable under policy wholly protected from creditors of insured provided beneficiary is spouse, child, or dependent relative of insured.

Applicable Section(s)

Tenn. Code Ann. § 56-7-203

TEXAS

Life Insurance Proceeds

Policy proceeds and cash values wholly protected from all creditors (subject to disagreement among courts as to interpretation and interaction of statute).

Applicable Section(s)

Tex. Ins. Code § 1108.051

UTAH

Life Insurance Proceeds

Exemption for proceeds or benefits paid to a spouse or dependent upon death of insured to extent reasonably necessary for support of beneficiary and dependents.

Maximum $5,000 exemption for owner's interest in unmatured life insurance.

Applicable Section(s)

Utah Code Ann. §§ 78-23-6 and 78-23-7

VERMONT

Life Insurance Proceeds

Owner's interest in unmatured policy (except credit life insurance) wholly exempt.

Beneficiary's interest in payment under policy insuring life of individual on whom debtor was dependent wholly exempt; otherwise exempt from creditors of owner and insured only.

Applicable Section(s)

Vt. Stat. Ann. Tit. 12 §§ 2740(18) and (19)(H) and Tit. 8 § 3706

VIRGINIA

Life Insurance Proceeds

Beneficiary's interest in proceeds wholly protected from creditors of owner and insured, provided that beneficiary is not owner or insured.

Applicable Section(s)

Va. Code Ann. § 38.2-3122

WASHINGTON

Life Insurance Proceeds

Beneficiary's interest in proceeds and avails wholly protected from all creditors.

Applicable Section(s)

Wash. Rev. Code § 48.18.410

WEST VIRGINIA

Life Insurance Proceeds

Beneficiary's interest in proceeds and avails wholly protected from all creditors of owner and insured, provided that beneficiary is not owner or insured.

Applicable Section(s)

W. Va. Code § 33-6-27

WISCONSIN

Life Insurance Proceeds

Maximum $4,000 exemption for debtor/owner's interest in unmatured policy (other than credit life insurance), if debtor, dependent, or individual of whom the debtor is a dependent is insured.

Beneficiary's interest in payment under policy insuring individual of whom debtor was dependent is exempt to extent reasonably necessary for support of debtor and dependents.

Applicable Section(s)

Wis. Stat. § 815.18

WYOMING

Life Insurance Proceeds

Beneficiary's interest in proceeds wholly protected from all creditors of owner and insured, provided that beneficiary is not owner or insured.

Applicable Section(s)

Wyo. Stat. Ann. § 26-15-129

Although the authors have attempted to interpret and reflect the most current and appropriate statutory authority, planners are urged to refer to the current statutes and court decisions in their jurisdictions.

Chapter Notes

1. The discussion in this chapter assumes, of course, that the purchase of the insurance contract does not constitute a fraudulent transfer under applicable federal or state law. Under that scenario, any protections that would otherwise be afforded are vitiated by the fact of the fraudulent transfer.

2. 11 U.S.C. §§ 522(d)(8).

3. Pursuant to 11 U.S.C. § 104(b) this amount is subject to periodic adjustment by a detailed formula for the purpose of avoiding the erosion of Bankruptcy Code protections by reason of periodic cost-of-living increases.

4. See 11 U.S.C. § 522(a)(1).

5. 11 U.S.C. § 522(d)(11)(C).

6. S.C. Code Ann. § 15-41-30(8).

7. S.C. Code Ann. § 38-63-40(A).

8. Wis. Stat. Ann. § 815.18(f).

9. Wis. Stat. Ann. § 815.18(i)(a).

10. Fla. Stat. Ann. § 222.14.

11. Fla. Stat. Ann. § 222.13.

12. Hawaii Rev. Stat. § 431:10-232(a).

13. La. Rev. Stat. Ann. § 22.647(A).

14. New York Insurance Law § 3212; see also New York Civil Practice Law and Rules § 5205(i).

15. The person "effecting the policy" under the New York statute need not have actually purchased the policy. See, for example, *Kaufman v. New York Life Ins. Co.*, 299 N.Y.S.2d 269 (1st Dep't 1969), *aff'd* 309 N.Y.S.2d 929 (Ct. App. 1970) (husband who purchased life insurance policies that were later assigned to debtor/wife was treated as agent of debtor/wife for purposes of New York exemption statute); contrast *In re Bifulci*, 154 F. Supp. 629 (S.D.N.Y. 1957) (where a husband takes out insurance on his own life and names his wife as a beneficiary but does not assign the policy to her, the proceeds are exempt from the husband's creditors [pursuant to New York Insurance Law § 3212(b)(2)], but they are not exempt from the wife's creditors [under the same statute], even if the policy was taken out at the instigation of the wife).

16. New York Insurance Law § 3212(b)(1).

17. This exemption for a life insurance policy that insures the life of the owner for the benefit of another has been held to be protected from the owner/insured's creditors notwithstanding the fact that a power to change the beneficiaries of the life insurance policy has been reserved. See, e.g., *In Re Messinger,* 29 F.2d 158 (2d Cir. 1928); See also *Hechtkopf v. Mendlowitz,* 282 NYS 328 (N.Y. City Ct., Kings Cty. 1935) (life insurance policies fell under exemption statute where debtor was originally owner, insured, and beneficiary but changed beneficiary designation to wife after judgment for purpose of obtaining exemption).

18. New York Insurance Law § 3212(b)(2).

19. Id.

20. New York Insurance Law § 3212(b)(3).

21. New York Insurance Law § 3212(b)(6).

22. 40 F. Supp. 616 (S.D.N.Y. 1941).

23. New York Insurance Law § 3212(a)(2).

24. 28 B.R. 736 (Bankr. W.D. Kentucky 1983).

25. Ky. Rev. Stat. § 427.110(1).

26. *Worthington, supra* at note 24 at 737.

27. *In re Beckman,* 50 F. Supp. 339 (N.D. Ala. 1943).

28. Id. at 344. See also *In re White,* 185 F. Supp. 609 (N.D. W.Va. 1960).

29. Id.

30. Id. at 611.

31. *Supra* at note 28.

32. Id. at 342.

33. *Worthington, supra* at note 24 at 737.

34. The reorganization of a debtor's holdings into exempt assets prior to bankruptcy for the purpose of shielding such assets from creditors, however, is generally held to be acceptable prebankruptcy planning rather than transfers fraudulent as to creditors. See, e.g., the legislative history underlying the enactment of the Bankruptcy Reform Act of 1978 (H.R. Rep. No. 595, 95th Cong., 1st Sess. 361, 1977).

35. See 26 U.S.C. § 2042. But see 26 U.S.C. §2035(a)(2), which will include in the settlor's gross estate the proceeds of any life insurance policies that were transferred within the three-year period ending on the date of the settlor's death.

36. A discussion of which is well beyond the scope of this chapter.

37. See, *e.g.,* Gideon Rothschild, "Coming in From the Cold—Estate Planning Using Alaska Trusts," *CCH Financial and Estate Planning* (August 1997); see also PLR 9837007 (gift by Alaska settlor to Alaska trust of which settlor was discretionary beneficiary deemed completed gift. However, the IRS refused to rule on whether the trust would be includible in the estate). Amounts transferred in excess of the gift tax exemption (currently $1 million) would, however, be subject to gift tax. If larger amounts of premiums are anticipated, the settler can make loans to the trust, which would be repayable upon the settlor's death.

38. Although state premium tax is generally paid by the insurer, the cost is then passed along to the life insurance policy owner.

39. Insurance Act (1978) of Bermuda, Art. 26. If it can be shown, however, that the insurance contract "was effected and the premiums paid with intent to defraud creditors of the insured, they shall be entitled to receive, out of the money payable under the contract a sum equal to the premium paid" (Insurance Act 1978 of Bermuda, Art. 35).

40. Insurance Act, 1996 of Barbados, § 128(1).

41. Bahamas' External Insurance (Amendment) Act, Part II § 3.

42. Cayman Islands' Insurance Law (1999 Revision) § 7(6)(b)(ii).

43. The insurance law of the British Virgin Islands is very similar to that of the Cayman Islands in this regard. See Insurance Act, 1994 of the British Virgin Islands, §§ 45(2) and (4).

CHAPTER 5

Estate Planning
When Insurance Tames Taxes

MIKE CHONG

People often mistakenly assume that an estate plan is simply a matter of the drafting and execution of one's last will and testament. In fact, estate planning is a much broader concept and a key component of wealth planning. Wealth planning is the combination of estate planning and financial planning. Indeed, the two are so interrelated that one cannot do a financial plan without undertaking estate planning.

Estate planning has three distinct planning elements: (1) wealth-accumulation planning for the extended family; (2) planning for lifetime consumption and/or conservation of wealth; and (3) planning for the transfer of wealth upon death. Life insurance is a key tool in any wealth planner's arsenal. It's flexible enough to have a role in numerous combinations of wealth- and estate-planning scenarios. It can be used to:

❑ Replace wealth due to the premature death of a primary wage earner
❑ Accumulate tax-deferred wealth
❑ Transfer wealth without the imposition of estate taxes or gift taxes
❑ Provide estate liquidity to pay estate settlement costs, thereby allowing other estate property to pass to heirs by "bequest." (A bequest is a transfer of tangible personal property instead of cash. The transfer of real estate or family heirlooms usually occurs by bequest.)

Taxes and Estate Planning

Many elements of estate planning relate to the management of the various taxes affecting an estate. Transfer-tax planning is an integral part of estate planning. Whenever wealth is transferred to another individual, certain types of transfer taxes apply. Proper estate planning will significantly reduce the application of such transfer taxes, both during the life and upon the death of the estate owner. There are various types of transfer taxes. The most significant are estate, gift, and generation-skipping taxes.

Estate Taxes

Federal estate taxes apply to an individual's gross estate upon its passage to heirs. The top estate tax rate is 48 percent in 2004, 47 percent in 2005, 46 percent in 2006, and 45 percent from 2007 through 2009. In 2010, estate taxes are scheduled to be completely repealed. However, unless Congress enacts additional legislation, the estate tax that existed in 2001 (that is, 55 percent plus an additional 5 percent tax designed to recapture the benefit of the lower marginal rates for large estates) will be reinstated for the years 2011 and beyond.

Fortunately, much like the standard deduction on the federal income tax form, the federal estate tax allows for an exemption amount. The federal estate tax applies to amounts in excess of this exemption. The exemption applies to each individual's estate and does not increase according to the number of heirs. Therefore, for wealthy families, the wealth-transfer need normally far exceeds the available exemption. The exemption amount is $1.5 million in 2004 and 2005, $2 million in 2006 through 2008, and $3.5 million in 2009. For the year 2010, the estate taxes are scheduled to be completely repealed so the exclusion amount is not applicable. Again, unless Congress enacts additional legislation, the estate tax will be restored to the rates and exemption that were in effect in 2001 (that is, a maximum exemption of $1 million and a top tax rate of 55 percent), which will then apply indefinitely starting in 2011.

Special provisions apply in the case of transfers to surviving spouses. Portions of the estate transferred to the decedent's surviving spouse qualify for the marital deduction, meaning that no estate taxes are payable on such a transfer.

State Death Taxes

In addition to federal estate tax, nearly every state and the District of Columbia impose a transfer tax on the distribution of a taxpayer's estate upon death. Various types of state transfer taxes apply, including estate, inheritance, legacy, and succession taxes (state death taxes). Before 2002, the practical impact of a state death tax normally was not significant because the federal estate tax provided a credit to the taxpayer for the amount of state death taxes paid. The amount of the credit varied with the value of the taxable estate. However, when Congress enacted the scheduled reduction in estate taxes beginning in 2002, it also enacted a corresponding "phase out" of the state death tax credit against the federal estate tax. In 2001, 100 percent of the credit was available. Thereafter, the credit was reduced to 75 percent in 2002, 50 percent in 2003, and 25 percent in 2004. In 2005 no credit is available. Instead, beginning in 2005, the amount of state death taxes paid can be deducted from the taxpayer's gross estate before computing the federal estate taxes. Since the reduction and elimination in the state death tax credit and the introduction of the state death tax deduction from federal estate taxes are tied to the overall reduction of the federal estate tax, unless Congress enacts additional legislation, the federal estate tax will be restored to the rates and exemption that existed in 2001, and the corresponding state death tax credit will also be restored and will then apply for the years 2011 and beyond.

Gift Taxes

One of the simplest methods of avoiding estate taxes is for a donor to give away as much "excess wealth" as possible during his or her lifetime. This reduces the dollar value of the donor's estate at death and thereby reduces the amount of estate taxes due upon the subsequent estate transfer to heirs. However, the federal gift tax was created to prevent a donor from gifting large portions of the estate immediately before death.

The federal gift tax rates track the estate tax rates—the rates are the same as the estate tax rates. This makes sense from a tax policy standpoint because the estate tax could be completely defeated if a donor could simply gift away all of his or her estate immediately before dying. To prevent this from happening, Congress enacted a gift tax that would apply to certain gifts. As mentioned earlier, the top gift tax rates are the same as the top estate tax rates. The top gift tax rates are 48 percent in 2004, 47 percent in 2005, 46 percent in 2006, and 45 percent from 2007 through 2009. Unlike the estate tax, however, the gift tax is not completely repealed in 2010. Instead, the rate is reduced to 35 percent in 2010, and unless Congress enacts additional legislation, the top gift tax rate, like the estate tax, will be restored to the 2001 level (that is, 55 percent) effective 2011. A few states have state gift taxes applicable to the donor. These states generally maintain rates and exclusions similar to federal income tax law.

Much like the federal estate tax exclusion, the federal gift tax also has an annual exclusion. The gift tax rate applies to amounts in excess of this exclusion amount. The annual exclusion amount is $11,000 gifted to any single individual per calendar year. This amount is indexed for inflation. As a result, the threshold at which the gift tax will apply is expected to increase in the future. The annual exclusion applies to an unlimited number of recipients and for an unlimited number of years. For example, an individual could gift $11,000 to ten different individuals in the same tax year for a total of $110,000 without incurring a gift tax. Any amounts gifted in excess of the $11,000 limit are subject to the gift tax at the rates specified above. For many wealthy donors, the annual exclusion is not sufficient to cover the ultimate wealth that the donor seeks to transfer. Therefore, most estate plans use techniques that maximize the use of the annual gift tax exclusion or the lifetime gift tax exemption.

The Estate- and Gift-Tax Connection

Gift tax rates track estate tax rates, except for the year 2010. But the gift tax and the estate tax also both have exemptions or exclusion amounts that are somewhat interrelated. In other words, if an individual makes a gift over and above the $11,000 per year annual exclusion, up to $1 million of the gift in excess of the annual exclusion will be used to reduce the applicable estate tax exemption. Provided the $1 million cap is not exceeded, no gift tax will be due on the amount of the excess gift. Therefore, an individual could make a gift of up to $1 million over and above the $11,000 per year annual exclusion with no gift taxes.

For example, suppose an individual makes an excess gift of $1 million in 2004. For 2004–2005, the estate tax exemption is $1.5 million. The excess gift is applied against the $1.5 million and no gift tax is due. If the individual dies in 2005, the estate tax exemption for the individual's estate would be $500,000. The excess gift in 2004 reduced the individual's estate tax exemption by $1 million, leaving $500,000 of the exemption intact ($1,500,000 - $1,000,000 = $500,000).

Generation-Skipping Taxes

In addition to the estate tax, generation-skipping taxes may apply if any portion of a taxpayer's gross estate is transferred to subsequent generations that are two or more steps removed from the taxpayer. For example, if the taxpayer transfers portions of his or her estate to grandchildren, the transfer will be subject to the generation-skipping tax.

The generation-skipping tax rate in 2004 is 48 percent for amounts in excess of an exemption. The exemption is $1.5 million in 2004 and 2005, $2 million in 2006 through 2008, and $3.5 million in 2009. In 2010, the tax is completely repealed. In 2011, however, the tax will be restored to the rate that applied in 2001 (that is, 55 percent with an exemption of $1,060,000) for the years 2011 and beyond. The generation-skipping tax is in addition to the estate tax. Therefore, a transfer to grandchildren could be subject to a 48 percent estate tax plus a 48 percent generation-skipping tax on the balance. This produces a combined effective tax rate of 78 percent. For example, a bequest in 2004 of $1 million to grandchildren in excess of the applicable exemptions would be subject to a combined estate and generation-skipping tax of $730,000.

Techniques for Reducing Estate Taxes

Every estate plan incorporates elements of tax-avoidance techniques, whether it is the complete or partial avoidance of gift tax, estate tax, income tax, or a combination of such taxes. Indeed, a majority of estate plans are designed to achieve three goals:

- ❏ Minimize the impact of the estate tax by gifting away portions of the estate during the lifetime of the taxpayer
- ❏ Minimize the impact of the gift tax when portions of the estate are gifted away during the lifetime of the taxpayer
- ❏ Maintain some level of control over the portions of the estate gifted during the lifetime of the taxpayer

Estate planners employ a range of techniques—some very simple, others quite sophisticated—to achieve these goals. One of the simplest is to give $11,000 per year in cash gifts to family members and others. This accomplishes the dual task of avoiding estate taxes and gift taxes. However, this method does not allow the taxpayer to maintain any control over the gift once it passes to another; nor does it maximize the use of the yearly $11,000 exemption.

More sophisticated estate-planning techniques allow a taxpayer to maintain some control over a gift upon its passage to others as well as maximize the use of the yearly $11,000 gift-tax exemption. Many of these techniques involve the use of trusts, closely held corporations, loans, discounts, leverage, life insurance, and annuities. Whether these techniques are appropriate for any individual depends on the individual's situation and on his understanding and appetite for complexity.

Trusts

Trusts are commonly used to remove assets from a taxpayer's estate before death to minimize estate taxes. The settlor (the person who establishes and funds the trust) can structure the trust in a manner that restricts or increases distributions to beneficiaries provided they act in certain ways. This approach allows the settlor to exert some control over the eventual disposition of trust assets. Trusts also allow the trustees the flexibility to determine when and how distributions of trust funds will be made to the beneficiaries. Trusts can be used to achieve other important estate-planning goals such as investment management, protecting assets from the creditors of beneficiaries, and preventing assets from being pledged or sold. The following are some common types of trusts used by estate planners.

Irrevocable Life Insurance Trust

An irrevocable life insurance trust (ILIT) can be structured so as to remove both the policy and its death benefit from the estate of the taxpayer. As a result, death benefits can pass to the beneficiaries free from both estate taxes and income taxes. Although life insurance can provide tax-deferred asset accumulation and an income tax–free death benefit, the death benefit proceeds are not ordinarily exempt from estate taxes. To avoid the application of the estate tax to the death benefit proceeds, the life insurance policy should not be owned by the taxpayer's estate at the time of the insured's death. In addition, the taxpayer should not retain any "incidents of ownership" in the policy before the death of the insured. From the standpoint of the Internal Revenue Service (IRS), if an individual or entity maintains power and control over property (such as a life insurance policy), that individual will be deemed to own that property, and all of the attendant taxation events flowing from the property will accrue to that individual or entity regardless of any structural formalities. By placing the life insurance policy in a life insurance trust, structuring the trust as irrevocable, and naming an independent trustee for trust administration, the taxpayer can effectively remove the policy and its proceeds from the taxpayer's estate resulting in death benefits passing to the beneficiaries free from estate taxes and income taxes.

Two practical issues that arise with the establishment of an ILIT are (1) funding the trust in a way that allows for the immediate use of the annual gift-tax exclusion, and (2) maximizing the annual gift-tax exclusion amount. Trusts normally provide for funds to accumulate (within the trust or in the life insurance policy) before any payment to trust beneficiaries. Since trust asset accumulations are not intended to be paid out until sometime in the future, gifts to the trust would not normally qualify for the $11,000 per beneficiary gift-tax annual exclusion on a current basis because they are not gifts of a "present interest." A present-interest gift is one that is completed during the current tax year. A gift may not be considered completed if there are conditions or restrictions on the gift. For example, let's assume the settlor of a trust were to provide gifts of $11,000 per year for five years to a trust, but the trust beneficiaries could not receive any of the funds until the fifth year. Since the beneficiaries could not access the funds until the fifth year, the gift was not completed until then. Therefore, the settlor did not make annual gifts of $11,000 per year for five years but rather a single gift of $55,000 in the fifth year. Fortunately, however, there is a common technique used to make gifts to trusts qualify currently for the annual gift-tax exclusion.

One method of ensuring that the funds will qualify as a present-interest gift and therefore be eligible for the immediate use of the gift-tax exclusion is to provide the ILIT trust beneficiaries with Crummey powers. The term "Crummey" is not a misspelled reference to the effectiveness or value of the trust but simply reflects the name of a court case in which this type of trust structure was first validated (*Crummey v. Commissioner,* 397 F.2d 82, 9th Cir. 1968). The most important Crummey power that must be provided to the ILIT trust beneficiary is the immediate right to withdraw funds that are contributed to the trust. The trustee should notify the trust beneficiaries within seven days of the trust's receipt of funds from the settlor. If the beneficiaries have at least 30 days immediately following their receipt of notice to withdraw funds contributed by the settlor to the trust, then the funds will qualify as a present-interest gift by the settlor. The present-interest gift qualification is not compromised if the trust beneficiaries do not exercise their right to withdraw the funds and their right to withdraw funds expires after 30 days.

Another issue that must be resolved is the extent to which an ILIT beneficiary's right to the funds contributed to the ILIT is, in itself, considered a property interest subject to estate and gift taxation. In other words, the trust beneficiary may have a property right that can be transferred to another by the beneficiary's failure to exercise his or her withdrawal right. Generally speaking, this issue may arise to the extent the beneficiary's withdrawal right exceeds the greater of $5,000 or 5 percent of the aggregate value of assets out of which the withdrawal right could be satisfied.

Several techniques that can mitigate this issue are available to estate planners. One commonly used strategy is to structure the trust to allow only the portion of the withdrawal right that does not exceed the $5,000 or 5 percent to lapse in any given year. Any excess withdrawal right carries over to successive years and would lapse only to the extent that it did not exceed the $5,000 or 5 percent limitation in successive years.

One method of maximizing the annual gift-tax exclusion of $11,000 is to include a spouse's annual exclusion so that the total exclusion available is $22,000. Another method is to include as many Crummey beneficiaries under the trust as possible. Since each beneficiary would be eligible for a $22,000 annual combined gift from the client and his or her spouse, naming three Crummey beneficiaries would increase the total gift-tax exclusion available for funding the trust to $66,000. Of course, the lifetime gift-tax exemption amount of $1 million can always be used in addition to the $11,000 annual exclusion. If the ILIT seeks to purchase PPLI policies with significant minimum premium amounts, use of both the annual exclusion and lifetime exemption may be warranted.

Dynasty Trust

A dynasty trust is a trust that's intended to benefit perpetual generations of the settlor. Estate taxes are minimized through the transfer of assets to the trust. Once assets are gifted to the trust, further accumulation of those assets will not be subject to estate tax assessed against the estate of the donor. Since the beneficiaries of the dynasty trust are intended to be the extended descendants of the trust settlor, most estate planners design the trust to take advantage of the generation-skipping tax exemption. Life insurance is an important tool that, if properly structured, may provide funding for the dynasty trust without the imposition of estate taxes, income taxes, gift taxes, or generation-skipping taxes. For example, an ILIT can be established and designed as a dynasty trust. Using the ILIT techniques described earlier, the proceeds of the ILIT can be passed to heirs without the imposition of estate taxes, income taxes, gift taxes, or generation-skipping taxes.

Spousal Bypass Trust

A spousal bypass trust preserves the estate tax exclusion afforded a marital partner while preserving some benefit to the surviving spouse. The trust allows a taxpayer to place an amount equal to the applicable estate tax exclusion into the trust in the year of the taxpayer's death. The surviving spouse then receives the balance of the estate. Because the marital deduction is unlimited, the portion of the estate passing to the spouse is received without estate tax. The bypass trust can pay income to the surviving spouse during his or her lifetime. At the time of the surviving spouse's death, the heirs receive the amounts in the bypass trust, which are not included in the surviving spouse's gross estate for estate tax purposes. If the bypass trust were to purchase life insurance on the life of the surviving spouse, the death benefit amounts received by the heirs would not be subject to either estate tax or income tax.

Qualified Terminal Interest (Q-TIP) Trust

A Q-TIP trust allows a marital partner to provide asset income to the surviving spouse while ensuring that the remaining assets go to those individuals specified by the marital partner when the surviving spouse dies. This type of trust is commonly used in the case of second marriages with combined families. The asset passing from the deceased spouse to the surviving spouse qualifies for the marital deduction. When the surviving spouse dies, the remaining portion of the asset passes to the heirs specified by the deceased spouse. However, the asset will be included in the surviving spouse's estate. The term *qualified terminable interest property* describes a situation in which (1) property passes from the decedent, (2) all the income is paid to the spouse for life, (3) income or principal cannot be distributed to anyone other than the spouse until the spouse's death, and (4) the executor of the estate makes an irrevocable election on the federal estate tax return to have the marital deduction apply.

A Q-TIP trust is most useful when a large estate is passed to the trust, thereby allowing the surviving spouse to derive sufficient income from the trust during his or her lifetime. One way of maximizing the size of the estate passed to the trust is to purchase life insurance on the life of the first spouse. The death benefits paid by the life insurance policy into the trust can be sizable enough to provide sufficient lifetime income to the surviving spouse. When the surviving spouse dies, the remaining portion of the asset can pass to the heirs specified by the deceased spouse.

Intentionally Defective Grantor Trust

An intentionally defective grantor trust incorporates a technique allowing trust income to be imputed to the settlor for income tax purposes yet allows the assets to remain outside of the settlor's estate. Most trusts must pay income taxes on any income retained in the trust, and the beneficiaries pay tax on trust income distributed to them. If the estate planner's goal is to remove as much as possible from the client's estate, an intentionally defective grantor trust will cause the settlor to be taxed on the trust income rather than the trust. As a result, the settlor pays the income tax, allowing the trust to accumulate income faster than it would if income taxes were paid out of trust assets.

A grantor trust is a trust in which the settlor retains certain interests or rights in the trust that cause the settlor to be considered the owner of the trust for federal income tax purposes. Under the Internal Revenue Code (IRC), a trust will be considered a grantor trust if the trust settlor retains certain rights or benefits under the trust, such as: (1) the right to alter, amend, or revoke the trust; (2) the right to control the disposition of trust income or assets; (3) the right to substitute assets of equal value; or (4) the right to use trust income to pay premiums for life insurance, such as on the settlor or spouse.

An ILIT may be structured as an intentionally defective grantor trust. However, the attorney responsible for drafting the trust must be careful to structure it so that trust assets remain outside of the estate of the settlor while simultaneously causing the trust income to become taxable to the settlor instead of to the trust. The manner and method of achieving this goal may vary depending on the goals and circumstances of the settlor.

For example, the right to alter, amend, or revoke the trust or the right to control the disposition of trust income or assets would cause the trust to be included in the settlor's estate; whereas, the right to substitute assets of equal value or allowing trust income to be used to pay life insurance premiums would not cause the trust to be included in the settlor's estate.

Three-Year Rule on Transfers

In general, gifts made within three years of the donor's death (other than gifts to members of the decedent's family, which qualify for the annual gift exclusion) will be included in the donor's estate upon death. Therefore, estate plans that call for the transfer of assets before death should be implemented as soon as possible.

Family Limited Partnership

Family limited partnerships, if established pursuant to a valid business, financial, or investment purpose, can be very useful tools in estate planning. There are many techniques available that use the partnership as a conduit whereby wealth is transferred to extended family members, with minimized gift- and estate-tax consequences, and also provide the client with some control over the wealth before death.

In a typical scenario, a client will transfer assets to the limited partnership in return for partnership interests. The client becomes the general partner of the partnership and thereby has the ability to exert some level of control over the partnership, including partnership assets. The client then gifts limited partnership interests to family members. As a result, the asset accumulation allocated to the gifted limited partnership interests is removed from the estate of the client, who is the general partner. However, care must be taken to ensure that the client does not retain too much control over the assets contributed to the family limited partnership. Otherwise, the transfer to the limited partnership may not be respected under the tax law and the asset may be considered to have remained in the client's estate.

For gift taxes, the value of the interests in the limited partnership gifted to family members may be less than the actual assets transferred by the client to the partnership. That's because the gift is not considered the actual asset transferred to the partnership. Instead, the gift is considered an interest in the limited partnership itself. Since the limited partnership interests can be structured so that the interests are not freely alienable or sold to others, the interests may be considered illiquid and may therefore be discounted. The net result is that the asset transfer is conducted at a discount.

For estate planning, the combination of a family limited partnership and the purchase of PPLI produce some very attractive results. For example, a family limited partnership may purchase PPLI on the life of the general partner. The general partner may transfer funds to the family limited partnership in an amount equal to the premium payments with no immediate gift-tax consequences. Thereafter, interests in the family limited partnership would be gifted to other family members. However, the amount of the gift would not be the premium payments but rather the value of the interest in the limited partnership. Since the value of the limited partnership interest can be discounted for illiquidity, the asset transfer is conducted at a discount and the death benefit proceeds of the life insurance are received without the imposition of income taxes or estate taxes (provided the client did not retain an impermissible level of control over the assets contributed by the client to the limited partnership).

Loans

Loans may sometimes be a more effective estate-planning tool than an outright gift of assets, depending on the donor's circumstances. For example, a loan may be appropriate when a donor either does not wish to use all of the available transfer-tax exclusions and credits or wishes to preserve these items for other transactions. The IRC requires a loan to be charged the applicable federal rate (AFR). There are short-term, mid-term, and long-term AFR rates. The short-term AFR rate applies to a demand loan or term loan of up to three years. The mid-term AFR rate applies to a term loan longer than three years but no more than nine years. The long-term AFR rate must be charged for a term loan longer than nine years. If a rate lower than the applicable AFR is charged, or if no interest is charged at all, the difference between the applicable AFR and what is actually charged constitutes a gift.

Most estate planners will structure a loan to be a demand loan so that it qualifies for the short-term AFR. The IRS updates each of the AFR rates (short, mid-term, and long-term) monthly. When interest rates are low, a donor's loan that is used by the recipient to purchase an income-producing asset can be an attractive gift-planning strategy.

Let's assume, for example, that a client establishes an ILIT, which plans to purchase PPLI. Since the ILIT initially has no funds, the client may either gift the premiums or loan the premiums to the ILIT. Instead of gifting the premiums, the client may instead make loans to the ILIT in the amount of each premium payment. If each premium-payment loan is structured as a demand loan, the interest payable on the loans will be the short-term AFR. Since the trust will not have the funds to pay the interest on the loan, the client will gift the interest to the trust, which will, in turn, pay the interest back to the client. If the ILIT is structured as a grantor trust, no income tax consequences will result from the ILIT's interest payments to the client (that is, no taxable income to the client and no deduction to the ILIT). As a result, the ILIT has sufficient funds to purchase a PPLI policy. The PPLI policy account values may increase each year outside of the client's estate. At the client's death, the ILIT pays the client's estate the principal amount of the loans.

In the end, the annual gift of loan interest may be less than gifting the amount of the premium payments. While this certainly can be advantageous, the estate planner should also understand that (1) AFRs change every year and higher rates increase the gifts; (2) the outstanding loan principal the trust owes to the client is included in the client's estate (this either decreases the estate tax advantage over time or requires the ILIT to select what is commonly known as death benefit option two under the life insurance policy—that is, the death benefit, which equals the specified amount plus account value under the policy—to ensure that the ILIT nets the specified amount under the policy); (3) increasing the insurance death benefit could increase the premiums and the loan amounts; and (4) interest is due on the loans each year until the loans are paid back by the ILIT.

Estate Settlement Costs

When an individual dies and leaves an estate to his or her heirs, even if there was an estate plan in place, there will usually be some amount of probate costs, federal, and state estate taxes, or generation-skipping taxes due in order to settle the estate. In many cases, the estate planner cannot anticipate whether there will be enough liquid assets to pay these costs. PPLI can be a useful tool for ensuring that there is enough cash on hand to pay these expenses.

It's not unusual for families to maintain real estate, vacation property, or family heirlooms that they wish to pass intact to their heirs. These assets are usually passed to heirs in the form of specific bequests. If the estate does not maintain enough cash to pay the expenses necessary to settle the estate, the beneficiaries must either furnish their own cash to pay them or one or more of these specific bequests will need to be sold to pay the expenses. To avoid a situation where specific bequests will need to be sold to pay estate settlement expenses, many estate planners advocate the purchase of PPLI to cover the cash necessary to settle the estate.

A Versatile Tool

Each stage of life requires a different type of wealth planning. These stages usually correspond to a major life event, such as marriage, having children, and purchasing a new home. Life events may also include divorce, remarriage, and providing for stepchildren or second families. People typically go through three wealth-planning stages in life—accumulation of wealth, consumption/conservation of wealth, and transfer of wealth upon death.

It's not a coincidence that the three elements of estate planning—(1) wealth-accumulation planning for the extended family, (2) planning for lifetime consumption and/or conservation of wealth, and (3) planning for the transfer of wealth upon death—actually correspond to each of the typical wealth-planning stages in a life. PPLI is a simple yet powerful estate-planning tool that can be used to implement all three elements of estate planning. PPLI is also flexible enough to meet the needs of the owner at each planning stage of life. With life insurance coverage, a person can initially use the policy to simply provide term life insurance coverage. As the owner accumulates funds in later years, additional excess premiums can be paid into the policy to grow tax deferred. Each premium paid into the policy can be counted as part of the owner's basis in the policy, thereby providing more tax-efficient withdrawal opportunities in the policy's later years. Of course, upon death the proceeds of the policy are paid to beneficiaries income tax–free.

Successful estate planning is highly dependent on a client's situation, technical understanding, and appetite for complexity. Estate planning is an art, not a science. What works well for one individual or family may be totally inappropriate for others. To fully leverage the talents of a good estate planner, the client should be able to relay personal information regarding wealth goals, personal goals, and family-planning goals to the estate planner—and keep the estate planning up to date when the client's circumstances or goals change. These are the foundations upon which an effective estate plan is built.

CHAPTER 6

Trust Administration
The Domestic Advantage

AL W. KING III AND PIERCE H. MCDOWELL III

The insurance industry is starting to attract larger and larger premiums on certain types of domestic private placement life insurance (PPLI) contracts—often well in excess of $1 million annually. Until recently, increased regulatory costs drove much of the PPLI business to the international branches of the major insurance companies. This is no longer the case. Now, because of competitive state premium taxes, consumer laws for insurance policies, and modern trust laws, policyholders are seeking jurisdictions other than their home states in which to have these policies issued. And many insurance companies have registered new policies to once again accommodate the needs of the sophisticated investor domestically.[1]

South Dakota has the lowest state premium tax (eight hundredths of 1 percent, or 8 basis points) in the United States for premium payments in excess of $100,000 combined with very favorable insurance laws, thereby attracting many of these larger policies.[2] Alaska also has a very low state premium tax (one tenth of 1 percent, or 10 basis points) for premium payments in excess of $100,000.[3] These are by far the two lowest premium tax states in the United States. The other states average between 1.75 percent and 2.5 percent. South Dakota and Alaska also have very favorable dynasty trust statutes. South Dakota has had a dynasty trust statute (that is, no rule against perpetuity) since 1983. Consequently, trusts governed by South Dakota law and administered by a South Dakota trustee can last forever, if desired.[4] Alaska implemented its dynasty trust statutes in 1997.[5]

Much of the advanced insurance planning is contained in dynasty trusts. However, these long-term trusts are only one of the many trust options used to take advantage of the beneficial South Dakota and Alaska laws.

Premium Taxes

Practitioners use a trust, limited liability company (LLC), or other legal entity located in either South Dakota or Alaska as the owner and purchaser of the PPLI policies. South Dakota's and Alaska's low state premium taxes for premiums over $100,000,[6] plus the fact that South Dakota waives the opportunity to charge a retaliatory tax for large cases (life or annuity cases where the first-year premium is equal to or greater than $1,000,000),[7] make these two jurisdictions the most popular in the United States. A retaliatory tax generally allows the state to whom the premium tax is paid to impose the premium tax of the state in which the insurance company is located if that rate is higher. (See **FIGURES 6.1 AND 6.2** for a summary of premium taxes.)

There are three major types of premium taxes for both offshore and/or onshore policies:[8]

❑ *Federal deferred acquisition cost tax (DAC tax).* The DAC tax is a one-time tax on the premiums paid into a domestic policy (issued by a U.S. company). The tax calculation is complex, but it essentially equates to 1 percent of the premiums. The life insurance

FIGURE **6.1** *Summary of Premium Taxes*

U.S. insurance company/ off-shore operation [953(d)]	DAC tax (1% average) No premium tax Have to travel to country
International insurance company [non–953(d)]	1% federal excise tax Have to travel to country
U.S. company	DAC tax (1% average) State premium tax (The two lowest statutes are South Dakota—8/100ths of 1%, or 8 basis points, and Alaska 1/10th of 1%, or 10 basis points)

company pays this tax directly from the premiums put into a policy.[9]

❑ *Federal excise tax on foreign premiums.* This is a one-time 1 percent tax on premiums paid into an international policy issued by a foreign insurance company (including a foreign subsidiary of a U.S. company) that has not otherwise filed an election to be treated as a domestic company (a 953(d) election). This excise tax is reported on Form 720. The fine for failure to file Form 720 and pay the excise doubles the tax due.[10]

❑ *State premium tax.* The state premium tax is based on the premium dollars paid into a policy. The rates range from eight hundredths of 1 percent to more than 2.5 percent. Historically, international policies sold to U.S. citizens were structured to eliminate this tax (at a minimum, the application must not be signed by the prospective policy owner and the insured in the United States).[11] However, because of changes in the

FIGURE **6.2**   *Selected State Premium Taxes for Large Insurance Premiums[12]*

STATE	NUMBER OF BASIS POINTS (BPS)	STATE	NUMBER OF BASIS POINTS (BPS)
Alaska	10*	Minnesota	200
Arizona	200	Nebraska	100
California	235	Nevada	175–350
Colorado	100–200	New Jersey	210
Connecticut	175	New York	150–360
Delaware	200	North Carolina	190
Florida	175	Ohio	140
Georgia	225	Rhode Island	200
Hawaii	275	South Dakota	8*
Idaho	275	Utah	225–425
Illinois	50	Virginia	225
Maine	200	Washington	200
Maryland	200	Wisconsin	200
Missouri	100–200	Wyoming	75

*On premiums in excess of $100,000

laws in states like South Dakota and Alaska, there has been a recent push to use domestic insurance companies.

Generally, offshore insurance is less appealing than onshore insurance because no life insurer licensed solely offshore can offer, solicit, or otherwise engage in life insurance business in the United States. However, no law prohibits U.S. citizens from going offshore to purchase their life insurance. The Internal Revenue Code (IRC) recognizes the potential for such transactions and imposes an excise tax on the purchase of insurance from a foreign insurance company. However, in all instances when PPLI is sold to a U.S. taxpayer, the policy must comply with all the same tax requirements as those policies purchased in the United States for the policy owner to defer income taxes on the inside buildup and to have the death benefit pass to the beneficiary free from any income tax.[13] This requirement, together with the taint now associated with offshore trusts for U.S. citizens, has caused many U.S. citizens to purchase PPLI from domestic companies. Additionally, many offshore PPLI policies are now being 1035 exchanged into domestic policies.

Insurance Statutes

States like South Dakota have favorable statutes that provide unique investment rules for PPLI. The IRC allows life insurance contracts to invest in a wide array of nontraditional assets.[14] However, consumer laws of most states, drafted primarily for traditional smaller retail cases, are not as flexible (that is, most retail variable account cases consist only of prepackaged mutual funds). Because of very short payment-of-claims periods, the current rules require that all assets be liquid on a daily basis. South Dakota law allows for the incorporation of certain changes in the PPLI policy contract that facilitate greater flexibility for investment options. Such flexibility is necessitated by the many sophisticated investment options that have certain illiquidity issues that would be in conflict with many of the current insurance code rules. Certain types of investments, for example, often having minimums in the millions of dollars, require investors to invest and subsequently liquidate the accounts monthly or quarterly. Although these investments may meet the IRC provisions, consumer laws regarding liquidation and the insurance code's payment-of-claims provision currently prevent these assets from being held in traditional policies. Several South Dakota law provisions address this issue, allowing for in-kind distributions during lifetime and at death for larger PPLI policies.[15]

The low on-shore South Dakota and Alaska premium taxes and favorable insurance statutes are the reasons that the onshore PPLI business has gained in popularity versus offshore. These states' trust laws are another reason for the momentum toward onshore PPLI policies and the 1035 exchange from foreign policies to domestic policies.

Trusts

Modern South Dakota and Alaska trusts are created with "open architecture," which means they are a collaborative relationship among beneficiaries and trustee, much like a partnership. Frequently, multiple trustees and managers assume duties once assigned to a single trustee (for example, specialization of function: investments, the purchase and monitoring of insurance, distribution, custody, administration, and accounting).[16]

The typical type of administration involving a modern trustee is a *directed trust.*[17] They're usually newly drafted trusts and can be either revocable or irrevocable. For example, the typical directed trust in South Dakota has a South Dakota trustee as an administrative trustee and/or custodian but a non-South Dakota investment adviser, or manager, who is responsible for the trust's investment management and/or the purchase and monitoring of a PPLI policy. The trust can be structured in many different ways, based on the client's needs. A South Dakota or Alaska directed trust combines the fiduciary expertise of the administrative trustee located in the respective state with the skills of one's own insurance and investment advisers. This combination of services provides exceptional management and administration of the trust combined with the comfort of maintaining the family's trusted insurance and investment advisers.

A distribution committee may also be established to determine when trust distributions should be made. Family members can serve on these distribution committees and determine most of the distributions of income and principal for "health, education, maintenance, and support" (HEMS). Any distributions that would be tax-sensitive still require the independent trustee. Typically, the trust instrument allows for the removal of an administrative trustee at anytime. Alternatively, if desired, the administrative trustee can step into any of the committee functions (that is, investment or distribution committees).

The typical modern directed trust structure is shown in **FIGURE 6.3**.

Dynasty Trust

Many advisers and clients are becoming more comfortable with the concept of a South Dakota or Alaska dynasty trust as a vehicle to purchase PPLI. The dynasty trust is an irrevocable trust drafted to last for multiple generations. The beneficiaries therefore are both living and future descendants of the trust's creators. If properly structured, the trust assets can be available to beneficiaries over the course of time (although Alaska's trusts may be limited to 1,000 years) but never exposed to transfer taxes (that is, gift-, estate-, or generation-skipping taxes).[18]

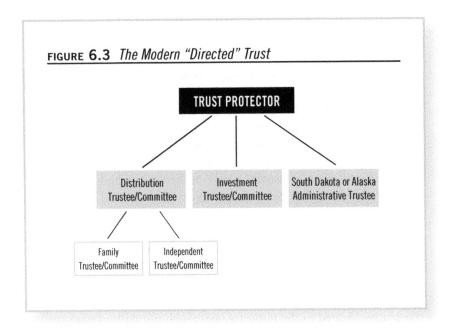

FIGURE **6.3** *The Modern "Directed" Trust*

The federal estate tax rates in 2004 are 48 percent with a $1.5 million exemption in 2004 and 2005 and are scheduled to decline by 1 percent annually to 45 percent in 2007 and ultimately scheduled to be repealed in 2010. The federal estate tax rate drops to 47 percent in 2005, but the exemption remains at $1.5 million. If properly structured, the South Dakota dynasty trust can avoid death taxes in perpetuity;[19] whereas, the Alaska dynasty trust is limited to 1,000 years, if a limited power of appointment is utilized.[20] Admittedly, the practical difference between the two is moot, but there are definitely other considerations.

The generation-skipping transfer tax is equal to the maximum federal estate tax rate. However, there is an important generation-skipping tax exemption ($1.5 million in 2004 and 2005) for each person, which, when properly used, allows the trust to continue for multiple generations. It's possible for families to leverage the $1.5 million generation-skipping exemption to pass multiple millions down through the generations without imposition of tax. Some of the leveraging techniques include one or more of the following:

❑ Loans
❑ Promissory note sales
❑ The sale of Walton GRAT remainders
❑ The sale of charitable lead trust remainders
❑ PPLI and/or other life insurance

The promissory note sale to a defective grantor dynasty trust provides an excellent strategy to accommodate the purchase of one or more large PPLI policies permitting freedom from gift, estate, and generation-skipping taxes. For example, husband and wife first make a taxable gift of $1 million each ($2 million total) in cash or other assets to a trust that's defective for income tax purposes (that is, the grantor, not the trust, pays the income taxes, but the trust is removed from the estate). No gift tax is due because the $2 million gift is covered by the husband's and wife's combined $1 million gift-tax exemptions ($2 million). And each uses $1 million of the respective $1.5 million generation-skipping exemptions, so that the trust can last for multiple generations (or even in perpetuity as is the case with South Dakota). They then form a family limited partnership (FLP) outside of the trust and contribute income-producing assets to the partnership in exchange for partnership interests. (They may also use an LLC.)

The husband and wife then sell $25 million in prediscount value worth of limited-partnership interests to the trust in exchange for a note. These interests are appraised at a 20 percent discount since they're nonvoting minority interests and unmarketable. After taking a 20 percent discount, the limited-partnership interests being sold have a fair market value of $20 million ($25 million discounted by 20 percent). The amount of the note sale is generally limited to 10 times the original funding amount ($2 million in the example, thus funding a $20 million note). Furthermore, the note typically matures in three to twenty years.

For example, for a seven-year interest-only note with a balloon payment at the end of the seventh year, the interest rate is 3.44 percent (the IRC §1274(d) federal mid-term rate for February 2004). The *nondiscounted* value is removed from the client's estate. At the beginning of the first year, the trust holds assets with a value to the clients of $27 million, which is computed by adding the initial gift of $2 million to the nondiscounted $25 million in real value that's removed from the couple's estate. The example assumes that the assets produce a 7 percent annual cash flow. Since the discount does not affect the cash flow, the 7 percent is multiplied by the entire $27 million to compute the income earned by the trust in the first year. The income earned is $1.89 million.

At the end of the year, the trust must pay the seller 3.44 percent of the initial fair market value of the property (the discounted note amount of $20 million), or $688,000. This is computed by multiplying 3.44 percent by $20 million. As a result of the defective nature of the trust (that is, the husband and wife paying income taxes on the trust), this interest payment paid to the couple is income tax–free to them. And the difference between the $1.89 million cash flow and the $688,000 interest payment inures to the benefit of the trust both gift- and GST tax-free. The difference

($1,890,000 - $688,000 = $1,202,000) can be used to pay a life insurance premium each year for the life of the note (seven years) without using any of the trust principal. This strategy can result in the purchase of a substantial PPLI policy without any gift, estate, or GST tax.[21]

PPLI is a great funding vehicle because of its tax-free growth and death benefit. And the $2 million initial trust funding amount may also be used to purchase PPLI. The cash value is then used as down payment for the promissory note sale technique. Since the trust is income tax–defective and the husband and wife have to pay income taxes on the trust, the purchase of PPLI in the trust would prevent the couple from having to pay income taxes because the cash value of life insurance is not taxed for income tax purposes. Caution should be taken not to create a modified endowment contract if tax-free withdrawals are required (see chapter 12). A similar strategy can also be used with loans to the trust versus a promissory note sale.

The family can leverage the PPLI policy for several generations. South Dakota was the first unlimited trust state (1983) with no state income tax.[22] Many advisers and clients struggle with the idea of creating a generation-skipping trust with an unlimited duration (a perpetual dynasty trust) because they're unaware of the advantages of creating such a trust and how flexible it can actually be.[23] Once they understand these benefits, many individuals frequently ask, "Why wouldn't I have an unlimited duration dynasty trust?" It's not enough to ask someone whether they want an unlimited duration dynasty trust without explaining the advantages, because the typical reaction is that 80 to 120 years is sufficient. If properly explained to them, most individuals choose the unlimited duration.[24]

A trust's maximum duration varies by state. In most states, trusts are subject to the "rule against perpetuities," which originated in the common law of trusts. The rule against perpetuities says that a trust must terminate no later than the end of a period that ends 21 years after the death of the last survivor of a class of persons who were alive at the creation of the trust (usually the beneficiaries identified in the trust, but sometimes defined as including other easily identifiable persons). In some states, the rule against perpetuity time limit is the longer of this defined length or 90 years.

Several states have abolished the rule against perpetuities in whole or in part so that the trust can last forever,[25] including Alaska,[26] Arizona,[27] Colorado,[28] Delaware,[29] Idaho,[30] Illinois,[31] Indiana,[32] Maine,[33] Maryland,[34] Missouri,[35] Nebraska,[36] New Hampshire,[37] New Jersey,[38] Ohio,[39] Rhode Island,[40] South Dakota,[41] Virginia,[42] Washington, D.C.,[43] and Wisconsin.[44] Delaware retains the rule against perpetuity for all investments in real estate (110-year limitation); however, Delaware has a statute that changes the character of real estate to personal (that is, intangible) property if placed in a partnership or LLC.[45] But there could be a problem if the partnership or LLC holding the real estate terminates or ends in a Delaware dynasty trust.

Several states have statutes limiting the duration of a dynasty trust: Florida,[46] 360 years; Utah,[47] 1,000 years; Washington,[48] 150 years; and Wyoming,[49] 1,000 years. Alaska also limits its rule to 1,000 years if limited powers of appointment are used.[50] Many advisers claim that there may be a problem by limiting the duration of a trust to 1,000, 360, or 150 years.[51] South Dakota does not have this issue.[52] Several of the states that have no rule against perpetuity allowing unlimited duration trusts also exempt their dynasty trusts from state income tax and capital gains, including Alaska, Delaware, Illinois, New Hampshire, Ohio (although has an accumulated earnings tax), South Dakota, and Wisconsin. Although Delaware, Illinois, New Hampshire (dividends and interest), and Wisconsin tax state residents who establish trusts in their respective states, they do not tax nonresidents who establish dynasty trusts in their respective states. The absence of a state income tax and capital gains tax on the trust can have a dramatic impact over time.[53] Other than South Dakota, with an 8-basis-point premium tax, and Alaska, with a 10-basis-point premium tax, all of the other dynasty trust states have high premium taxes, making them less than ideal places to purchase PPLI within the dynasty trust.[54]

Many individuals create dynasty trusts not only for possible income, premium, estate-, and generation-skipping tax savings, but also to maintain family values. This results in the promotion of fiscal and social responsibility within the family for several generations. The trusts act as "family banks," ensuring the perfect inheritance, which, according to Warren Buffett, is "leaving family members enough money so they do something, but not enough so they do nothing." Consequently, PPLI funds the family bank upon the payment of the death benefit and also provides an opportunity for income tax–free loans to the family during the life of the insured.

Clauses in these trusts that might be used to support a family's values include the following:

❑ distributions of $1 of trust income for $2 earned of earned income

❑ distributions to supplement the income of a family member who works for charity or stays at home to care for young family members

❑ rewarding good grades in school as well as graduations at all levels

❑ provisions for medical expenses, for example, chemical warfare and West Nile virus

❑ providing for enhanced distributions from the trust as a result of marriage and/or starting and maintaining families (vesting schedules)

❑ floating spouse clauses for in-law beneficiaries (the in-laws float in and out as beneficiaries if they separate or divorce the family member beneficiary)
❑ restrictions on distributions to beneficiaries at certain net-worth levels and/or without prenuptial agreements

Additionally, many of the trusts require that distributions be made by family members directly to charities once the trust attains certain levels. These types of clauses, as well as the asset protection afforded the modern trust, make them attractive vehicles for promoting both fiscal and social responsibility within a family as well as ensuring that the great-great grandparents and their values will never be forgotten.

The trusts also contain *jurisdiction-skipping clauses* so that the trust can move anywhere in the United States, offshore, or even intergalactically for clients who believe we will be living on Mars someday or those fearful about the threat of asteroids. There can be provisions for the trust law of the trust to change as well as the situs—meaning place or location—in many situations.[55]

Lastly, the dynasty trust strategy provides total flexibility as it relates to the uncertainty of the federal estate tax such that no estate, gift, or generation-skipping taxes will be due upon the formation of the trust if properly structured. The trust property and the appreciation on that property will remain in trust out of the family's successive estates and will remain asset protected. However, the flexibility of South Dakota and Alaska law allows for the termination of the trust if that were desired after careful evaluation. This dissolution is usually accomplished by the proper use of trust protectors. South Dakota has the oldest trust protector statute in the United States.[56] Consequently, flexibility is maintained with the current tax law as well as with repeal and/or modification to that law.[57]

Other Trust Techniques

The dynasty trust is one of many vehicles available to provide for the purchase of large PPLI policies by families that gain the benefits of South Dakota's and Alaska's favorable premium taxes, trust, and insurance laws. Other vehicles are the irrevocable life insurance trust (ILIT), the revocable insurance trust, the self-settled irrevocable life insurance trust, the beneficiary-defective/beneficiary-controlled trust, and the LLC.

Irrevocable Life Insurance Trust (ILIT)

A South Dakota or Alaska irrevocable insurance trust will typically be used for families that are not interested in intergenerational planning but are instead looking to remove the PPLI policy from their estates as well as garnering the favorable South Dakota or Alaska premium taxes, trust, and insurance laws. These trusts are usually drafted as "directed," with the investment committee given the exclusive power to both purchase and monitor the policy and the underlying cash value.

If life insurance continues to require payment of premiums after the initial gift to a typical irrevocable life insurance trust, the insured will generally make annual gifts to the trust to cover the premium payments. To make those gifts qualify as "present interest gifts" and therefore come within the 2004 and 2005 $11,000-per-donor-per-beneficiary annual exclusion from gift tax, the trust often will have a Crummey withdrawal power granted to the beneficiaries (usually the children and/or the grandchildren with a generation-skipping trust).

With a Crummey withdrawal power, each time a contribution is made to the trust, the beneficiary has a right to demand withdrawal from the trust. If the demand right is not exercised, the annual transfer for that year remains in the trust for management by the trustee. If the demand is made, the trustee must deliver the funds to the beneficiary. Generally, the beneficiary will realize that such a withdrawal may affect the grantor's decision as to future transfers to that trust and the beneficiary may therefore not make a demand. Once the withdrawal right lapses, the trustee is then free to use the funds that were contributed to pay the premiums on the life insurance policies. The name "Crummey trust" comes from the name of a party to a lawsuit, *Crummey v. Comm.,* 397 F.2d 82 (9th Cir. 1968). Usually Crummey gifts are not sufficient to fund large PPLI cases in ILITs. Consequently, large PPLI premiums are not funded by Crummey gifts but by a combination of large upfront gifts as well as loans to the trust and/or promissory note sales if the ILITs are established as income tax–defective.[58]

Generally, there are two levels of trust administration associated with irrevocable insurance trusts both during the insured's lifetime and at the insured's death. Trust administration during the insured's lifetime involves establishing the trust account to purchase a PPLI policy, paying insurance policy premiums, possibly sending Crummey notices to the trust beneficiaries (not usually the case with the purchase of large PPLI policies by the trust), and monitoring the insurance company and policy.

Once a policy is purchased, the trustee has an obligation to monitor and evaluate the financial performance of the insurance company, the underlying cash value, and the exercise of various policy options. Many trustees do not want to act as a trustee until the insurance policy "matures," leaving family members with the previously mentioned burdens. These duties may be and are frequently delegated, or directed, to the families' insurance advisers via an investment committee or trust adviser, which is allowed by both South Dakota and Alaska trust law. The one main drawback of the ILIT is that the client cannot have access to the cash value during his or her lifetime; consequently, if access is desired, other types of trusts are generally chosen—revocable insurance trust, self-settled trust, or the beneficiary-defective/beneficiary-controlled trust.

Revocable Insurance Trust

A revocable trust with its own tax ID number, drafted pursuant to South Dakota or Alaska law, and administered by a corporate trustee, or co-trustee, provides the family or the beneficiaries with access to the PPLI cash values during their lifetimes by taking tax-free loans from the policies for retirement or other purposes. This trust structure also accommodates the family's desire to take advantage of the low premium tax and favorable insurance laws in South Dakota and Alaska. The trusts typically use *trust advisers* or investment committees to assist with the selection of the proper PPLI policy, authorize the South Dakota or Alaska trustee to purchase such a policy, and monitor the PPLI policy.[59]

Pursuant to South Dakota statute, the trust adviser or investment committee is a party to whom certain powers are reserved by the trust instrument to the exclusion of another fiduciary acting under the instrument. Alaska has a similar type of statute. A trust adviser also includes any party who accepts the delegation of a fiduciary's power to direct the acquisition, disposition, or retention of any investment. The trust adviser may be an investment adviser and/or insurance professional who directs that the South Dakota trustee purchase the PPLI. Such trust advisers will generally be responsible for monitoring the PPLI as well.

Any trust adviser who is given authority to direct, consent, or disapprove a fiduciary's investment decision or proposed investment decisions shall be considered a fiduciary unless the trust instrument provides otherwise. Typically, the South Dakota or Alaska trustee is exonerated from any blame for the actions of the trust adviser.[60] The trust adviser may also be used with an irrevocable trust, but generally a directed trust with an investment committee is a better alternative for an irrevocable trust.

Self-Settled Irrevocable Insurance Trust

Another option to provide the client with possible access to the PPLI policy's cash value is a self-settled insurance trust. Self-settled trusts are commonly known as domestic asset-protection trusts. They're spendthrift trusts that the settlor forms for his or her own benefit (the settlor is a beneficiary as well as the settlor). The settlor can convey assets to the trust, and after the conveyance, the assets (inside the PPLI) will be protected from creditors and spouses of the settlor. Most states do not recognize self-settled spendthrift trusts.[61] However, Alaska,[62] Delaware,[63] Nevada,[64] Rhode Island,[65] and Utah[66] have enacted such statutes. Colorado,[67] Missouri,[68] and Oklahoma[69] also have limited statutes. Except for Alaska, all of these self-settled trust states are high-premium-tax states. Consequently, clients looking to establish such trusts for the purchase of large PPLI policies usually choose Alaska.

Alaska permitted self-settled trusts as of April 2, 1997.[70] The drafters of the Alaska law intended to provide a vehicle for both asset protection and estate planning. The initial issue of whether Alaskan self-settled trusts can provide similar asset-protection features to those provided by offshore trusts has received a mixed response from many professional advisers. However, many advisers believe that even if the asset-protection statutes are ineffective, estate-planning advantages can be obtained by the use of a self-settled trust, such as a self-settled irrevocable insurance trust.

Such a trust would provide the grantor with asset protection on the policy, a low premium tax, access to the policy cash value, and possible removal from the estate is yet questionable to its legal standing . Many advisers claim that such a planning strategy is untested in the courts and is fraught with possible estate tax, generation-skipping tax, and possible constitutional issues.[71] The only certainty with the trusts is that the IRS has ruled in Private Letter Ruling 9827007 that a gift to a self-settled trust is a completed gift. This ruling was silent as to the estate tax and generation-skipping-tax consequences. Lastly, many advisers claim that if you are a resident of Alaska, you have a better chance of the statute working for asset protection than if you're not a resident. Consequently, it's also an untested statute for providing asset protection to nonresidents.

Beneficiary-Defective/Beneficiary-Controlled Trust

The beneficiary-defective/beneficiary-controlled trusts are generally a better, more firmly established alternative to the self-settled insurance trust.[72] The beneficiary-defective/beneficiary-controlled trust also addresses the client's desire to use PPLI for retirement planning or other purposes during the client's lifetime. It allows the estate owner both access to the internal buildup as well as the ability to keep the death benefits from estate taxes and provides asset protection without the issues associated with the self-settled trust.

The beneficiary-defective/beneficiary-controlled trust circumvents estate tax because it's created by someone other than the client, usually the parent of an adult child. The trust is income tax–defective to the beneficiary rather than the trust creator (that is, grantor defective), meaning the beneficiary would pay the income taxes on the trust during its defective status.

The income tax–defective status for the beneficiary-defective trust is obtained by violating IRS Section 678(a) using a Crummey power of withdrawal and not by violating any IRC provision that would tax the trust to the trust creator. Since the parent of an adult child establishes the beneficiary-defective/beneficiary-controlled trust, the adult child can be both the trustee and primary beneficiary of the trust, if properly structured, without negating its favorable tax and asset-protection features.[73] Please note that the child cannot gift funds to the parent for the purpose of funding such a trust.

If the PPLI purchased by the trustee of the beneficiary-defective/beneficiary-controlled trust is on the beneficiary's life, the beneficiary may not be a trustee who makes decisions with regard to the insurance;[74] nor can the beneficiary have a power of appointment as to the insurance portion of the corpus without creating an estate tax problem. Consequently, if insurance on the beneficiary/trustee's life is an asset of the trust, a special or independent trustee (that is, a directed or trust adviser working in combination with a South Dakota or Alaska trustee) would need to be appointed to deal with the life insurance. This would generally be the case for low-premium-tax purposes. However, the beneficiary can also have the right, with some limitations, to fire and replace the corporate trustee.

If the PPLI purchased by the beneficiary-defective/beneficiary-controlled trust is on the life of a person other than the beneficiary (the beneficiary's child or grandchild), then the trust could be used as a tax-exempt accumulation vehicle with possible future tax-free withdrawals from the trust via PPLI loans provided a modified endowment contract is not created.[75] Generally, this is accomplished by the South Dakota or Alaska corporate trustee (other than a trustee who is also insured), who borrows the cash value of the PPLI, then loans the money to the beneficiary. The interest payments made by the beneficiary or his or her spouse during the beneficiary's lifetime do not generally have any income tax consequences because the loan is from a trust that is an income tax–defective trust to the beneficiary. Any unpaid loan balance at death will also generally be deductible as a debt of the estate. However, any unpaid interest will be taxable when paid, since grantor-trust status will have ceased.[76]

The trustee can also purchase other assets from the beneficiary. Assets can be sold to the beneficiary-defective trust (and from it) without gain as a result of its defective status.[77] The beneficiary-defective/beneficiary-controlled trust established by a parent for an adult child is a great PPLI planning tool without the uncertainty of the self-settled trust regarding asset-protection planning as well as estate and generation-skipping taxes.

Reforming an Older Trust

South Dakota law also includes a statutory procedure for the modification or reformation of older irrevocable trusts, making it possible to modernize them and allow them to purchase PPLI.[78] The statutes permit a trustee or beneficiary to petition the court to modify administrative or dispositive terms of the trust or terminate the trust if circumstances not anticipated by the owner have arisen and the modification or termination of the trust would substantially further the trust or its purpose for creating the trust. The procedure can also be used to convert the trust to a directed trust or add a trust adviser provision to the trust.[79]

South Dakota has adopted a series of statutes designed to facilitate the administration and court supervision of trusts that have disabled (including a minor), unborn, or unascertainable beneficiaries. With regard to all legal matters, including court proceedings, it's unnecessary for the court to appoint a guardian *ad litem* (a guardian appointed to protect the interests of individuals unable to protect themselves) to represent the interests of this class of beneficiary, provided persons having the same interests are deemed to represent these beneficiaries. If there is no person having the same interest as the beneficiary, the court is required to appoint a guardian ad litem to protect the beneficiary.[80]

LLCs

Another option that some clients and advisers choose as a means of taking advantage of the low South Dakota and Alaska premium taxes and related insurance statutes is a limited liability company. In South Dakota, for example, such an LLC must have a managing member (trust company) in South Dakota purchase the PPLI policy. Fortunately, South Dakota's LLC filing fees are very reasonable.[81]

The filing fees are generally based on the agreed amount of capital contributed to the LLC (a capital contribution of $1 million will generate a filing fee of $300).[82] South Dakota is a Uniform LLC Act state, having adopted the NCCUSL Uniform Act in 1998.[83] This also makes South Dakota a great state in which to form an LLC, because there are no income, intangibles, franchise, or personal property taxes on such an entity.[84] Alaska has similar LLC statutes.[85]

Location, Location, Location

Many international/foreign offshore PPLI policies can be converted to a domestic policy and/or trust via a 1035 exchange, thereby fueling PPLI's popularity. But domestically, South Dakota and Alaska are the two most favorable trust jurisdictions for the purchase of PPLI for four reasons:

1 Both have the lowest premium taxes in the United States (8 basis points and 10 basis points, respectively, for premiums over $100,000). This low premium tax would generally apply whether a properly drafted irrevocable trust, revocable trust, or LLC is used.

2 South Dakota statutes allow for in-kind distributions from a PPLI policy during life and at death so that the underlying investments (for example, hedge funds and private equity) do not have to be liquidated.

3 Both states have dynasty trust statutes as well as other favorable modern trust statutes.

4 Both states' directed trust and trust adviser statutes provide for the flexibility families desire when establishing trusts.

Chapter Notes

1. Grant Markuson, "Insurance as a Domestic and International Tax Planning Strategy," *Markuson and Neufeld* 2001.

2. S.D. Codified Laws § 10-44-2.

3. Alaska Statute § 21.09.210.

4. S.D. Codified Laws § 43-5-8.

5. Alaska Statute § 34.27.050 (Lexis 2000) (Repealed 2000). § 34.27.100(a).

6. See notes 2 and 3.

7. S.D. Codified Laws § 58-6-70, Alaska Statute § 21.09.270, § 21.09.210.

8. Grant Markuson, "Summary of Important Concepts and Tax Provisions for Private Placement Life Insurance," *Markuson and Neufeld* 2000.

9. Internal Revenue Code (IRC) Section 848.

10. IRC Section 4371.

11. See note 8.

12. "2004 State Tax Handbook," *CCH Incorporated* (November 2003). (Note: 100 basis points [bps] equals 1 percent.)

13. IRC Section 7702, 7702(g), 72(e)(1), 101(a)(1).

14. IRC Section 817(d),(h).

15. S.D. Codified Laws § 58-15-17.
    S.D. Codified Laws § 58-15-26.
    S.D. Codified Laws § 58-15-26.2.
    S.D. Codified Laws § 58-15-33.

16. S.D. Codified Laws § 55-1B, Alaska Statute § 13.36.110.

Al W. King III, "Death Tax Uncertainty Makes Flexible and Family Value Estate Planning More Important than Ever," *Trust & Estates* (January 2001).

Al W. King III, "The Modern Dynasty Trust: Flexibility Is More Important Than Ever," *Trust & Estates* (January 1998).

17. See note 16.

18. Daniel G. Worthington, Pierce H. McDowell III, and Joseph T. McKay, "The South Dakota Difference: Family Wealth Preservation through Charitable and Dynastic Planning," *The Law School Foundation* 1, no. 3 (November 1995); Al W. King III, Pierce H. McDowell III, and Dr. Daniel Worthington, "Dynasty Trusts: What the Future Holds for Today's Technique," *Trust & Estates* (April 1996); Al W. King III, "The Modern Dynasty Trust; Al W. King III, "South Dakota Dynasty Trust," *Millionaire* (June 2000); Al W. King III, "Smart Start—Establishing a Dynasty Trust in South Dakota," *Departures Magazine* (November 2000); Al W. King III, "Trust Planning: Expert's Critical Analysis of the Dynasty Trust, a Unique Planning Device to Preserve and Create Wealth," *CCH Insights and Strategies* (June 1996); Al W. King III, "Dynasty Trust," *The CPA Journal* (September 1996).

19. S.D. Codified Laws § 43-5-4, § 43-5-8; Thomas H. Foye, "Using South Dakota Law for Perpetual Trusts," *Probate and Property* (January/February 1998).

20. See note 5.

21. Steven J. Oshins, Al W. King III, and Pierce H. McDowell III, "Sale to a Defective Trust: A Life Insurance Technique," *Trusts & Estates* (April 1998); also see notes 5 and 19.

22. S.D. Codified Laws § 43-5-4, §43-5-8.

23. Al W. King III, "A Generation-Skipping Trust: Unlimited Duration? Why Not?" *Trusts & Estates* (June 1999); Al W. King III, "The Modern Dynasty Trust."

24. See note 23.

25. Garrett Moritz, "Dynasty Trusts and the Rule against Perpetuities," *Harvard Law Review* 116, no. 8 (June 2003).

26. See note 5.

27. Ariz. Rev. Stat. Ann. § 14-2901(A)(I)(West Supp. 2002).

28. Colorado Rev. Statute § 11-11-1101 et. seq.

29. Del. Code Ann. Fit. 25, § 503(a)(b), § 504 (Supp. 2000).

30. Idaho Code § 55-111 (Michie 2000).

31. 765 Ill. Comp. Stat. Ann 305/4 (a), 305(4)(a)(8), 305/3/a-5 (West 2001).

32. IND. H.B. 116(2003).

33. Maine Rul. Stat. Ann. Fit 33, § 101, § 101A (West 1964).

34. Maryland Code Ann. Est. & Trusts § II-102(e)(2001).

35. Missouri Revised Statutes § 456-236.

36. Nebraska Laws Section § 76-2001-2008.

37. N.H. Rev. Stat. Ann § 547:3-k and 546:24 (West, Westlaw through 2003 Sess.).

38. New Jersey Statute Ann. § 42:2 F-9, 46:2 F-10 (West Supp. 2000).

39. Ohio Statutes §2131.08, § 2131.09.

40. Rhode Island Gen. Laws § 42:2 F-9, 46:2 F-10 (West Supp. 2000).

41. See note 4.

42. Virginia Code Ann. § 55-13.3(c) (Michie Supp. 2002).

43. D.C. Code s. 19-109(10)(2002).

44. Wisconsin Stat. § 700.16(5) (1999).

45. Delaware Code Ann. tit., § 503(b), §504.

46. Florida Statute Ann. § 689.225(2)(a)(I) (West Supp. 2003).

47. Utah Statutes § 9-8-505, §75-2-1201, § 75-2-1208.

48. Washington Rev. Code Ann. § II.98.130 (West 2000).

49. Wyoming Statute § 34-1-39.

50. See note 5.

51. Dr. Daniel G. Worthington, "Is Florida's New Rule against Perpetuities a Generation-Skipping Transfer Tax Trap for the Unwary?" *Trusts and Estates* (December 2000).

52. Thomas H. Foye, "Using South Dakota Law for Perpetual Trusts," *Probate and Property* (January/February 1998); Dr. Daniel G. Worthington, "Is Florida's New Rule against Perpetuities a Generation-Skipping Transfer Tax Trap for the Unwary?" *Trusts and Estates* (December 2000).

53. Max Gutierrez Jr. and Frederick R. Keydel, "State Taxation on Income of Trusts with Multi State Contacts," *The American College of Trust and Estate Counsel ACTEC Studies* (September 2001); "2004 State Tax Handbook," *CCH Incorporated* (November 2003).

54. See notes 2 and 3.

55. Al W. King III, "A Generation-Skipping Trust: Unlimited Duration? Why Not?" Al W. King III, "Death Tax Uncertainty."

56. S.D. Codified Laws § 55-1B.

57. Al W. King III, "Death Tax Uncertainty."

58. Al W. King III, "When to Consider a Corporate Trustee: Part I," *AICPA Planner* (November 1995); Al W. King III, "When to Consider a Corporate Trustee: Part II," *AICPA Planner* (December/January 1996); Steven J. Oshins, Al W. King III, and Pierce H. McDowell III, "Sale to a Defective Trust."

59. S.D. Codified Laws § 55-113, Alaska Statute § 13.36.110.

60. See note 59.

61. Roy M. Adams, "How to Protect Your Assets and those of Others Under Applicable State and Federal Laws," *Cannon Financial Institute Inc. and Sonnenschein Nath and Rosenthall 2003 Estate Planning Teleconference Series.* June 24, 2003.

62. Alaska Statutes § 13.36.390, § 13.36.035, § 34.40.110, § 09.60.010.

63. Delaware Statutes 12 Del. C. § 3575, § 3570, § 3572, § 3573.

64. Nevada Rev. Statutes § 166.150, § 166.170.

65. Rhode Island General Laws § 18-9.2.

66. Utah Statutes § 25-6-14.

67. Colorado Rev. Statute § 38-10-111 (2002).

68. Missouri Statute § 456.080. RSMO.

69. Okla. Stat. tit. 31, § 10 et. seq.

70. See note 62.

71. M. Roy Adams, "A Comparison of Domestic and Foreign Trusts for Meaningful Creditor's Protection Planning and Other Relevant Uses," *Cannon Financial Institute, Inc. and Sonnenschein Nath & Rosenthal.* August 20, 2002.

72. Richard A. Oshins and Noel C. Ice, "The Inheritor's Trust: The Art of Properly Inheriting Property," *Estate Planning* 30, no. 9 (September 2003); Richard A. Oshins, "Defective Trusts Offer Unique Planning Opportunities," *CCH—Financial and Estate Planning* (August 20, 1998); Richard A. Oshins and Steven J. Oshins, "Protecting and Preserving Wealth into the Next Millennium," *Trusts & Estates* (September/October 1998); Richard A. Oshins, "In Search of the Perfect Estate Plan: A Pipe Dream Can Become a Reality," *CCH—Financial and Estate Planning* (November 1998).

73. See note 72.

74. See note 72.

75. See note 72.

76. See note 72.

77. See note 72.

78. S.D. Codified Laws § 55-3-24 et. seq.

79. S.D. Codified Laws § 55-3-32, § 55-3-37.

80. S.D. Codified Laws § 55-3-37.

81. S.D. Codified Laws § 47-34A-212.

82. See note 81.

83. S.D. Codified Laws § 47-34.

84. See note 83.

85. Alaska Statute § 10.50.070.

CHAPTER 7

Executive Benefits
The Plan That Pays Its Way

LESLIE N. BROCKHURST

Regardless of a company's size or sector, or whether it's publicly owned or privately held, its most valuable asset is likely to be its people. Competition for high-caliber executives has never been more intense. Although industry reputation, geographic location, corporate culture, and career fit are important to recruitment and retention, the most critical factors are likely to be compensation and benefits.

The best companies offer competitive compensation along with benefit plans designed to meet the needs and expectations of their employees at every salary level. Benefit plans fall into two main categories—qualified and nonqualified—depending on how the plans are viewed for tax purposes. Qualified plans include retirement plans that meet requirements of the Internal Revenue Code and, as a result, are eligible to receive certain tax benefits. Qualified plans generally must be available to all employees and funded with a trust. Nonqualified plans receive different tax treatment, are generally available to highly compensated employees, and may be informally funded with a specialized trust.

Regardless of the type, all benefit plans create costs and liabilities. This chapter looks at vehicles currently being used to recover these costs and liabilities. Among those vehicles are corporate-owned life insurance (COLI) and a specialized form of COLI called private placement life insurance (PPLI).

Qualified Benefit Plans

In a defined-benefit plan, the employee's benefits are determined through a formula, with the investment risk borne by the employer. For example, the plan may provide the employee a certain dollar amount each month at retirement, with the amount based on a percentage of the employee's average salary and the benefit offset by projected Social Security earnings.

In a defined-contribution plan, the company pays a specific amount into a trust for the benefit of the employee. The amount may be determined by a formula tied to salary or a profit-sharing contribution, which may be allocated pro rata. Unlike a defined-benefit plan, the investment risk in a defined-contribution plan is borne by the employee, and the benefit at retirement is the account balance.

Defined-contribution plans, such as 401(k) plans, have become familiar to many employees. Because 401(k) plans contain annual contribution limits, however, they tend to discriminate against highly compensated executives. For example, the 2004 contribution limit of $13,000 would represent 26 percent of the before-tax compensation of an employee making $50,000 a year, but just 2.6 percent of the before-tax compensation of an executive earning $500,000. This disparity creates a sizable shortfall of retirement savings for higher paid employees. In addition, the maximum salary considered for any qualified plan in 2004 is $205,000, whereas the maximum employer contribution to a defined-contribution plan is $41,000. The maximum annual benefit that can be derived from a defined-benefit plan is $165,000, with the excess amount liable to a 15 percent excise tax.

As a result of such restrictions, qualified plans severely limit the amount of retirement income that may be available to highly compensated executives. For example, an employee earning $50,000 a year at age 45, with an average annual increase of 5 percent, would have a final salary of $126,347 at age 65. Assuming a qualified benefit plan with 60 percent salary replacement without a Social Security offset, the employee would receive $75,808 in retirement income.

An employee earning $250,000 at the same age with the same 5 percent annual increase (and assuming that the IRS limit increases 3 percent per year) would have a final salary of $631,738 at age 65, but would receive just $215,681 in retirement income, or roughly 34 percent of his or her final salary. The point is clear: the more an executive makes, the more his or her retirement income must come from savings or sources other than qualified plans.

As a result of such inequities, companies of all sizes have increasingly turned to nonqualified benefits, including nonqualified deferred-compensation (NQDC) plans, as a way to restore benefits that have been limited by legislation. In this way, the corporation can provide incentives that help recruit and retain senior-level employees. In 2003, in its tenth annual survey of executive benefits plans, Clark Consulting found that 93 percent of 227 Fortune 1000 companies surveyed had instituted NQDC plans.

Nonqualified Benefit Plans

NQDC plans allow an executive to defer pretax compensation into investment alternatives similar to those in a 401(k) plan. In NQDC plans, the employer may provide a match or other contribution but does not receive a tax deduction until the benefit is paid out, at which time the employee is taxed.

NQDC plans were established under the "top hat" exemption offered to corporations by the Department of Labor. NQDC benefits are general assets of the employer and are subject to creditor risk. In addition, to avoid current taxation, the employee may not take constructive receipt of the benefit. In supplemental executive retirement plans (SERPs), the employer funds a plan to either restore pension limits or mimic a defined-benefit or defined-contribution plan. When the benefit is paid, the employer deducts the payment as compensation.

Also included among nonqualified plans are bonus arrangements that enable the employer to provide an additional benefit, often a life insurance policy with cash values. The employee owns the policy and the employer may receive a current tax deduction if the total compensation does not violate IRC restrictions. Other nonqualified benefit plans include stock-incentive plans, death-benefit-only plans, and split-dollar life insurance arrangements.

PPLI

Life insurance companies created COLI in the 1980s for sale to corporations as vehicles for funding employee and executive benefit plans. Typically, COLI products were competitively priced for institutional use and provided a fixed rate of return. In the 1990s, as insurance companies began to merge with asset-management firms, fixed-rate COLI products were joined by variable universal life (VUL) products that featured a portfolio of cash value investment options offering equity and fixed-income yields.

The demand for COLI products has increased as executive compensation levels have risen and qualified plan benefits become increasingly insufficient. At the same time, the executive benefits marketplace has become more sophisticated, with deferred-compensation plans becoming more creative, more user-friendly, and offered to more employees beyond the executive suite. Traditionally, deferred-compensation plans had been relatively small, applying to only a few key executives in an organization, and the investment alternatives were quite limited. Today, deferred-compensation plans may cover many employees, allowing them to select investment options from a menu of funds—even though, technically, they do not own the assets.

Requests from corporate benefits planners for a funding vehicle with even more investment options and flexibility than COLI led to the creation of PPLI products. These highly customized products are designed to meet the needs of specific benefit plans. PPLI products typically offer additional investment options, which are designed to meet IRS diversification and investor-control requirements. In addition, PPLI policies provide more ways to structure loads to better fit the plans they're informally funding. Today, PPLI has captured a large share of the COLI marketplace—perhaps as much as 50 percent, according to some estimates.

Advantages

Like other corporate-owned life insurance, PPLI is often used to informally fund employee and executive benefit plans because life insurance provides an excellent match to such long-term benefit liabilities. As one example, the cash value growth closely matches the change in a deferred-compensation account balance. The death benefit provides an excellent match for health costs for the terminally ill as well as cost recovery of other post-retirement benefits. In addition, because the growth or "inside buildup" of the policy's cash value is tax deferred, the cash value grows more quickly than the cash value of a taxable investment portfolio and therefore is attractive to corporations. As with traditional life insurance, the death benefits paid are generally received free of income tax by the corporation. These death benefits come at a time when the employer may have incurred substantial health/medical plan costs prior to the employee's or retiree's death. The principal attraction of PPLI, however, is that it offers corporations flexibility that is not possible with standard COLI products. A typical COLI universal life contract's fund selection may not fit the corporation's needs. PPLI offers a greater variety of funds, which may be especially attractive to companies that want to mirror the number and style of funds offered in a 401(k) plan.

Disadvantages

Although PPLI has features that make it an effective way to informally fund many kinds of employee and executive benefit plans, there may be certain disadvantages. For example, the transaction must be large enough to warrant the insurance company's participation. In addition, the sponsoring corporation must be willing to develop or secure the expertise necessary to design the plan, determine the method of funding, and negotiate the transaction.

Typical PPLI transactions today involve an annual premium as high as $5 million, a custom set of funds (most often selected to match an existing 401(k) plan), and a product design with loads and charges that were set to specifically meet certain requirements. PPLI also requires a private placement memorandum (PPM). This document resembles a prospectus but is more complex. PPLI customers are also asked to fill out a private placement questionnaire (PPQ), which asks investment-related questions. The corporation must be large enough and sophisticated enough to qualify for these products. These two documents can be intimidating, especially if the company has had little experience with PPLI or does not have access to expert advice. For that reason, the choice of a consultant and broker is of paramount importance.

The Role of the Consultant

Because PPLI transactions typically are large and can be complicated, depending on the benefit plans involved, considerable expertise is required to help navigate each step from design of the plan through determination of the correct policy terms, selection of the carrier, and negotiation of the transaction. Companies should solicit the services of outside attorneys, accountants, consultants, and insurance specialists with experience in this area.

Generally, the best results are obtained when the benefit-plan design and funding determinations are managed by a team that includes representatives of the corporation, outside counsel, and a consultant and/or insurance specialist with broad benefit-plan expertise. It's essential that the team have the legal and financial expertise needed to evaluate benefit-plan options and recommend the most appropriate informal funding solutions.

The insurance specialist should have access to a number of PPLI products and be able to assist the company with decisions on the product design, load structure, and funds available from each carrier. Likewise, the carrier must have extensive experience and possess the administrative capabilities necessary to handle the flexibility of PPLI products. The insurance specialist, who is usually paid a commission by the insurance companies, can assist in these determinations.

PPLI Regulation

PPLI contracts must be carefully designed to meet rules established by the IRS for life insurance. Among the criteria are diversification requirements and investor-control issues (see chapter 12). Care must be taken not to overfund the policy, which may subject the policy owner to taxation on the full amount of some policy distributions, including policy loans.

Because the corporation wants to avoid high-risk investments, venture capital investments are not normally included in 401(k) or nonqualified plans. Hedge funds are normally employed only in extremely large cases or for the funding of SERPs or VEBAs (voluntary employees benefit associations use life insurance structures to supplement various employee benefits using largely unlimited tax deductible contributions). In addition, company stock is typically not offered as an option within COLI and PPLI policies for a variety of reasons but mainly because corporations can easily offer stock options as a separate part of the executive's compensation package.

The Future of PPLI

The role of PPLI is likely to continue to grow as corporate consolidations generate the need for larger benefit plans and more efficient vehicles to informally fund them. In addition, PPLI's flexibility makes it increasingly attractive to smaller firms that are seeking ways to improve both their benefit plans and their financial strength. Most important, PPLI's future is bright because it represents a vital tool for helping companies of all kinds remain competitive by retaining key employees.

PART TWO

A Vital Investment Vehicle

Although private placement life insurance (PPLI) can meet wealth-management goals in many situations more effectively than conventional choices, it is not a stand-alone solution. The investor's overall investment-policy document guides the selection of PPLI to address particular tax, asset-protection, estate-planning, and other issues. PPLI's role in the overall portfolio is played out over the long-term horizon, an area often neglected in portfolio design. This section explains how a PPLI portfolio is constructed and the investment choices that can thrive within it.

With its long-term focus, the policy's underlying investments can target asset classes with high historical returns and high tax exposure. Indeed, alternative investment classes are a perfect fit for these portfolios, with hedge funds at the core and private-equity and single-strategy funds in satellite positions.

Of course, selecting alternative investment managers is a much more rigorous process than selecting traditional equity and fixed-income managers, and this section explains the work involved. Due diligence on such investments requires not only experience in judging a firm's added value against the fund's higher fees but also the ability to understand investment processes, manager capabilities, and risk exposures in areas that veer far afield from traditional asset classes. The same skill and diligence are needed after investment options are selected; indeed, the portfolio's ongoing monitoring and adjustments are the most important activities for long-term portfolio viability.

CHAPTER 8

Toward a More Powerful Portfolio

KIRK LOURY

rivate placement life insurance (PPLI) is much more than an insurance policy. It represents the most powerful investment vehicle
available in the high-net-worth investor marketplace. Executed
within a trust and estate program, PPLI moves far past its immediate
tax-deferral features to an investment horizon reaching beyond 40 years—
a horizon akin to that of an endowment or a foundation.

Like any long-term investment program, PPLI requires an active portfolio construction plan, defined in an investment-policy document that
guides the application and management of the underlying investments.
This is particularly true for PPLI, given that a variety of management
and support personnel are tasked with achieving the investor's objectives
established at the policy's formation. An investment-policy document provides a framework to consistently evaluate the effectiveness of the policy's
portfolio over time, a critical feature in light of PPLI's long life span. Here,
the components needed to build an effective PPLI portfolio are identified with an eye toward ensuring that the PPLI portfolio will serve the
investor's or family's overall investment portfolio.

PPLI in the Investor's Portfolio

PPLI's flexibility makes it a powerful solution for a variety of needs. The
policies support five main applications:

Wealth preservation. PPLI provides two levels of wealth preservation. First, a non-MEC (modified endowment contract) policy owner

may choose or need to access the cash value through loans and with-drawals. Therefore, the portfolio must select investments that preserve sufficient wealth in anticipation of such outflows. Second, in both MEC and non-MEC policies in good standing, the estate's wealth is preserved through the death benefit. In effect, until the policy's cash value reaches the death benefit, the insurance company *bears the entire downside risk* of the portfolio's performance. The policy's key goal in wealth preservation is to *minimize portfolio declines in support of the policy owner's liquidity needs and integrate the death benefit in calculating the estate's anticipated value.*

Wealth creation. Every investment portfolio must strike an appropri-ate balance between the need to preserve wealth and the need to create it. PPLI supports an array of high-return, wealth-creating assets such as hedge funds and private equity, which are wholly unavailable through traditional insurance products. The policy's key goal in wealth creation is to *provide protection against inflation's erosive effects for current and future generations.*

Asset protection. PPLI, as a separate-account product, protects as-sets from an insurance company's creditors. More important, in certain jurisdictions (see chapter 4), creditors or litigants are unable to access the policy's cash value or death benefit. This advantage applies itself to many different trust and estate-planning approaches. The policy's key goal in asset protection is to *provide protection from creditors and/or litigants aris-ing from unforeseen, adverse events.*

Tax management. PPLI's protection of income and capital gains from taxation offers high-net-worth investors the ability to create extreme tax efficiency within the policy. Such tax efficiency accelerates wealth creation as the tax savings are compounded on top of the investment portfolio's rate of return. The policy's key goal in tax management is to *achieve high tax efficiency to drive accelerated wealth creation.*

Wealth transfer. By issuing policies on the lives of younger genera-tions, PPLI provides a highly efficient means to transfer wealth within a family. PPLI can also serve as an outstanding funding source for an indi-vidual's or family's philanthropic desires or a company's executive benefit programs (see chapter 7). Indeed, the longer a policy's horizon, the greater the amount of wealth that accumulates. This wealth transfer is not a fixed process, but it allows the policy owners to access the wealth through with-drawals and loans on a similarly tax-free basis, when the policy is struc-tured as a non-MEC. The policy's key goal in wealth transfer is to *establish a strong financial foundation for subsequent generations.*

The actual application employed on behalf of a high-net-worth investor or family is a customized process arising from the combined leadership of the trust and estate attorney, accountant, investment, and/or insurance advisers. Given the array of applications PPLI can support, a team approach is strongly encouraged so that all of a family's needs can be addressed.

Portfolio Construction Principles

Historically, PPLI has been executed as a stand-alone initiative. The best strategy, though, is to fully integrate PPLI into the investor's overall investment plan so that the policy's unique features are engaged in solving the investor's or family's comprehensive financial needs.

Three portfolio construction principles govern how PPLI should be integrated into the overall portfolio:

1 Use PPLI to support the investor's long-term financial needs
2 Select asset classes that have historically produced the greatest return
3 Allocate to asset classes that benefit most from PPLI's structure

Using PPLI to support long-term financial needs. In this context, the overall portfolio is reoriented to match asset classes to a needs-based approach. **FIGURE 8.1** illustrates that asset and need horizons must be matched to adequately support the investor's assorted portfolio objectives.

The key theme rests on the importance of identifying and targeting investments best suited to the investor's differing needs. In an extreme,

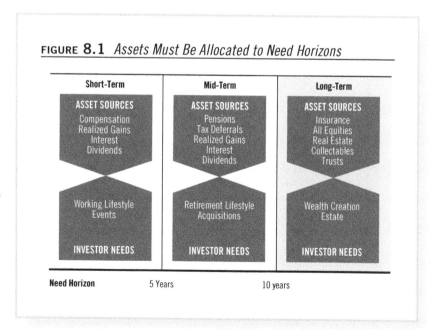

FIGURE **8.1** *Assets Must Be Allocated to Need Horizons*

Short-Term	Mid-Term	Long-Term
ASSET SOURCES	**ASSET SOURCES**	**ASSET SOURCES**
Compensation	Pensions	Insurance
Realized Gains	Tax Deferrals	All Equities
Interest	Realized Gains	Real Estate
Dividends	Interest	Collectables
	Dividends	Trusts
Working Lifestyle Events	Retirement Lifestyle Acquisitions	Wealth Creation Estate
INVESTOR NEEDS	**INVESTOR NEEDS**	**INVESTOR NEEDS**
Need Horizon	5 Years	10 years

Source: Spencer Trask Asset Management

misaligned sense, an art collection is no more expected to support the investor's day-to-day cash needs than interest income is destined to create long-term wealth.

PPLI serves the overall portfolio for the investor's long-term needs. These needs are often encapsulated in the trust and estate plan that, by design, references multiple generations. This elongated horizon assigns PPLI portfolio construction a different set of objectives than those used to guide the investor's non-PPLI portfolio (the portfolio that incorporates short- to mid-term financial needs and not the trust and estate plan's legacy needs).

Selecting asset classes with the greatest returns. PPLI's long-term horizon gives rise to the most prominent difference between the overall portfolio and the specific PPLI portfolio—the vastly lessened need to consider return volatility as a decision criterion for an asset class.

This long horizon establishes one of PPLI's great privileges: to focus on wealth-creating (high-return) investments. High-return potential is the constant that drives the selection of PPLI's portfolio investments. Salomon Smith Barney developed **FIGURE 8.2**, which clearly shows the progression in added return that specific investment strategies take as volatility, or risk, is increased. In other words, the greater the risk, the greater the return. PPLI's portfolio, then, becomes the main repository for relatively high-return hedge funds, private equity, and venture capital.

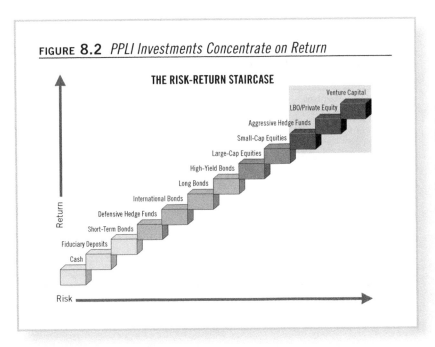

FIGURE **8.2** *PPLI Investments Concentrate on Return*

THE RISK-RETURN STAIRCASE

Venture Capital
LBO/Private Equity
Aggressive Hedge Funds
Small-Cap Equities
Large-Cap Equities
High-Yield Bonds
Long Bonds
International Bonds
Defensive Hedge Funds
Short-Term Bonds
Fiduciary Deposits
Cash

Return

Risk

Source: Salomon Smith Barney Consulting Group; IBC Conference April 13, 2003.

FIGURE **8.3**　　*Matching PPLI's Goals to Investment Characteristics*

PPLI GOAL	IDEAL INVESTMENT CHARACTERISTIC	EXPLANATION
Wealth Preservation	Predictability	Except for those few policy owners that plan on tapping the cash value via loans and withdrawals, PPLI preserves wealth through the tax-free death benefit, a guaranteed commitment from the insurance company.
Wealth Creation	High Return	Wealth creation arises from compounding the tax savings of high-returning assets.
Asset Protection	High Return	Assets with the highest historical return produce the largest long-term value and become the most attractive to creditors and/or litigants.
Tax Management	Large Tax Exposure	Intolerable tax exposure results from (1) ordinary income taxed at the highest rates and (2) the realization of large investment gains.
Wealth Transfer	High Return	Intergenerational asset transfers elongate the investment horizon two to three times, thus requiring the investments to counteract inflationary erosion.

Asset-class allocation. Without PPLI, the value of a portfolio of high-return investments would be dampened because of the extremely large tax exposure that typically results from a focus on wealth creation. This marriage of a very long-term investment horizon with the policy's extreme tax efficiency establishes a unique foundation upon which to build the portfolio. **FIGURE** 8.3 illustrates how the goals supporting PPLI's five main applications align with the investment characteristics needed to deliver on the goals.

FIGURE 8.4 ranks the asset classes in a high-net-worth investor's total portfolio according to performance over the 10-year period ending in 2003. This 10-year period serves as a solid time comparison because it

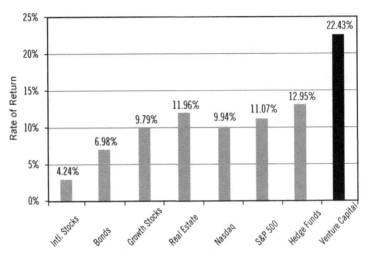

FIGURE **8.4** *PPLI Investors Freely Pursue Return*

Note: Although the statistics presented here are not current, the relative relationships between asset classes and the resulting conclusions remain consistent.

Source: www.InvestWorks.com; Spencer Trask Asset Management; Thomson Financial; HFR; NAREIT

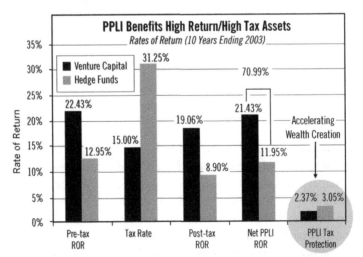

FIGURE **8.5** *PPLI Accelerates Wealth Creation*

Note: Although the statistics presented here are not current, the relative relationships between asset classes and the resulting conclusions remain consistent.

Source: www.InvestWorks.com; Spencer Trask Asset Management; HFR Corp.

covers a wide range of positive and adverse geopolitical, economic, and financial circumstances.

FIGURE 8.5 brings together the high historical performance of hedge funds and venture capital and shows how PPLI's extreme tax efficiency comes into play. PPLI accelerates wealth creation in hedge funds and venture capital through the compounding of the tax savings, compared to the same investments in a taxable portfolio.

On the surface, it may be surprising that venture capital, with its relatively tax-efficient 15 percent capital gains rate, benefits so greatly from PPLI. However, when one considers that venture capital produces pretax rates more than 73 percent greater than those of hedge funds, the tax savings are substantial even at the much lower tax rate. Through PPLI, venture capital's historical return is even more pronounced; it's 79 percent higher than the historical return of hedge funds in a PPLI portfolio.

Figure 8.5 shows how PPLI's tax savings works. The figure takes both wealth-creating investment classes—venture capital and hedge funds— and compares the large tax consequences for each asset class and the great boost that the PPLI tax protection provides. Venture capital produced large returns of 22.43 percent (the Pre-Tax ROR bar) during the 10 years ending in 2003. As a long-term investment, it carries a 15 percent capital gains tax rate (the Tax Rate bar). Combined, venture capital's after-tax return is reduced to 19.06 percent (the Post-Tax bar)—a tax loss of 3.37 percent (22.43 percent – 19.06 percent).

Although venture capital is already fairly tax efficient, historically it has generated such strong returns that the actual tax payments can be comparatively high. Subtracting the PPLI return of 21.43 percent (the Net PPLI ROR), which allows for a 1 percent charge for policy expenses from the Post-Tax ROR of 19.06 percent yields an additional return of 2.37 percent. In other words, figure 8.5 shows that the same venture capital investment within a PPLI portfolio generates well over 2 percent of additional compounded return simply as a result of PPLI's tax protection.

Hedge funds, notoriously tax inefficient from the short-term gains generated by active trading strategies, have similarly dramatic PPLI benefits. Although hedge funds have a substantially lower return than venture capital, the tax rate is much higher. Working through the same investment in a PPLI portfolio using figure 8.5 yields an additional 3.05 percent compounded annual return.

Aligning PPLI with the Overall Portfolio

Various government and private-sector studies have shown that approximately 70 percent of a high-net-worth investor's portfolio is devoted to supporting his or her working and retirement lifestyle needs, and 30 percent of the portfolio represents assets that are *not* targeted for any specific purpose. This latter asset pool represents the bulk of the assets backing a family's trust and estate plan. Moreover, as wealth increases, the greater this free-standing asset pool becomes relative to the total portfolio.

PPLI presents a simple question to wealth investors: *If such long-term assets are not backing any particular lifestyle need, why subject them to taxes as well as to potentially adverse situations?* **FIGURE 8.6** addresses this question.

The answer to this question ultimately resides in the trust and estate-planning document. Clearly, many issues need to be addressed in identifying the various funding sources for the plan. An important purpose of the portfolio construction process is to ensure that investments best suited to PPLI are effectively managed according to their intended role in the overall investment plan.

Essentially, PPLI holds many of the high-risk assets contained in the 30 percent wealth-creation slice from figure 8.6, while the lower-risk assets supporting the investor's lifestyle needs represent the remaining 70 percent of the portfolio. It's impractical to take all of the portfolio's high-return/high-risk assets and immediately establish a PPLI policy of commensu-

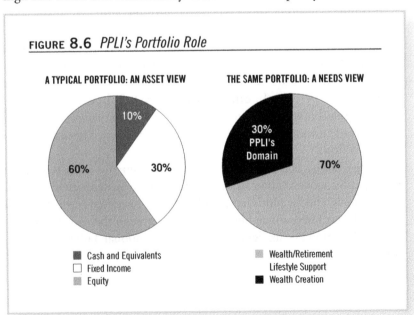

FIGURE **8.6** *PPLI's Portfolio Role*

A TYPICAL PORTFOLIO: AN ASSET VIEW

10%
60%   30%

■ Cash and Equivalents
□ Fixed Income
▨ Equity

THE SAME PORTFOLIO: A NEEDS VIEW

30%
PPLI's
Domain   70%

▨ Wealth/Retirement
   Lifestyle Support
■ Wealth Creation

Source: Spencer Trask Asset Management

rate value. PPLI is one of several tools at the disposal of the investment-planning team. In addition, these considerations must be part of the reallocation process that funds the policy from the overall portfolio:

❑ Assets such as collectibles cannot be included in PPLI's portfolio because of legal and regulatory limitations (see chapter 14).

❑ Assets such as closely held or restricted stock under direct investor control are not permitted in a PPLI contract.

❑ Investments in limited partnerships cannot simply be converted to a PPLI portfolio. The IRS has mandated that any PPLI investment choice must have only assets that fund insurance policies (that is, "insurance dedicated" (see chapter 14).

Nonetheless, the investor and his or her advisory team should equally recognize that the tax-free compounding of high-return investments in a PPLI policy mandates its use for PPLI-eligible investments, primarily hedge funds and private equity. The inherent growth derived from the policy's extreme tax efficiency will generate extraordinary wealth and make the policy's proportion of the investor's total net worth substantially larger over time. Of available liquid assets to fund PPLI's premium, experience says that 10 percent to 30 percent of the investor's total portfolio will be held in PPLI; the wealthier the investor, the greater the PPLI percentage of the investor's total portfolio.

Building the PPLI Portfolio

A wealthy investor's portfolio already has sizable allocations to the asset classes that meet PPLI's ideal investment characteristics. In a study of 105 family offices cosponsored by the Family Office Exchange (FOX) and Mellon Bank and published in January 2003, respondents representing some of the world's most sophisticated investors proved that allocations to alternative investments—hedge funds, private equity, and real estate—have already been established as vital components of the portfolio. **FIGURE 8.7** shows the target allocations among the respondents as of year-end 2002.

The focus at this level is on asset-class allocations, not investment-manager allocations. The specific investment firm selected for an asset class is a function of the insurance company's alternative-investment roster (see chapter 13) or of the willingness of a manager to create an insurance dedicated fund or become part of an existing insurance dedicated fund of funds. That said, while a favored hedge fund or private-equity manager may not offer an insurance- and tax-compliant product, best-of-breed substitutes previously approved by PPLI insurance companies will be used. If the investor chooses, the noncompliant but

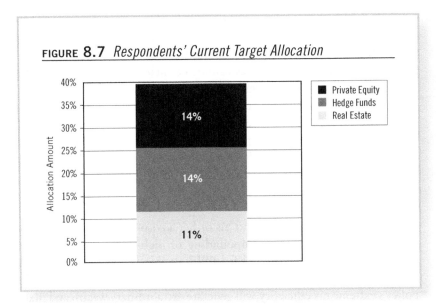

FIGURE **8.7** *Respondents' Current Target Allocation*

Source: Family Office Exchange; Alternative Investing Practices by Family Enterprises; January 15, 2003

favored manager simply stays on the taxable side of the investor's overall portfolio. Keep in mind that the ultimate portfolio must conform to the diversification requirements in the tax code, mandating at least four investments, with no single investment making up more than 55 percent of the assets; no two making up 70 percent; no three making up 80 percent; and no four making up 90 percent (see chapter 12). Therefore, the investor must take care in using any single, insurance-dedicated hedge fund in a portfolio.

Moreover, the FOX study reveals that, on average, 80 percent of all respondents have had at least 10 years' experience with private-equity and hedge funds in the overall portfolio. Large percentages have had experience in these asset classes since the 1980s. The point is that investors will be quite comfortable with a PPLI portfolio made up of these alternative investments.

PPLI Investment Portfolio Objectives

A PPLI portfolio, as a component of an investor's total portfolio, is designed with investments exhibiting these characteristics:

❑ High historical returns
❑ High tax exposure
❑ Low relative correlation
❑ Competitive investment management fees

Turning these characteristics into PPLI portfolio objectives guides not only the portfolio's initial construction but also its ongoing reporting and monitoring. The investment characteristics restated as portfolio objectives are:

- ❑ Investment strategy diversification
- ❑ Avoidance of highly correlated assets
- ❑ Ongoing compliance with tax laws and insurance regulations
- ❑ Investment manager's ongoing satisfaction of institutional standards of investment practice

Investment Manager Characteristics

In building a portfolio, there's a constant temptation to jump into the manager-selection process, since it's the investment choices that activate a plan. However, as with most plans, the most thoughtful one will have the best result. We've listed the characteristics of ideal PPLI investments. What about the characteristics of an appropriate PPLI investment firm? The following set of investment firm characteristics are based on the truism that an investor buys a firm that manages a product and not the product itself.

Full alignment of interests. The greatest evidence of common interest is a commitment of the investment manager's own capital to the same investment strategy for which the firm is being hired. This alignment of interests ensures commitment and continuity over the long-term horizons indicative of PPLI's structure.

Historical performance exceeding industry benchmarks. An investment manager must demonstrate the ability to succeed in its investment style across market cycles. Such success gives the investment firm the financial foundation to weather the difficult times that occur during negative market conditions.

Investment-style purity. A huge risk to a portfolio arises when an investment manager fails to maintain its chosen investment style (see chapter 10). Often these style variances demonstrate inherent weakness in the manager's investment approach and discipline. Moreover, a well-constructed portfolio expects the interplay of investment styles to achieve the portfolio's objectives. An investment manager who deviates from the designated style can corrode the portfolio's effectiveness.

Strategic commitment to the PPLI marketplace. Because of PPLI's legal and regulatory requirements, an investment manager must demonstrate firmwide commitment to this marketplace (see chapter 14). In the past, investment managers have viewed the PPLI market opportunistically, but to drive success, PPLI requires the manager to have a truly strategic emphasis.

Due diligence review and approval. Only investment firms that have demonstrated a PPLI market commitment by seeking and gaining approval from a variety of insurance carriers, research firms, and/or fund of funds need to be considered. The strength of an investment firm's business model and operations is evident in the approval from sophisticated external evaluators who possess the resources and responsibility to be highly rigorous.

PPLI's tax and regulatory standards force insurance companies to undertake intensive due diligence (see chapter 13). Certainly, the more times an investment firm has been reviewed and approved, the less likely it will be that any adverse or unseemly circumstances will surface later.

Comprehensive investor communications and reporting structure. Investment managers working with high-net-worth individuals understand best the reporting demands that this market has, compared to institutional investors. Beyond reporting performance numbers, investment managers must facilitate, through the insurance company, the appropriate reporting, monitoring, and educational material valuable to the investor and the advisory team.

Competitive investment management fees. The higher an investment manager's fees, the lower the return to the investor. Insurance companies have been able to use institutional clout to negotiate competitive advisory fees and investment access from an array of highly attractive alternative investment firms. The institutional pricing structure of both the investment advisory fees and the policy itself (see chapter 16) allows much more of the investor's premium to compound than does that of a retail insurance product.

Portfolio Management Pitfalls

A well-constructed PPLI portfolio does not just manage according to favorable characteristics; it must also manage to avoid inappropriate investment behaviors. Two particularly damaging portfolio behaviors are:

Frequent reallocations. Changing the investment mix too often can create investment drag on the portfolio. This investment drag will affect the very compounding that the policy delivers. Generally, the adviser looking after the PPLI portfolio should revisit allocations annually and make changes only when severe imbalances occur. Unlike portfolios supporting lifestyle needs, PPLI's portfolio is built with a long-term horizon in mind and it needs a much longer runway to build momentum. As described earlier, short-term market cycles are unlikely to affect the long-term results the portfolio was designed to provide.

Lack of vigilance. Given PPLI's long-term nature, a lack of monitoring intensity can result. In fact, a PPLI policy should be treated with the same rigor as those of institutional investors with similar horizons. The insurance company and the policy owner's advisory team must remain vigilant in monitoring the portfolio so that any investment or regulatory missteps can be uncovered and the policy's long-term viability ensured.

Core/Satellite Investment Structure

A well-grounded portfolio-building strategy is to establish a core investment position representing the broad market that the portfolio seeks to mimic. PPLI's core portfolio is an investment, through fund of funds vehicles, in a diversified set of hedge fund strategies (see chapter 9). This diversified approach is combined with sufficient investment manager depth *in each strategy* to minimize specific manager risk.

Around this core, allocations are made to specific high-growth strategies—satellites—that complement the hedge fund core. The primary complementary characteristics will be low correlation to the core and high historical returns. Also, for a satellite investment to achieve its intended purpose in the portfolio, it must be of sufficient size to have an impact, but not so large that it causes a disruption in meeting the portfolio's *long-term* objectives. Satellites ranging in size from 10 percent to 25 percent of the PPLI portfolio are recommended. The core/satellite structure is illustrated in **FIGURE 8.8**.

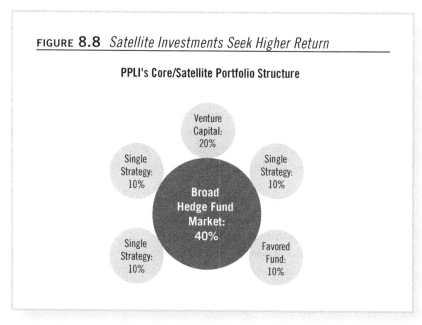

FIGURE 8.8 *Satellite Investments Seek Higher Return*

PPLI's Core/Satellite Portfolio Structure

Venture Capital: 20%

Single Strategy: 10%

Single Strategy: 10%

Broad Hedge Fund Market: 40%

Single Strategy: 10%

Favored Fund: 10%

FIGURE **8.9**   *Total Portfolio Impact of PPLI Satellites*

PPLI SATELLITE ALLOCATION	PPLI % OF TOTAL PORTFOLIO	SATELLITE % TO TOTAL PORTFOLIO
10%	10.0%	1.0%
10%	20.0%	2.0%
10%	30.0%	3.0%
25%	10.0%	2.5%
25%	20.0%	5.0%
25%	30.0%	7.5%

Venture capital is a good example of a high-growth strategy used in a satellite. Venture capital has far exceeded the performance of any other asset class (see figure 8.4) while exhibiting some of the lowest correlations to different hedge fund strategies. According to Van Hedge Fund Advisors International, for the 10-year period ending in 2003, venture capital had the second-lowest correlation to nondefensive hedge funds; the lowest correlation strategy was short selling. These characteristics lead to the venture capital satellite carrying the high-impact, wealth-creating role for the PPLI portfolio.

Above all else, PPLI's portfolio should be built within the context of the investor's overall portfolio. **FIGURE 8.9** calculates how an allocation to a PPLI satellite investment relates to the investor's overall portfolio allocation. For example, if an investor chooses to invest 30 percent of his or her assets into PPLI and the satellite allocation is 25 percent of the total PPLI allocation, the investor still has only 7.5 percent of his total portfolio allocated to wealth-creation strategies, as reflected in the last line in figure 8.9.

Using this approach can reassure the investor and the advisory team that a satellite allocation within a PPLI policy will not significantly skew the investor's overall portfolio structure.

Other satellite allocations involve the more aggressive hedge fund of fund strategies such as macro, managed futures, and long/short equity, which employ significant leverage. If an investor has a favorite single-hedge-fund-strategy manager *that has an insurance-dedicated fund ap-*

proved by the insurance carrier, that may also be a satellite candidate. And as the PPLI market matures and real estate, LBO, and other alternative investment managers engineer funds for the policies, advisers can look to expand the use of different satellite investments.

PPLI Funding Tactics

The FOX study identified that the respondents' target portfolio allocations required significant funding as reflected in **FIGURE 8.10**, which shows the amount to be invested as a percent of the investor's total portfolio.

The premium funding a PPLI policy—whether in a MEC or non-MEC structure—must be in cash. As shown in figure 8.10, funding a non-MEC policy requires a combination of "Committed, Not Yet Invested" capital (often in the form of cash or liquid investments) and liquidated capital from the "Already Invested" allocation. For the planned allocations to hedge funds and venture capital, the following tactics illustrate one funding methodology:

Hedge funds. To fund the policy premium, the investor may choose to liquidate existing hedge fund investments and use the resulting proceeds to make allocations in appropriate PPLI-approved hedge fund substitutes. Using the core/satellite methodology, 40 percent or more of the premium will be allocated to a hedge fund portfolio to make up the core. Favored hedge fund managers that are not PPLI compliant and/or inappropriate PPLI hedge fund strategies would continue residing in the investor's taxable portfolio.

Venture capital. Venture capital is the only private-equity class that has been approved for PPLI investing thus far. Fifty percent of the FOX study respondents' private-equity allocation target is dedicated to venture capital. The remaining allocation is spread among LBO (22 percent), ex-

FIGURE **8.10**	Alternative Asset Allocations and Funding		
ASSET CLASS	TARGET ALLOCATION	ALREADY INVESTED	COMMITTED, NOT YET INVESTED
Private Equity	14.0%	6.7%	7.3%
Hedge Funds	14.0%	8.3%	5.7%
Real Estate	11.0%	6.2%	4.8%

pansion capital (10 percent), special situations (8 percent), and mezzanine financing (5 percent).

In figure 8.10, the venture capital allocation represents 7 percent of the private-equity portfolio target (14 percent target allocation times the 50 percent venture capital portion of private equity). To come up with the venture capital allocation that is "Committed, Not Yet Invested," the 7 percent venture capital target is multiplied by the 52 percent of private equity not yet invested (7.3 percent "Committed, Not Yet Invested" divided by 14 percent "Target Allocation"). This yields 3.6 percent of the desired venture capital allocation that needs to be invested.

Because PPLI gives venture capital tax-free compounding of returns and a non-MEC policy's loans and withdrawals *give liquidity to a venture capital allocation that it otherwise wouldn't have,* PPLI will be the repository for the investor's diversified venture capital portfolio investments going forward. The 3.6 percent "Committed, Not Yet Invested" portion of venture capital will be funded through the initial PPLI premium payments. To translate this 3.6 percent into a PPLI allocation, we go back to figure 8.9.

A 3.6 percent total portfolio allocation is slightly more than a 30 percent satellite allocation of a policy, which represents 10 percent of the investor's total portfolio and between a 10 percent and 20 percent satellite allocation of a policy representing 25 percent of the total portfolio. In either case, this is a highly manageable allocation to make from the PPLI premium payments.

What can be done with the investor's current illiquid venture capital limited partnerships? Most of these investments were made in the 1999 and 2000 technology bubble, during which commitments to venture capital were unprecedented. An investor's limited partnerships that have not already been liquidated because of poor performance will be allowed to self-liquidate. A typical venture capital partnership has a legal life of 10 years before it goes through a forced liquidation. Therefore, a 1999 vintage-year partnership has already consumed much of its useful life and will liquidate in five years or less. (Note: an investor's venture investments in single companies are not PPLI-eligible because of investor control exposure; these investments will remain in the investor's taxable portfolio.)

Real estate is not an approved option for PPLI, so the investor's target allocation will remain as a component of the investor's taxable portfolio.

Execution Practices

For PPLI policies to remain in force, they must be compliant with current Internal Revenue Service (IRS) standards for insurance, diversification, and investor control (see chapter 12). The policies must also be compliant with appropriate state and/or offshore insurance regulations. In addition, the investor's advisory team must insist on best practices for reporting and monitoring investment portfolios. In total, a well-executed PPLI policy will have these characteristics:

- ❑ Insurance-dedicated investment options
- ❑ Appropriate diversification, with a minimum of five approved investments per policy
- ❑ Monthly valuations
- ❑ Quarterly reporting
- ❑ Annual reporting
- ❑ Monitoring of investments according to the investment manager's stated objectives and processes
- ❑ Ongoing review of newly approved investment managers
- ❑ Continued strong relationships with the insurance carriers
- ❑ Ongoing interaction with legislative and regulatory bodies

A Portfolio for the Ages

PPLI provides high-net-worth investors and the advisory marketplace with an investment vehicle that can change the course of productivity in an investor's portfolio. Such productivity not only assists the current generation but also benefits multiple generations and other designated beneficiaries thereafter.

To maximize PPLI's productivity, the underlying portfolio must be constructed to take advantage of PPLI's unique structures. Using PPLI's long-term horizon to establish a diversified portfolio of high-returning investments, the future wealth of individuals and families can be dramatically improved.

CHAPTER 9

Who's Afraid of Hedge Funds?

GEORGE VAN AND DANIEL T. HAYDEN

T he performance of a private placement life insurance portfolio results directly from the returns of its investment components. A wide variety of investments may be used in PPLI policies, but as hedge funds continue to grow rapidly worldwide, both in numbers and assets, they are rapidly finding a place in PPLI. Hedge funds are very attractive candidates for a PPLI portfolio; this chapter explains why. We begin by describing the funds' characteristics and the process for selecting them as portfolio components as well as the legislation that affects the construction of PPLI portfolios. An integral part of choosing the funds is a detailed examination of all proposed investment managers as well as their strategies. Though both exhaustive and time-consuming, due diligence is critical to successful hedge fund investing.

A Burgeoning Industry

The hedge fund industry has expanded dramatically in the past 16 years, growing at an average annual rate of more than 20 percent. During that time, high-net-worth and institutional investors have found it increasingly easy to gain access to the wide array of hedge funds. In the mid-1990s, hedge funds were the domain of the sophisticated wealthy who knew how to find them. Today, some hedge funds are registered with the U.S. Securities and Exchange Commission as investment companies and are available for investment to any individual who qualifies. The minimum invest-

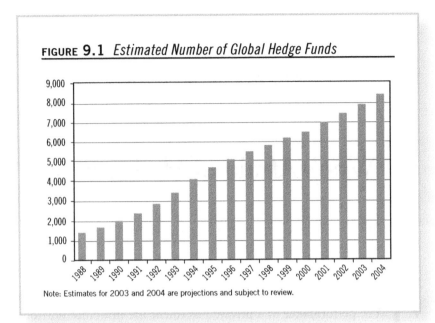

FIGURE 9.1 *Estimated Number of Global Hedge Funds*

Note: Estimates for 2003 and 2004 are projections and subject to review.

Source: © 2004 by Van Hedge Fund Advisors International, LLC and/or its affiliates, Nashville, TN

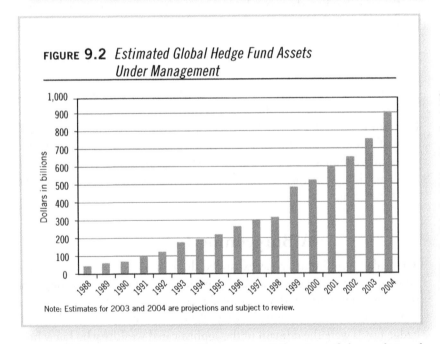

FIGURE 9.2 *Estimated Global Hedge Fund Assets Under Management*

Note: Estimates for 2003 and 2004 are projections and subject to review.

Source: © 2004 by Van Hedge Fund Advisors International, LLC and/or its affiliates, Nashville, TN

ments of these companies typically are a small fraction of the traditional minimum hedge fund investment of $200,000 to $1 million.

FIGURE 9.1 shows the estimated growth in the number of hedge funds over the years.

The assets managed by hedge funds also have been increasing steadily, as shown in **FIGURE 9.2**. These amounts are expected to continue to grow through the end of the decade as more and more investors allocate higher percentages of their portfolios to alternative investments.

The Hedge Fund Edge

What caused this dramatic—and continuing—increase in hedge fund popularity? The answer is straightforward: over time, hedge funds have provided superior returns with less risk than most other types of investments for numerous reasons, including these:

❑ Even as hedge funds have the potential to provide profits in rising markets, their short positions (that is, gaining a return on an expectation that a stock's price will decline) provide cushioning against market downturns.

❑ Arbitrage strategies used by many hedge funds are not as dependent on equity-market fluctuations as equity-based funds (although they're subject to their own specific market influences—for example, interest-rate movements for many strategies).

❑ The performance-based compensation of hedge funds attracts many of the best and brightest money managers.

❑ Hedge funds generally are kept much smaller than traditional long-only strategies, allowing the managers to concentrate on the most attractive market niches.

❑ Managers of hedge funds often have a significant percentage of their net worth invested in their own funds, creating an intensity and alignment of interest that is often lost when only outside assets are managed.

❑ The hedge fund manager's compensation is directly tied to the performance of his fund, providing him an added incentive to perform well.

These structural and investment benefits have allowed hedge funds to produce, on average, superior returns and lower risk than traditional investments, and the funds are widely regarded as important diversification tools within portfolios. As a result, their inclusion in a PPLI or other investment portfolios can both increase returns and reduce risk. **FIGURE 9.3** illustrates the degree to which hedge funds outperformed traditional benchmarks from 1988 to 2003.

Another way to illustrate the superior characteristics of hedge funds over traditional investments is to plot the statistics from figure 9.3 in reward-risk space, as shown in **FIGURE 9.4**.

FIGURE 9.3 *January 1, 1988–December 31, 2003*
Hedge Fund Returns* Compared to Traditional
Benchmarks

INDEX	COMPOUND ANNUAL RETURN (%)	SHARPE RATIO (%)	STANDARD DEVIATION (%)
Van Global Hedge Fund Index	15.9	1.6	8.6
MSCI World Equity Index	6.2	0.3	16.4
S&P 500 Index	12.5	0.7	15.5
Average Equity Mutual Fund Index	9.9	0.6	16.0
Lehman Brothers Aggregate Bond Index	8.3	1.5	4.4

*Based on quarterly returns

FIGURE 9.4 *Reward-Risk Characteristics of Hedge Funds*
January 1, 1988–December 31, 2005

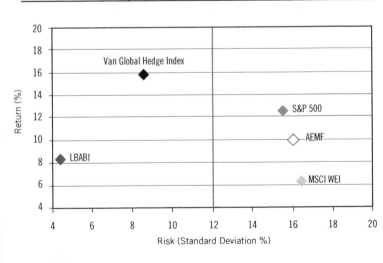

Source: © 2004 by Van Hedge Fund Advisors International, LLC and/or its affiliates, Nashville, TN

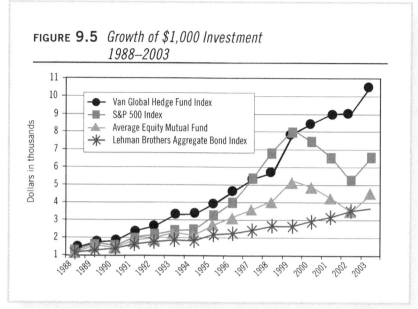

FIGURE **9.5** *Growth of $1,000 Investment 1988–2003*

During the bear market that began in 2000, hedge funds outperformed traditional benchmarks even more significantly, as illustrated in **FIGURE 9.5**.

For example, in the second quarter of 2002, when the S&P lost 13.4 percent, the average hedge fund, as measured by the Van Global Hedge Fund Index, lost only 1.2 percent. **FIGURE 9.6** (see page 130) shows the compelling difference in returns for hedge funds compared to mutual funds during losing quarters for the S&P.

Beta and Alpha

Note the beta and alpha of hedge funds and mutual funds to the S&P in **FIGURE 9.7**. Together, beta and alpha determine an investment's overall return. Beta measures the degree of market-based return. If an investment vehicle has a beta of 1.25 to the S&P 500, its return will change 1.25 percent for every 1 percent change in the S&P 500. Alpha measures manager skill or the value added by an individual manager in excess of the market-based returns of the beta. An alpha of 5 percent to the S&P 500 means that the manager's skill is adding 5 percent to the return, over and above the return accounted for by the movement of the S&P 500 (the beta). Beta and alpha may be positive or negative.

Using quarterly returns from the first quarter of 1988 through the fourth quarter of 2003, figure 9.7 shows the beta and alpha of hedge funds and mutual funds to the S&P.

FIGURE **9.6** *Performance of Hedge Funds and Mutual Funds in Down S&P 500 Quarters 1Q88–4Q03*

	S&P 500 (%)	VAN GLOBAL HEDGE FUND INDEX (%)	AVERAGE EQUITY MUTUAL FUND %
1Q90	–3.0	2.2	–2.8
3Q90	–13.7	–4.1	–15.4
2Q91	–0.2	2.3	–0.9
1Q92	–2.5	5.1	–0.7
1Q94	–3.8	–1.2	–3.2
4Q94	–0.02	–2.0	–2.6
3Q98	–10.0	–7.0	–14.9
3Q99	–6.2	1.6	–3.4
2Q00	–2.7	–0.9	–3.2
3Q00	–1.0	2.0	0.6
4Q00	–7.8	–2.0	–8.1
1Q01	–11.9	–0.4	–12.7
3Q01	–14.7	–2.6	–17.2
2Q02	–13.4	–1.2	–10.7
3Q02	–17.3	–3.1	–16.7
1Q03	–3.1	0.7	–3.7
Cumulative Return	**–69.4%**	**–10.7%**	**–70.9%**

Source: © 2004 by Van Hedge Fund Advisors International, LLC and/or its affiliates, Nashville, TN

Based on this analysis, hedge fund returns are less dependent on the overall market than are mutual funds. Beta, which measures the degree of market-based return, is 0.98 for mutual funds. This means that for every 1 percent of market return, mutual funds return 98 basis points (or 98 percent of the S&P 500's return) on average. The average hedge fund, with a beta of 0.41, derives from the market a portion of its return equal to 41 percent of the S&P's return. Alpha, which measures manager skill,

FIGURE **9.7** *Hedge Funds versus S&P 500 Index*
January 1, 1988–December 31, 2003

	BETA	ALPHA
Van Global Hedge Fund Index	0.41	10.40%
Average Equity Mutual Fund	0.98	-2.05%

is 10.40 percent for hedge funds; whereas mutual funds actually subtract 2.05 percent from market return.

Correlations

A correlation coefficient measures the extent to which two investments move in lockstep in response to market changes. If they move together in perfect coordination, the correlation is 1.0. If they consistently and perfectly move in opposite directions, the correlation coefficient is –1.0. If their movements are totally random to each other, the correlation will be 0.0.

The low correlation of many hedge fund strategies both to each other and to market benchmarks provides opportunities to construct portfolios that will not be primarily market driven but rather will produce returns that are somewhat independent of market direction. The correlation of hedge fund strategies to the S&P 500 range from a correlation of –0.8 for short selling to 0.8 for aggressive growth and value strategies.

Research has shown that the addition of hedge funds to a diversified portfolio can increase the portfolio's return and decrease its risk, as illustrated in **FIGURE 9.8**.

According to figure 9.8, it appears that a desirable portfolio would include at least 60 percent hedge funds. This is the far-left point, representing the highest return for the lowest risk (standard deviation). The majority of investors are not yet comfortable with such a high allocation to hedge funds, but we expect allocations to hedge funds to increase substantially by the end of the decade as the industry continues to mature. Some well-known institutional investors such as Harvard University and the University of Notre Dame have considered hedge funds an essential part of their portfolios for many years. Although these institutions have been in the minority, things are changing. In the past five years, many institutions have added alternative investments as a standard part of their

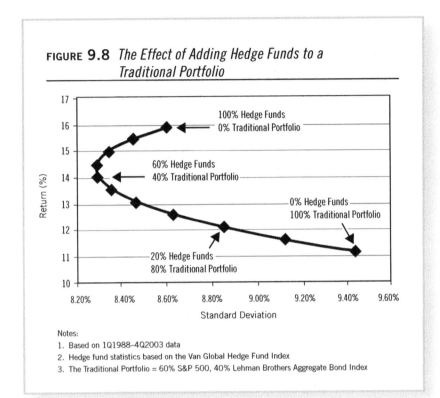

FIGURE **9.8** *The Effect of Adding Hedge Funds to a Traditional Portfolio*

Notes:
1. Based on 1Q1988–4Q2003 data
2. Hedge fund statistics based on the Van Global Hedge Fund Index
3. The Traditional Portfolio = 60% S&P 500, 40% Lehman Brothers Aggregate Bond Index

Source: © 2004 by Van Hedge Fund Advisors International, LLC and/or its affiliates, Nashville, TN

portfolios, and several leading universities, including the University of North Carolina, have allocated 20 percent or more of their portfolios to alternative investments.[1]

Hedge funds are more complex and rewarding instruments than traditional investments, but with complexity comes potential pitfalls. Hedge funds have a number of potential disadvantages that warrant careful attention (see "Additional Screening," page 140, and "Due Diligence," page 145; also, the appendix to this chapter, page 151, describes some of the most common mistakes that hedge fund investors make along with steps they can take to avoid them). For one, the funds are usually not tax-friendly, because their gains frequently are short-term. However, using hedge funds in PPLI permits the investor to enjoy the funds' investment advantages in combination with the favorable tax benefits of life insurance.

Insurance Rules and Investment Selection

For an investment to qualify as appropriate for an insurance portfolio, it must meet specific criteria. Two rules in particular need to be described here because they directly affect investment selection.

Rule 1: Diversification

The first rule is a diversification test. No single investment may represent more than 55 percent of the value of total assets in the policy; no two investments may make up more than 70 percent; no three, more than 80 percent; and no four, more than 90 percent. In other words, insurance regulations require a minimally diversified portfolio, with at least five investments. Current rules allow one to "look through" the structure of a nonregistered investment partnership (such as a U.S. hedge fund) and count its underlying investments (such as stocks) for purposes of meeting this requirement. However, even if it passes the diversification test, a single U.S. hedge fund does not provide adequate portfolio diversification. A more prudent approach would be to invest in at least five hedge funds.

There is no look-through provision for offshore funds structured as corporations. In this case, an investor would have to invest in at least five hedge funds (or several hedge funds plus other investments) to satisfy the test. If there is not enough equity to invest in at least five individual hedge fund managers, then an investor should consider several fund of funds (FOFs).

A hedge FOF invests in individual hedge funds. U.S. FOFs are structured as pass-through vehicles, so generally a single U.S. FOF would meet the diversification test because most FOFs invest in more than five individual hedge funds. With offshore corporate FOFs, as with individual offshore corporate hedge funds, there is no look-through and one would have to invest in at least five FOFs.

Rule 2: The Insurance Portfolio

The second rule is a 2003 IRS Revenue Ruling related specifically to the use of hedge funds in an insurance portfolio. The ruling attempts to specify that only hedge funds that are insurance-dedicated (that is, only variable life insurance policies and variable-annuity contracts may invest in them) may be used in a policy. Because revenue rulings typically reflect the position that the IRS will take on audit and in litigation, the most prudent course of action for an investor looking to access hedge funds through an insurance contract is to invest only in insurance-dedicated funds (see chapter 14). Unfortunately, few individual hedge fund managers have set up cloned funds that are insurance-dedicated. There are some insurance-dedicated FOFs, however, and the number is growing. Fortunately, the hedge fund industry usually responds with new products to service new markets. We can expect to see more insurance-dedicated hedge fund clones springing up to satisfy investor demand and IRS requirements.

There is a significant difference in the due diligence conducted by insurance companies (see chapter 13) compared to that conducted by hedge fund consultants or FOF providers. The insurance company typically tends to focus primarily on business risk, whereas hedge fund specialists usually spend a great deal of time on performance issues (that is, producing portfolios designed to meet reward and risk targets).

Strategy and Manager Selection

Once the decision has been made to include hedge funds in the PPLI portfolio, the next step involves selecting appropriate hedge fund strategies and combining them to achieve specified investment objectives. Although certain legal and structural features are common to hedge funds, managers trade a wide variety of strategies with dramatically different reward-risk profiles. Thus, it's important to clearly define the objectives and risk tolerance of the investor before beginning the selection process. Another important consideration is the investment time horizon. In the case of PPLI, investors should have a longer-term horizon. This will enhance the opportunity to construct a quality portfolio (see chapter 8). Once the strategy is settled, superior funds from those strategies can be selected.

Strategy Selection

Selecting the right strategies for the investment mandate is crucial to building a portfolio that will perform to benchmark expectations. If performance will be measured against an equity benchmark such as the S&P 500, selecting truly market-neutral strategies would be unlikely to yield the desired results. Hedge fund strategies more highly correlated to the S&P would be preferable. Conversely, if capital preservation over a short time horizon were a primary investment objective, investing in highly volatile strategies would be unwise. **FIGURE 9.9** shows how differently two strategies may perform over time.

The popular conception of hedge funds is the classic hedge fund model, a trading philosophy designed to produce absolute returns uncorrelated to general market movements while limiting volatility, that is, superior returns in good times and bad. This strategy is designed to identify undervalued stocks that are likely to rise in value relative to the market. It also is designed to identify overvalued stocks to help produce profits in falling markets. The cost of hedging associated with this approach makes it useful to add a certain amount of leverage to amplify returns.

In reality, fund managers employ a great variety of strategies to generate excess return (alpha), which include trading many of the market and derivative instruments available. Different strategies can exhibit very different reward-risk profiles, as illustrated in **FIGURE 9.10**.

FIGURE **9.9** *Contrasting Hedge Fund Strategies Growth of $1,000 Investment*

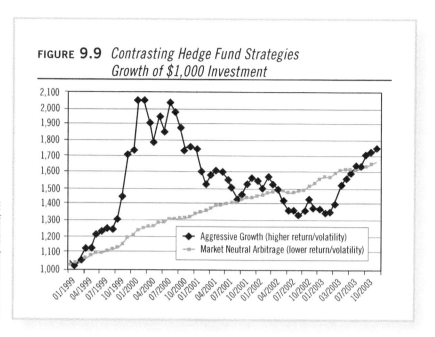

FIGURE **9.10** *Reward-Risk Characteristics of Various Hedge Fund Strategies January 1, 1988–December 31, 2003*

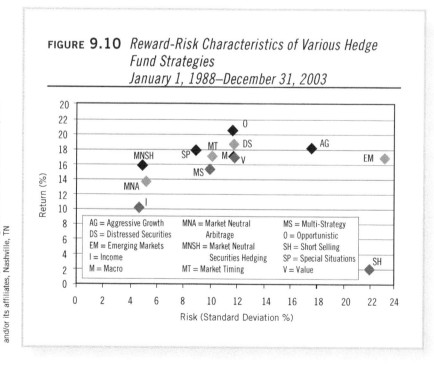

FIGURE 9.11 *Market Opportunities and Relevant Hedge Fund Strategies*

MARKET OPPORTUNITIES	RELATED HEDGE FUND STRATEGIES
1. Identification of under- or overvalued securities	Distressed Securities, Market Neutral Securities Hedging, Short Selling, Value
2. Arbitrage opportunities created by market inefficiency	Market Neutral Arbitrage
3. Anticipated moves in market direction	Emerging Markets
4. Trends in stock or sector movements	Aggressive Growth, Market Timing
5. Anticipated economic events	Macro
6. Steady income opportunities	Income
7. Other events that trigger changes in market valuations	Special Situations

Managers typically identify a niche and a trading strategy based on many years of experience in their field. Their funds are run in a specific style to use their skills and knowledge. Hedge fund managers seek to exploit several general categories of opportunities. **FIGURE 9.11** lists categories of opportunities and matches them with various hedge fund strategies.

Figure 9.11 aligns typical opportunities and strategies. This is not a precise exercise because some hedge fund strategies can fit into more than one market-opportunity classification. Two hedge fund strategies listed in figure 9.10 are not shown in figure 9.11. One is multistrategy, which describes the use by a hedge fund manager of several stated strategies. These few selected strategies can vary from one multistrategy manager to another. The second, the opportunistic strategy, refers to a manager's ability to use any of the hedge fund trading strategies at different times. The market-neutral arbitrage strategy encompasses, among others, these important substrategies: convertible arbitrage, fixed-income arbitrage, merger arbitrage, and statistical arbitrage.

Each strategy has its own unique risk-and-reward profile. Some managers trade based on the classic balanced long-short model; others pursue strategies that are not strictly market neutral. Within each general strategy grouping, each manager will have his own targets for return and volatility. Essential to selecting funds is a general understanding of the strategies available and, for each one: (1) the general pattern of trading, (2) the instruments traded, and (3) the historical returns of the trading strategies under consideration.

There are several commercial providers of hedge fund strategy indices. These indices represent the aggregate returns and risks of a pool of hedge funds practicing that strategy (see chapter 10 for a discussion on the use of indices in evaluating managers). Although none represents the entire universe of such managers trading, each index has its strengths and weaknesses.

❑ Some providers construct indices based on a limited selection of funds that they deem to be "style pure"; others choose to be more broadly based.

❑ Some providers classify funds based on the instruments traded (for example, equities).

❑ Other providers classify funds by the methodologies employed to select the securities.

❑ Some indices are calculated on an asset-weighted basis, and some are not.

❑ Certain indices impose material restrictions for fund inclusion; others do not.

In the traditional world of unhedged investments, stock indices usually are intended to serve as barometers either of the overall equity or bond markets or of specific segments within them. Different index sponsors favor different methodologies for choosing stocks for their indexes. The S&P 500, for instance, which tracks 70 percent of all U.S. equity, is composed of stocks chosen for their market size, liquidity, and sector. In contrast, the Dow Jones Industrial Average uses only 30 stocks, representing a price-weighted average of mostly industrial blue-chip equities. [2]

Hedge fund indices exhibit similarly diverse methodologies. Some attempt to serve as barometers of performance of the overall hedge fund industry; others have different goals, for example, representing only funds with "purity of style." Some indices track sufficient funds to reasonably represent not only the overall universe but also constituent strategies; others do not.

To understand the performance history of the various strategy alternatives, consider all of the information available. At least one of the index sources consulted should track a large enough number of funds to reasonably represent performance of both the overall hedge fund universe and its constituent strategies. It is also helpful if the index labels its strategies in the same terms as those used by managers—which makes it easier to compare the manager's performance to the index substrategy. A long track record is also useful in an index because it provides the investor with information on how the strategies performed through different market cycles and stressful periods. Different strategies have their own cycles and will perform better or worse depending on the market environment. Short selling, for instance, was a winner during the 2000–2002 bear market but was pummeled during the 2003 market recovery. To the sophisticated hedge fund observer, this is precisely how one would expect a short-selling strategy to perform—positive returns in down markets and negative returns in rising markets. Looking at strategy index returns also will provide useful guidance on how returns correlate between strategies. How strategies interact with one another, as evidenced by their correlations, is a key determinant for a successfully constructed portfolio (see chapter 8).

Indices that have been calculated consistently for many years have another advantage: they will reflect the returns as they occurred at the time and minimize "survivorship bias." Survivorship bias refers to the bias created in a sample by omitting funds that are now defunct or out of business. A hedge fund index started in 1995, for instance, will have access only to funds open at that time. The index provider will not have access to the data for the considerable number of funds that went out of business before 1995. The index sponsors, in this example, typically will request that the funds they contact provide their pre-1995 performance history. Thus, aggregate performance for the pre-1995 years will not show the poor results for the funds that have failed.

From the historical index information accumulated, investors can determine the long-term return parameters of each trading strategy, the volatility to be expected, and the extent of potential drawdowns. Analyze this information over an extended period of time—three to five years—and consider performance during stress points in the market. A stress point is a period in the equity or debt markets during which conditions make it difficult for hedge funds to operate well. Because hedge funds have equity or debt components, or both, they will be affected by such unfavorable market conditions. August 1998 and all of 2002, for example, were difficult times for most hedge funds. In August 1998, worldwide turmoil in both equity and fixed-income markets affected equity- and bond-based hedge fund strategies. In 2002, since primarily the equity markets were affected, equity-based hedge fund strategies suffered while arbitrage strategies, many of which use bonds, performed much better.

Difficult market conditions notwithstanding, hedge funds have almost always performed better in these periods than their traditional long-only equity or bond counterparts. For example, one study shows that from the beginning of the recent bear market, on April 1, 2000, through July 31, 2002, the average U.S. hedge fund gained 1.9 percent net while the returns of the major indices were down: the S&P 500, –37 percent; the NASDAQ, –71 percent; the Dow –17 percent; and the average equity mutual fund, –36 percent. [3]

After analyzing strategies, decide which of them to use and in what proportion. One of the considerations should be how the proposed selection affects the profile of the entire portfolio.

Manager/Fund Selection

Once strategies are identified, the search for individual funds must be thorough. Two primary factors can be used as an initial screen:
- ❑ Potential for attractive returns
- ❑ Consistency of returns

Potential for attractive returns. Specific managers should be identified as attractive based on their historical returns. The axiom that "past performance does not ensure future returns" is true, but some information knowledgeably interpreted is better than none. A record of superior past performance, though cautiously viewed, is certainly better than poor past performance. These figures can provide insight regarding the investment discipline that has been exercised.

Consistency of returns. Consistency of returns speaks to the manager's ability to manage his hedging programs to produce absolute returns, versus returns linked to the markets. A comparison of manager performance versus benchmarks both in favorable market conditions, such as in 2003, and in periods of market dislocations or "shocks," such as the one in August 1998, can yield further insight into the manager's trading skill. The industry has devised a variety of risk measures including the standard deviation of returns and the Sharpe ratio. The Sharpe ratio, the one most widely cited, measures the extent to which the return of an investment exceeds the volatility of its returns. In other words, the Sharpe ratio asks: "How much return does an investor get per unit of risk taken?" It's useful as a relative measure to compare one potential investment with another. There are several other useful barometers of risk including the standard deviation of returns (volatility), downside deviation, and drawdown analyses. Using several measurements can help facilitate the interpretation of risk and reduce the volatility of a portfolio and its risk of loss. A thorough discussion of these different risk factors is beyond this chapter's scope, but it's clear that using a variety of measures provides deeper insight into the true riskiness of an investment.

Although there is no single definitive source of information for the universe of alternative funds, several consulting organizations maintain hedge fund databases. A basic Internet search for "hedge fund" will yield several such sources. Access to the broadest and deepest information available will improve the selection process and allow for measurement of fund performance versus those of peers and other benchmarks. A typical peer group review compares funds using similar strategies for both absolute return and standard deviation. **FIGURE 9.12** illustrates a typical peer group review chart.

Statistical analyses should be supplemented by a review of the raw data—the reported return stream throughout the fund's trading history. Some issues, such as painful loss periods, may stand out more here than in aggregate statistics.

Additional Screening

After the top-performing managers are identified, preliminary review of other characteristics of the fund must be done to determine whether an investment is appropriate. Such factors include:

- ❑ Fund capacity and size
- ❑ Length of track record
- ❑ Extent and method of hedging employed
- ❑ Concentration of positions
- ❑ Amount of leverage

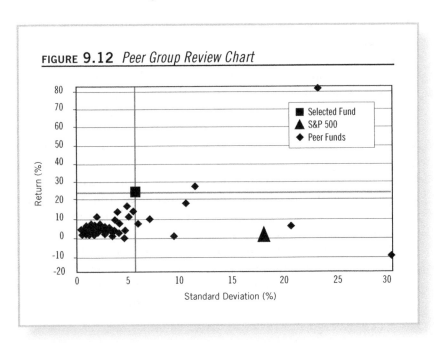

FIGURE **9.12** *Peer Group Review Chart*

❑ Use of derivative securities
❑ Liquidity provisions
❑ Personnel turnover and strategy drift
❑ Sophistication of the organization and risk controls
❑ Fees

(For more detail on items in this list, see "Due Diligence," page 145.)

Fund capacity and size. A fund's being at or near capacity may preclude an investment. The fund manager must have a clear plan for the fund's growth and an understanding of the market opportunity even if he claims that capacity is not a current concern. Profit generation often is retarded by growth in fund size when the manager has to allocate capital to trades in which he has less conviction, or whose reward-risk ratio is not favorable. Having to close a fund to new investment because it has reached its trading capacity is a hallmark of a successful manager. The manager must understand the practical research capacity of the firm. It's also important to evaluate the fund's total net assets in relation to the total investment likely to be made in the near future. No investor should become too large a percentage of any fund.

Track record. It also is important to consider the length of the track record of the manager at the current fund and at previous firms where he has traded the same strategy. He should have a clearly demonstrated ability to succeed in various market conditions. An attractive short-term track record can be misleading if markets have been uniformly favorable throughout that time frame. Success should be viewed differently for different strategies.

Extent and method of hedging employed. To hedge generally means to protect against risk of loss. Within reason, the greater the degree of hedging, the safer the portfolio—as long as the manager can still produce acceptable returns. That's because hedging generally has a cost attached to it. The manager's skill lies in hedging enough for reasonable safety without the cost of hedging unduly eating into the profits of the fund. The classic way for a hedge fund manager to hedge against risk is to take on short positions that are intended to produce profits as the market falls. With the continuing proliferation of strategies and the growing ingenuity of hedge fund managers, many more forms of hedging are now being employed. Examples of new techniques increasingly popular among traders include the use of options and futures instead of stocks, as well as the use of ETFs (exchange-traded funds) in market timing.

Not all hedge funds are market neutral or are significantly hedged against all relevant negative return possibilities. If absolute-return profiles are desired, the manager's hedging program should be understood. The types of risks the manager assumes will help indicate the volatility of future returns. To what extent has the fund been long and short on both a gross and net basis?[4] Are these percentages based on a consistently applied risk-management philosophy or do they vary widely based on manager perception of market conditions?

Concentration of positions. This characteristic refers both to the number of positions and to the percent of the fund's assets in single positions. Typically, the higher the concentration of assets, the higher the risk. Generally, for long/short hedge funds, a minimum of at least 25 positions, with no position ever being greater than 10 percent of the portfolio, is desirable. Within reason, the greater the number of positions and the smaller the percentage of assets allowed within a single position, the smaller the risk.

It is an axiom of investing that portfolio diversity is a key factor in reducing aggregate risk. It takes significantly more skill to manage risk in a highly concentrated portfolio. Most quality money managers will have strict policies that dictate portfolio diversity to minimize concentration. How many positions does the fund typically hold, long and short? What is the maximum percentage of the portfolio allowed in the top positions, and what are the policies for trimming back positions as they grow outside of stated guidelines? Most hedge fund investors will choose to avoid highly concentrated portfolios.

Amount of leverage. Leverage refers to the practice of borrowing money to add to an investment position. Occasionally, an imprudent hedge fund manager may leverage too highly, exposing his investors to undue risk. However, the investor has several ways to protect himself from this eventuality: checking the manager's track record on use of leverage, verifying the historical volatility of the portfolio (higher leverage equals increased volatility), and verifying the manager's confidential memorandum regarding restrictions on leverage.

Leverage is an important tool that hedge fund managers use to help produce excess returns. The extent of appropriate leverage varies widely by strategy and the risk profile of the individual trades executed. There are, however, norms for individual strategy groupings. High-risk, directional traders would generally not employ leverage. Certain arbitrage traders may employ leverage of 10 to 1 or more. These arbitrage opportunities usually generate only small profits per trade, but the risk of loss is generally low. Leverage allows the manager to magnify profits in these situations.

Use of derivative securities. More and more hedge fund managers are using derivatives in their trading. Many such derivatives are leveraged by their very nature. Each dollar invested in futures, for example, can result in many dollars of market exposure, in addition to the fund's borrowings. This adds risk beyond the leverage represented by the borrowings of the fund and should be taken into account.

Liquidity provisions. This characteristic can refer both to the frequency with which investors can withdraw money as well as the ease with which the manager can liquidate some or all of the portfolio.

What are the fund's liquidity provisions? They may include lock-ups, number of redemption dates offered per year, hold-back provisions, and other restrictions imposed. Certain funds also assess redemption fees that expire after a specified holding period or remain in perpetuity. Even if the terms appear favorable, remember that most fund documents provide for the potential suspension of redemptions during periods of duress. The liquidity of the fund's underlying portfolio affects the likelihood of this eventuality. An assessment should be made as to whether the fund's investing methodology and its holdings are consistent with the stated liquidity provisions.

The ease with which investors can withdraw money from their hedge funds keeps improving. A few years ago, the majority of hedge funds had a first year of investment "lock-up," during which no money could be withdrawn. The number of funds with such lock-ups is diminishing rapidly. Similarly, biannual or quarterly withdrawals were once fairly common. Now, we're seeing more and more funds with monthly withdrawal privileges.

Liquidity of positions within a manager's portfolio is also an important consideration. The faster positions can be sold without large losses, the better. Insufficient ability to liquidate positions can expose the fund to large losses.

Personnel turnover and strategy drift. Since the initial screening of the funds to be used is based on the reported returns and risk, investors should determine whether that performance was produced by the current team executing a consistent strategy. All organizations evolve, but turnover in key personnel or significant strategy drift may negate the possibility that future performance can be implied from past results.[5]

Sophistication of the organization and risk controls. Quality funds are run by individuals who have demonstrated trading talent and a desire and ability to create the infrastructure necessary to execute a long-term business plan. Such managers build organizations compatible with the scope of operations, provide for strong internal controls and procedures, and have appropriate risk-management systems.

Fees. Although net returns should be the priority for the investor, the type of fee structure employed may influence the motivation of the manager and the volatility he's willing to accept. Managers of stand-alone hedge funds typically charge a 1 percent annual fee based on net assets and a fee calculated at 20 percent of net profits. Managers of FOFs (ready-made portfolios of hedge funds) typically charge 1 percent on assets; some also charge 10 percent of profits in addition to what the underlying funds charge.

Different characteristics will be of lesser or greater importance to an individual investor, but they all should be part of the winnowing process.

FIGURE **9.13** *Hedge Fund Characteristics*

Use of Leverage (ratio of dollars invested to dollars of equity)	None = 27%	Low (<2.0:1) = 45%	High (≥2.0:1) = 28%
Minimum Investment Required	Mean = $630,000	Median = $500,000	Mode = $1 million
Management Fee (charged on client's total invested assets)	Mean = 1.3%	Median = 1.0%	Mode = 1.0%
Performance Allocation (charged on gains produced for client)	Mean = 16.8%	Median = 20.0%	Mode = 20.0%
Audited Financial Statements and/or Audited Performance	Yes = 90%	No = 10%	
Frequency of Entry Dates (fund subscriptions)	Monthly (or more often) = 73%	Quarterly = 24%	Less often than quarterly = 3%
Frequency of Exit Dates (fund redemptions)	Monthly (or more often) = 43%	Quarterly = 39%	Less often than quarterly = 18%

Source: © 2004 by Van Hedge Fund Advisors International, LLC and/or its affiliates, Nashville, TN

The final short list of funds that will be considered for investment should be constructed based on the totality of the understanding gained about the characteristics of the fund, rigorous peer group analysis, and analyses of how the addition of the funds selected will affect aggregate portfolio performance. **FIGURE 9.13** lists selected hedge fund characteristics.

Due Diligence

Once investment candidates are selected, rigorous due diligence is required before making an allocation to a manager. For a hedge fund-of-funds manager delivering a PPLI insurance-dedicated portfolio, the process described here is far more detailed than the investment due diligence carried out by the insurance company on the manager itself (see chapter 13). The insurance company focuses more on business risk; the hedge fund-of-funds manager focuses on manager and investment risk. Nevertheless, an investment approved by both the fund manager and the insurance company has undergone a level of scrutiny that far exceeds what any adviser would likely undertake.

All of the factors critical to fund selection should be reviewed and verified. Hedge funds are subject to certain regulatory scrutiny, but just like the PPLI policy itself, as private investment vehicles targeted to ac-credited and qualified investors, most are structured to be exempt from SEC registration and certain provisions of the Investment Company Act of 1940. They have less governmental oversight and far more operating latitude than do mutual funds. Due diligence must be conducted to de-termine whether there is some reason to believe that the manager has the background and skill to produce alpha and whether the management firm has sufficient safeguards and controls to minimize the risk of loss. Effective due diligence answers these two important questions: Why is this fund the right investment? Why is it not the right investment? Procedures should cover the following areas of inquiry and verification:

- ❑ Review of fund specifications
- ❑ Examination of the manager's specific strategy and trade execution
- ❑ Review of the fund's risk parameters, risk controls, and risk-man-agement systems
- ❑ Transparency
- ❑ Infrastructure: review of the firm's business structure, internal con-trols, and operations
  - —Examination of the quality of the fund's policies, procedures, and principal service providers
  - —Review and verification of the manager's background, work his-tory, and education

- ❏ Portfolio valuation procedures
- ❏ Verification of the regulatory standing of the fund, the firm, and the manager
- ❏ Review and examination of the fund's audited financial statements
- ❏ On-site examination of the firm's offices and a face-to-face meeting with the manager

Although this examination list is not exhaustive, the proper level of inquiry and verification will provide a reasonable basis for making an investment.

Reviewing fund specifications. In considering the fund's specifications, it's necessary to supplement the information gathered during the fund selection process with a thorough review of all the legal documents associated with the investment company. These include the private placement memorandum, subscription documents, and the articles of association. Any discrepancies between the legal provisions of the fund and previous representations made by management, or those included in the marketing presentations, should be explained.

Strategy. An interview with the portfolio manager at the fund can provide an understanding of the strategy being executed and the types of instruments traded. These discussions should include:

- ❏ A description of the value proposition and where the fund derives its opportunity
- ❏ What the manager views as his edge. What skill set he has to create alpha
- ❏ What differentiates the fund from its peers
- ❏ The process whereby investment decisions are made
- ❏ The trading discipline employed
- ❏ The consistency with which the strategy has been executed (are there any pending changes?)
- ❏ Methods and extent of hedging employed
- ❏ The types of instruments traded and how they're used
- ❏ Complexity (that is, "the number of moving parts" of the strategy). The more complex the strategy, the harder it is for investors to understand it and the more likely it is that—other things being equal—the manager will make mistakes.

Risk management. What are the risks undertaken by the manager, and what are his guiding principles for risk control? What risks are specific to this strategy? Superior managers have a clear understanding of the market factors that affect performance and have guiding principles for risk control. Risk factors might include interest-rate movements, equity-market direction, credit cycles, volatility, and economic conditions.

The fund should have strict policies to control risk. Limits should exist for leverage, liquidity, concentration of positions, and the extent of hedging. Tactical trading controls such as stop/loss limits and profit-taking disciplines should be defined. Additionally, the firm should have risk-management systems commensurate with the complexity of the trading operation and the level of risk assumed. Various models and techniques may be employed.

Transparency. Transparency refers to the extent to which the manager is willing to divulge his portfolio positions. Many knowledgeable investors wish to know the composition of a portfolio. Although many managers are unwilling to disclose all their positions to their investors, most will compromise in one of several ways: by providing detailed positions for prior periods, thus giving a flavor of their investment style but avoiding having their strategy replicated; by revealing their largest positions; or by providing the percent of their holdings according to sector. Each investor will have a different need for transparency. It's not a significant issue for most individual investors, but it can be a deal killer for institutional investors who need at least some transparency to assess risk. A PPLI sponsor would be well advised to insist on some reasonable level of transparency, both to better understand the fund and to demonstrate a good level of due diligence.

Infrastructure. A key determinant of long-term success for managers is their ability to build a sound, well-controlled business environment to nourish their trading acumen. Staffing, systems, and internal controls should be adequate to support the business plan. Policies and procedures should be documented, especially in larger organizations. Internal systems should be supplemented by relationships with quality service providers. The fund should have good working relationships with prime brokers, custodians, and administrators. A satisfactory working relationship with these firms should be confirmed by checking professional references.

Any evaluation of a fund and fund manager includes a determination as to whether the individual managers have the skills, background, and experience to profitably conduct the trading style employed. A significant piece of this evaluation is the quality and length of tenure of his previous trading experience and the formal educational training he has received. Given that, it's essential to verify work history and educational background. References should be checked and should include professional colleagues, fund investors, and others who can speak to the manager's background and integrity.

Portfolio valuation. Can investors rely on the portfolio performance the manager provides? If the portfolio consists of publicly traded instruments, the manager may use these public valuations to value the overall portfolio. However, if the portfolio is composed in whole or in part of privately traded (nonpublic) instruments, it's important that the portfolio valuations be arrived at objectively. One or more independent third parties should value the portfolio before performance is provided to investors. Although such independent valuation increasingly is the norm, a few hedge fund managers still value their own portfolios in the case of esoteric strategies with thinly traded investments. The potential for material misstatements of reported returns should be carefully evaluated.

Regulatory checks. Although most funds are private investment companies, their principals and the management firms that operate the funds often are registered with a governmental or quasigovernmental agency and are subject to its regulations. Prudence dictates checking with a variety of sources to ascertain whether there is any history of regulatory or legal problems. These checks should include verifications with the Securities and Exchange Commission, the National Association of Securities Dealers, the National Futures Association, and the appropriate jurisdictional authorities. There are also various ways to check criminal and civil court records to ascertain whether the managers have been the subjects of any litigation. With the availability of information from Internet sources, it's easy to search for relevant news items that may disclose information material to the investment decision. Unlikely sources should not be discounted. Problems with one large hedge fund manager were initially reported in the tabloid press before any financial publication became interested in the story.

Audits. Avoid funds that are not audited. Though the information presented in audited financial statements reflects only the financial condition of the fund at a given point in time, the discipline involved in keeping financial records to a standard that renders them auditable is valuable. The mere fact that a competent third party will subject accounting decisions to review helps ensure that reporting and record keeping are maintained at a high standard, that critical issues such as position pricing will be dealt with, and that accounting problems will be considered. Obtain a copy of at least the most recent audit and review the information presented to determine that it's consistent with management representations of the fund's operations. Review the footnotes for evidence of pricing discretion, illiquid securities, related-party transactions that create conflicts of interest, off-balance-sheet exposure, and other items that affect the quality of fund assets and reported returns.

On-site visit. Due diligence is not complete without a face-to-face meeting with the portfolio manager, preferably at the fund's offices. This is the ideal opportunity to gain valuable insight about the manager and observe the working environment, the level of professionalism, the staff, and the technology. At this point, any remaining issues can be resolved. This is also a good time to meet the firm's investor-relations staff to develop a channel for future service requests and ongoing conversations about fund returns.

In these areas for investigation, different investors will have quite different tolerances. Generally speaking, however, the findings in any single area could be a reason not to invest. For instance, the leverage and resulting risk to a fund could be too high for the investor. Or there may be too high a concentration of fund assets in only a few positions. Or too high a percentage of the fund is in illiquid securities such that, when the investor redeems from the fund, he might not be able to obtain the value of his holdings because the manager can't sell them.

Fund of Funds

A significant percentage of all new hedge fund investments are placed through multimanager funds of funds (FOFs). In this type of vehicle, the manager identification, selection, and due diligence (for individual funds) are the responsibilities of the firms that manage and advise the fund. A FOF manager is paid to conduct prudent due diligence. The process should be extensive and address the elements we've presented.

FOFs are valuable investment vehicles both for individuals and institutional investors because of the diversification they provide. Diversified multistrategy funds of this type will often include allocations to 15 to 20 managers. Most studies indicate, and most practitioners would agree, that the value of diversification begins to decline dramatically beyond that point unless the fund has specialized correlation goals. A direct investment in each underlying fund would require the investor to meet the large minimum investment each fund requires. The FOF investor can achieve this diversification with a relatively small capital commitment.

Certain FOFs are strategy-specific. These funds seek to create manager diversity while maintaining a style purity to meet very specific investment goals. Investors use these vehicles as part of a larger investment plan to diversify aggregate portfolio risk. For example, an investor may have a traditional portfolio that's overweighted to stock- and bond-market–correlated instruments. A diversified portfolio that includes managers with like correlations may not improve the portfolio's characteristics. A strategy-specific arbitrage fund may be suitable in this case. Strategy-specific funds may also be used in conjunction with a broadly diversified fund in a core/satellite approach in which an investor builds a broadly diversified core portfolio supplemented by satellite holdings designed to produce excess return in anticipated market conditions. Manager diversity is important even with strategy-specific allocations. A hedge fund investment is an investment not only in a strategy but also in the skills of a specific manager. Individual manager performance can be affected by a variety of nonmarket-correlated factors.

To invest in a FOF, the investor pays an additional level of fees. These vary from fund to fund, but typically there will be an annual management fee of 1 percent of assets. Some also charge a performance fee of 10 percent of profits. A certain level of due diligence on the FOF manager is necessary and on the investment advisory firm if applicable. Here, track records are very important. A pro forma history of the combined underlying proposed funds has limited value. How that manager behaved in real time and how successful he was in producing returns when money was actually invested are much better indicators of future success. This makes an investment in a new FOF with simulated returns problematic. In these cases, it's useful to examine the individual funds and their return and risk profiles.

Any FOF manager should be able to describe his investment philosophy and the discipline he employs to set strategy allocations for the portfolio. How are these allocations driven by the risk-and-return benchmarks of the fund? He may employ various portfolio-optimization tools. The manager also should have a clearly stated benchmark, and the portfolio should be constructed to meet or exceed the performance of the benchmark.

The manager should also be able to describe his fund identification and selection process. How does he deal with the fundamental principles we've listed here? A manager's approach may be to select underlying funds that each individually meet the aggregate fund mandate. Others may select a group of managers whose performance in concert meets the investment guidelines. Both methods can produce a sound portfolio, but a greater level of skill and monitoring are required to be successful with the latter.

INVESTING IN HEDGE FUNDS is not a passive exercise. Of the thousands of alternatives in the investment world, a relatively small number of managers are generally suitable and an even smaller subset is suitable for any particular mandate. Care and diligence are required to obtain a successful result. Know the risks and rewards available from the various broad trading styles. A broad universe of potential fund candidates must be developed. Adequate consideration should be given to performance- and nonperformance-related factors that make each fund unique. Finally, the information acquired from managers in the fund selection process must be verified with extensive due diligence.

Appendix

Common Mistakes of Hedge Fund Investors

The following are the ten most common mistakes investors make when investing in hedge funds:

1 Not performing adequate due diligence
2 Not performing adequate ongoing monitoring and due diligence
3 Relying solely on historical performance
4 Chasing last year's high returns
5 Not building a diversified portfolio
6 Investing in a fund whose strategy the investor does not fully understand
7 Using an insufficient sample from which to choose hedge funds
8 Having poorly diversified strategies
9 Using too few funds
10 Not recognizing a fund's inherent weak risk control

Not performing adequate due diligence. Because hedge funds are less regulated than public investments such as mutual funds, the risk of manager fraud is higher with hedge funds than with regulated investment entities. Many investors fail to sufficiently investigate funds in which they are considering an investment. The manager's background, experience, and track record are key factors that need to be verified. If possible, one also should speak to current investors about their experience with the fund, verify education and employment history of the key managers, and thoroughly review all fund documents. Most managers are willing to speak with investors about the investment strategy and fund operations. Visit the fund's headquarters and meet the manager before allocating substantial capital.

The amount of due diligence to be performed is usually too great for most individuals or companies who do not specialize in hedge funds. Some companies typically spend one to three weeks on initial due diligence before approving a fund, in addition to the extensive time required for subsequent monitoring and ongoing due diligence on the same managers.

Not performing adequate ongoing monitoring and due diligence. Extensive due diligence before investing is only the first step. Once an investment has been made, the hedge fund must be monitored in light of changing market conditions or changes to the investor's personal financial situation. "Style drift," whereby the manager does not adhere to his mandate, usually is an important danger signal.[6] For example, a market-neutral manager with equal dollars in long and short positions decides to take a chance that the market will rise and becomes 75 percent net long. Beware. The majority of *hedge fund legal documents* allow the manager far greater latitude than his *marketing materials* may suggest. Therefore, review the fund's performance and strategy to ensure that there is little or no style drift. If a manager does stray from his stated strategy, determine how that could affect the investor's overall portfolio and whether the fund still meets the investor's needs.

Relying solely on historical performance. Although the quantitative aspects of a fund are very important, the qualitative aspects of potential funds and the strategy for different market conditions are also important. Many key factors determine whether a fund is a suitable investment for an individual investor: the investment strategy, the fund's liquidity, and its use of leverage. Many funds may have a phenomenal track record but may have assumed greater levels of risk than a particular investor desires. The returns of two funds following the same strategy should also be examined and compared. One fund may have outperformed the other by 25 percent, but it may have done so using twice the leverage. This would tend to indicate that the skill of the lower-returning manager actually is superior to that of the one using twice the leverage and may be a better indicator of which fund will provide positive returns in the future with less risk.

Chasing last year's high returns. Another mistake hedge fund investors often make is constantly reallocating to the latest and greatest manager. Too often, yesterday's upside outlier is tomorrow's downside outlier. A more prudent course of action is to look for funds with consistent acceptable performance relative to their stated strategy. Look for managers with concentration limits and risk controls in place that will improve their likelihood for absolute returns with low volatility in future market environments.

Not building a diversified portfolio. As with traditional investing, it is very important to construct a well-diversified hedge fund portfolio. Because of high investment minimums, many investors cannot afford to allocate capital to more than one hedge fund manager or may choose to make just one investment to test the waters. Investing in only one hedge fund exposes the investor to the risk that the individual manager will run into difficulty as well as the risk that the chosen fund's strategy will not perform well. If an investor is planning only one hedge fund investment, it's much safer to invest in a fund of funds that will provide diversification across several strategies and managers. The entry fee typically is no greater than that for a single hedge fund.

Investing in a fund without understanding its strategy. Understanding the manager's strategy before investing in a hedge fund is important on two levels. First, if a manager cannot adequately convey his investment strategy to investors, it may signal that he's either not capable of successfully implementing the proposed strategy or, in extreme cases, he's trying to hide aspects of his strategy. Second, if the investor does not understand the fund's strategy, he will be unable to conceptualize its expected return and its risks in varying market conditions. As a result, he'll be unable to diversify with investments that will have offsetting returns in a particular market environment.

Using an insufficient sample from which to choose hedge funds. The statistics that hedge fund index producers provide monthly are based on the average hedge fund performance reported for the month. There is a wide range of performance around this mean; to find the better-performing hedge funds, a large selection of hedge funds is needed. Because there is no central repository for hedge fund performance information, it's difficult to build and maintain a comprehensive hedge fund database. In the not-so-distant past (and for some, still today), hedge funds' main marketing tool was word-of-mouth references at cocktail parties. This can be a dangerous way to invest in a hedge fund. It's highly useful to compare characteristics of an individual hedge fund to those of other hedge funds using the same strategy. Without a large sample from which to select and compare managers, that's impossible to do.

Having poorly diversified strategies. Many investors attempt to diversify by using numerous managers but do not incorporate enough hedge fund strategies. Managers with the same strategy will be affected similarly by market conditions. Ideal is a portfolio of hedge funds constructed so that it can provide returns in all market conditions and be adequately insulated from market shocks. Most investors do not have the expertise to accurately predict the performance of each strategy under varying market conditions and therefore to properly construct a diversified portfolio.

Using too few funds. One of the biggest mistakes investors make is not including enough hedge funds in their portfolios. Many investors who can afford only one or two hedge fund investments are attracted by the stellar track record of an individual hedge fund when the most prudent investment would be a FOF. Because of the lack of regulation and use of leverage, their short selling, and the derivatives they hold, many individual hedge funds have an inherent level of risk that mutual funds do not. Unless an investor has enough available capital to construct a properly diversified hedge fund portfolio, a FOF is strongly recommended.

Not recognizing a fund's weak risk control. An investor should consider many factors in addition to the performance history and background of hedge fund managers. Often overlooked are the fund's risk controls, including concentration limits, operational controls, leverage limitations, liquidity of investments, and extent of hedging. These risk controls are usually tested only in market crises, and many less experienced managers have not been through enough market cycles to fully appreciate their necessity.

Although hedge fund investments can significantly improve the overall performance of an investment portfolio, there are potential pitfalls for non-experts. Using the services of a hedge fund consultant and investing in a diversified portfolio of funds can help each investor achieve his investment goals. Consulting fees typically range up to 1 percent of assets, depending on the amounts invested.

Chapter Notes

1. Gregory Zuckerman, *Wall Street Journal*, "Money & Investing," October 7, 2002, C1, C5.

2. Investorwords.com.

3. "Hedge Funds Shine Throughout Bear Market," study by Van Hedge Fund Advisors International, Inc., September 4, 2002.

4. The company's hedge fund index information is based on information received (and not audited or independently verified) from the hedge funds in an affiliate's databases and may not be representative of all hedge funds. Hedge fund returns are net of fees and performance allocations. The timing of the deduction of such fees and performance allocations may affect the reported performance. Different statistics may be based on different numbers of funds. Averages are not dollar-weighted. Past results are not necessarily indicative of future performance. AEMF is based on data provided by Morningstar.

5. Gross long exposure is expressed as a percentage and refers to the total dollars invested in long positions divided by investor's equity. Gross short exposure refers to the total dollars invested in short positions divided by investor's equity. Net exposure is defined as gross long minus gross short exposure.

6. Style drift refers to a fund changing its strategy in a significant way. It usually refers to a situation in which the manager does not disclose the change to investors.

CHAPTER 10

In Search of Skilled Investment Managers

RONALD J. SURZ

T he trouble with high-return investments is they can trigger some high costs. Hedge funds generate large amounts of ordinary income that's taxed at the highest rates. Private equity may enjoy a relatively low 15 percent capital gains rate, but it produces historically large returns that result in substantial tax exposure. But put either of these alternative investments into a private placement life insurance (PPLI) portfolio, and the landscape changes dramatically. Indeed, hedge funds and private equity benefit even more than do traditional equity products from the tax efficiency of a PPLI policy.

A PPLI portfolio, gaining substantial tax-deferred growth on historically high-performing assets, can result in stunning cash values in the not-too-distant future. Simply growing a $5 million PPLI portfolio 10 percent per year (after fees), for example, yields the policy cash values shown in **FIGURE 10.1**.

Generally, once a PPLI policy is set in place, little attention is given to the ongoing task of monitoring and managing the portfolio. But the PPLI policy, with its vital role as both a wealth preserver and wealth creator for current and future generations, deserves as much attention as the rest of a wealthy family's portfolio. Fortunately, the skills and techniques used by the investment advisory team to monitor and report on the overall portfolio apply just as well to the assessment of the PPLI portfolio's performance. There is, however, one very important distinction.

A portfolio made up of alternative investments requires a shift in the way it's evaluated. Rather than studying its performance relative to a broad

FIGURE **10.1** *Cash-Value Growth*

YEAR	CASH VALUE
0	$ 5,000,000
1	$ 5,500,000
5	$ 7,320,500
10	$11,789,738
20	$30,579,545
40	$205,723,889

benchmark, such as the S&P 500, the emphasis is placed on understanding a manager's skill. You might wonder why management skill would be any more important in alternative investments than it is in traditional long equity. Certainly, an investor wants only skillful managers, but one key difference is in play for an alternative investment manager: performance that can justify high fees.

Superior long-equity managers have no choice but to "ride the markets," expecting to secure marginal return and gain a relative advantage over the returns of their peer group. Consequently, a long-equity manager who is 1 percent better than the peer group—even at –20 percent return to the peer group's –21 percent—can still rank as a skilled manager.

Skilled hedge fund managers are altogether different animals. Their trading skill becomes apparent in their ability to capture positive return when the market is going up or down. In effect, their performance is decoupled from the market's momentum. They have nowhere to hide.

Similarly, successful private-equity managers deliver return solely on their ability to find and build winning companies. Indeed, in the investment business, private equity is a pure alpha play. Here, little market benefit is derived from producing return because the technologies typically found in fledgling companies take years to make their way into the mainstream equity markets. Venture capital is purely an arbitrage of information in which a highly skilled manager interprets the information embodied in today's trends better than the market itself does. In this game, value accrues only to the skillful.

The price paid to gain access to the unique return characteristics of alternative investments is the managers' performance fees. At 20 percent for a hedge fund manager and 20 percent to 30 percent for a private-equity firm, the performance fee greatly rewards the top managers. And since the investor pays substantially more for high-end skill, the manager must consistently deliver high-end performance.

Traditional Analyses of the Nontraditional

This chapter examines three types of investment structures—hedge funds, funds of hedge funds (FOFs), and private equity—with an eye toward distinguishing form from substance when it comes to understanding the difference between structure and value-added. Form is the structure of the investment, such as long-short or merger arbitrage. Substance is the skill the manager brings to the table in exchange for the fees. In many cases, there's nothing extraordinary about the form; you can create it yourself without active management. So you need to know why you're paying a professional to do it.

Hedge funds use a variety of strategies. The broad group of strategies we'll focus on is called long-short investing. Here, the manager is actually running two portfolios: a portfolio of companies in which he has a "long" position because he expects them to increase in value, and another containing companies that he "shorts" because he expects them to decline in value or to underperform the longs.

FOFs are similar in concept to portfolios of stocks, except that the manager is choosing individual hedge funds rather than individual companies. Private equity is like a traditional long-only portfolio, except the holdings are generally not publicly held and are therefore illiquid and difficult to value. Let's begin with traditional long-only concepts and then apply them to these three nontraditional areas.

The growing popularity of hedge funds and FOFs has fostered a tendency to confuse form with substance. Because of the fees involved and the degree of latitude afforded to hedge fund managers, they need to be even more skilled than traditional managers. Indeed, the hedge fund vehicle is an excellent one for skillful managers because they can implement efficient choices based on their insights. In all the moving parts of a hedge fund (as depicted in **FIGURE 10.2**), skill is the fuel that keeps them going. As a result, some investors equate hedge funds with skill, even calling them "skill-based strategies." The trouble is, skill isn't necessarily part of the picture, and the substance may in reality be missing from some hedge funds.

Several key elements play a role in measuring management performance. Style and attribution analyses begin by looking independently at

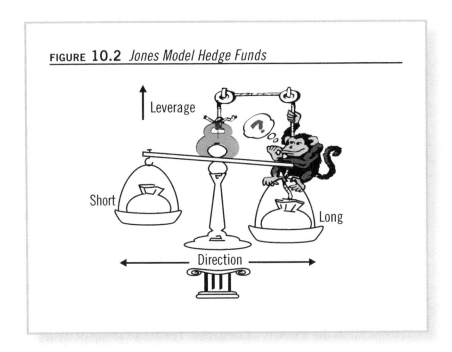

FIGURE **10.2** *Jones Model Hedge Funds*

the short and long portfolios, just as if they were each long-only portfolios. Performance evaluation and attribution analyses blend the two portfolios, adding in the effects of directional bets, which are amounts of deviation from the target long and short exposures for the fund. The final level of evaluation and attribution is leverage. Here we measure the effects of the targeted leverage as well as any deviations from this target. As in traditional analysis, the end game is persistence (that is, consistent success) in one or more of these sources of value added because only persistence confirms the skill of the people, process, and philosophy of the manager.

Similarly, the fund of hedge funds (FOF) managers are evaluated on the basis of their ability to allocate to strategies and managers. This approach is analogous to evaluating traditional managers according to their ability to allocate to economic sectors and individual companies. In both cases, style plays a crucial role because we don't want to make the common and costly mistake of confusing style with skill.

Style is also central to evaluating private-equity managers, but here the benchmarks are even less well defined than they are in the hedge fund world, primarily because each pool tends to be quite different. We'll offer guidance on evaluating private placements, but ultimately you can't manufacture these offerings passively, so you're left with a risk-reward assessment, rather than a clear reading on the manager's skill per se, primarily because there's not much to compare the manager to.

The Search for Skill

Two questions must be addressed before any evaluation begins: (1) Does skill have anything to do with investment management? and (2) If it does, can the managers who have it be identified?

Just a few short years ago, these questions could not be answered—at least not with confidence. The motto of professional investment performance evaluators has long been, "Evaluate skill, not luck," and for years everybody attempted to make this distinction by using modern portfolio theory (MPT). But it didn't work, primarily because the focus of MPT is solely on broad market effects—an arena alternative in which investment managers don't play. Identifying skill has long been problematic because it has routinely been confused with style. Witness the numerous firings of value managers that occurred as the growth stock bubble of the late 1990s inflated. Accordingly, the motto for 21st century evaluators is gradually becoming, "Evaluate skill, not style." The evolution beyond MPT has been slow.

About five years ago, however, researchers discovered the significance of investment style in identifying skill. (A list of some of these studies is provided in the appendix.) Skill, it turned out, could be properly identified only if we first lift the thick clouds of style that routinely distort our perspective, in addition to accounting for the broad market effects dictated by MPT. It was more complicated than MPT would suggest, but not that much more. For traditional equity portfolios, good growth equity managers tend to continue to be good growth equity managers; ditto for value. But if you're looking only at broad market effects, you'll never see this parallel.

Let's look at skill the way professional evaluators do. They have an advantage over the academic researchers who have discovered style-adjusted persistence in performance, because professional evaluators understand the other three Ps beyond performance: people, process, and philosophy. Accordingly, they can use style-adjusted alpha (that is, manager skill) as a first cut in their search for skill. This determination of positive risk and style-adjusted value added is called *performance evaluation.* Professional evaluators can then determine the reasons for the alpha and verify that these reasons substantiate the other three Ps.

Examining the reasons for performance is called *attribution analysis.* The reasons revealed by attribution analysis are stock selection and sector allocation or, in the case of FOFs, strategy allocation and manager selection. To make sound decisions, evaluators look for persistence over time in these sources of added value. Furthermore, they confirm that the value added is coming from a source consistent with the management process. If the management process is predominantly top-down, one would expect

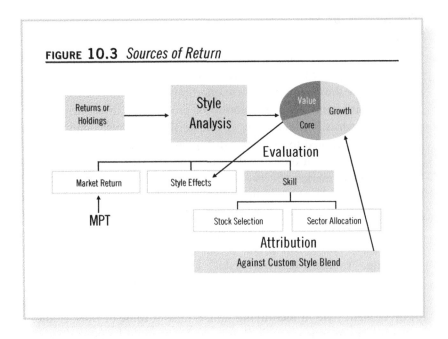

FIGURE **10.3** *Sources of Return*

alpha to derive primarily from sector or strategy allocation. Similarly, a bottom-up manager should excel in stock or manager selection. This total performance evaluation and attribution picture is shown in **FIGURE 10.3**.

Figure 10.3 applies to traditional long-only portfolios. The extension to private-equity portfolios is a straightforward concept, but it's challenging in practice because it requires the estimation of a natural style return to an illiquid concentrated portfolio. The extensions to hedge funds and FOFs are easier. To extend figure 10.3 to hedge funds, apply the indicated decompositions individually to the long portfolio and the short portfolio. To extend the figure to FOFs, substitute "strategy blend" for "style."

Although alpha, or skill, can be estimated using either holdings or returns, holdings are required to complete the picture with the components of skill, or attribution analysis. Style must be taken into account in both performance evaluation and performance attribution.

As a practical matter, the search for skill ought to begin at the macro level with managers whose performance is good. Then due diligence can proceed with an understanding of the people, process, and philosophy that produced the good performance (see chapters 9 and 13). Last, but not least, performance attribution confirms that the sources of this good performance are consistent with the people, process, and philosophy. Throughout this process, the resultant decisions are all about the future, even though we use the past as a guide.

Performance Evaluation

Is a manager's performance good or bad? The answer depends on yet another question: Relative to what? The traditional investment industry has two answers to the second question: passive alternatives and peer groups. Most evaluators use both of these benchmarks. Passive alternatives are indices or combinations of indices. Peer groups are collections of other managers that could have been hired instead of the active manager selected. Both of these benchmarks have problems, but there are appropriate solutions.

Peer Groups

How do you avoid the problems that traditional peer groups present in both traditional and nontraditional performance evaluation? The investment industry has been using peer groups for so long that no one thinks to question them, except for the occasional discussion about survivor bias, which seems to be the only bias that people know and understand. Survivor bias raises the bar by including only those portfolios that have remained in business for the entire evaluation period, which is generally five years or more.[1] Survivor bias is said to be even more pronounced in nontraditional investments than in traditional. But this may not be the case, because nontraditional managers who are closed to new business are also absent from most databases, thereby offsetting the failed managers that create survivor bias.

In fact, peer groups suffer from a collection of biases, only one of which is survivor bias, and each peer group has its own unique set of idiosyncratic distortions. As a result, the exact same performance number will rank differently against different peer groups, even when all of the peer groups are for the same management mandate, such as large-cap growth. In the nontraditional world, these peers are often aggregated to create an index.

Even if a bias-free peer group existed, it would not qualify as a valid investment-performance benchmark as defined by the criteria established by Richards & Tierney, a Chicago-based investment consulting firm specializing in custom benchmarks, and supported by the CFA Institute. Those criteria for good benchmarks include:

- ❏ **Unambiguous:** Names and weights of securities are clearly stated.
- ❏ **Investable:** Investors have the option to forego active management in lieu of a passive alternative.
- ❏ **Measurable:** The benchmark's return can be calculated on a reasonably regular basis.

- ❑ *Appropriate:* The benchmark accurately represents the manager's approach.
- ❑ *Reflective of current investment opinions:* The manager has current knowledge of the securities constituting the benchmark.
- ❑ *Specified in advance:* The composition of the benchmark is agreed to and constructed before the start of all evaluation periods.

Traditional and alternative investment peer groups meet none of these criteria, except possibly that of the measurability of a benchmark's return. Performance evaluation is all about making a judgment as to whether performance is good or bad. This judgment ought to be made relative to a passive alternative. *It doesn't matter how other managers in a particular peer group have fared,* because they too should each be evaluated against their respective passive alternatives. This measure leads to a great temptation for managers performing poorly in relation to the peer group: if you don't like your ranking in one peer group, choose another. Since the nontraditional investments we're discussing here are generally unregulated, the potential investor needs to be particularly diligent in assessing the claims of these managers and the opportunities for creative benchmarking.

What matters is the degree of success or failure relative to the benchmark. This difference can only be captured through a relatively new technique that creates all of the portfolios that could have been held by the manager, selecting from stocks in a benchmark that meet the criteria. The approach combines the better characteristics of peer group measures with those of passive alternatives, while eliminating the problems of each. A manager's ranking in this scientific universe indicates the degree of his success or failure.

The technique can be extended to the nontraditional. For hedge funds, keep figure 10.2 in mind. All of the possible long portfolios are created, as are all of the possible short portfolios and all combinations of these two portfolio sets, where the allocations to each side are guided by the hedge fund's direction, that is, the amount long and short. The amount of leverage is overlaid on this opportunity set to produce an unbiased scientific backdrop for evaluation. Similarly, FOF universes are created by drawing portfolios of hedge funds at random, tailored to the strategy mix employed by the FOF. The approach does not extend to private equity, however.

Passive Alternatives (Indices)

Scientific universes bridge the gap between peer groups and passive alternatives. Passive alternatives have two problems: definitions and waiting time. The industry's efforts at manager performance evaluation have led it to conclude that most managers use a blend of styles. This conclusion was reached with the help of a relatively new technology called returns-based style analysis (RBSA). RBSA solves for the blend of style indices that has been most reflective of the manager's choices and identifies this blend as the manager's effective style mix. This approach to evaluation is similar to what's applied to a normal portfolio. RBSA can also be applied separately to both the long and the short portfolios in a hedge fund, and it has been applied to FOFs, substituting strategies for styles.

Another approach, holdings-based style analysis (HBSA), examines the stocks actually held in the investment portfolio and maps these into styles at points in time. Once a sufficient history of these holdings-based snapshots is developed, an estimate of the manager's average style profile can be developed and used as the custom benchmark. HBSA, like normal portfolios, starts with individual securities and both normal portfolios and holdings-based style analysis examine the history of holdings. They part ways when it comes to blending.

Normal portfolios blend stocks to create a portfolio profile that's consistent with investment philosophy, whereas HBSA makes an inference from the pattern of point-in-time style profiles and translates the investment philosophy into style. For a PPLI portfolio, HBSA is not practical, because the typical hedge fund or private-equity manager is reluctant to reveal holdings. This lack of transparency is giving way to full transparency among alternative managers, which is demanded by investors, but until there is widespread agreement, HBSA will be severely handicapped.

Normal portfolios are custom benchmarks designed to capture the essence of an individual manager's process and philosophy. Sometimes called information-neutral portfolios, these designer benchmarks were intended to reflect the portfolio to which the manager would retreat if one day he had no insights or ideas to implement. Almost everyone agreed at first that "normals" were a great idea, but it turned out that only a few consulting firms could construct them properly. The cost and effort involved prevented normal portfolios from catching on. In contrast to normal portfolios, which are composites of individual securities and extremely difficult to construct, effective mix portfolios are blends of styles that are easy to create. The old idea of designer benchmarks is back, and this time it's actually doable. It's called returns-based style analysis.

The collection of style indices used in RBSA is called a "style palette." It must be created with care so that the analysis will be reliable. Like a color master for creating custom-blended paint, RBSA uses return history and optimization techniques to determine the blend of styles that most closely mimics the behavior of the investment portfolio.

As with any statistical process, data problems in RBSA may go unde-tected, leading to faulty inferences. One such problem is multicollinear-ity, which occurs when the style indices used in the regression overlap in membership. Multicollinearity invalidates the regression and usually pro-duces spurious results. Although most users of RBSA focus on optimal fit, good style palettes should also possess the characteristics listed below. The first two have been put forth as requirements by the developer and creator of RBSA; the last two are my own.

Characteristics of Good Style Palettes

- *Mutually exclusive:* No stock is categorized into more than one style, thereby minimizing multicollinearity.
- *Exhaustive:* All stocks are classified. Some index vendors throw out data, for example, stocks with negative earnings or small com-panies. Finding a good fit is impossible if any of the portfolio's stocks have been eliminated.
- *Inclusion of core:* This continues to be a novel idea. It's a way to deal with stocks in that gray area between value and growth. Most index providers deal with this problem by throwing out these stocks, violating the exhaustive rule, or by classifying them into multiple styles and violating the mutually exclusive rule. Inter-estingly, core doesn't always perform between value and growth. Sometimes it's better than both, and sometimes it's worse.
- *Quarterly rebalancing:* Things change rapidly. Calling a cheap high-tech stock "growth" because it had a high price/earnings ratio a year ago doesn't make sense. Of course, more frequent rebalanc-ing makes an index harder to track because its composition is changing.

A properly constructed style palette can be applied to hedge funds in one of two ways: The RBSA can be instructed to allow short sales, in which case negative style allocations may enter into the solution. Or the performance histories of the long and short portfolios can be run separate-ly, thereby identifying the individual style on each side. To run RBSA on a FOF, the style palette can be set with hedge fund strategy benchmarks.

Regardless of the style palette, the resultant style blend meets the criteria for a good benchmark and represents a portfolio that the investor could have purchased for a low fee instead of hiring an active investment manager, so the problem of defining the benchmark has a contemporary solution.

The next problem is somewhat more difficult to solve. It takes many decades to develop statistical confidence in the manager's ability to beat his benchmark. For example, if your manager's return is 12 percent per year, and the custom style mix has returned 10 percent, you'll have low confidence that this 2 percent annual spread is a matter of skill if it occurred over a five-year period. You might still have insufficient confidence even with a 55-year period. That's because it takes a long time to develop confidence in the parameters that define the underlying statistical process.

Operating in the cross section (that is, across all possible funds) solves the problem of time span. Forming all of the portfolios that could have been formed from the passive style blend makes it possible to determine statistical significance in a very short time. It's classic statistics. For example, say you want to test the hypothesis that the manager has succeeded. You let the computer form portfolios at random. If a manager's performance is in the top 10 percent of this random distribution, you would accept the hypothesis with 90 percent confidence, and you would do so even if the measurement period were as short as a few months or weeks. This technique is the Monte Carlo simulation that has become so popular in the advisory community.

Let's put it another way. If a manager delivers a 50 percent return in a month and his custom index is flat, there is a good chance that this is a significantly good return and you shouldn't have to wait decades to come to this conclusion. Cross-sectional performance evaluation produces the statistical backdrop necessary to make this determination, while traditional cross-temporal regression approaches (alpha) do not.

The alpha problem is particularly acute in nontraditional investing because the benchmark is generally ill defined, causing some to proclaim that the industry is buying beta, not alpha. The idea is this: Since hedge funds and FOFs are hedged, their betas (risk exposures) are lower. In periods of declining markets, this reduced risk exposure should protect the portfolio, but it's not necessarily a reflection of skill or alpha. Even if the benchmark is resolved, the waiting-time problem in alternatives is still there; you'll wait decades for the statistics to settle down. Monte Carlo simulation solves this waiting-time problem for both traditional and nontraditional investors.

So performance is best evaluated against a scientific universe formed from all of the portfolios that the manager could have held, selecting stocks from his custom style blend or, in the case of FOFs, his custom strategy blend.

Performance Attribution

Like performance evaluation, performance attribution has evolved. The performance-measurement industry is fairly young, having started in the 1970s. Much of the attribution analysis used until recently was developed in the 1980s, when we were only beginning to understand that there was

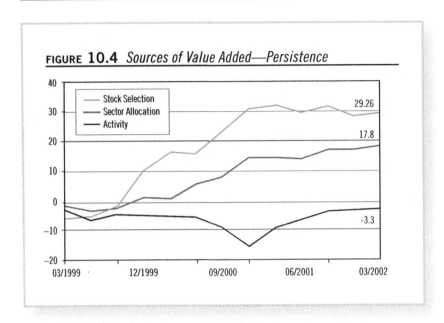

FIGURE **10.4** *Sources of Value Added—Persistence*

more to life than MPT. We knew back then that characteristics like capitalization, price/earnings ratio, and dividend yield mattered, but we hadn't figured out how to best integrate these factors into attribution analysis. Consequently, we wrote slicers and dicers that segmented the portfolio and the benchmark by whatever characteristics we chose. Want to see how the segment of your portfolio with high P/Es fared against the comparable segment of stocks in the S&P 500? No problem. Just draw the P/E line wherever you want, and voilà, there you have it.

The problems with these old approaches are standardization and benchmark inflexibility. For example, if you draw the P/E line at 15 and I draw it at 20, we'll each get different insights. Also, as already described, we'd like to use a custom style blend as the benchmark, but we can't do so with the 1980s technology because it doesn't allow us to customize the benchmark as a blend of indices. So, with the old technology we can peel the apple like an orange or slice the orange like an apple, but all we've got to show for it is a rotten fruit salad.

By contrast, contemporary technologies encourage the use of custom style-blended benchmarks and standard style definitions so there is comparability across managers. In this way, a manager's stock-selection and sector-allocation skills are not confused with his style. **FIGURE 10.4** summarizes this evolution.

In the search for skill, we look for persistence in the reason(s) for good performance and for confirmation of the people, process, and philosophy.

Figure 10.4 shows the performance of a manager who has consistently added value through stock selection, although the amount of value added has slowed somewhat in the recent past. This particular manager is a bottom-up stock picker, and the attribution analysis confirms his skill in this endeavor. Sector allocation has also added some value, which is consistent with bottom-up stock picking. Only trading activity has had a modest negative effect on performance. Trading activity measures the intra-period effects on performance of transactions executed during the period. If this manager were looking for ways to improve performance, the trading desk would be a place to start.

In attributing performance for hedge funds, figure 10.4 is used separately for the long and short portfolios. Separate analyses are also conducted to track the effects of directional bets and leverage. As noted, this is not always practical in light of the lack of transparency in these investments, but nonetheless the tools are available when the data are available.

These relatively new tools give the professional evaluator the insights needed to determine whether good performance is likely to continue into the future. The search for investment manager talent puts a lot of emphasis on recent past performance. Unfortunately, in evaluating past performance, style is routinely confused with skill. In nontraditional investing, beta and strategy allocations can be confused for skill. After general market effects, the most important determinant of performance is style, followed by a distant third residual that we use to find manager skill. Detecting skill is tough for this reason. Although it's easy to confuse style with skill, it's difficult to make good decisions once this mistake has been made.

Appendix

Studies Finding Evidence of Persistent Style-Adjusted Excess Return

Daniel T. Coggin and Charles A. Trzcinka, "A Panel Study of U.S. Equity Pension Fund Manager Style Performance," *Journal of Investing* 9 (Summer 2000): 6–12.

Martin J. Gruber, "Another Puzzle: The Growth in Actively Managed Mutual Funds," *Journal of Finance* 51, no. 3 (1996): 783–810.

Roger Ibbotson and Amita Patel, "Do Winners Repeat With Style," Ibbotson Associates research paper, November 2001.

Ronald N. Kahn and Andrew Rudd, "The Persistence of Equity Style Performance: Evidence from Mutual Fund Data," *The Handbook of Equity Style Management*, 2d ed. (New Hope, PA: Frank J. Fabozzi Associates, 1997).

Scott D. Stewart, "Is Consistency of Performance a Good Measure of Manager Skill?" *Journal of Portfolio Management* 24, no. 3 (1998): 22–32.

Chapter Notes

1. The analogy that's frequently used to describe survivorship bias is the marathon with 1,000 runners and 100 finishers. Is the 100th finisher dead last, or in the top decile? He's in the top decile.

PART THREE

Under the Hood—
The Essentials on PPLI

The wealth manager is to investment choices for the affluent what the conductor is to a symphony orchestra. The conductor knows the qualities of each instrument and how best to integrate them to make beautiful music, but the conductor does not play each one himself.

A wealth manager contemplating private placement life insurance (PPLI) to meet a client's needs should be conversant with the basic elements of this investment vehicle—its structure, costs, jurisdiction, investment choices, regulation, and due diligence—but the complexities involved make it necessary to leave the details to the experts, primarily the insurance adviser. To avail a client of PPLI's advantages, the wealth manager must know the key questions to ask and must have a solid enough understanding of PPLI to interpret whether the answers indicate that PPLI may, in fact, be the right choice.

Equally important in terms of using resources efficiently and adhering to "best practices" is knowing at which point to engage outside expertise. This section provides that solid grounding—and more—for wealth managers as it addresses both the basics and the subtleties involved in building a PPLI policy.

CHAPTER 11

Policy Structure
The Good, the Bad, the Ugly

PAUL F. BERLIN

M ost advisers understand the value of private placement life insurance (PPLI) in the high-net-worth marketplace. The income tax advantages of cash accumulation, income tax–free death benefits, and professionally managed cash value accounts are the big draws. But how many advisers fully understand the product's chassis? How many will audit the insurance product every year to verify charges? Will they monitor net amount at risk to maximize returns? Or would a new structure that requires much less servicing be a better alternative? The answers to these questions will help advisers in determining whether a product with a traditional chassis best suits the investor's needs.

PPLI and Retail Products

PPLI shares several characteristics with retail variable life insurance:
- Payment of cash premium is required to establish the policy.
- IRC § 7702 describes the maximum cash value buildup of the investment options in relation to the death benefit.
- The mortality elements are the same.
- The underwriting process is the same.
- Both products require extensive medical underwriting.
- Underwriting classifications are the same—preferred, standard, or rated.
- The maximum death benefit is a function of medical and financial underwriting.

PPLI differs from retail variable life insurance in important ways:

Loads and surrender charges
❑ Most state regulators allow load structure to be negotiated; therefore, PPLI loads are much smaller than a retail product's and most PPLI contracts have no surrender charges.

Flexibility in investment options
❑ Hedge fund strategies are aimed at reducing volatility and private equity creates wealth (see chapter 8). It's also possible to add and customize options without a lengthy filing and SEC registration process.

Different compliance issues
❑ Virtually no sales material is permitted for PPLI; nor is advertising allowed.
❑ PPLI purchasers must be accredited, as defined by Regulation D of the Securities Act of 1933. Under these provisions, suitability requires that the purchaser have a minimum net worth of $1 million, or $200,000 of annual income in the past two years, with anticipation of reaching the same level in the future. Investment products accepting such investors are known as 3c(1) funds, and fewer than 100 accredited individuals are permitted to invest.
❑ An investment fund in a PPLI portfolio may contain an exemption using the 3c(7) stipulation of the 1933 Act, which permits up to 500 investors. This exemption, also under the 1940 Act, defines a "qualified purchaser" as a natural person with $5 million of investable assets or an entity with $25 million of net worth.
❑ An investor can invest only after receiving and reading a private placement memorandum (PPM). The PPM functions in the unregulated Reg. D market as a prospectus for registered products and states whether the investment is intended for 3(c)-1 or 3(c)-7 investors.

The PPLI Investment

The separate account. The investment options underlying PPLI are held in a separate account through the insurance company. These accounts have the following characteristics:
❑ Separate accounts need not be registered as investment companies as defined under Section 2(a) 51 of the Investment Company Act of 1940.

❑ PPLI cash values in the separate accounts are segregated from the insurance company's general account (see chapter 1), thereby providing protection from the insurance company's creditors.

❑ PPLI assets are owned by the insurance company and are used to satisfy obligations of the insurance company to the policy owner.

PPLI regulations. Insurance is a highly regulated investment product with tax legislation and IRS regulations clearly defining the resulting tax benefits. Key regulations give life to PPLI.

IRC § 817(h) diversification test. PPLI separate account assets must be diversified in accordance with § 817(h) or the tax-deferred cash buildup will be forfeited. The diversification test requires that no single investment constitute more than 55 percent of the value of each division of the separate account; no two investments more than 70 percent; no three investments more than 80 percent; and no four investments more than 90 percent. Beyond 90 percent of each division of the separate account, an unlimited number of investments greater than four is permissible.

Limits to policy owner's control over investments in the separate account. When an individual buys a life insurance policy, the individual is the client of the life insurance company and the life insurance company is the client of the investment manager. The boundaries are clear and must not be violated.

The policy owner cannot direct the separate account investment manager's investment decisions, but the policy owner can make allocations across the available separate accounts.

PPLI Death Benefit

Whether the goal is tax-efficient cash accumulation or wealth transfer, as a matter of routine, PPLI products are maximally funded. That means the premium paid into the contract will be right at the IRS maximum death benefit permitted. This produces the greatest degree of tax-efficient cash accumulation within the policy and the greatest cash-on-cash rate of return.

Death benefit sale. The controlling sections of IRS regulation 7702 require that to enjoy the tax-deferred inside buildup of cash value, the policy must also provide a certain amount of death benefit in relation to the policy's cash value. The extent to which premiums can be paid into the policy must take into account one of two tests which act like valves restricting the flow of permitted premium payments into the policy based on the continually changing ratio of the policy's actual death benefits to its accumulating cash value. The life insurance company is free to use either of these tests in the administration of the product for tax compliance.

However, the adviser needs to be aware that additional changes to the death benefit after initial funding can alter the taxation of the policy. This is important to understand, as we will see later.

Cash value tests. The guideline premium test (GPT) closes or reduces the flow of premiums that can be paid into the policy once the payment of a premium causes the policy cash value to become too large (as defined by IRS) in relation to the death benefit. Assuming the policy is going to be maximally funded, this test requires the policy to provide an initial death benefit for the given premium. This guideline premium test produces high death benefits in the early years. The adviser needs to determine if this result is consistent with the client's goals. Once the cash value growth reaches what's called the "corridor," the death benefit increases. (The corridor is the ratio of the cash value to the death benefit. For a policy to be in compliance, the cash value and death benefit must be adjusted to stay within the corridor's boundaries. The corridor changes as the policy owner ages.) The cost of insurance (COI) charge affects the guideline premium pricing (see "Misleading Illustrations," page 182). The policy performs best once the corridor is reached, because the corridor represents the lowest spread between the cash value and death benefit.

The cash value accumulation test (CVAT) allows an unrestricted flow of premiums to be paid into the policy, provided the policy death benefit routinely increases to whatever amount of insurance is needed to meet the minimum death-benefit-to-cash-value ratio required under IRS Code 7702 rules. Assuming the policy is going to be maximally funded, this test will generate a smaller initial death benefit than using a GPT, but it will generate larger death benefits in the long run. Since life insurance death benefits are income tax–free, this will benefit the client's estate and preserve the maximum amount of wealth.

Conversely, the CVAT design provides much higher early cash values because the death benefit is initially lower than the GPT. Then again, some people may desire the higher initial death benefit that the use of this test offers. That's why it's important for the adviser to analyze both and understand the advantages and potential disadvantages of each to determine which is more suitable for the client.

Some insurance companies offer a choice of which test to use in the design of the policy. But once the choice is made, it becomes irrevocable. How do you determine which test method is best for a given client's objectives? The following section presents the variables to consider, but note that the way in which these variables interact makes the testing differ from policy to policy.

Determining the Proper Course

It's up to the insurance adviser to understand both types of testing. Most PPLI products in the market are priced using the guideline premium test, and it's incumbent on the client's insurance adviser to monitor the spread between the premium and death benefit.

The initial death benefit will be larger using a guideline premium chassis than it would be using a CVAT chassis. Suitability considerations should dictate how to proceed. The GPT product does not allow for the reduction of death benefit during the first 15 years without the potential force-out of cash value. A force-out means that the spread between the cash value and death benefit has become too narrow, and section 7702 is violated. To avoid disqualification, the cash value must be reduced or forced out. This is important to understand if the early earnings in the policy go down.

Both product designs share a common set of fees that are important for the adviser to understand (see chapter 16). Here's how the fees are defined and how they operate:

- ❑ The annual mortality and expense (M&E) fee represents the profit to the insurance company and its fee for administering the mortality element of the policy.
- ❑ The monthly cost-of-insurance charge is based on net amount at risk. The COI is an outgrowth of the medical underwriting process described in chapter 15, and it depends on age, gender, and the underwriting rating.
- ❑ The pure death benefit charge for the net death proceeds varies based on age and net amount at risk.
- ❑ State premium taxes vary by state and range from 10 basis points to 4 percent.
- ❑ Deferred acquisition (DAC) tax is a federal premium tax and is either 1.25 percent or 1.3 percent of premium.
- ❑ Investment-management fees, charged by the investment manager for the designated investment services in the separate account, may be shared with the insurance company.
- ❑ Distribution charges may be included in the M&E charge and are used to compensate an insurance adviser in lieu of the exorbitant commissions paid on a retail product.

Illustrations

The best way to understand how these fees interact is to use an illustration, even though the results can be cloudy. Illustrations are common sales tools in the purchase of life insurance. In the PPLI marketplace, where the average premium is high, an illustration has become a means to compare different product structures. All illustrations are run at a constant rate of return. With volatile capital markets, we know that this is highly unlikely to occur.

To combat fixation on a faulty scenario, the adviser must request illustrations run at various rates of return, including zero years, negative years, and positive years. The adviser must review these illustrations at the insurance company's current charges, guaranteed charges, and somewhere in the middle. A current-charges illustration is the insurer's presentation of current experience and a projection of that experience for all years. The adviser must alert the client that the option to change the charges based on a different future experience is at the insurance company's sole discretion. An illustration is not a binding agreement and is not useful in determining how much the policy might be worth in the future. Such an analysis, though, is key to showing PPLI's long-term benefits.

An illustration can't be predictive because both M&E charges and COI are changeable if the insurer determines it's not realizing its experience or return expectations. Assumptions from insurance companies can change over the years. With a slight change in mortality or expenses associated with the PPLI contract, the desired goal of the client may not be achieved. It's the adviser's job to monitor the insurance company's changing mortality assumptions and explain to the client the potential effect the changes will have on the performance of the contract.

For the policy to remain in good standing, a PPLI insurance adviser must maintain vigilance over the policy, particularly during major market cycle shifts. **FIGURE 11.1** is a sample illustration from a leading insurance company and shows the range of mortality costs that the company can charge. This illustration simply represents the insurance company's current estimated mortality charge compared to its guaranteed mortality charge. Notice the huge difference in what's projected versus what's guaranteed. This difference can cause many servicing headaches later on.

The COI charges aren't the only figures the insurance company can change. It can also revise the M&E fee. **FIGURE 11.2** is an illustration used by a leading insurance company in the PPLI market. Again, the illustration is the insurance company's current projected charges based on steady 8 percent earnings. This is a typical projection. The adviser would show this to a client with the implication that the policy's costs would be in the 40-basis-point range.

Now let's see how one negative year affects costs in this illustration (see **FIGURE 11.3**). Here, the same illustration is used but with a change in investment results. The loads in this illustration have been taken out, based on the assumption that the adviser is receiving a fee pass-through from the

FIGURE 11.1   *PPLI Sample Illustration:*
Current versus Guaranteed

Assumptions: Male age 65, 10 percent return, $5 million single premium; costs are mortality (COI) charges, not M&E.

YEAR	DEATH BENEFIT CURRENT	DEATH BENEFIT GUARANTEED	MORTALITY CHARGE CURRENT	MORTALITY CHARGE GUARANTEED
1	9,770,000	9,770,000	9,215	114,643
2	9,770,000	9,770,000	12,657	127,595
3	9,770,000	9,770,000	16,296	128,977
4	9,770,000	9,770,000	17,641	128,120
5	9,770,000	9,770,000	16,971	124,623
6	9,770,000	9,770,000	14,764	117,981
7	9,783,288	9,770,000	11,908	107,120
8	10,483,973	9,770,000	8,836	90,457
9	11,232,152	9,770,000	8,810	65,567
10	12,031,221	10,357,960	8,231	39,673
11	12,884,568	11,065,322	7,227	31,021
12	14,060,689	12,042,360	8,412	37,215
13	15,342,651	13,101,353	10,557	44,422
14	16,739,465	14,248,610	13,363	54,744
15	18,261,340	15,490,719	16,493	62,460
16	19,911,615	16,834,411	27,041	73,987
17	21,707,966	18,286,521	32,265	87,795
18	23,662,836	19,853,801	38,390	104,528
19	25,789,647	21,542,943	45,573	124,807
20	28,102,675	23,360,895	54,156	148,961
25	43,038,241	34,648,602	127,383	339,165
30	63,574,315	49,892,793	40,602	109,350

FIGURE **11.2** *Standard Market Chassis Illustration*

CERTIFICATE YEAR	AGE	GROSS PREMIUM	PREMIUM LOAD	CONTRACT CHARGES	COST OF INSURANCE	COST ADDITIC BENEF
1	50	5000000	89883	4780	6565	0
2	51	0	0	4780	19327	0
3	52	0	0	4780	29102	0
4	53	0	0	4780	31258	0
5	54	0	0	4780	31492	0
6	55	0	0	4780	33537	0
7	56	0	0	4780	37934	0
8	57	0	0	4780	38533	0
9	58	0	0	4780	39449	0
10	59	0	0	4780	40270	0
TOTAL		5000000	89883	47803	307466	0
11	60	0	0	180	41567	0
12	61	0	0	180	43743	0
13	62	0	0	180	44405	0
14	63	0	0	180	43417	0
15	64	0	0	180	40828	0
16	65	0	0	180	43718	0
17	66	0	0	180	36450	0
18	67	0	0	180	35872	0
19	68	0	0	180	40135	0
20	69	0	0	180	44723	0
TOTAL		5000000	89883	49603	722325	0
21	70	0	0	180	49614	0
22	71	0	0	180	50659	0
23	72	0	0	180	50350	0
24	73	0	0	180	48248	0
25	74	0	0	180	43791	0
26	75	0	0	180	36218	0
27	76	0	0	180	42817	0
28	77	0	0	180	50668	0
29	78	0	0	180	59934	0
30	79	0	0	180	70820	0
TOTAL		5000000	89883	51403	1225446	0
31	80	0	0	180	83602	0
32	81	0	0	180	98519	0
33	82	0	0	180	115748	0
34	83	0	0	180	135679	0
35	84	0	0	180	159194	0
36	85	0	0	180	186871	0
37	86	0	0	180	219253	0
38	87	0	0	180	257022	0
39	88	0	0	180	300981	0
40	89	0	0	180	351518	0
TOTAL		5000000	89883	53203	3133832	0

8% all years; Current COI—not guaranteed; Curent M&E—not guaranteed

investment managers in the portfolio in lieu of any compensation from the policy owner.

In a perfect world, with a constant rate of return as we have just seen, the insurance company projects the policy to have annual charges in the

	TOTAL DEDUCTION			NET RATE OF RETURN 8.00%	
CHARGES FOR EXTRA RATINGS	MORTALITY AND EXPENSE CHARGES	SUM	PERCENTAGE OF CASH VALUE	CASH VALUE EOY	LIFE INSURANCE BENEFIT EOY
0	8942	110170	2.14%	5281833	19168000
0	9608	33715	0.62%	5669286	19168000
0	10304	44187	0.75%	6076817	19168000
0	11045	47083	0.75%	6513935	19168000
0	11842	48115	0.71%	6984951	19168000
0	12699	51016	0.70%	7490627	19168000
0	13617	56331	0.73%	8031219	19168000
0	14602	57915	0.70%	8613412	19168000
0	15663	59892	0.67%	9240124	19168000
0	16805	61855	0.65%	9914931	19168000
0	125127	570279			
0	15463	57210	0.56%	10648553	19168000
0	16608	60531	0.55%	11437404	19168000
0	17840	62425	0.53%	12287391	19168000
0	19170	62767	0.49%	13205023	19168000
0	20606	61614	0.45%	14197270	19168000
0	22154	66052	0.45%	15264260	19168000
0	23828	60459	0.38%	16422452	19542718
0	25641	61693	0.36%	17672114	20853094
0	27591	67905	0.37%	19015286	22247885
0	29687	74589	0.38%	20458960	23732393
0	343715	1205526			
0	31939	81734	0.38%	22010695	25312300
0	34364	85203	0.37%	23682969	26761755
0	36978	87508	0.36%	25486640	28290170
0	39799	88227	0.33%	27433874	29902923
0	42847	86818	0.30%	29538376	31606063
0	46143	82541	0.27%	31815719	33406505
0	49697	92694	0.28%	34264689	35977924
0	53519	104367	0.29%	36897436	38742308
0	57626	117741	0.31%	39726890	41713234
0	62040	133040	0.32%	42766782	44905121
0	798667	2165399			
0	66781	150563	0.34%	46031632	48333214
0	71872	170572	0.36%	49536849	52013691
0	77337	193265	0.38%	53298864	55963807
0	83201	219061	0.40%	57334992	60201741
0	89491	248865	0.42%	61662985	64746135
0	96333	283284	0.44%	66301386	69616456
0	103457	322890	0.47%	71296923	74833105
0	111192	368394	0.50%	76587941	80417338
0	119469	420630	0.53%	82277329	86391196
0	128320	480018	0.56%	88360024	92778025
0	1746023	5022940			

Source: ©2004 Executive Planning, Inc.

40-basis-point range. Of course, even 17 years into the future a constant rate of return is assumed—a highly unlikely scenario. This assumption leads to the policy reaching the corridor in the seventeenth year.

FIGURE **11.3** *Current Illustration*

Age 65	CV	$15,264,260
	DB	$19,168,000
	COI Charge*	$36,450
	Net Amt Risk	$3,903,740
	Illustrated Charge including M&E	45 basis points

* Projected, not guaranteed

FIGURE **11.4** *Current Cost of Insurance Column*

CERTIFICATE YEAR	AGE	GROSS PREMIUM	PREMIUM LOAD	CONTRACT CHARGES	COST OF INSURANCE	COST OF ADDITIONAL BENEFITS
11	60	0	0	180	41567	0
12	61	0	0	180	43743	0
13	62	0	0	180	44405	0
14	63	0	0	180	43407	0
15	64	0	0	180	40828	0
16	65	0	0	180	43718	0
17	66	0	0	180	36450	0
18	67	0	0	180	35872	0
19	68	0	0	180	40135	0
20	69	0	0	180	44723	0

Let's look at what would happen if the portfolio dropped 20 percent in the sixteenth year, the year before the corridor is reached. The illustration for this scenario, **FIGURE 11.4**, reveals that it may take an additional four or five years to hit the corridor.

Age 66	Market goes down 20 percent	
	CV	$12,211,408
	DB	$19,168,000
	COI Charge*	$81,271
	Net Amt Risk	$6,986,592
	Illustrated Charge	45 basis points
	Actual Charge	81 basis points

CHARGES FOR EXTRA RATINGS	MORTALITY & EXPENSES CHARGES	SUM	PERCENTAGE CASH VALUE	CASH VALUE EOY	LIFE INSURANCE BENEFIT EOY
0	15463	57210	0.56%	10648553	19168000
0	16608	60531	0.55%	11437404	19168000
0	17840	62425	0.53%	12287391	19168000
0	19170	62767	0.49%	13205023	19168000
0	20606	61614	0.45%	14197270	19168000
0	22154	66053	0.45%	15264260	19168000
0	23828	60459	0.38%	16422452	19542718
0	25641	61693	0.36%	17672114	30853094
0	27591	67905	0.37%	19015286	22247885
0	29687	74589	0.38%	20458960	23732393

Furthermore, a decline in the cash value portfolio means that the net amount at risk increases, leading to an increase in the COI, the charge that the insurance company leaves on the net amount at risk. Compounding the COI increase from a portfolio decline is the aging policy owner. The

COI will increase not only in the year the market decreases but also as the insured ages, causing COI increases in all the years that follow (due to the increase in net amount at risk).

Misleading Illustrations

The adviser must monitor the net amount at risk in the policy. The adviser servicing a policy that has suffered a portfolio decline less than the assumed constant return can lower the death benefit to minimize the COI. But if the market has some good years following the reduction in death benefit, the policy may force out cash because it wouldn't qualify as life insurance anymore. The forced-out cash is taxed at ordinary rates, which is clearly undesirable.

If conditions diverge from any of the initial assumptions illustrated, new illustrations need to be run annually. If the market decreases in the first 15 years, the desired 38-basis-point charge that we reviewed before will probably never be met, leading to a more expensive product than the client thought he was purchasing at the outset. If the original 38-basis-point assumption turns into a 110-basis-point charge, PPLI still makes sense simply because of the compounding tax savings. Regardless, sudden turns in the road are what investors dislike about insurance purchases. All possibilities must be presented upfront. At the time of purchase, the adviser needs to show the client various rates of return in the proposal. He must properly explain the net amount at risk. These are serious questions that neither the client nor the adviser wants to revisit once the policy is in force.

Net Amount at Risk

Now that we have reviewed the COI, or the mortality charge, we see the importance of monitoring the net amount at risk. This amount is the difference between the cash value and death benefit. For example with a $1 million death benefit, the cash value is $500,000 and the net amount at risk is $500,000. Should the market go down 10 percent the next year, the amounts would change: For a $1 million death benefit, the cash value would be $450,000 and the net amount at risk would be $550,000.

When the net amount at risk increases, so does the COI. Consequently, the adviser needs to monitor the net amount at risk annually. Given such a drop in the market, the adviser might lower the death benefit to reduce the COI charge. It can be a complicated process that requires the adviser to carefully monitor the policy—not only the performance of the separate accounts but also the life insurance charges. Certainly, an insurance adviser working in the PPLI market will be familiar with the net amount-at-risk analysis, the needed adjustments, and the ongoing service requirements.

A New PPLI Design

A new PPLI contract has been designed (with a patent pending) that solves the fluctuating net-amount-at-risk problem. In effect, the death benefit floats and there are no COI charges. The insurance company has created an actuarial formula to translate the COI charges into an asset-based M&E charge. In other words, the COI charge varies as the value of the separate account portfolio changes. This is a familiar arrangement to investors and investment advisers, whereby the fees charged change with the market value. In addition, this new policy chassis charges a fixed asset-based fee that's contractually guaranteed.

What does this new design mean? The chassis eliminates the uncertainty that the insurance company will change the M&E or COI charges, or both. When the cash value decreases, so does the internal fee because it's asset based. With all other PPLI chassis on the market, when the cash value decreases, the net amount at risk increases and therefore so does the COI.

But for now at least, the insurance adviser must show a series of illustrations under different market conditions, discuss the possible COI fluctuations, and describe the scenarios that can occur with declines in portfolio values. This kind of service is a major consideration in selecting an insurance adviser. No PPLI, or retail variable life policy for that matter, should ever be viewed as a simple "buy it and put it in the file" sale. It's an important financial asset that deserves the same annual monitoring as other, noninsurance investments.

What if the policy owner does not want a lot of service interaction with the policy? Or what if there are questions about the long-term commitment to the service relationship? What if the policy owner wants to keep it simple, that is, keep the focus on gaining PPLI's substantial tax advantages? For these reasons and others, the new chassis structure is an attractive alternative. The new design eliminates the need for illustrations. The client simply gets a death benefit factor page that provides the ratio of death benefit to cash value. To calculate the death benefit, the cash value is multiplied by the death-benefit factor (see **FIGURE 11.5**). The new chassis eliminates the need to service and monitor the net amount at risk and COI, so new illustrations are not required each year.

For the client who does not want to be involved with complexities, this new chassis takes a complex investment and translates it into a simple formula. It's a lot easier to tell a client that the total charge, for example, is 100 basis points per year guaranteed, rather than to explain that the insurance company could charge 50 basis points, but it could change that to 150 basis points later on, depending on how the portfolio performs.

But be aware that this chassis may not be appropriate for the client who is looking for a larger initial death benefit. In that case, a traditional

FIGURE **11.5** *Death-Benefit Factor Illustration*

ATTAINED AGE	MALE NONSMOKER	SMOKER	FEMALE NONSMOKER	SMOKER
40	3.5713	2.9501	4.0108	3.5585
41	3.4547	2.8594	3.8811	3.4484
42	3.3419	2.7722	3.7571	3.3434
43	3.2337	2.6889	3.6372	3.2432
44	3.1296	2.6090	3.5222	3.1464
45	3.0296	2.5323	3.4108	3.0537
46	2.9331	2.4590	3.3038	2.9646
47	2.8401	2.3887	3.2008	2.8789
48	2.7509	2.3212	3.1007	2.7963
49	2.6647	2.2565	3.0043	2.7166
50	2.5817	2.1943	2.9118	2.6401
51	2.5021	2.1347	2.8225	2.5665
52	2.4258	2.0778	2.7365	2.4955
53	2.3523	2.0231	2.6538	2.4269
54	2.2823	1.9712	2.5745	2.3614
55	2.2149	1.9217	2.4979	2.2982
56	2.1506	1.8744	2.4242	2.2371
57	2.0890	1.8293	2.3531	2.1782
58	2.0299	1.7861	2.2845	2.1211
59	1.9735	1.7448	2.2181	2.0655
60	1.9194	1.7052	2.1537	2.0114
61	1.8678	1.6673	2.0916	1.9590
62	1.8183	1.6311	2.0317	1.9082
63	1.7713	1.5968	1.9742	1.8596
64	1.7265	1.5641	1.9193	1.8131
65	1.6839	1.5333	1.8668	1.7688
66	1.6434	1.5040	1.8168	1.7264
67	1.6049	1.4762	1.7689	1.6859
68	1.5682	1.4496	1.7229	1.6466
69	1.5331	1.4242	1.6785	1.6086

ATTAINED AGE	MALE NONSMOKER	SMOKER	FEMALE NONSMOKER	SMOKER
70	1.4998	1.3999	1.6358	1.5718
71	1.4682	1.3768	1.5947	1.5362
72	1.4382	1.3548	1.5554	1.5021
73	1.4099	1.3341	1.5181	1.4698
74	1.3835	1.3147	1.4829	1.4392
75	1.3587	1.2965	1.4497	1.4105
76	1.3355	1.2797	1.4185	1.3835
77	1.3138	1.2639	1.3891	1.3581
78	1.2932	1.2491	1.3613	1.3341
79	1.2738	1.2349	1.3350	1.3113
80	1.2554	1.2214	1.3102	1.2896
81	1.2379	1.2086	1.2867	1.2690
82	1.2214	1.1964	1.2646	1.2496
83	1.2061	1.1849	1.2440	1.2313
84	1.1919	1.1743	1.2250	1.2144
85	1.1787	1.1645	1.2073	1.1987
86	1.1666	1.1552	1.1909	1.1841
87	1.1553	1.1464	1.1757	1.1705
88	1.1447	1.1379	1.1614	1.1576
89	1.1346	1.1297	1.1480	1.1453
90	1.1247	1.1214	1.1351	1.1333
91	1.1148	1.1128	1.1226	1.1216
92	1.1047	1.1036	1.1103	1.1098
93	1.0941	1.0935	1.0978	1.0977
94	1.0827	1.0825	1.0850	1.0850
95	1.0704	1.0704	1.0717	1.0717
96	1.0576	1.0576	1.0583	1.0583
97	1.0452	1.0452	1.0455	1.0455
98	1.0366	1.0366	1.0366	1.0366
99	1.0265	1.0265	1.0265	1.0265
100+	1.0100	1.0100	1.0100	1.0100

FIGURE 11.6   *Chassis Comparison*

	GUARANTEED CHASSIS	TYPICAL PPLI
Can Charges Change	No	Yes, COI increases annually with age, insurance companies have a "current" and guaranteed set of charges. M&E has a "current" and "guaranteed" set of charges.
Sales Load	To be determined by adviser	To be determined by adviser
Premium Tax	State by state	State by state
DAC	1.25	May or may not include a DAC charge
Surrender Charges	None	Usually none
Other Charges	None	May impose a charge for certain policy transfers (new hedge fund because old manager left, etc.)
Illustrations	None (Death Benefit Factor Page)	Level interest assumption— needs to be reproduced annually

PPLI product will be of more use. Nevertheless, a client who seeks a larger death benefit in later years will find the new chassis of interest because the death benefit can be substantially larger even at quite advanced ages.

FIGURE 11.6 illustrates the new chassis. The constant and guaranteed asset-based charge allows the adviser to eliminate complicated illustrations. The client/adviser simply multiplies the cash value by the factor to determine the death benefit. The core of the design is simplicity.

PPLI IS AN EXCELLENT vehicle for accumulating wealth. Once the adviser determines the client's goals, he can put a policy in place to meet them. Once the policy is set, the appropriate insurance chassis can be recommended. The sale process should be needs based and strip the unnecessary complexity from PPLI's use in the investment and estate plans. A skilled insurance adviser will be able to educate the client about the various moving parts and make appropriate comparisons to the new, simplified chassis to determine the most appropriate solution. Doing so will allow the focus to remain squarely on PPLI's benefits.

CHAPTER 12

Getting It Right
A Regulatory Overview

MAUREEN NELSON

Owners of life insurance contracts and annuities obtain several U.S. federal income tax benefits under the Internal Revenue Code (the Code),[1] most notably the deferral of taxation on earnings (inside buildup) credited to policy values prior to distribution[2] and the exclusion from taxation of proceeds of a life insurance contract paid by reason of death of the insured.[3] In addition, although the Code does not permit a policyholder to deduct the premiums paid to purchase a life insurance or annuity contract,[4] because taxable income upon the surrender of a life insurance[5] or annuity contract is calculated by reference to the excess of the contract's cash surrender value over the policyholder's "investment in the contract"[6] and because the policy's cost of insurance and administrative charges levied by the insurer decrease a policy's cash surrender value, earnings credited to policy values will escape taxation, even upon surrender, to the extent they were used to satisfy such charges.[7] Finally, amounts paid as an annuity after the annuity start date of an annuity contract are treated as consisting in part of nontaxable return of the invested capital in the annuity contract and in part taxable ordinary income pursuant to an "exclusion ratio,"[8] thereby permitting policyholders to avoid the "income first" treatment afforded to owners of other types of debt instruments.[9]

These tax benefits also extend to the type of life insurance contracts sold in private placements, referred to as private placement life insurance (PPLI) contracts, but the contract must first qualify as a life insurance contract and then as a variable life insurance contract under section 817(d) for the policyholder to obtain these benefits. (See page 192 for an explanation of section 817(d).) The same qualification path is required for a private placement deferred annuity (PPDA) contract; it must qualify as an annuity under section 72 and as a variable annuity under section 817(d) for the policyholder to obtain these benefits. And although it may seem a bit circular, a contract that qualifies as a life insurance contract or annuity and as a variable contract will nonetheless lose its status as a life insurance or annuity contract (and the policyholder will lose the previously described tax benefits) if the variable contract is deemed to be inadequately diversified under section 817(h).[10]

The Internal Revenue Service (IRS) maintains that a policyholder holding a life insurance or annuity policy that qualifies as a variable contract and satisfies the diversification requirements may still be taxed currently on the earnings credited to the policy's cash value if the policyholder is determined to possess "investor control" over the assets purchased by the insurance company to support the policy's value. Thus, if you are involved in the design, administration, or marketing of a variable contract or an investment program to support variable contracts, it's important that you understand the federal tax rules—as well as the unresolved questions with respect to those rules—that are critical to ensuring that PPLI and PPDA policyholders will continue to enjoy the tax benefits attendant to ownership.

Tax Rules for Structuring PPLI and PPDA

Qualifying as a Life Insurance or Annuity Contract

To qualify as a life insurance contract under the Code, the contract must satisfy the requirements of section 7702. Section 7702 is a relatively recent addition to the Code; it was enacted in 1984 by a Congress concerned that modern-day life insurance products had become too investment oriented, a goal that arguably did not justify the tax benefits accorded to life insurance products.[11] Although a detailed discussion of section 7702 is beyond the scope of this chapter, in essence it contains a two-part test.

First, the contract must qualify as a life insurance contract under applicable law, meaning the law of the state or foreign jurisdiction in which the contract was deemed to have been issued. Second, the contract must meet one of two tests designed to limit the investment features of the contract—the cash value accumulation test of section 7702(a)(1) or the guideline premium and cash value corridor requirements of section 7702(a)(2). In essence, one of these tests is satisfied if either (a) the contract's cash value (net of surrender charges) does not at any time exceed the net single premium that a policyholder would have to pay at that time to purchase the future benefits promised under the contract; or (b) if the sum of all premiums paid under the contract does not at any time exceed the greater of the amount calculated under one of two guideline premium tests and the death benefit is equal to or greater than a statutorily prescribed multiple of the contract's cash value, which varies depending on the age of the insured.[12]

Section 72 sets forth most of the rules regarding the taxation of annuity contracts,[13] but does not specifically define what qualifies as an annuity for all purposes.[14] It is possible, however, to glean a working definition applicable in the context of variable contracts from the statute, the regulations, court cases, and IRS published revenue rulings and private letter rulings on related issues;[15] they generally provide that for a contract to be treated as an annuity contract in the hands of an individual policyholder, the contract must provide for the periodic liquidation of an invested sum of money over a period of time.[16] For example, for a policyholder, section 72(b) provides an exclusion ratio for taxing amounts received as an annuity that divides each payment into nontaxable return of investment (as long as there is unrecovered investment in the contract) and taxable ordinary income, but the regulations merely provide that this treatment is afforded to contracts that "are considered to be … annuity contracts in accordance with the customary practice of life insurance companies,"[17] without specifying what that might be. In addition, section 72(j) excludes from annuity treatment amounts "held under an agreement to pay interest thereon." Thus, if the contract distributes only interest and returns the invested principal later, instead of systematically liquidating both the principal and the earnings generated by that invested capital, then the contract will not qualify as an annuity.[18]

Finally, section 72 contains some disqualifying provisions that provide that in certain instances contracts otherwise qualifying as annuities will not be treated as annuities. Specifically, section 72(s) imposes specific distribution requirements for the contract to be treated as an annuity contract in the event that the holder of the annuity dies, and section 72(u) eliminates from annuity treatment (other than with respect to Subchapter L of the Code, which contains the provisions applicable to insurance companies), with certain limited exceptions, annuities not held by natural persons.[19] It's possible, however, for a contract that does not qualify as an annuity in the hands of the holder under section 72(u) (such as a deferred annuity held by a tax-exempt organization) to nonetheless be treated as a contract that provides for the payment of annuities for purposes of section 817.[20]

Qualifying as a Variable Contract

Section 817(d) defines a variable contract as one that (1) provides for the allocation of all or part of the amounts paid to the issuer to an account that, "pursuant to state law or regulation, is segregated from the general asset accounts of the company" (that is, a separate account); (2) provides for the payment of annuities or is a life insurance contract (or a contract that provides for funding of insurance on retired lives, a category of variable contract not relevant to the discussion herein); and (3) in the case of a life insurance contract, provides that the amount of the death benefit or the period of coverage is adjusted on the basis of, and in the case of an annuity contract, provides that the amounts paid in or the amounts paid out reflect, the investment return and the market value of the assets held in each "segregated asset account" that supports the contract.[21]

Rules to this effect have been in place since Congress amended the Code in 1962 in recognition of various states' enactment of separate account legislation, a move designed to permit the insurance industry to compete with other financial institutions for pension plan money.[22] Insurance companies are well acquainted with these rules, and those offering variable products have established separate accounts under state law and developed contracts that readily fit within these rules. In other words, technical compliance with section 817(d) has not been an area of IRS concern.

Nonetheless, one issue of relevance to the world of PPLI and PPDA has recently arisen under section 817(d). Recall that the definition of variable contract under section 817(d) refers to a contract that is issued pursuant to certain state laws or regulations. In a recent private letter ruling[23] involving a contract issued by a life insurance company domiciled outside the United States, which had elected under section 953(d) to be taxed as a U.S. taxpayer,[24] the IRS, noting that "state" is defined in the Code so as to be limited to one of the 50 states and the District of Columbia,[25] indicated that but for the foreign insurer's election to be taxed as a U.S. taxpayer, the contract would not have been characterized as a variable contract under section 817(d), despite the fact that the contract otherwise complied with section 817(d). The implication by the IRS is if a foreign insurer does not have a section 953(d) election, its variable contracts might not be respected as variable contracts under section 817. This suggests that mutual funds and partnerships that are insurance dedicated (but that have sold interests to the separate accounts of foreign insurers without a section 953(d) election) might not qualify for the application of the look-through rule (discussed below), which could thereby potentially cause domestically issued variable contracts invested therein to fail diversification. Until this issue is clarified, it's important to ensure that any life insurance company investing in a fund or in a fund in which a policy owner's separate account is invested be domiciled in the United States or have in effect a valid election to be taxed as a U.S. taxpayer. It's typical for subscription agreements to require the insurer to make such representations.

Diversification Requirements and Investor Control

In the 1970s, the IRS began scrutinizing recent products designed by insurance companies to encourage current and prospective policyholders to keep or invest capital with the insurance industry by offering potentially higher after-tax yields than those obtainable outside of an insurance or annuity policy's cash value. Reacting to some of the transactions it reviewed, the IRS began issuing rulings intended perhaps to stop the marketing of what it viewed as variable contracts with too much emphasis on investment to warrant the tax benefits afforded to insurance contracts.

These rulings are known as the *investor-control* rulings. They're also known as the "wraparound" rulings because they addressed insurance arrangements that the IRS deemed to consist of no more than a customer's chosen investments with an annuity "wrapped around" those assets in order to cloak them with the tax benefits of a variable contract. In those rulings, the IRS described different variable contract arrangements and concluded in several instances that either the policyholder's control over the insurer's separate account assets supporting the variable contract's policy values or the acquisition by the insurance company of an investment in support of a variable contract that the policyholder could have obtained without the purchase of an insurance contract meant that the policyholder possessed inappropriate investor control over those assets. As a result, the assets—and the income generated by those assets—were deemed by the IRS to belong to the policyholder and not to the insurance company, and the policyholder was responsible for reporting any taxable income generated by those assets.

In reaction to the concerns expressed by the IRS in the investor-control rulings, in 1984 Congress enacted the diversification requirements codified in section 817(h). According to the legislative history:

> The diversification requirement is provided in order to discourage the use of tax-preferred variable annuities and variable life insurance primarily as investment vehicles. The committee believes that, by limiting a customer's ability to select specific investments underlying a variable contract, the bill will help ensure that a customer's primary motivation in purchasing the contract is more likely to be the traditional economic protections provided by annuities and life insurance.[26] ... In addition, the conference agreement allows any diversified fund to be used as the basis of variable contracts so

long as all shares of the funds are owned by one or more segregated asset accounts of insurance companies, but only if access to the fund is available exclusively through the purchase of a variable contract from an insurance company. The fact that a similar fund is available to the public will not cause the segregated asset fund to be treated as being publicly available. In authorizing Treasury to prescribe diversification standards, the conferees intend that the standards be designed to deny annuity or life insurance treatment for investments that are publicly available to investors and investments, which are made, in effect, at the direction of the investor.[27]

Notwithstanding the enactment of the diversification requirements of section 817(h), the IRS still maintains that investor control is another weapon it may employ to tax policyholders on income attributable to assets supporting variable contracts that would otherwise pass muster under section 817(h).[28] It's therefore necessary to understand the investor-control rulings issued before the enactment of section 817(h), the diversification requirement contained in section 817(h), the regulations promulgated (and in part withdrawn) pursuant to section 817(h), and the recent rulings issued by the IRS in this area to find the answers to a prospect's questions about how PPLI or PPDA products may meet all of the federal tax requirements. Of course, there are still unanswered questions, but identifying the questions that require additional guidance is useful as well.

Prediversification Rules Investor-Control Rulings

The first investor-control ruling, Rev. Rul. 77-85,[29] was issued after the IRS had issued and then revoked a private letter ruling[30] that had blessed the identical transaction. In the ruling, the assets supporting the variable annuity's policy values were held in a custodial account formed pursuant to an agreement among the policyholder, the insurance company, and the custodian. Although the policyholder could select only investment assets from a list preapproved by the insurer, the policyholder could direct the custodian to sell assets from the account, to vote the underlying securities in a specific manner, and to exercise any options. The IRS ruled that the policyholder "possessed significant incidents of ownership over the assets" and therefore was taxable on the income generated by those assets.

One insurer offering a variable annuity like that described in Rev. Rul. 77-85 successfully convinced a federal district court that the IRS erred in concluding that policyholders of such an annuity should be deemed to own the underlying assets, but this victory was in effect reversed when the appeals court ruled against the insurer on procedural grounds.[31] The IRS continued to issue investor-control rulings.

In the next ruling, Rev. Rul. 80-274,[32] the IRS introduced the concept of what is now referred to as "publicly available" investments into the notion of investor control. This ruling involved an annuity supported by interest-bearing term deposits with a savings and loan association at a rate and maturity selected by the policyholder. Observing that the policyholder's economic position with respect to the annuity was substantially identical to the economic position the policyholder would have had with the deposits had he invested directly with the savings and loan association, the IRS ruled that the policyholder was the owner of the term deposits for tax purposes and taxable currently on the interest credited.

The next investor-control ruling, Rev. Rul. 81-225,[33] is the ruling most often cited by the IRS when discussing or applying the investor-control doctrine. This ruling involves five slightly different scenarios, but each is predicated on the same platform—a policyholder buys a variable annuity policy and an insurance company allocates premiums to a separate account, which is organized as a unit investment trust registered under the Investment Company Act of 1940 (the 1940 Act).[34]

In situation one, the insurance company purchases shares of a mutual fund that is managed by an asset manager independent of the insurance company, whose fund shares are sold directly to the public through registered broker-dealers. In situation two, the mutual fund is managed by the insurance company or by an asset manager related to the insurance company, and again the shares are available to the general public. In situation three, the separate account has five subaccounts, each of which purchases shares of a different mutual fund; again, the fund shares are available to the general public. In situation four, the shares of the mutual fund are available only to policyholders through the purchase of the policy or to customers of the insurance company's investment plan account. In situation five, the mutual fund shares are not available except to a policyholder through the purchase of a variable contract.

The IRS ruled that, in situations one through four, the policyholder had investor control over the assets and was therefore currently taxable on the earnings because in each situation the policyholder's contract was supported by assets that were available to the policyholder without the acquisition of an insurance or annuity policy. According to the IRS, "the policyholder's position in each of these situations is substantially identical to what his or her position would have been had the mutual fund shares been purchased directly (or indirectly as in Situation 4)." In contrast, however, in situation five, the sole function of the mutual fund was "to provide an investment vehicle to allow [the insurance company] to meet its obligations under its annuity contracts" and therefore the insurance company was deemed the owner of the shares.

The reasoning of Rev. Rul. 81-225 was challenged in court and the IRS ultimately came away the victor, but only after first losing in federal district court.[35]

In Rev. Rul. 82-54,[36] the last investor-control ruling issued before the enactment of the diversification rules, policyholders were permitted to allocate their premiums and policy values among three mutual funds managed by the insurance company, the shares of which were available exclusively to the insurer's separate account in support of variable contracts. One fund invested in equities, one in bonds, and one in money market instruments. The IRS ruled that the ability of the policyholders to choose among "broad, general investment strategies" did not constitute inappropriate investor control in light of the fact that the fund shares were not available to the public except through the purchase of a variable contract.

The Diversification Rules of Section 817(h)

In the Tax Reform Act of 1984 (TRA of 1984),[37] Congress responded to IRS concerns with wraparound variable contracts by enacting the diversification rules of section 817(h). Section 817(h) provides that a life insurance, endowment, or annuity contract (other than a pension plan contract) that otherwise qualifies as a variable contract shall not be treated as a life insurance, endowment, or annuity contract for any period and for all subsequent periods for which the investments made by any "segregated asset account"[38] in which the contract was invested were not adequately diversified. In other words, if a variable contract is deemed to fail the diversification test, all of the tax benefits of owning a life insurance or annuity policy will be lost. And a PPLI or PPDA contract that has any portion of a variable contract invested for even one day in a segregated asset account that is not adequately diversified will no longer qualify as a life insurance or annuity contract. In addition, nondiversification is not so easy to cure: once nondiversified, a contract remains nondiversified until the IRS deems the diversification failure remedied, which is a costly exercise,[39] no matter how much the asset mix supporting the contract has been changed in the interim. Thus, it is essential that the diversification rules are understood and followed.

The Test for Diversification

Congress left it to the Treasury Department to provide specific rules for adequate diversification. The statute does, however, set forth a statutory safe harbor for diversification, which borrows by cross reference from what were then the more established statutory diversification requirements under section 851 for regulated investment companies (RICs, mutual funds, or funds).[40] Before final regulations were issued, Congress amended section 817(h) in 1986 to add section 817(h)(4), the "look-through" rule, and the final regulations reflect the enactment of this rule.

The basic diversification rule allows no more than 55 percent of a segregated asset account's total asset value to be represented by any one investment; no more than 70 percent by any two investments; no more than 80 percent by any three investments; and no more than 90 percent by any four investments.[41] Under an alternative formulation, which is applicable only to variable life insurance contracts (and not to variable annuity contracts), these percentages are increased based on the value of the segregated asset account's investments represented by Treasury securities. Indeed, a variable life insurance contract (but not a variable annuity contract) may be completely supported by Treasury securities and satisfy section 817(h).[42] The statutory safe harbor, borrowed from the RIC statute, provides yet a third formulation for diversification.[43] Under this safe harbor rule, no more than 5 percent of the total asset value may be invested in the securities of any one issuer, nor may such investment account for more than 10 percent of the outstanding voting securities of such issuer. In general, this "5 percent and 10 percent" safe harbor excludes cash, cash items (including receivables), investments in government securities,[44] and investments in securities of RICs. Moreover, these excluded items, together, must not themselves exceed 55 percent of total asset value of the segregated asset account.[45]

For purposes of these diversification requirements, all securities of the same issuer, all interests in the same real property project, and all interests in the same commodity are each considered a single investment of a segregated asset account.[46] "Security" includes a cash item and any partnership interest registered under a federal or state securities regulation, but does not include any other partnership interest, an interest in real property, or an interest in a commodity.[47] A "Treasury security" is a direct obligation of the U.S. Treasury.[48] "Interest in real property" includes the ownership of land or improvements and leaseholds and options to acquire same but does not include mineral, oil, or gas royalty interests.[49] A "commodity" means any type of personal property other than a security, and "interest in a commodity" includes the ownership of any type of personal property and any put, call, straddle, option, or privilege on any type of personal property other than a security.[50] With respect to government securities, each government agency or instrumentality counts as a separate issuer.[51] "Value" for assets for which market quotations are readily available is the market value, and for assets for which a market quotation is not readily available, "value" is "fair value as determined in good faith by the managers of the segregated asset account."[52] To the extent not inconsistent with section 817(h), the terms used in that section have the same meaning as in section 851, which addresses regulated investment companies.[53]

Each segregated asset account must be adequately diversified on the last day of each quarter of a calendar year (that is, March 31, June 30, September 30, and December 31) or within 30 days after such last day.[54] A start-up grace period for diversification is contained in the regulations, which provide that a segregated asset account (other than a "real property account"[55]) will be considered adequately diversified until the first anniversary of the date on which any amount received under a life insurance or annuity contract is first credited to the account.[56] A segregated asset account that is a real property account on its first anniversary is deemed to be adequately diversified until the earlier of its fifth anniversary or the anniversary on which it ceases to be a real property account.[57]

A Segregated Asset Account

Note that section 817(h) requires the segregated asset account (or accounts—the regulations specifically refer to variable contracts based on "one or more segregated asset accounts")[58] and not the contract itself to be adequately diversified, so it may be useful to digress momentarily from the discussion of how adequate diversification is determined to ascertain the meaning of the term "segregated asset account." It is a term of art in section 817 that is specifically defined in the Treasury regulations, and it does not necessarily mean the same thing as a "separate account" (although the assets of a segregated asset account will, under state law, be held by the insurer in a separate account). Appreciating just what qualifies as a segregated asset account is critical to structuring investment options for insurers. The offering documents can then be properly drafted so that all parties to the transaction will be able to prevent a diversification failure.

The regulations define a "segregated asset account" as "consist[ing] of all assets the investment return and market value of each of which must be allocated in an identical manner to any variable contract invested in any such assets."[59] Examples in the regulations illustrating the meaning of this term put the focus on a group of assets, the value and yield of which are shared and disseminated ratably among the policyholders whose contracts are supported by that particular group of assets, and provide that a customer's ability to choose among groups of assets as investment options (usually partnerships or mutual funds) causes each of those groups of assets to be characterized as comprising a separate segregated asset account.

In the examples, the insurance company invests the policy values of its variable contracts in two different types of investments—a managed portfolio of publicly available debt securities that satisfies the diversification requirements and a publicly registered partnership, the assets of which also satisfy the diversification requirements. When the policyholder may choose between the managed portfolio and the partnership, the interests in the portfolio and the interests in the partnership are treated as separate segregated asset accounts. When the policyholder may not choose between the two types of investments and every policyholders' policy values are allocated between the two types of investments in the same proportion, then the assets of the managed portfolio and the assets of the partnership together make up one segregated asset account.[60]

Here is a simple example to illustrate how this definition works. Assume the insurer offers policyholders three different investment strategy options—a large-cap growth fund, a mid-sized value fund, and an international equities fund, interests in each of which are sold exclusively to insurance companies to support variable contracts.

A customer may allocate any part of his or her policy value and premiums to any investment strategy. To keep track of policy values, the insurer may employ a record-keeping device without independent legal significance, such as subaccounts, and each subaccount corresponds to each of the investment strategies. The insurer allocates a policyholder's policy values to the appropriate subaccount within its separate account when so directed to invest in a particular strategy, and the amounts so allocated are then used to buy shares of the corresponding fund.

Those shares are credited to the corresponding subaccount, but as a state law legal matter they are deemed held in the separate account. Every policyholder that has shares of a particular fund supporting his or her variable contract policy values on any particular day receives, on a per-share basis, the same value and yield from those shares as every other policyholder with policy values supported by those fund shares on that day.

Under the regulatory definition of segregated asset account, each subaccount in this example is a segregated asset account because the value and yield of the assets held by the subaccount are shared ratably by all of the policyholders who have policy value allocated to that subaccount at that time and because the policyholders were in effect permitted to choose among subaccounts. The assets of the segregated asset account are the fund shares—although if the look-through rules discussed below apply, the assets of each of the segregated asset accounts will consist of a pro rata portion of all of the assets owned by each subaccount's corresponding fund (see discussion of look-through rules).

In the foregoing example, each subaccount purchased shares of one mutual fund. Suppose, however, that the insurer had offered three investment strategies but had used the funds allocated to a particular subaccount by each policyholder to purchase shares of two large-cap growth mutual funds, and policyholders had no ability to allocate policy value to one particular fund but could only select the large-cap growth investment strategy. In that event, the assets of the segregated asset account would consist of shares of both funds held in the subaccount (and the underlying investments of both funds if the look-through rules were to apply) and those assets collectively would be tested for diversification.[61]

Thus, if the mutual fund manager is representing to the insurance company that the fund will be managed in accordance with the diversification rules, it is very important to draft the relevant agreements to ensure that insurers do not structure their investment choices for policyholders in a manner that effectively commingles different fund shares within one segregated asset account, because it is possible that the two funds' assets, when combined, will cause the segregated asset account not to be adequately diversified. As a practical matter, this should not be difficult, but it does require the advice of experienced legal counsel who can make sure the operating documents are properly drafted to effect that result.

The Market Fluctuation Rule

Under a market fluctuation rule contained in the regulations, if a segregated asset account satisfies any of the diversification requirements set forth above as of the last day of any calendar quarter (or within 30 days after the end of such calendar quarter), the segregated asset account will "not be considered nondiversified in any subsequent quarter because of a discrepancy between the value of its assets and the diversification requirements unless such discrepancy exists immediately after the acquisition of any asset and such discrepancy is wholly or partly the result of such acquisition."[62] Stated more plainly, once the segregated asset account's investments establish compliance with any of the diversification tests on the last day of a quarter or within 30 days thereafter and no assets are thereafter acquired, subsequent market fluctuations that cause the value of existing investments to exceed the diversification limitations will not cause the segregated asset account's investments to be considered nondiversified.

In other areas with similar or identical market fluctuation rules, if diversification has been met and then market fluctuation of the value of owned assets causes nondiversification, it may be possible to buy or sell other assets without being deemed nondiversified.[63] Although the IRS has not ruled on this point in the section 817(h) context, it is fair to expect that the same result would obtain were the IRS to address the issue, but experienced tax counsel should be consulted before proceeding in reliance upon the guidance issued in other areas.[64]

The Look-Through Rule

Treasury Regulation § 1.817-5(f) contains a look-through rule that applies to certain legal structures or entities in certain situations to assist a segregated asset account that is invested therein to comply with the diversification requirements. If the look-through rule applies to an entity in which a segregated asset account has invested, then a pro rata portion[65] of each asset owned by the entity will be treated, for purposes of the diversification requirements of section 817(h), as an asset of the segregated asset account.[66] In other words, if the look-through rule applies, the segregated asset account gets to look through the assets it holds, such as fund shares, to the assets owned by the fund. As a result, a segregated asset account that has purchased one investment—for example, shares of a mutual fund eligible for application of the look-through rules—will be adequately diversified as long as the fund itself is diversified in a manner consistent with section 817(h).

The look-through rule is the reason insurance companies usually require independent asset managers[67] to represent that their funds or partnerships will be adequately diversified, even though technically it is the segregated asset account—the parameters of which will be defined by how the insurer structures the investment options offered to policyholders—that must be adequately diversified under section 817(h). Because the scope of the segregated asset account in any particular situation is under the control of the insurer, a well-advised asset manager required to represent that its fund will be adequately diversified requires in return that the insurer represent that the interests in the RIC or partnership will constitute all of the assets of a single segregated asset account and then limits its diversification representations to situations in which the insurer's representation is accurate.

Under the current formulation of the regulations, the look-through rule applies to any structure or entity described in at least one of the following clauses: (i) a RIC, real estate investment trust (REIT), partnership, or grantor trust (collectively, RIC or partnership), if all the beneficial interests of the RIC or partnership are held exclusively by one or more segregated asset accounts of one or more insurance companies and public access to such RIC or partnership is available exclusively through the purchase of a variable contract from an insurance company (the exclusively held look-through rule); or (ii) a partnership if the partnership interests therein are not registered under a federal or state law regulating the offering or sale of securities (the private placement look-through rule);[68] or (iii) a grantor trust if substantially all of its assets are Treasury securities.[69]

On July 30, 2003, the Treasury Department and the IRS announced their proposal to amend the regulations to revoke the private placement look-through rule, a move that was not opposed by those in the industry (although substantial comments were filed outlining other areas in which the regulations under section 817(h) could be improved), but at present the regulation has not been withdrawn.

The preamble to the proposed regulations contemplates that the revocation will be effective on the date the final regulations are published, and it will apply to all investments in all private placement RICs and partnerships, including those made prior to the revocation. Variable contracts invested therein will be deemed to be adequately diversified, however, if they were adequately diversified prior to the revocation and if by the end of the last day of the second calendar quarter ending after the effective date of the amended regulations, those contracts are brought into compliance with the new regulations.[70] Because it is expected that the private placement look-through rule will be withdrawn soon (or perhaps was withdrawn after this text went to press), the following discussion will address structuring issues based on the premise that the private placement look-through rule is no longer available, while mentioning areas of concern during the era of the private placement look-through rule.

An insurance-dedicated RIC or partnership will be considered to be exclusively held even if certain other investors own interests in the fund or partnership, but this is a very small world of permitted other investors. Specifically, interests may be owned by (1) the trustee of a qualified pension or retirement plan;[71] (2) the general account of a life insurance company or a corporation related[72] to a life insurance company if a segregated asset account of that life insurance company also holds or will hold a beneficial interest in the entity; (3) the manager (or a corporation related to the manager in the same manner described in note 72) of the RIC or partnership, but only if (a) the holding of the interests is in connection with the creation or management of the entity, (b) the return on such interests is computed in the same manner as the return on an interest held by a segregated asset account is computed (determined without regard to expenses attributable to variable contracts), and (c) there is no intent to sell such interests to the public.[73]

According to the legislative history to this rule, these latter two permitted investors were included "to allow for the ownership of fund shares by an insurance company or fund manager for administrative convenience, in operating an underlying investment fund."[74] Thus, it is permissible for the asset manager (or a related corporation, although arguably not a related partnership or limited liability company) forming an insurance-dedicated fund or partnership to own an interest in the fund or partnership, for example, to seed the fund, but that interest may not be used to provide performance bonuses because the return on the interest would not then be computed in the same manner as the return to the segregated asset accounts.

The asset manager should be compensated with fees, not interests in the underlying fund or partnership, unless the asset manager is prepared to earn the same yield on such interests as all other interest holders. Note that the revocation of the private placement look-through rule may cause a RIC or partnership sold exclusively to segregated asset accounts (but relying on the private placement look-through rule because the asset manager receives a profits interest) to become ineligible for look-through treatment despite being sold exclusively to segregated asset accounts, a perhaps unintended consequence of the revocation.

Interests in an exclusively held RIC or partnership may also be owned by another exclusively held RIC or partnership without the former losing its status as exclusively owned.[75] Such an arrangement is common in so-called "fund of funds" arrangements (although not all funds of funds invest in exclusively owned RICs or partnerships), discussed below.

To preserve the exclusively owned status of a RIC or partnership, the manager of an insurance-dedicated RIC or partnership must ensure that the insurance company separate account does not distribute its interests in the RIC or partnership to policyholders or to anyone else. It is common, therefore, for subscription agreements to contain a restriction on transfers of interests and a prohibition on in-kind distributions to policyholders. A similar restriction should be in place to prevent the asset manager of a fund of funds from making in-kind or other transfers of its interests in an underlying insurance-dedicated fund.

An unanswered question is whether the exclusively owned status of a RIC or partnership is lost when an investor-control problem unique to one (or even more than one) policyholder causes that policyholder, and not the insurance company separate account, to be deemed to own the interests in the RIC or partnership. Because neither an insurer, which would be concerned with protecting the tax benefits of its policyholders, nor the investment manager of the RIC or partnership, which would be concerned with protecting its exclusively owned status for other investing insurance companies, would want to risk such an onerous result, it is common to see subscription agreements or other operating documents contain language designed to avoid the potential that the IRS may find that some policyholder exerted inappropriate investor control. (See the discussion of investor control, page 205.)

Funds of Funds

A growing segment of insurance-dedicated asset management is involved with "funds of funds," that is, RICs or partnerships (the first-tier RIC or partnership) that invest in several other RICs or partnerships (the second-tier RICs or partnerships). Such a structure enables the manager of the first-tier RIC or partnership to offer a segregated asset account an investment that combines efficiencies in fund management and cost savings with a high degree of diversification (at least from a literal perspective, if not from the point of view of section 817(h)). If the first-tier RIC or partnership is exclusively held but the second-tier RICs or partnerships are not, then for purposes of testing for adequate diversification, the assets of a segregated asset account invested in the first-tier RIC or partnership (the fund of funds) will be limited to the shares or interests in the second-tier RICs and partnerships.

Under that arrangement, it is necessary to test the segregated asset account's compliance with the diversification rules by valuing and counting the various interests in the second-tier RICs or partnerships held by the fund of funds.[76] (It is also possible, although perhaps not very common, to structure a fund of funds using a single-member limited liability company (LLC) owned exclusively by the insurance company separate account that in turn invests in multiple RICs or partnerships. As long as the LLC does not elect to be taxed as a corporation, it should be treated as a disregarded entity and its assets in the second-tier RICs or partnerships will be imputed to the segregated asset account invested therein, without the need to resort to the look-through rules.[77]) If the second-tier RICs or partnerships are also exclusively held, however, then a "double look-through" results—that is, the segregated asset account invested in the fund of funds will look-through the first-tier RIC or partnership *and* through the second-tier RICs or partnerships owned by the first-tier RIC or partnership to the underlying investments owned by those second-tier RICs and partnerships, all of which will be aggregated and attributed to the segregated asset account for purposes of measuring diversification.[78]

This double look-through has been very helpful in enabling an asset manager that operates a fund of funds that invests in second-tier RICs or partnerships also managed by that asset manager (or by a related asset manager or by asset managers that operate insurance-dedicated funds and that are familiar and compliant with the section 817(h) rules) to provide a highly diversified investment to a separate account. But while the private placement look-through rule was [is] in effect, the double look-through [has] also provided some structuring difficulties to managers of funds of funds seeking to invest in publicly available RICs or partnerships to which the private placement look-through rule applied (such as most hedge funds) because although a hedge fund is likely to be highly diversified, if such partnership is not intended to be insurance-dedicated, it might not be "adequately diversified" on the last day of a calendar quarter or within 30 days of the end of the calendar quarter, as required by section 817(h). Or the hedge fund manager might not be prepared or willing to share the composition and value of the assets held by the hedge fund with the fund of funds asset manager on a basis that would permit the fund of funds manager to test his or her RIC or partnership for diversification.

To avoid this measuring difficulty, many fund of fund managers chose to invest in entities not eligible for the look-through rule, such as offshore corporate entities ineligible for look-through treatment (that is, passive foreign investment companies, or PFICs). The diversification problem caused by the potential application of a double look-through was [will be] alleviated, however, with the rule's repeal. After the repeal of the private placement look-through rule, a fund of funds invested in a RIC or partnership that is not exclusively owned is [will be] deemed to own one investment, thus making it necessary for such a fund of funds to own interests in several different of such funds (or other assets) in the correct proportion to be adequately diversified. (Such a fund of funds would seem to be the functional equivalent of the managed portfolio of debt securities described in the examples in the regulations and should be a permissible structure that does not violate the deemed investor control rule,[79] although it is always wise to seek the advice of informed counsel in this regard.)

The Return of the Investor-Control Issue

The repeal of the private placement look-through rule should also result in less confusion about when a segregated asset account structure will be deemed to have an investor-control problem. Recall that in Rev. Rul. 80-274 and Rev. Rul. 81-225, the IRS ruled that when the separate account invested in a mutual fund that was available to a policyholder without the purchase of a variable contract, the policyholder would be deemed to have investor control (as opposed to actually exercising investor control, as in Rev. Rul. 77-85).[80] As a result, the fund shares would be deemed to be owned directly by the policyholder and the policyholder would be taxed on the income and gain from the fund.

Although these rulings were never withdrawn or limited by the IRS, Congress's enactment of the diversification rules in 1984 was viewed by some in the industry as supplanting the investor-control rules, an entirely reasonable view notwithstanding the claims of the IRS to the contrary. Nevertheless, the IRS continued to remind the world that investor control was alive and kicking, although such reminders were for many years found either in caveats appended to the end of diversification private letter rulings or in favorable private letter rulings that found no investor control when an exclusively owned RIC or partnership invested in one or more publicly available RICs or partnerships.[81]

In PLR 200244001 (November 1, 2002) (often referred to as the Keyport ruling; see note 80), however, the IRS ruled that a policyholder who owned a variable contract supported by a segregated asset account that invested in a publicly available but private placement partnership would be deemed to possess investor control over the partnership interest and would be taxed currently on the income and gain from that partnership interest. The insurer argued that Example 3 of the regulations[82] seemed to sanction such an investment by according look-through treatment to the segregated asset account invested in a private placement partnership that was publicly available, without identifying any investor control problem. The IRS rejected this argument and observed that, as in Rev. Rul. 81-225, the policyholder had merely purchased the same investment through a variable contract that he could have obtained without purchasing a variable contract. The IRS also rejected the insurance company's argument that when Congress adopted the diversification rules it intended effectively to overrule the investor control doctrine, citing the following language from the legislative history to section 817(h): "In authorizing Treasury to prescribe diversification standards, the conferees intend that the standards be designed to deny annuity or life insurance treatment for investments that are publicly available to investors."[83]

The IRS followed PLR 200244001 with a pair of revenue rulings intended to demonstrate reasonable levels of policyholder investor participation in choosing assets to support a variable contract, thereby effectively establishing safe harbors, and impermissible levels of investor control over such assets. In Rev. Rul. 2003-91, 2003-33 I.R.B. 347 (July 30, 2003), the insurer established 13 subaccounts,[84] each of which had an identified and distinct investment strategy. The insurer represented that it may increase or decrease the number of subaccounts it offers, but it would never offer more than 20 subaccounts at any one time. The investments of each subaccount were managed by an independent investment adviser and the investments of each subaccount were adequately diversified. Access to the subaccounts could only be obtained through the purchase of a variable contract from the insurer. The insurer permitted policyholders to allocate premiums among the subaccounts and to change premium allocation at any time; balances could be transferred from one subaccount to another once per 30-day period without charge and thereafter by paying a fee.

After considering all of the facts and circumstances, the IRS ruled that the policyholder in Rev. Rul. 2003-91 would not possess investor control. In particular, the IRS noted the following:

> Holder [policyholder] may not select or direct a particular investment to be made by either the separate account or the subaccounts. Holder may not sell, purchase, or exchange assets held in the separate account or the subaccounts. All investment decisions concerning the separate account and

the subaccounts are made by IC [insurance company] or adviser [independent investment adviser] in their sole and absolute discretion.

The investment strategies of the subaccounts currently available are sufficiently broad to prevent holder from making particular investment decisions through investment in a subaccount. Only IC may add or substitute subaccounts or investment strategies in the future. No arrangement, plan, contract, or agreement exists between holder and IC or between holder and adviser regarding the specific investments or investment objective of the subaccounts. In addition, holder may not communicate directly or indirectly with adviser or any of IC's investment officers concerning the selection, quality, or rate of return of any specific investment or group of investments held by separate account or in a subaccount.

Investment in the subaccounts is available solely through the purchase of a contract, thus, subaccounts are not publicly available. The ability to allocate premiums and transfer funds among subaccounts alone does not indicate that holder has control over either separate account or subaccount assets sufficient to be treated as the owner of those assets for federal income tax purposes.

The second investor-control ruling issued that day, Rev. Rul. 2003-92, has many of the same facts as Rev. Rul. 2003-91, viz., the policyholder purchases a variable contract and may allocate premiums and policy values to one of several subaccounts within the insurer's separate account, and the policyholder may reallocate policy values among the subaccounts at any time. Situation one involves a life insurance contract, situation two involves an annuity contract, and in both situations, each subaccount purchases an interest in a private placement partnership that is publicly available. In the third situation, each subaccount purchases an interest in an exclusively owned partnership. Each partnership has an investment manager that selects the partnership's specific investments, and a policyholder may not act as an investment manager or independently own any interest in any of the partnerships. In addition, policyholders have no voting rights with respect to any partnership interest held by any subaccount.

The IRS ruled that in the first two situations the policyholders would be treated as owning the interests in the partnerships purchased by the subaccounts because each subaccount held an interest in a partnership that was available other than through the purchase of a life insurance or annuity contract. In contrast, because the subaccounts in situation three invested only in exclusively owned partnerships, the insurer would be treated as the owner of the partnership interests for tax purposes.

Although some may characterize Rev. Rul. 2003-92 as shutting down an arguably abusive area of practice where an insurance contract was merely wrapped around a publicly available investment, relatively few in the industry structured PPLI and PPDA in that manner and Rev. Rul. 2003-92 did not take away what the regulations seem to permit—a segregated asset account should still be able to offer a mix of assets that includes or consists entirely of publicly available assets as long as the particular mix of assets that the segregated asset account holds is available exclusively through the purchase of a variable contract. After all, that is the composition of an exclusively held RIC or partnership that is investing in publicly available securities. But it is important to make sure that an asset manager independent of the policyholder is truly selecting the particular mix of assets owned by the segregated asset account (which is why it is also important to understand what comprises the segregated asset account in a particular context), and it is also important to make sure that all parties agree that neither the asset manager nor the insurer will take investment advice or direction from the policyholder. Of course, advice of experienced counsel in this regard is critical.

So what do we learn from these two new revenue rulings and from the previous rulings that can enable an insurer and an asset manager to structure a product and execute operating documents designed to prevent investment-control issues from arising? Although we already were aware of most of the points the IRS made in the rulings, a few are arguably new. We know that:

❑ A policyholder should not be telling the insurance company what specific assets to purchase for or sell from the segregated asset account.

❑ The insurance company must retain the right to keep or change investment strategies and managers for each segregated asset account or to add or delete investment strategies.

❑ No arrangement, plan, contract, or agreement should exist between the policyholder and the insurer or between the policyholder and the investment adviser regarding what assets to place in the segregated asset account or any RIC or partnership in which the segregated asset account is invested.

❑ The policyholder should never communicate directly or indirectly with the insurer's investment advisers or with the independent asset manager concerning the selection, quality, or rate of return of any specific investment or group of investments. Well-advised insurers and asset managers should include language in their operating documents designed to ensure that neither the asset manager, the insurer, nor the policyholder crosses these lines of investment authority. An insurer can offer at least 20 different investment options for a policyholder, as long as each represents a different investment strategy. (Perhaps if an insurer were to offer multiple choices of the same investment style of RIC or partnership, the IRS may deem that to be tantamount to providing investments that the policy-holder could purchase without purchasing a variable contract.)

❑ A segregated asset account cannot invest in a single RIC or part-nership that is publicly available and expect to avoid an investor-control problem. Of course, after the repeal of the private placement look-through rule, a segregated asset account that invests solely in a single publicly avail-able RIC or partnership would have a diversification problem anyway, so that problem should be eliminated with the change to the regulations.

THERE ARE STILL unanswered questions in this arena. For example, it has been posited that the legislative history from the TRA of 1984 Act per-mits the development of insurance-dedicated funds that mimic publicly available funds without an investor-control problem.[85] Although the IRS appears to have permitted clone funds that do indeed mimic publicly available funds,[86] the degree to which such funds have been blessed is unclear—is it acceptable if the clone fund uses the same asset manager employing the same investment strategy as a publicly available fund as long as the clone fund is a legally independent RIC or partnership? What if the particular mix of assets is identical between the two funds—has a line been crossed? What about exclusively held funds that have such a fairly specific investment strategy—for example, the 10 corporations with the largest market capitalization? Is that too specific? If so, does that mean an exclusively held S&P 500 index fund is not permitted? Are single-investor separate accounts permitted? Although the IRS has ruled that no investor-control problem existed in a situation where the insurer held the assets supporting each policyholder's variable contracts in a different sepa-rate account,[87] this ruling sets a precedent only for the taxpayer to whom it was issued. Whether the IRS, with its renewed concern about investor control, would issue the same ruling today is unclear. And what about a policyholder that has a pre-existing relationship outside the insurance context with an independent asset manager of an exclusively held RIC or partnership—may the policyholder engage in discussions with the asset manager regarding the investments obtained outside the variable contract without the parties being deemed to have an "arrangement, plan, contract, or agreement" with respect to the assets supporting the variable contract?

As is apparent, it is difficult to know exactly where to draw the lines. Because the consequences of diversification failure and investor-control violations are so adverse, it is critical to obtain advice from a well-informed adviser before treading in these waters.

Chapter Notes

1. All references to the Internal Revenue Code (Code) are to the Internal Revenue Code of 1986, as amended, 26 U.S.C. § 1 et seq. All section references are to the Code unless otherwise indicated.

2. Inside buildup is not currently taxed because the policyholder is deemed not to be in actual or constructive receipt of the earnings so credited. See *Cohen v. Comm'r*, 39 T.C. 1055 (1963), acq. 1964-2 C.B. 3. In effect, section 7702(g) codifies this treatment for life insurance contracts by providing rules that specifically tax policyholders on inside buildup (referred to in the statute as "income on the contract") on life insurance contracts that fail to satisfy either section 7702(a)(1) or section 7702(a)(2). Note, however, that section 7702(g), unlike section 72(e), charges the policyholder for the cost of life insurance protection provided under the contract when calculating the amount of income taxed to the policyholder. A contract structured as a deferred annuity that does not qualify as an annuity contract is treated as a debt instrument subject to the original issue discount rules of sections 1272–1275. See note 9.

3. See section 101(a). A detailed discussion of amounts paid under a life insurance policy that are *not* paid by reason of the death of the insured or paid under an annuity before the annuity start date or not paid as an annuity is beyond the scope of this chapter. In general, however, if the cash surrender value of a life insurance contract or annuity is paid upon complete surrender of the policy, then the proceeds are ordinary income to the extent they exceed the policyholder's "investment in the contract." Section 72(e)(5)(E); Treas. Reg. § 1.72-11(d)(1). This treatment applies to deemed payments to policyholders, such as amounts used to repay policy loans, as well as to actual distributions to policyholders. If the cash surrender value of a life insurance policy is paid (actual or deemed payments) in part prior to the death of the insured or if amounts are paid from an annuity contract but are paid before the annuity start date and in neither instance is the payment in full discharge of the insurer's obligation under the contract upon its complete surrender, the owner must report as ordinary income those amounts that are less than the excess of (1) the cash surrender value of the policy immediately before distribution over (2) the "investment in the contract," with the balance being treated as a tax-free return of capital [section 72(e)(2)(B)]. In other words, proceeds of a partial surrender are treated as distributions of income on the contract until that income is exhausted and then return of capital, whereas proceeds of a complete surrender are treated as return of capital first and then ordinary income. See notes 6 and 7.

4. See section 264.

5. If the life insurance contract is also a modified endowment contract (MEC) as defined in section 7702A, then proceeds of a partial *or* complete surrender are treated as taxable income to the extent the cash value of the policy before the surrender exceeds the investment in the contract. In other words, distributions are treated as income first, then return of investment. In addition, if amounts are

deemed distributed from a MEC and the recipient is not yet age $59^1/_2$, the distributions are subject to a 10 percent penalty tax under section 72(v). Although a discussion of MECs is beyond the scope of this chapter, in general a MEC is a life insurance contract that at any time during the first seven years of the contract has accumulated premiums that exceed the sum of the seven level annual premiums needed on or before that time to pay the benefits promised under the policy. See section 7702A(b). Some life insurance contracts are structured to be classified as MECs; but a life insurance contract that inadvertently becomes a MEC may be "cured" by effecting a written agreement (closing agreement) with the IRS pursuant to Rev. Proc. 2001-42, 2001-2 C.B. 212.

6. Section 72(e)(6) in essence defines "investment in the contract" as the sum of all premiums or other consideration paid for the contract, reduced by all amounts previously received under the contract that were excluded from income (such as premium refunds).

7. See section 72(e)(2), which includes in gross income amounts received prior to the annuity start date to the extent such amounts exceed the investment in the contract. Section 72(e)(2) also applies to surrender proceeds of a life insurance contract and would in effect pick up all surrenders prior to maturity. Note that administrative charges levied against policy value that are not properly charged to the contract, such as fees paid to an independent investment adviser retained by the policyholder, may be deemed to constitute amounts not paid as annuities and taxable as ordinary income under the rules of section 72(e)(2)(B), described in note 3. See PLR 9342053 (July 28, 1993).

8. See section 72(b).

9. Although an annuity is in an economic sense a debt instrument, most annuities are excluded from the definition of the term "debt instrument" under the original issue discount (OID) rules of sections 1271–1275. See section 1275(a)(1)(B). Without that exclusion, a deferred annuity would be subject to the OID rules and the policyholder would be taxed currently on income attributed to the contract, even if no distributions were received. A discussion of the OID rules is beyond the scope of this chapter, but please be aware that although section 1275(a)(1)(B) excludes from the characterization of a debt instrument an annuity contract to which section 72 applies, this exclusion may not be available if (1) the annuity contract was not issued by an insurance company unless, in a meaningful way, the annuity depends in whole or in part on the life expectancy of one or more individuals [see section 1275(a)(1)(B)(i) and Treas. Reg. § 1.1275-1(j)]; or (2) if it was issued by a foreign insurance company not subject to U.S. federal income tax under Subchapter L of the Code. See section 1275(a)(1)(B)(ii) and Treas. Reg. § 1.1275-1(k). Whether a PPDA issued by a non-U.S. insurance company will be respected as an annuity or will be subject to the OID rules depends upon the particular facts of the insurer, for example, if the insurer has in place an election to be taxed as a U.S. taxpayer under section 953(d). Additional guidance on this point should be sought from knowledgeable tax counsel.

10. Section 817 is relevant in the calculation of a life insurance company's taxable income, not a policyholder's. When a variable contract is properly structured, the income, gain, and loss attributable to the assets in the separate account (a creditor-remote account of the insurance company that holds assets supporting variable contracts) are reflected on the insurance company's tax return and not on the policyholder's. As a practical matter, however, a life insurance company is largely tax indifferent to the income, gain, or loss of separate account assets because recognized taxable income (or loss) attributable to separate account assets will be offset by deductions (or income) attributable to life insurance reserve increases (or decreases) under section 807 occasioned by the increase (or decrease) in policy values, and the asset basis adjustment rules of section 817(b) will prevent an insurer from realizing taxable gain or loss upon the disposition of appreciated or depreciated separate account assets. There is an exception to this tax indifference and that is due to a tax rule applicable to insurance companies called "proration," which effectively prevents an insurer from taking a full deduction for the cost of increasing life insurance reserves to the extent those reserves are funded by tax-exempt interest and limits the amount of dividends eligible for the dividends received deduction allowed under sections 243 and 805(a)(4). See Technical Advice Memorandum (TAM) 200330002 (July 24, 2003), in which the IRS ruled that short-term capital gain distributions from a regulated investment company to a separate account maintain their status under section 852 as dividends and are therefore subject to the proration rules, and they are not treated as capital gain items eligible for the basis adjustment rules of section 817(b). Although the interaction of the basis adjustment rules of section 817(b) and the rules governing passive foreign investment companies (PFICs) is not entirely clear, section 817(b) should operate to protect an insurance company that holds interests in PFICs from the penalty interest rules of section 1291 without the need to make an election under section 1295 to have the PFIC treated as a qualified electing fund (QEF). No guidance specifically addressing the interplay of the PFIC rules and section 817 has been issued by the IRS, however, so an insurer considering investing in a PFIC on behalf of its separate account should seek the advice of qualified counsel.

11. See Andrew Pike, "Reflections on the Meaning of Life: An Analysis of Section 7702 and the Taxation of Cash Value Life Insurance," 43 Tax L. Rev. 491 (1988), for an in-depth discussion of the history and operation of section 7702.

12. Insurers with failed life insurance contracts have reporting and withholding obligations under section 3405 on the deemed income distributions to policyholders. See Rev. Rul. 91-17, 1991-1 C.B. 190. Section 7702(f)(8) permits the IRS to waive a failure under section 7702 if such failure is due to reasonable error and reasonable steps are being taken to remedy the error. Section 7121 permits the IRS to execute a written agreement (a closing agreement) under which the IRS will waive any penalties for failing to comply with section 3405 when a waiver under section 7702(f)(8) is not available, provided the insurer pays any tax the policyholders would have owed on the deemed income distributions and any

interest owing on such tax. See Rev. Rul. 91-17, above; see also Notice 99-48, 1999-2 C.B. 429.

13. A discussion of annuities issued under a qualified plan is beyond the scope of this chapter, although section 72 speaks to them as well.

14. The regulations under section 72 provide that a contract may be taxed as an annuity under section 72 despite not being issued by an insurance company. See Treas. Reg. § 1.72-2(a)(1). As the discussion of the variable contract requirements of section 817 makes clear, however, a *variable* annuity (and a variable life insurance contract) may be issued only by an insurance company operating under a statute that provides for separate accounts.

15. Under section 6110(k)(3), private letter rulings (unlike IRS published rulings, such as revenue rulings) may not be used or cited as binding precedent. Private letter rulings may be a useful indication of the prior thinking of the IRS, however.

16. In a recent private letter ruling issued to an insurance company under section 817, the IRS looked to the regulations under section 72 and concluded that for a group annuity contract to qualify as an annuity contract for purposes of qualifying as a variable contract under section 817(d), it had to be funded with amounts that were not "held under an agreement to pay interest thereon," it must provide for payments in periodic installments at regular intervals over a period of more than one full year from the annuity starting date, and the total amount payable under the contract had to be determinable as of the annuity starting date either directly from the terms of the contract or indirectly by the use of either mortality tables or compound interest computations, or both. See PLR 200248021 (Nov. 29, 2002). See also, for example, *Ingleheart v. Comm'r,* 10 T.C. 766 (1948), *aff'd* 174 F.2d 605 (7th Cir. 1949).

17. See Treas. Reg. § 1.72-2(a)(1).

18. It seems that pension trusts holding pension plan contracts as defined by section 818(a) may hold annuities notwithstanding the lack of contractual language providing for periodic payments, which arguably protects distributions under such contracts from constituting unrelated business taxable income under section 512, as long as the annuity contracts are not debt financed. See section 817(e), which provides that "[a] pension plan contract that is not a life, accident, or health, property, casualty, or liability insurance contract shall be treated as a contract which provides for the payments of annuities for purposes of [section 817]."

19. Detailed discussion of these rules is beyond the scope of this chapter. For a more complete discussion of annuities, see John T. Adney, Joseph F. McKeever, III, and Barbara N. Seymon-Hirsch, *Annuities Answer Book* (Panel Publishers, 3d ed., 2000).

20. See PLR 200248021 (Nov. 29, 2002).

21. See section 817(d). In PLR 200248021 (Nov. 29, 2002), the IRS ruled that

contracts that otherwise met the requirements of section 817(d) would not fail to be treated as variable contracts even though the separate accounts holding the assets supporting those contracts also held assets that supported contracts issued to tax-exempt organizations and the contracts owned by the tax-exempt organizations did not qualify as annuities due to section 72(u).

22. See former section 801(g). See also Howard Stecker, Frederic Gelfond, and Friedrich von Rueden, "Separate Account Products: A Story of Natural Selection Along the Insurance Product Continuum," 13 Ins. Tax Rev. 2027 (December 1997), for a description of the historical underpinnings of the development of the variable contract industry.

23. PLR 200246022 (Nov. 15, 2002).

24. The life insurance company was a "controlled foreign corporation" (that is, with sufficient U.S. shareholder ownership) eligible to make the election to be taxed as a domestic insurance company under section 953(d).

25. See sections 7701(a)(9) and (10).

26. See Staff of Senate Comm. on Finance, 98th Cong., Report on P.L. 98-369 (Comm. Print 1984).

27. See H.R. Rep No. 98-861, at 1055 (1984).

28. See, for example, Rev. Rul. 2003-92, 2003-33 I.R.B. 350. See also the preamble to the temporary regulations under section 817(h) issued in 1986: "The temporary regulations in this document do not ... provide guidance concerning the circumstances in which investor control of the investments of a segregated asset account may cause the investor, rather than the insurance company, to be treated as the owner of the assets in the account.... Guidance on this and other issues will be provided in regulations or revenue rulings under section 817(d), relating to the definition of variable contract." T.D. 8101.

29. Rev. Rul. 77-85, 1977-1 C.B. 12.

30. See PLR 7747111 (Aug. 29, 1977), revoked by PLR 7817018 (Jan. 24, 1978).

31. See *Investment Annuity, Inc. v. Blumenthal,* 442 F.Supp. 681, 689 (D.D.C. 1977), *rev'd on other grounds* 609 F.2d 1 (D.C. Cir. 1979).

32. Rev. Rul. 80-274, 1980-2 C.B. 27.

33. Rev. Rul. 81-225, 1981-2 C.B. 12.

34. 15 U.S.C. § 806-1 et seq.

35. See *Christoffersen v. U.S.,* 749 F.2d 513 (8th Cir. 1984), *rev'g* 578 F. Supp. 398 (N.D. Iowa 1984).

36. Rev. Rul. 82-54, 1982-1 C.B. 11.

37. Pub. L. No. 98-369, 98 Stat. 484 (codified as amended in scattered sections of 26 U.S.C.).

38. "Segregated asset account" is a defined term in the regulations and it does not mean the same thing as a state law separate account. Indeed, under the regulations, a single separate account may hold numerous segregated asset accounts, and a single variable contract may be supported by many such accounts, each of which must meet the diversification test at all times. These points will be discussed in the text below.

39. If the failure to diversify was inadvertent, the nondiversification was rectified within a reasonable period of time after discovery, and the issuer or holder of the variable contract agrees to pay to the IRS an amount "based upon the tax that would have been owed by the policyholders if they were treated as receiving the income on the contract," plus interest on the tax, then the IRS will execute a closing agreement in which the nondiversification is deemed not to have occurred. See Treas. Reg. § 1.817-5(a)(2); see also Rev. Proc. 92-25, 1992-1 C.B. 741, which sets forth the procedures and requirements for effecting a closing agreement and calculating the penalty.

40. Section 817(h)(2).

41. Treas. Reg. § 1.817-5(b)(1).

42. See section 817(h)(3); see also Treas. Reg. § 1.817-5(b)(3), which provides that the percentage of the value of total assets represented by Treasury securities is multiplied by 0.5. This product is then added to each of the percentage limitations in Treas. Reg. § 1.817-5(b)(1), creating new ceilings for investment in one, two, three, or four investments. Assets that are not Treasury securities are then tested against these increased ceilings (without counting Treasury securities in total assets). Thus, Treasury securities can make up any portion of a life insurance segregated asset account's investment as long as the remaining assets, taken as a group, meet the adjusted ceilings of the alternative diversification requirements. Treas. Reg. § 1.817-5(b)(3).

43. Treas. Reg. § 1.817-5(b)(2).

44. "Government security" is defined for these purposes in Treas. Reg. § 1.817-5(h)(1) as "any security issued or guaranteed or insured by the United States or an instrumentality of the United States; or any certificate of deposit for any of the foregoing." That regulation also provides that if the United States guarantees only a part of the security, then only that portion will be treated as a "government security." Note that in Rev. Proc. 2004-48, 2004-21 I.R.B. 984 (May 7, 2004), the IRS stated that a RIC may treat a repurchase agreement as a government security for purposes of the RIC diversification test under section 851(b)(3). Although no mention is made of the section 817(h) "safe harbor" in that revenue procedure, it is likely the same treatment would be accorded a repurchase agreement in the context of section 817(h) in light of the specific cross-reference to section 851(b)(3) contained in section 817(h).

45. Treas. Reg. § 1.817-5(b)(2); section 851(b)(3).

46. Treas. Reg. § 1.817-5(b)(1)(ii).

47. Treas. Reg. § 1.817-5(h)(6).

48. Treas. Reg. § 1.817-5(h)(2).

49. Treas. Reg. § 1.817-5(h)(7).

50. Treas. Reg. §§ 1.817-5(h)(5) and (8).

51. Treas. Reg. § 1.817-5(b)(1)(ii).

52. Treas. Reg. § 1.817-5(h)(9).

53. Treas. Reg. § 1.817-5(h)(10).

54. Treas. Reg. § 1.817-5(c)(1).

55. An account is a real property account if, on the anniversary of the date on which any amount received under a variable contract was first credited to the account or on the date on which a plan of liquidation is adopted, not less than the applicable percentage of the total assets of the account is represented by real property or interests in real property. The applicable percentage is 40 percent on the first anniversary, 50 percent on the second, 60 percent on the third, 70 percent on the fourth, and 80 percent on the fifth and thereafter. Treas. Reg. § 1.817-5(h)(4).

56. Treas. Reg. § 1.817-5(c)(2)(i) and (iii). Note that this rule does not apply if more than 30 percent of the amount allocated to the account as of the last day of a calendar quarter is attributable to contracts entered into more than one year before such date. For this purpose, amounts transferred from another account or as a result of an exchange of contracts that qualifies for nonrecognition treatment under section 1035 do not count as attributable to contracts entered into more than one year before such date. Treas. Reg. § 1.817-5(c)(iv). This rule also applies to the grace period for real property accounts, discussed in note 55, but by substituting five years for one year.

57. Treas. Reg. 1.817-5(c)(2)(ii).

58. See Treas. Reg. § 1.817-5(a).

59. Treas. Reg. § 1.817-5(e).

60. See Treas. Reg. § 1.817-5(g). Note also that these examples, which illustrate both the meaning of "segregated asset account" and the application of the look-through rules, discussed in the text, also provide that when all the beneficial interests in the partnership are owned only by insurance company segregated asset accounts and access to such interests is available only through the purchase of a variable contract, the segregated asset account may look though its interest in the partnership to the assets of the partnership to test for diversification.

61. See Treas. Reg. 1.817-5(g), Ex. (4). See also PLR 200119036 (May 11, 2001), in which the IRS ruled that investment profiles established by the insurer's investment management affiliate, each of which acquired shares of multiple insurance-dedicated mutual funds, constituted the segregated asset account for the variable contracts held by policyholders who had enrolled in the asset-management program sponsored by the insurer with the affiliate. Critical to the ruling is the fact that the policyholders had no ability to allocate among funds but instead were put into profiles by the investment adviser and then each policyholder assigned to one particular profile shared ratably in the particular group of assets assigned to that investment profile.

62. Treas. Reg. § 1.817-5(d).

63. See PLR 199920036 (May 24, 1999). Assets purchased must not create a new discrepancy between the diversification rules and the value and mix of the assets owned, nor exacerbate the discrepancy that was caused by the market fluctuation.

64. The market fluctuation rules under section 817 are drawn verbatim from the market fluctuation rules affecting RICs, and the rules for real estate investment trusts (REITs) are the same. Accordingly, most tax practitioners look to these rules when applying the market fluctuation rules under section 817. For example, in PLR 8707033 (Nov. 17, 1986), the IRS relied on the REIT market fluctuation rules to rule that a RIC that had satisfied the diversification requirements and then became nondiversified due solely to the change in market value of securities of one particular issuer would not be deemed to be nondiversified if it purchased or sold securities of yet another issuer if that purchase or sale would not, by itself, have caused the RIC to become nondiversified. In addition, unlike the REIT or RIC rules, there are alternative tests for segregated asset account investment diversification, two of which contain different valuation ceilings. Thus, it would be wise to consult a tax professional before relying on the market fluctuation rule if any of the alternative means of satisfying diversification are being used.

65. For this purpose, a partnership investor's pro rata portion of each asset of a partnership to which the look-through rule applies will be determined in accordance with the partnership investor's capital interest in the partnership. Treas. Reg. § 1.817-5(f)(1).

66. Section 817(h)(4); Treas. Reg. § 1.817-5(f).

67. Section 817(h)(5) specifically permits the use of independent investment advisers.

68. In PLR 9847017 (Nov. 20, 1998), discussed at note 86, the IRS ruled that a Delaware business trust taxed as a partnership, interests in which were not registered under the Securities Act of 1933, 15 U.S.C. § 77a et. seq. (the 1933 Act) but instead were sold exclusively to qualified accredited investors under Regulation D of the 1933 Act, was not eligible for the private placement look-through rule because the trust was registered under the 1940 Act. Query whether this was a proper denial of the look-through rule while the private placement look-through

rule in the regulations was in effect, an inquiry that will become moot when the regulation providing the private placement look-through rule is revoked.

69. Treas. Reg. § 1.817-5(f)(2).

70. See Notice of Proposed Rulemaking, Fed. Reg. Vol. 68, No. 146, p. 44689 (July 30, 2003).

71. In Rev. Rul. 94-62, 1994-2 C.B. 164, the IRS identified eight specific categories and one general category of arrangements that are qualified retirement or pension plans for purposes of Treas. Reg. 1.817-5(f)(3)(iii). In PLR 200223012 (June 7, 2002), the IRS extended that treatment to simple retirement accounts under section 408(p) and Roth individual retirement accounts under section 408A, which did not exist in 1994 when Rev. Rul. 94-62 was issued. It is unclear whether an exclusively held RIC or partnership would lose such status were a qualified pension plan investor to lose its qualification.

72. Specifically, two corporations are related in an appropriate manner if they are part of a chain of corporations underneath a common parent corporation where the members of such chain of corporations are connected by at least 50 percent stock ownership (determined by vote or value). For purposes of applying the 50 percent stock ownership test, constructive ownership rules and other special rules apply. See Treas. Reg. 1.817-5(f)(3)(ii); see also section 267.

73. Treas. Reg. § 1.817-5(f)(3)(ii).

74. S. Rpt. No. 99-313, p. 976.

75. See PLR 200115028 (April 16, 2001).

76. See PLR 9851044 (Dec. 18, 1998), in which the segregated asset account was invested in an exclusively held RIC that in turn invested in numerous other RICs, shares of which were offered to the general public. The IRS ruled that the look-through rule applied to the first-tier fund but not to the second-tier funds. The IRS also ruled that as long as the variable contracts did not otherwise violate the investor control rules as set forth in Rev. Rul. 81-225 and Rev. Rul. 82-54, they would not be deemed to violate those rules merely because the first-tier fund invested in publicly available second-tier funds. See also PLR 200025037 (June 26, 2000).

77. See PLR 200025037 (June 26, 2000).

78. See PLR 200115028 (April 16, 2001).

79. See Treas. Reg. § 1.817-5(g). See also ruling 5 in PLR 200025037 (June 26, 2000), in which the IRS specifically ruled that the fact that an exclusively held RIC or partnership in turn invested in publicly available RICs or partnerships would not in itself cause an investor control problem under Rev. Rul. 81-225.

80. For an excellent discussion of investor control in general and in particular the deemed versus "actual" notions of investor control, see David S. Neufeld, "The 'Keyport Ruling' and the Investor Control Rule: Might Makes Right?" *Tax Notes*

Jan. 20, 2003, reprinted in *The Insurance Tax Review*, March 2003.

81. See PLR 9851044 (Dec. 18, 1998), discussed in note 76, and PLR 200025037 (June 26, 2000), discussed in note 79.

82. Treas. Reg. § 1.817-5(g), Ex. 3. Note that the proposed revocation of the private placement look-through rule also contemplates the revocation of Ex. 3.

83. See H.R. Rep No. 98-861, at 1055 (1984).

84. The ruling says 12 but then identifies 13.

85. According to that legislative history, "[t]he fact that a similar fund is available to the public will not cause the segregated asset fund to be treated as being publicly available." See H.R. Rep No. 98-861, at 1055 (1984).

86. See PLR 9847017 (Nov. 20, 1998), which involved a series trust that was established as a business trust under Delaware law and taxed as a partnership, that was registered under the Investment Company Act of 1940, 15 U.S.C. 80a-1 et seq. (the 1940 Act) and two separate series of RICs, Portfolio 1 and Portfolio 2 (each series a fund). The funds in Portfolio 1 were publicly available; the funds in Portfolio 2 were exclusively held. The investment objectives and strategies of each fund in Portfolio 2 corresponded to the investment objectives and strategies of a fund in Portfolio 1. Each series of the series trust corresponded to the investment objectives and strategies of a fund in both Portfolio 1 and Portfolio 2 (that is, each Portfolio 2 fund was a clone fund). Each Portfolio 1 fund and each Portfolio 2 fund with the same investment objective would invest in the corresponding series. The IRS ruled that the segregated asset account invested in a fund of Portfolio 2 could look through that interest to the underlying investment of that Portfolio 2 fund, but the fund itself could not look through its underlying investment, the series, because the series qualified for neither the exclusively held look-through rule (because a Portfolio 1 fund was also invested in the series and Portfolio 1 was publicly available), nor the private placement look-through rule (because the series was registered under the 1940 Act). The IRS ruled, however, that for purposes of satisfying the various asset holding and diversification rules applicable to RICs, each Portfolio 2 fund, as a partner in the corresponding series, should take into account its proportionate share of the series' underlying assets. The IRS did not identify any investor-control problem for variable contract owners invested in a Portfolio 2 fund, despite the fact that the Portfolio 2 funds were identical to publicly available Portfolio 1 funds.

87. See PLR 9433030 (May 25, 1994).

CHAPTER 13

Investment Due Diligence
Beyond the Questionnaire

KEVEN DE LA CRUZ

W hy does an insurance company feel obliged to do extensive due diligence on funds it may offer through private placement life insurance (PPLI)? Arguably, the company is making no investment representation about the funds offered. After all, separate-account variable products were designed to shift the risks and rewards of investing away from the insurance company to the individual policyholder. An insurance company making such a variable product offering is not managing the money and is not promising any investment results. Rules of the game aside, no one wants to be personally named or have his employer named on New York Attorney General Eliot Spitzer's must-call list. And no one responsible for due diligence wants to have to explain why a fund was approved while its head trader is doing the "perp walk."

Analyzing and understanding the portfolio-management strategies that a fund manager uses is one part of the process, but understanding the business practices and compliance culture of a prospective fund is equally important. A thorough due diligence process is one of an insurance company's basic responsibilities to clients and policyholders. The insurance company is picking not only a manager for a long-term investment offering but also a business partner.

The business partnership between an insurance company's variable life policy and the fund manager may last 30 years or more. The insurance company often has the most to lose, because in many product offerings, the insurance company is the one with the deep pockets. That's why it insists on meticulous due diligence.

The due diligence process begins with a questionnaire. To understand the process, one needs to understand the questions that need to be asked and what answers to expect. The questionnaire should cover key aspects of the manager's investment strategy, portfolio-management techniques, trading skill, business operations, legal structure, treasury operations, compliance culture, business plan, and technological infrastructure. In part, the questionnaire is undoubtedly a cover-your-assets (CYA) activity. The due diligence team members may not get a straight answer, but they can always say they asked. Indeed, the team is not doing its job if key questions are not asked. But to do a good job, the team has to go beyond the questionnaire. To dig deeper, there's no substitute for face-to-face interviews, which need to be conducted by experts in the asset class, focusing on key aspects of the fund.

Shades of Gray

Even an extremely thorough due diligence effort ends with some doubts. Coming to a judgment about such a complex topic relies on clear quantitative measures like asset size and performance track record, but quality plays a big role. Does the manager have a good reputation? Does the portfolio manager seem clear, focused, and motivated?

In the end, the evaluation must reach a conclusion after weighing many factors. Whether the decision to approve an investment was a wise one or not can only be determined over time. The life cycle of a hedge fund can be surprisingly short; funds close their doors every day. The cost of implementing a fund that later fails can be high, both in terms of lost opportunity cost and the potential damage to the insurance company's reputation.

The due diligence ultimately comes down to three simple questions:
- ❑ Has the due diligence process been meticulous, thorough, and sound?
- ❑ Is the fund worthy of approval?
- ❑ Does the fund become a success, or does it melt down and become nothing more than an embarrassing story in the newspaper?

This distillation (see **FIGURE 13.1**) allows us to think a little like a game theorist and view a complex process reduced to a handful of possible answers. Understanding the impact on the insurance company of each of these possible outcomes explains a great deal about how insurance companies approach the due diligence process. Ranking the outcomes from best to worst reveals how the people on the due diligence team will view their role.

Clearly, insurance company employees are not engaged in due diligence to pick winners but rather to avoid disasters. At its worst, the due diligence process is a time-wasting CYA exercise. At its best, real value is brought to the fund selection process, providing protection for the insurance company and its policyholders. The key to a successful process is to be as thorough as possible within a limited time frame. This is the only way for the due diligence team leader to avoid the worst worse case—having no job and an embarrassing resume.

How Much Diligence Is Due?

The correct level of detail and thoroughness in due diligence depends on the type of fund being considered. In the case of a plain vanilla money market fund or an index fund offered by an experienced fund manager with a sterling reputation, there is very little risk to the insurance company. It may be important to consider the level of fees, examine whether investment assets will benefit from expense breakpoints, and understand the benefits and limitations of commingled funds. But there is very little downside to the insurance carrier in these types of funds, and the goal of due diligence really should be to create the appropriate documentation and move on quickly. Other funds present different challenges.

Plain vanilla with sprinkles. The vanilla-with-sprinkles fund may be an insurance-dedicated clone of a registered mutual fund with a long track record. In this category, more consideration needs to be paid to the fund's structure and to the firm itself rather than to the specifics of the strategy. The treatment of expenses and fees is also critical. But if the fund manager has made a registered offering, the fund has already generated a body of compliance documentation. The due diligence team can review these documents without having to do the work that generated them.

Rocky road. This category covers the more highly flavored fund options—the hedge fund of funds (FOF), a common alternative investment option in a PPLI product. A hedge fund of funds can be seen as a firm that itself specializes in due diligence. True, many FOFs add value through portfolio construction, optimization, and asset allocation, but basically the FOF manager picks other managers.

Certain structural considerations—for instance high leverage, lack of liquidity, and insufficient diversification—may make a particular FOF a bad fit for an insurance product. Careful scrutiny should also be paid to the fee structure, because FOF offerings have been criticized as "fee of fee" structures. But for the most part, the due diligence on a FOF offering can be less rigorous than the due diligence required on a direct hedge fund. Essentially, the additional layer at the top provides

FIGURE **13.1** *Outcomes*

DUE DILIGENCE PROCESS IS ...	FUND IS ...	FUND IS ...
1 sound	approved	successful

This is the best case, and the result will be a long-term successful business relationship between the fund manager and the insurance company. Of course, gaining happy policyholders is an important result.

2 flawed	approved	successful

Sometimes it's better to be lucky than good. If the fund is a long-term success, despite a sloppy due diligence process, no one is likely to go back into the files and criticize the due diligence team. All's well that ends well.

3 sound	not approved	a failure

In this case, the due diligence process functioned exactly as intended, and the insurance company avoided a bad outcome, which is the primary goal of due diligence. As a whole, due diligence at an insurance company is not about picking the winners. In fact, with most insurance companies offering scores of funds in their variable products, one or two winners won't have a huge impact. But one or two embarrassing failures can have a dramatic impact on the insurance carrier and on the careers of the team responsible for due diligence.

4 flawed	not approved	a failure

In this case, the insurance company was lucky enough to dodge a bullet, and the due diligence team will take credit for superior intuitive judgment, even if the actual work done was sketchy.

5 sound	not approved	successful

This is a case of missed opportunity, and it happens. It's a bad but defensible outcome. Even the best due diligence process can't predict the future. Interestingly, a fund that goes on to be a big success for a rival insurance company will be used by the marketing department as an example of why the due diligence process should be less selective.

built-in due diligence, and this is what the FOF manager is paid to do.

An insurance company's due diligence process has a different goal than that of the FOF manager, whose goal is to pick fund managers that will

DUE DILIGENCE PROCESS IS ...	FUND IS ...	FUND IS ...
6 flawed	**not approved**	**successful**

Another missed opportunity. The likely outcome within the insurance company is a lot of griping in the marketing department not only about how the fund went on to be a success for someone else but also that the due diligence process is broken. It puts the due diligence team in a position that's hard to defend. But the impact to the insurance company is really just a lost opportunity and potentially a setback to its reputation.

7 sound	**approved**	**a failure**

Like the missed opportunity, this happens to even the most thorough insurance company. Despite the team's best efforts, the company's reputation can be damaged. There might be a negative financial impact on the company, but at least the due diligence team can point to a thick due diligence file. Is the file's thickness a sufficient defense here? How about pointing out that the failure often results not from the due diligence process undertaken but from a lack of understanding about the trading strategies (as was the case with Long-Term Capital)? Or, in the case of Gotham Partners, from a well-reasoned investment plan undercut by managers with poor ethics?

8 flawed	**approved**	**a failure**

This is the worst worse case for the insurance company as well as for the individual due diligence team members. The company is financially hurt and left with egg on its face. The team faces a career-ending situation. The team gets no direct reward when it picks a winning fund, but it will get punished for approving a fund that turns out to be a loser. No one wants to have to admit in his next job interview that he was the one responsible for due diligence at XYZ insurance company when it approved Long-Term Capital.

outperform and generate significant alpha (see chapter 9); an insurance company's due diligence team is simply looking for funds that will not melt down. Doing due diligence on a fund of funds—which in itself spe-

FIGURE **13.2** *Discounting and Payment*

HEDGE SUB INDICES	VALUE	JAN 04	YTD (%)	1 YEAR (%)	AVG ANNL[1] (%)	STD DEV[2] (%)	SHARPE[3]
Convertible Arbitrage	275.06	1.42	1.42	11.14	10.56	4.76	1.36
Dedicated Short Bias	71.17	−1.73	−1.73	−31.90	−3.32	17.95	−0.41
Emerging Markets	203.66	2.53	2.53	32.61	7.31	17.70	0.18
Equity Market Neutral	277.48	0.82	0.82	7.62	10.65	3.06	2.14
Event Driven	300.64	2.16	2.16	19.89	11.53	6.02	1.23
Distressed	359.94	2.42	2.42	24.26	13.54	6.97	1.35
E.D. Multi-Strategy	271.86	2.01	2.01	17.22	10.43	6.34	1.00
Risk Arbitrage	226.33	0.83	0.83	10.31	8.44	4.44	0.98
Fixed Income Arbitrage	195.51	1.23	1.23	7.93	6.88	3.94	0.70
Global Macro	392.42	1.45	1.45	17.32	14.52	12.07	0.86
Long/Short Equity	321.22	2.00	2.00	19.70	12.27	10.96	0.75
Managed Futures	200.23	1.09	1.09	8.77	7.13	12.09	0.25
Multi-Strategy	251.58	1.60	1.60	15.20	9.84	4.53	1.26

1. Index data begins January 1994.
2. Monthly standard deviation annualized.
3. Calculated using the rolling 90-day T-bill rate.

cializes in due diligence—can seem redundant. For this reason, we'll focus here on the due diligence process as applied to a direct hedge fund.

Italian gelato. With the direct hedge fund, we come to the more exotic flavors, at least compared with the investment options available inside of variable insurance products. A wide range of direct hedge funds—literally thousands—is available in the alternative investment asset class. The CSFB/Tremont Hedge Fund Index Sub Indices provides a valuable snapshot of this asset class (see **FIGURE 13.2**).

Tremont Advisers is involved in a joint venture with Credit Suisse First Boston to form the CSFB/Tremont Hedge Fund Index. The CSFB/Tremont Hedge Fund Index is the hedge fund industry's first asset-weighted index. The index was designed and built to provide a new standard for tracking and comparing hedge fund performance against other major asset classes. (Data are available from CSFB/Tremont Index LLC at http://www .hedgeindex.com/.)

More or Less Than Meets the Eye

Clearly, certain types of hedge funds may never be suitable for the long-term nature of a PPLI insurance offering. But equally revealing in the subindices data is that a number of segments of the hedge fund asset class display surprisingly low volatility. An argument can be made that these types of funds expose investors to much less risk than the traditional, long-only mutual funds more commonly offered inside PPLI products. If insurance companies have accepted the level of volatility inherent in long-only mutual funds, then in terms of investment risk, they should be even happier with direct hedge funds. Which type of fund—and more important, which fund in particular—becomes the key question.

Hedge funds face few regulatory restrictions in terms of investment strategy, leverage, liquidity constraints, diversification, and reporting transparency—and this freedom has raised concern at the Securities and Exchange Commission (SEC). In a September 2003 report, the SEC identified a number of areas of concern regarding hedge funds: lack of SEC information about hedge funds and their advisers' activities; lack of prescribed and uniform disclosure by hedge fund advisers; valuation and other conflict of interest issues; the potential for increased investment by less-sophisticated investors, directly or indirectly, in hedge funds; and despite the relatively low absolute number, an increase in the number of enforcement actions regarding hedge fund advisers. Many of these concerns arise from the unregulated status of hedge funds, which generally allows them to operate without SEC oversight.[1]

In this kind of "Wild West" environment, a complete and thorough due diligence process becomes essential. As an asset class, hedge funds can reduce risk. And picking the right fund can reduce policyholder asset volatility, but picking the wrong one can expose policyholders to an investment that literally goes to zero.

The due diligence a hedge fund requires depends on the type of fund and the degree of risk that the issuing insurance company perceives. The due diligence process isn't designed to uncover any single red flag. Rather, what due diligence should provide is a sensitivity to clues that might reveal a lack of consistency, an internal contradiction in the response to different due diligence questions, or unrealistic expectations on the part of the fund manager. To quote from Warren Buffett's 2003 chairman's letter: "Investment managers often profit far more from piling up assets than from handling those assets well. So when one tells you that increased funds won't hurt his investment performance, step back: His nose is about to grow."

The hedge fund world is filled with small, lightly regulated start-up businesses. Every year hundreds of new funds are created. Many will never seek to create an insurance-dedicated fund for inclusion in a PPLI product. But if the insurance company's goal is to gather assets to its PPLI fund, the small, young, and growing fund is precisely the type of option that might be most attractive in an insurance product. The largest, most established hedge funds are less likely to be concerned with attracting assets. In fact, many are probably closed to new investments. Still, the young, growing fund may be the first to suffer a business or operations setback. For this reason, a fund needs to be evaluated in terms of its portfolio management and its viability as an ongoing business. To review a fund as a small business, questions need to explore business strategy, pricing policy, compliance, infrastructure and trading systems, as well as simple business income and expense ratios.

Of course, understanding the investment risk management guidelines used to manage the portfolio is critical. These guidelines may be quantified, and there may be an analytical method to verify compliance. Metrics used may include risk tolerance, value at risk, or tracking coefficients to specific benchmarks. The due diligence team might look for fund volatility, style drift, a shift in markets traded, liquidity, or leverage.

These measures may be a comfort to the mathematicians on the team, but care should be taken that there is not an overly simplified reliance on analytical measures. Consider, for example, that a fund could develop a sophisticated value-at-risk analysis that quantified potential market risk at the end of every trading day, but if a manager is engaging in intraday arbitrage, it's entirely possible that all positions are closed out at the end of the day. The VAR may be zero at the end of each day, but the fund could still be losing money daily. Any purely analytical risk-measurement technique needs to be considered in light of some common sense.

"Appendix I: Areas of Inquiry" and "Appendix II: The Fifty-Seven Questions"—available at www.bloomberg.com/ppli—offer ways to interpret the information you uncover as well as suggested questions that cover a lot of territory. Is asking the portfolio manager these 57 questions sufficient to detect fraud, judge the future success of the investment fund, or even evaluate the investment firm's business plan? The answer to that question has to be a qualified no. But engaging the portfolio manager in a dialog is the most effective way of coming to understand the philosophy of the investment firm. Not asking the questions is clearly a mistake. It's critically important that insurance companies enter these business relationships armed with more than a hunch.

The funds considered for a PPLI product should be suitable for an insurance product. Highly volatile "swing for the fences" hedge funds are probably not appropriate. A PPLI policy may be in force for 25 years or more. The credibility and sustainability of the investment firms managing the assets are vitally important to the policy's success.

For an insurance company, the due diligence process is more about avoiding losers than it is about picking winners. At its worst, due diligence can be a time-consuming CYA activity. Both quality and quantity must be considered. In today's investment environment, neither can be ignored; a failed business relationship can cause serious harm to a company's reputation as well as severe financial penalties. The long-term nature of a policyholder relationship makes effective due diligence essential for insurance companies. It helps build sustainable products and a strong reputation in the industry.

References

Stephen Brown, William Goetzmann, and Bing Liange, 2002, "Fee on Fees in Funds of Funds," Yale ICF Working Paper No. 02-33, http://papers.ssrn.com/so13/papers.cfm?abstract_id=335581.

Chapter Notes

1. Based on testimony of William H. Donaldson, Chairman, U.S. Securities & Exchange Commission, taken September 30, 2003, on Commission activity to enhance investor protections.

CHAPTER 14

Creating and Administering an Insurance-Dedicated Fund

BRENT KINETZ

If you're a hedge fund or fund-of-hedge-funds manager looking for an edge, few opportunities are quite as tempting as eliminating current taxation from returns without changing investment strategy. Even if this opportunity required your investors to pay a small additional cost— one that's just a fraction of the taxes they've been paying—the choice is still a classic "no brainer."

Such is the allure of creating an insurance-compliant version of a fund, a so-called insurance dedicated fund (IDF). The fund is designed to hold the cash value of private placement life insurance (PPLI) and private placement annuity policies and deliver returns to the policy owner. Because of the tax preferences afforded to life insurance and annuities, these returns are not taxable as current income to the policy owner. Given the advantages of private placement programs, every high-net-worth and institutional U.S. taxpayer who owns life insurance or hedge funds should be allocating meaningful capital to them. Indeed, the clarity of IRS rulings has compelled even the most conservative practitioners to feel comfortable that properly structured and managed insurance-dedicated funds are tax compliant. Nevertheless, the insurance-dedicated-fund market remains severely underpenetrated.

Does that mean a fund manager should drop everything to set up an IDF? Not really. In fact, unless your fund has a clear distribution strategy, the opportunity to create an insurance-dedicated fund is one you should pass up. Not only is there already a core of IDFs in the market, but the task of building PPLI distribution support and expertise—not to mention the operational complexity of managing a fund—can be very difficult, costly, and time consuming.

Insurance-Dedicated Funds Defined

An insurance-dedicated fund is an independent legal structure that's open only to investments from insurance carriers. An IDF can either be a registered investment company or a nonregistered entity, such as a Delaware limited partnership, a limited liability company, or a managed account. This chapter focuses on nonregistered entities—specifically, hedge funds—but other asset classes such as venture capital and commodities are being added as PPLI investment options to gain the policy's great investment and structural advantages.

The insurance carrier investing in an IDF is typically making an investment on behalf of a PPLI or annuity policy owner who has cash value in his policy. The insurance carrier first puts the policy owner's cash value in a separate account owned by the insurance carrier. The policy owner then instructs the carrier to allocate the cash value to one or more investment alternatives approved and offered by the insurance carrier. Once the allocation instruction is signed, the carrier invests the cash value in the IDFs as directed by the policy owner (see **FIGURE 14.1**).

This definition of an IDF differs from the structure often referred to as an "asset allocator," or "managed separate account." With an allocator

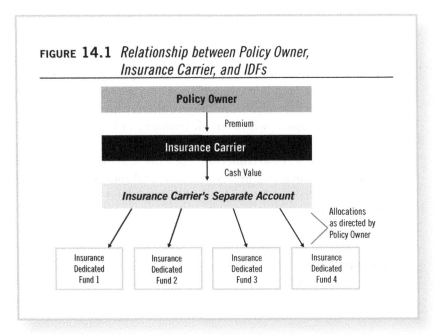

FIGURE 14.1 *Relationship between Policy Owner, Insurance Carrier, and IDFs*

Source: SALI Fund Services

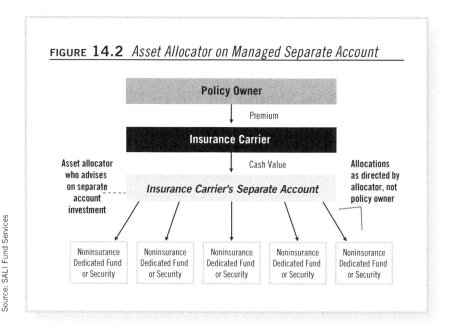

FIGURE **14.2** *Asset Allocator on Managed Separate Account*

structure, the insurance carrier hires an independent manager, the allocator, to manage the allocations within its separate account on behalf of the policy owner. The policy owner can direct the insurance carrier to allocate cash value to any approved allocator but cannot direct the allocator's investment selections in any way (see **FIGURE 14.2**).

From a compliance perspective, the main difference between the two strategies is the type of fund in which the insurance carrier's separate account ends up investing. With the IDF strategy, the insurance carrier is investing in a fund that accepts investment only from insurance carriers—an IDF. Under the allocator strategy, the insurance carrier is typically investing directly in funds that accept investment from noninsurance carrier investors—not an IDF. Although Revenue Ruling 2003-91 has deemed a properly structured and managed IDF structure to be compliant, there is still a material degree of uncertainty in the IRS's comfort with the allocator structure because of the carrier's resulting direct investment in noninsurance-dedicated funds. This issue is regularly debated, and the nuances on each side are beyond the scope of this chapter, but there is little debate that a properly structured IDF is the most compliant approach to this market.

An IDF can be structured as either a hedge fund or a fund of hedge funds. The vast majority of existing IDFs are structured as fund of hedge funds, but that doesn't mean this market has no appetite for single-manager hedge funds. Any single-manager hedge fund that's successful in raising capital directly from high-net-worth individuals or institutions should consider the opportunity of creating an IDF that would trade pari passu with one of its noninsurance funds.

Who Should Set Up an IDF?

The logic of why a significant percentage of qualified U.S. taxpayers should acquire private placement insurance or annuities funded by hedge funds may be compelling; nevertheless, hardly anyone in this market has profited from setting up an IDF—except for the policy owners. Not the carriers. Not the current IDFs. Not the intermediaries. As sensible as a low-cost, income tax–efficient life insurance or annuity program may sound, each transaction is still extremely complex and difficult to implement. But the market is moving toward simpler policy structures (see chapter 11) that will satisfy individuals with needs that are more typical. Nonetheless, before jumping in and creating an IDF, a manager needs to carefully consider how challenging it is to raise assets from high-net-worth individuals. One should not anticipate that if an IDF is built, new money will rain down. But if a manager already has strong relationships with sophisticated and productive distribution channels and is willing to do some work to help them orchestrate a life insurance or annuity distribution strategy tied to the manager's IDF, creating an IDF could be very helpful in setting the manager's business apart from others as well as providing a ready answer to any tax inefficiency in the investment strategy.

To maintain a belt-and-suspenders approach with regard to insurance rules and to reasonably dilute the manager's pass-through costs, a realistic distribution strategy should be in place that results in five to ten unrelated policy owners allocating at least $30 million in aggregate to the IDF. This will not happen on day one, but it should be realistic to expect it will happen within 12 to 18 months of launching the fund (see **FIGURE 14.3**).

So why hesitate? Why not just go ahead and create an IDF? It can't be too difficult, right? Wrong. It will be difficult and expensive if you're starting from scratch. A manager should plan on spending substantial hours becoming familiar with the domain of insurance and annuities, substantial amounts of money on legal fees to create the IDF structure and its offering documents, and significant time (and more money on legal fees) to negotiate and maintain relationships with insurance carriers. Outside legal fees typically run a minimum of $50,000, and many firms have spent more than $100,000. The opportunity cost of internal resources also needs to be factored in.

What makes the process so complex? Several hurdles separate the manager's decision to build from the realization of a funded (and hopefully profitable) IDF: investor control, diversification, liquidity, the subscrip-

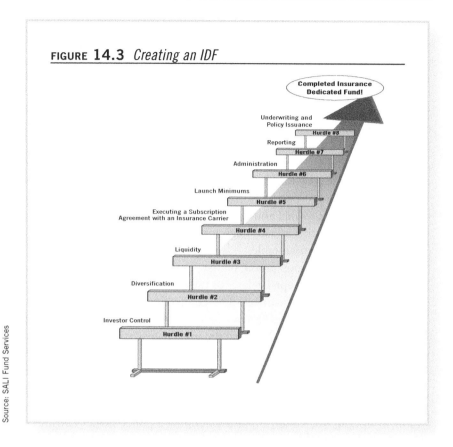

FIGURE **14.3** *Creating an IDF*

Source: SALI Fund Services

tion agreement, launch minimums, administration, reporting, and under-writing and policy issuance. Managers must consider all of these issues in advance and plan for ways to address them. Let's look at each one.

Investor Control

The business of getting a fund off the ground would be a lot easier if policy owners could simply buy a policy and allocate their cash value to their favorite hedge funds—basically maintaining full control over their cash value. Such control, however, would be a violation of the investor-control doctrine, which says policy owners may allocate only to IDFs.

The doctrine of investor control and its implications are discussed in more detail in chapter 12. But it's worth repeating here that the manager of an IDF must have full discretion over the investments and cannot al-low policy owners to influence investment decisions. The policy owner is supposed to be allocating to an IDF because of confidence in the IDF manager, not merely because of the specific investments that are going to be made.

For many would-be IDF managers, this is not a material concern. The idea of an investor controlling investment decisions in any way runs absolutely contrary to the way they operate. But in most circumstances, the agreements an IDF must execute with a carrier require IDF managers to take on a certain degree of liability for any actions with regard to inter-actions with policy owners—a liability that must be clearly understood. Appropriate controls need to be implemented at the IDF to avoid trigger-ing any liability.

Regulators designed these rules to prevent would-be IDF managers from generating fees by working with prospective policy owners to simply recreate an investment portfolio inside a tax-advantaged insurance or an-nuity wrapper that's owned and managed outside of insurance. Any man-ager contemplating this as a strategy for attracting assets to an IDF will find this hurdle insurmountable.

Perhaps a less obvious aspect of the investor-control doctrine—and one more difficult to accept—relates to the fact that an IDF's relationship to the policy owner is not direct. The connection is through the insur-ance carrier. There is no direct agreement between the policy owner and the IDF. Rather, the IDF is hired by the insurance carrier to represent an investment-allocation option to its policy owners. With very short notice, the insurance carrier can generally terminate its relationship with an IDF at any time. This is partly a result of the insurance carrier's desire to main-tain flexibility. But, just as important, a carrier is not offering any set in-vestment options as a condition of maintaining a policy owner's business. This disconnect is generally thought to be an important characteristic in complying with the investor-control doctrine. What is the significance of this exposure? It means an IDF manager can be fired and lose the fee income generated from policy owners that were attracted to the insurance policy in the first place. The ability to reconnect with those policy owners' allocations through another insurance policy at another carrier is a chal-lenging proposition that would require the manager to get hired by a new insurance carrier, the policy owner to qualify for the new policy at the new insurance carrier, and the policy owner to incur new acquisition fees for the new policy.

There is no way to fully avoid the risk of being fired by the carrier and losing a policy owner/investor base. But certain carriers will represent that they will limit their cause for termination to a list of factors that are largely under the manager's control. For example, the carrier will represent that it will fire the manager only if the manager has been found guilty of breaking a rule or regulation under which it's bound or if the manager violates the terms of its agreement with the carrier. As a result, the carrier cannot ter-minate a manager simply because it found another, more appealing one.

(For more on insurance-carrier relationships, see the section "Subscription Documents with an Insurance Carrier," page 241.)

Diversification

Although diversification is not a significant hurdle, regulations do require investments in at least five different securities, and they limit the percentage of the total fund assets invested in any one security or combination of securities may represent (see chapter 12). The good news for fund-of-hedge-fund managers is that pending regulations are almost certain to pass, clarifying that a hedge fund is deemed to be a security for purposes of diversification. That would mean any IDF that allocates to at least five underlying funds without any significant concentration meets the diversification requirements.

Specifically, an IDF must have the following minimum level of diversification:

❑ no more than 55 percent in any one security/fund
❑ no more than 70 percent in any two securities/funds
❑ no more than 80 percent in any three securities/funds
❑ no more than 90 percent in any four securities/funds

What obviously falls out of this math is that every IDF must have at least five different securities or funds, which is clearly not a problem for most would-be IDF managers. Cash and certain government securities are treated differently under these rules, generally allowing investment managers to have greater concentrations in such securities if required. (The diversification requirements are based on IRC § 817(h) and are discussed in chapter 12.)

So why is diversification a hurdle worth mentioning? It comes down to the responsibility of tracking and monitoring diversification. Because the policy owner and the insurance carrier have no way of ensuring that an IDF maintains compliance with the diversification standard under section 817(h), the IDF manager takes on full responsibility. The impact of an IDF's failing these standards is significant in that the contract allocating to a failed IDF can cease to be qualified as an insurance or annuity policy—forever—even if the diversification failure is corrected. An IDF manager should expect that the firm will have to take full responsibility for meeting this standard in its investment-management agreement with the insurance carrier.

Chapter 12 discusses a pending IRS ruling that permits an underlying hedge fund of an IDF to be treated as a single security and cannot be "looked through" for purposes of measuring compliance with section 817(h). As a result, an IDF that's structured as a fund of funds must have at least five underlying funds, each of which will generally be considered a single security for purposes of complying with section 817(h). An IDF manager should ensure that any agreement signed with an insurance carrier be structured to comply with these new regulations.

Liquidity

The less liquid the IDF is, the more flexibility the manager has in pursuing the investment strategy. But an IDF manager must plan for liquidity events. IDFs may be relatively illiquid when satisfying reallocation liquidity and may generally have lockups, irregular liquidity points, and long notice periods. But death/surrender liquidity can trip a manager up. Generally, insurance regulations require carriers to satisfy their obligations to beneficiaries of policies in short order and in cash when the insured dies or when policy owners surrender their policies. This is a hurdle for many.

Two considerations—marketing and compliance—are associated with liquidity. The marketing issue is pretty straightforward because generally the market for hedge fund strategies within life insurance and annuity policies is willing to accept the same liquidity terms from an IDF that the market outside of insurance accepts. So if a manager is planning on building an IDF based on a successful noninsurance-dedicated fund, there is no reason, for marketing purposes, not to offer the same liquidity parameters. Compliance is another story.

The compliance considerations stem from a complex and varied set of issues. Meeting the liquidity standards required by insurance-carrier investors has been one of the most difficult hurdles to overcome. These standards protect against two different events. The first occurs either when an insured on a life insurance policy or the measuring life on an annuity policy dies, or when the owner of a life insurance or annuity policy terminates a policy. Either one of these situations, referred to as forfeiture events, requires enhanced liquidity (typically mandating cash payouts within five months of the forfeiture event and a waiver of any lockup).

The second type of event, a reallocation event, is triggered when a policy owner instructs the insurance carrier to reallocate all or a portion of the cash value from an IDF to some other investment. Generally, this happens when reallocation to a different IDF is desired, but a policy owner's request to take a portion of the policy's cash value in the form of a withdrawal or loan can also trigger it. Insurance regulations often allow carriers to offer policy owners more restrictive liquidity in reallocation events than in forfeiture events. As such, forfeiture events are more stressful than reallocation events for the IDF manager.

It's tempting to ignore the risk of forfeiture events. One of the attractions to this market for many IDF managers is the lure of "sticky money" in insurance and annuity policies. Policy owners make their decision to own insurance or annuity policies based on long-term financial planning principals. Therefore, policy owners are not actively trading in and out of different policies, which would create a forfeiture event. In addition, life insurance policies often insure the policy owner and require the insured to medically qualify before the policy is issued. As a result, the average life insurance policy owner has a significantly lower chance of dying, and thereby creating a forfeiture event, than does the average noninsurance investor. Finally, the wise policy owner attempts to find liquidity through the policy only as a last resort since the policy owner will lose the tax-free compounding benefits on withdrawn assets. Despite the temptation, the stakes are high and the possibility of a forfeiture event is real, so a manager must plan wisely and address this complexity before launching an IDF.

Forfeitures would be a much simpler matter if there were one general set of insurance regulations, but such is not the case. Insurance carriers are regulated by state insurance departments. What's more, offshore carriers are regulated by the offshore jurisdiction in which the carrier is domiciled.

State regulations have two stipulations to which the carrier must conform: First, each carrier must be domiciled in just one state, which is referred to as its state of domicile. Second, each carrier must meet the requirements of the state in which products are offered. For example, consider a situation in which a carrier is domiciled in Delaware and offering a policy to a potential policy owner based in Connecticut. This policy will have to conform to certain rules of the state insurance departments in both Delaware and Connecticut.

It's difficult for an IDF to offer the liquidity required by the carrier to meet the generic state regulations in forfeiture events. Carriers under most jurisdictions are obligated to satisfy claims from forfeiture events in cash within three to five months of the notice of the event. Achieving such a level of liquidity in an IDF holding positions in underlying hedge funds or directly in sophisticated trading positions is often challenging for new IDF managers. The challenge is further exacerbated by the fact that new IDFs will likely receive an allocation from a very small number of policies, typically one—making the possibility of a 100 percent liquidity event very real. Also, new IDFs structured as a fund of hedge funds are making new allocations to underlying funds, which usually means they will be subject to an initial lockup. Unfortunately, current market activity is not substantial enough—even for the most successful IDFs—to rely on regular cash flows in and out of the fund to satisfy liquidity needs. But managers should take heart because there are solutions that can work for most IDFs.

The most basic solution is for a manager to design its IDF so that it offers its insurance-carrier investors enhanced liquidity should a forfeiture event occur. This solution works for some strategies that invest in liquid funds or securities, but often is not possible for hedge fund strategies.

A second solution is to find an alternative funding source for the liquidity. In essence, the manager would either self-fund the liquidity or open up a third-party credit line to create it. The IDF manager using this strategy is required to take the market risk on the portion of the portfolio that's paid out between the time the manager satisfies the redemption request from the insurance carrier in cash and the time the underlying IDF positions are liquidated to pay down the credit line.

Another way of addressing liquidity is for insurance carriers to ask the state insurance departments for exceptions to the general liquidity requirements in forfeiture events. Certain states have been willing to issue such exceptions in the form of riders to the life insurance or annuity policy. Assuming the policy owner acknowledges acceptance of such a rider, it can be an elegant solution. Certain states, however, will not agree to such exceptions, and as a result, illiquid IDFs cannot be offered there. When a prospective policy owner wishes to buy a policy, they sometimes set up a third-party ownership vehicle, often a trust, in a state that allows such liquidity flexibility. Among other potential advantages, this has the effect of giving the policy owner the benefit of a broader range of potential investment options within the policy.

Offshore, the situation is more straightforward in that the offshore jurisdictions generally have very lenient requirements for carriers in terms of satisfying both forfeiture events and reallocation events. This flexibility partially accounts for the early success of offshore transactions compared to onshore transactions (see chapter 17). So it follows that another strategy for an IDF manager struggling with meeting the liquidity requirements of insurance regulations is to limit investors to offshore carriers. But this limitation would leave out a significant segment of the emerging market for their product. Although there are material advantages to owning insurance or annuity policies offshore, certain policy owners will not be willing to go through the time, expense, or complexity of executing an offshore policy.

One liquidity strategy that seems to have fallen out of favor is for IDFs to satisfy liquidity requirements through a distribution of assets, often referred to as "in kind" distributions. The IDF manager faced with satisfying the liquidity requirements of a forfeiture event simply transfers interests in the IDF's underlying investments to the insurance carrier, which in turn transfers such interests to the owner or beneficiary of the insurance or annuity policy. More recent guidance from the IRS has caused many carriers to believe that satisfying its obligations in any form other than cash to be considered aggressive within the context of the investor-control doctrine and insurance regulations. As a result, this approach is unlikely to be a realistic solution to the liquidity issues.

Subscription Documents with an Insurance Carrier

Subscription documents are generally the most challenging hurdle to overcome. How can a manager efficiently become enough of an insurance expert to operate responsibly in this space? What does the manager have to do differently to develop its IDF structure and its offering documents? How can the manager find outside counsel with real experience in this area? How can the manager effectively wade through the bureaucracy of a large insurance carrier?

Many would-be IDF managers have spent considerable time, energy, and money trying to create the finished product. But the reality is that very few IDFs actually exist relative to the total hedge fund universe. The typical reasons for this are twofold:

Communication challenges. A substantial gap in domain expertise exists between the insurance carrier staff and the would-be IDF manager. The typical insurance carrier is a very large company, with all the bureaucracy inherent in such an organization; a would-be IDF manager is usually part of a much smaller, entrepreneurial organization. The gap is not insurmountable. Many carriers committed to this market have invested significantly to build a well-trained and effective staff prepared to work with new IDFs. Still, the learning curve can be frustrating for the manager, and this has certainly been the case with many IDFs that have fallen off track.

Motivation. The task of starting an IDF is extremely difficult when there is no policy owner eagerly awaiting the formation of the IDF and prepared to allocate capital sufficient to launch and seed the new fund. Since building an IDF has not been a means for fund managers to attract new capital without a substantial marketing effort, the manager typically has a hard time prioritizing the completion of the IDF until a committed policy owner is in the pipeline. And the staffing in most carriers' private placement life and annuity departments is relatively sparse. Often, members of the staff have multiple responsibilities that go well beyond adding new IDFs. The key to overcoming these two hurdles lies primarily in organizing a strategy that starts with a true business plan for both creating and marketing the IDF. The manager should ensure its distribution strategy is matched up with a compatible carrier. It's important to know the people at the carrier and to gain a basic understanding of their operating platform and business objectives. Next, the manager needs to communicate both its marketing strategy and fund differentiation.

Working with the carrier, the manager should build a very specific development and implementation timeline with clearly designated objectives, target dates, and responsible parties. For best results, attack the most challenging issues first, keep the momentum going by holding weekly meetings with the carrier during the development phase, and focus on completing weekly deliverables. This requires having a champion at the manager's firm to lead the initiative.

If a manager chooses to engage outside counsel to prepare its offering documents, working with a law firm that has completed IDFs, preferably with the same carrier, is far more efficient. Speaking to the law firm's other IDF managers to ensure basic competency is time well spent. Once a team has been assembled and contact made with a carrier, the specifics of building the IDF are in the offing.

Due diligence. Every carrier will perform due diligence on a prospective IDF manager. The level and nature of the due diligence varies widely and will consist of both initial and ongoing requirements. Due diligence is an excellent place to get the details on the table early on, because this is a point where the relationship can break down. At the very least, the manager will have to complete a questionnaire. At most, the manager will have to undergo on-site visits by either the carrier's investment team or a specialist that reports to the team. In some cases, carriers can demand a level of transparency and reporting requirements that may be either uncomfortable or impossible for the manager to meet.

The carriers seek through their due diligence to avoid reputation risk and, in some cases, avoid conflict with any internal asset managers that may be part of the insurance carrier's existing IDF portfolio. As the market for hedge fund managers inside insurance has matured, the carriers have also attempted to become increasingly familiar with the nuances of the hedge funds on their platform so as to better assist their distribution partners and policy owners in distinguishing one IDF from another. If a prospective IDF manager is not distinctive from other managers already on the platform, the carrier may choose not to move forward.

Many carriers focus due diligence primarily on noninvestment issues, such as management experience, assets under management, public records searches for known rules violations, operational infrastructure, technology, and redundancy. Certain carriers extend themselves much more broadly, into the area of investment due diligence—wanting to know exactly how the managers achieve their returns.

Ongoing due diligence typically consists of an informal dialogue, coupled with whatever reporting the carrier requires. It may also include annual updates to the carrier's due diligence file, and in some cases, an annual on-site visit by the carrier.

It is important to gain a precise understanding of the nature of the carrier's due diligence requirements up front. If they're not acceptable, move on to another carrier.

Creating the new legal entity. IDF managers use both limited partnerships and limited liability companies. Most are formed in Delaware, and although it's counterintuitive, the same fund, if properly structured, can be used to manage money from multiple contracts, issued on multiple policy structures (for example, both life insurance and annuities), issued in multiple jurisdictions (including both onshore and 953d qualified offshore carriers), and through multiple insurance carriers. So if an IDF is set up properly, the manager should be able to grow and evolve substantially over time without having to create additional IDFs (see **FIGURE 14.4**).

Creating the legal offering documents. The documents used to offer the IDF are very similar to those used with noninsurance dedicated funds. They include the offering memorandum (typically referred to as a private placement memorandum—PPM), a limited partnership agreement, and subscription documents. The limited partner in the IDF is the insurance carrier, not the policy owner. So very few LPs subscribe, but each can provide assets to manage from several different policy owners.

In naming the IDF, it's best to leverage the manager's name and reputation; some managers identify the IDF for its intended purpose (for example, the XYZ Insurance Fund).

Certain carriers subscribe to the IDF using the firm's standard subscription document. Others want to have more control over the terms of the relationship and require the use of the carrier's subscription document, typically referred to as a participation agreement. This document generally governs all others; review its terms very carefully to understand the manager's obligations. The key terms to consider in the manager's relationship with the carrier involve liquidity, investor control and diversification responsibility, qualification of life insurance and annuities, and qualification of policy owners. The carriers require specific liquidity terms to meet their obligations under the insurance regulations. These legal documents define the liquidity terms (see the section on "Defining the liquidity terms," page 246).

Investor control and diversification responsibility need significant review. In these documents, the parties represent how they will take responsibility for these two very critical standards. Certain carriers will require the IDF manager to indemnify the carrier against failure to meet these standards. The manager must know exactly what its responsibilities are in this area and establish the appropriate internal controls to meet such standards.

A manager would expect the carrier to ensure that the standard structural regulations of life insurance and annuities are met, including

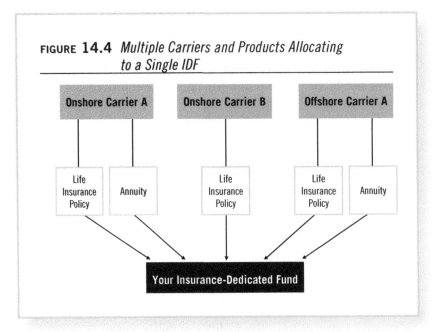

FIGURE **14.4** *Multiple Carriers and Products Allocating to a Single IDF*

Source: SALI Fund Services

making certain that appropriate insurance risk and other terms exist in the contract so that it qualifies as insurance. If a carrier fails to structure a policy properly and the policy owner has an unexpected negative result, the manager will want it understood that the IDF manager is not at fault. In addition, the manager will also expect the carrier to take responsibility for qualifying the policy owners who make allocations to the IDF as either qualified purchasers or accredited investors. Since the IDF manager will have no direct relationship with the policy owners, it's impossible for the manager to take responsibility for that.

Another aspect of qualification rests on the policy owner's and the advisory team's understanding of the role that the manager's IDF will play in the portfolio (see chapter 8). One obvious means of minimizing the number of reallocations mentioned earlier is to have the carrier affirm that the policy owner attests to reading the offering documents and initialing the pages describing the IDF's investment policy, practices, and risk/ reward expectation. The manager should work with its counsel to specify risk factors in the IDF. These risk factors should include commentary on investor control and the type of behavior that's required to avoid its negative impact. They should also include a discussion of the diversification requirements under section 817(h).

There are other documents related to the life insurance or annuity transaction that the manager probably won't need to be concerned with if the core IDF documents are structured properly. These include the offering documents for the policy, the marketing materials for the policy, illustrations of the policy performance and pricing, the forms the prospective policy owner uses to apply for the policy, and the policy contract itself. Although the manager should discuss them with its counsel, these documents are reviewed extensively, often by state insurance departments, and are not likely to hinder the manager's relationship with its investor, the insurance carrier.

Setting the fee schedule. IDF managers have pursued all the traditional ways of charging fees on hedge fund strategies, from a simple asset-based management fee to asset-based management fees plus a performance fee, with or without a high-water mark, and some have also added hurdle rates. Whatever the final fee schedule, setting one in an IDF involves two considerations: marketing and administration.

To cover the increased costs of managing and marketing an IDF, managers sometimes choose to charge more for their IDF than they would for the noninsurance product. The increased costs can result from the added complexity of operating an IDF and the fee-sharing arrangements many IDF managers use to encourage carriers and/or their agents to make allocations. Managers who are considering charging more for their IDFs should review the following questions:

❑ How comfortable is the manager in charging more for one fund than another?

❑ Is the manager going to need new methods of distribution or will existing distribution relationships suffice?

❑ Will the market tolerate higher fees in the IDF?

A word of caution: although the economic proposition of owning tax-inefficient investment strategies through PPLI or annuity programs is extraordinarily compelling, the manager must not fall under any illusions that fat margins will result. Policy owners and their advisory teams represent some of the most sophisticated purchasers in any market and any attempt to enhance margins will be quickly negotiated away.

The second consideration is fee administration, particularly with regard to the fair allocation of performance fees. If a manager charges a performance fee, it's a charge to its investor, the insurance carrier. The carrier must then allocate this fee fairly among its policy owners. If the carrier has only one policy owner, this is not an issue. But consider the following example: A carrier has an investment in an IDF on January 1 on behalf of one policy owner, Policy owner A. The manager delivers 15 percent year-to-date performance through November 31. On December 1, a second policy owner, Policy owner B, allocates money to the same IDF. For this portion of the year, the IDF's returns are negative 2 percent and the full-year return ends up at 13 percent. So the manager charges its 10 percent performance fee, or 1.3 percent, against the carrier's investment balance. Let's assume that the carrier allocates this charge equally based on its policy owners' account balances, and Policy owners A and B both have the same cash value. Policy owner A would pay 0.65 percent in performance for year-to-date performance of 13 percent—a better deal than expected. But Policy owner B would pay the same, 0.65 percent in performance for year-to-date performance of negative 2 percent, certainly not what would have been expected. So if the manager is going to charge a performance fee in its IDF, it's important to understand the carrier's performance fee allocation methods.

The range of solutions used includes everything from carriers' administering performance fees fairly by building such functionality into their own administration systems, to IDFs taking on that responsibility and reporting to carriers on how to administer the fees, to IDFs and carriers allowing the inequity to exist—typically after disclosing it as a risk factor of the fund. Another solution, pursued by certain funds, includes simply converting the expected performance fee to an asset-based management fee.

Determine the fee-sharing strategy. Certain carriers may require the manager to share fees for its IDF in exchange for offering it as an investment option within their policies. Other third-party distributors, such as insurance agents focusing on this market, may promote the IDF more aggressively to clients if the manager shares a portion of the fees with them. Indeed, a fee-sharing program makes perfect economic sense given the inability of the manager to work directly with the policy owner and needing a long-term policy service relationship. The insurance adviser effectively becomes the eyes and ears of the manager for its PPLI client base.

To date, the offer of fee sharing has not created a windfall of new assets under management for any IDF. Assets for IDFs have been raised mainly through the same methods managers are using outside of insurance products, whether this means using internal resources at the fund or through third-party relationships with private banks, broker-dealers, or registered investment advisers. Although insurance agents are playing a vital role in actually getting private placement programs designed, implemented, and serviced successfully, they have been, with rare exceptions, unable to steer their clients into one fund or the other.

Defining the liquidity terms. A most difficult hurdle to clear is providing the carrier with appropriate liquidity in the event of the need to satisfy claims of a policy owner surrendering a contract or the beneficiaries expecting the contractual death benefit. The manager needs to remain vigilant in managing to the policy's required liquidity. The terms that must be considered for liquidity include:

❑ *Lockup.* Typically this is set at one year, with a waiver in the event of policy surrender or death of an insured. Setting it any longer than one year or not offering the waiver may significantly reduce the jurisdictions where the IDF may be offered.

❑ *Liquidity intervals.* Typically, withdrawals are allowed quarterly with no waiver. They may be set less frequently without a significant impact on the jurisdiction availability if a waiver is offered.

❑ *Liquidity notice period.* This period is generally set at 60–90 days. Again, it may be set at longer intervals without a significant impact on the jurisdiction availability if a waiver is offered.

The manager must also consider whether its investment minimums and lockup terms should apply to the investor (the insurance carrier) or the beneficial owner of the investment (the policy owner). Insurance carriers will often negotiate for the terms to apply to them, so that once they've met the minimum and cleared the lockup, subsequent policy owners desiring to make an initial allocation are not subject to the manager's initial allocation minimum, but rather to the often lower subsequent minimum-allocation requirement. Carriers also use this strategy to avoid being subject to any lockups once the initial investment lockup is cleared.

Although changing the minimum allocation may be fine, consider the implications of giving investors access to investment expertise at lower investment minimums—and without lockups inside insurance—than those offered outside insurance. For some managers, this is an unacceptable compromise.

Understanding the budget. The manager setting up an IDF should expect to spend at least $50,000 in hard costs, primarily legal fees, and significant internal opportunity costs before the first allocation is accepted. Many IDFs spend substantially more than this before crossing the finish line. To a large extent, the balance between hard costs and opportunity costs depends on the manager's delegation of work to outside counsel. If internal staff works with the carrier and outside counsel drafts and reviews documents, the hard costs will be lower. The opportunity costs will still be significant. Becoming comfortable with the rules of managing money for insurance companies takes significant time and energy. Of course, the manager can delegate the work to outside counsel, but the hard costs then go up. That's why the manager must understand the marketing opportunities for its IDF before committing the time and money required launch it.

Launch Minimums

Once the manager has formed and integrated its IDF with at least one carrier, it's time to launch the fund. This requires that the manager find enough seed capital to run its strategy. Whether structured as a fund of funds or a single-manager fund, the manager will need at least enough initial capital to own five securities or funds, so that the fund complies with the IRC § 817(h) diversification regulations. It is uncertain whether an IDF's general partner, which is typically not an insurance carrier, can invest capital to launch a fund without potentially tainting its insurance-dedicated status. Also, principals of the IDF who may have the capital to purchase a policy and allocate their cash value to their own IDF to provide the launch capital would generally be violating investor-control rules with such an allocation. As a result, meeting the launch minimum typically requires a substantial allocation from the initial policy owner.

IDFs structured as fund of funds have launched with as little as $1 million, requiring the fund manager to negotiate exceptions to the typical minimums of the underlying funds. Other IDF managers refuse to launch with less than $15 million because of concern that the strategy will not achieve the required risk diversification and breadth of investment exposure. In the end, the required minimum to launch an IDF is the manager's decision.

Clearly, the tricky part of getting past the launch hurdle is lining up the first policy owner and getting an allocation of the required amount of capital. Many insurance programs are funded over several years, so even if a policy owner is committing $10 million to the program, the premiums may be paid in over time, for example only $2.5 million per year for four years. As a further complication, the policy owner may believe it's best to allocate to more than one manager, which could further reduce the initial capital seen from the first premium. It's the classic chicken-and-egg dilemma. Can a manager justify the time and energy to set up its IDF not knowing how it will initially be funded? On the other hand, how can you expect a policy owner to commit to an allocation if the manager does not have an official offering that's approved on at least one carrier platform? There is no magic answer. The best strategy is to build a fund as cost efficiently as possible, while never losing focus on nurturing the marketing strategy.

Another harsh reality is that IDFs are often fully formed in terms of legal structure, offering documents, and the conceptual terms of the relationship with the insurance carrier but are never truly up and running—meaning executing subscription documents with the carrier—until a policy owner wants to allocate to the IDF. It's at that magic moment that the parties involved suddenly pull together and push themselves across the finish line.

Administration

The administration of an IDF is similar in most respects to that of a non-insurance fund. Some areas, however, differ materially.

Coordination of new money coming from the carrier. Key steps need to be covered between the point at which a policy owner confirms an intention to allocate to a fund and the actual allocation. This process is discussed in greater detail in the "Underwriting and Policy Issuance" section, page 253, and should be clearly understood by the IDF's administrative staff. The manager will need to be prepared to have people on its staff who are familiar with this process and can work closely with the carriers to ensure the money flows are received from the carrier within a time frame that allows an allocation to the underlying investments timely enough to meet the policy owner's expectations.

Investor-control representations and monitoring. The manager needs to represent, generally quarterly, to the insurance carrier that the investor-control doctrine has not been violated. Administratively, it's a simple matter of signing a form. But the appropriate internal controls to prevent actual violations from occurring must be put in place in advance. This means that the manager must not allow any of the policy owners allocating to its IDF to have any influence on the management of the IDF's investment strategy or allocations. Beyond this, there are several nuances related to communication and transparency that need to be reviewed with counsel and the insurance carrier to ensure compliance.

Diversification representations and monitoring. The manager must represent to the insurance-carrier investors at the end of each calendar quarter that the IDF meets the diversification requirements of section 817(h). The form used for this representation will vary from carrier to carrier. On the simpler end of the spectrum, a signed form representing that the manager is diversified will meet the carrier's requirements. In other words, the manager's confirmation is good enough for the carrier to be assured that it's meeting the required fiduciary responsibility. Other carriers may require enough transparency to actually prove the manager is diversified. The manager should seek to understand these requirements in the early stages of its discussions with a carrier to ensure that the manager of a fund of funds can exact appropriate compliance from the underlying funds.

In the event that the fund does not meet the diversification test, all may not be lost. The code provides two potential outs. The first is to fix the noncompliance within 30 days of the end of the calendar quarter. This may or may not be feasible, depending on the liquidity provisions of the manager's investments. If the IDF is structured as a fund of funds, this is important to remember when negotiating terms with the underlying funds. The manager may want to have a side letter that provides enhanced liquidity if the survival of the IDF is at stake. The second out is that the code states that no IDF shall fail diversification if market fluctuations are the cause of the diversification failure. Therefore, the primary solution is to not allocate outside of the parameters allowed by section 817(h). Be sure to set up administrative procedures with the internal staff that would prevent such an allocation mistake from occurring.

Ongoing due diligence and transparency. All carriers conduct some form of ongoing due diligence monitoring to meet their fiduciary responsibilities. Like initial due diligence, the form and depth of this process varies from carrier to carrier, and it pays for the manager to understand this up front and ensure its ability and willingness to support the process.

Accounting/valuation timing. Insurance carriers are generally required by regulators to report values to policy owners regularly. This can take the form of a policy statement delivered to policy owners within a given time frame after the end of each month. As a result, most IDFs are required to report values to the insurance carrier limited partners within the first 10 to 20 days of the month. Reasonable estimates are generally acceptable as long as the practice is disclosed in the offering materials. The manager must ensure its ability to meet the requirements of the carriers.

The form in which the carrier requires valuations varies. Some carriers may ask for a simple account balance for the aggregate portfolio. Others may want the account balance tracked by the policy owner. Still others may want the manager to report unit values each month. Most carriers are relatively flexible, but it pays to understand the requirements up front and ensure that a process is in place to comply.

Tracking of minimums, lockups, and allocation of performance fees. If the manager decides to track these items by policy owner, the required administration system must be set up to track the policy owners as subinvestors.

Custody issues. Regulations now make this a broader issue than just insurance, but the manager should understand any custody requirements that the carrier and/or regulators have. It's been a challenge for many fund of funds to find qualifying custodians to support operations.

Errors and omission (E&O) insurance coverage. Certain carriers require that the manager acquire and maintain a certain amount of E&O insurance coverage, and in some cases, to name the IDF as the direct beneficiary. This is an important point to explore early in the process.

Paying insurance policy fees. Insurance and annuity policies have two types of fees: upfront fees and ongoing fees. The upfront fees are always deducted from premiums paid into the policy and cover items like sales loads, premium taxes, and other distribution charges. Ongoing fees cover any mortality risk as well as the carrier's asset-based fee requirements, typically referred to as M&E fees. Together, these two fees can range from 50 to 100 basis points per year, but they may be higher in the early years and will often be collected by the carrier quarterly. IDF managers should have no great concern about the upfront fees, although the fees will slightly reduce the net amount of investable assets. But the manager does need to understand how the carrier funds its ongoing fees. Two options exist: (1) setting aside 12–24 months worth of fees in a separate money market fund not affiliated with the IDF, to be drawn down as required; or (2) investing fully into the IDF fund and getting enhanced quarterly liquidity from the manager to pay the carrier's stated fees. The difference to the policy owner in the two alternatives should not be material. The manager should simply know which of the two methods the carrier uses and set up the appropriate processes ahead of time. The manager and the carrier must avoid a call for a fee payment just after the manager invested in a number of illiquid positions.

Tax returns. Even though the carrier should not be required to pay taxes on the gains experienced in the IDF fund, the carrier will need a schedule K-1 (for its tax reporting).

Audit. The IDF must be audited annually.

Offshore funds. Offshore funds are a hotly debated topic for IDFs structured as funds of funds. Can a Delaware-based IDF invest in an offshore fund? Many carriers prohibit IDFs from doing so on the grounds that it's not entirely clear that earnings from offshore funds will enjoy the tax benefits policy owners expect. Other carriers allow the investments, believing that such earnings will be protected inside insurance. If a manager expects such investing to be part of the fund, the help of competent counsel is essential before the IDF's implementation. Such a risk must be disclosed in the offering materials.

Side letters with underlying funds. If the manager is structuring an IDF as a fund of funds, the manager's obligations to the carrier must be established in turn with the underlying funds. Side-letter examples include: valuation timing, enhanced liquidity in the event of surrender or death, and transparency of the fund's holdings. It is vital that this step be accomplished early in the implementation process.

Getting into closed underlying funds. If the IDF is structured as a fund of funds, the manager should understand that because the IDF is a new legal entity, it requires a new subscription to the target underlying funds. It's not a foregone conclusion that the IDF will gain access to these funds. This hurdle often prevents fund of fund managers from creating an IDF clone of a noninsurance fund of funds.

Understanding the "slot" issue. As a Regulation D offering, the IDF provides for 99 accredited and 499 qualified purchaser slots. Although the number of slots a carrier takes is not entirely clear, the best approach is to count each policy that makes an allocation to an IDF as an investor. To a large extent, the counting methodology depends on how the carrier sets up each policy's separate account. This issue should be discussed with competent counsel and the insurance carrier to understand any limitations that may affect compliance with Regulation D.

For IDFs structured as fund of funds, a corollary issue is the question of how many slots the IDF counts to the underlying funds. Generally, this should be considered in the same way inside insurance as it is outside insurance. In other words, if more than 40 percent of an IDF's assets are allocated to an underlying fund, the manager must look through the IDF to count the investors. This could include looking through the insurance carrier to the policy owners for determination of a count. Under the Investment Company Act of 1940, assuming no single underlying fund receives an allocation greater than 40 percent of the IDF's total capital and the IDF does not represent more than 10 percent of the underlying fund's total capital, the IDF should count as one investor. Again, this is an area that should be discussed with competent counsel to fully understand the nuances of the rules.

Section 3(c)(1) vs. section 3(c)(7) exemption under the Investment Company Act of 1940. The formation of the IDF as a 3(c)(1) fund or a 3(c)(7) fund should be determined in tandem with the development of the marketing strategy. The pluses and minuses of each are the same inside insurance as they are outside, and the manager should be aware that carriers can generally invest in either structure with no problem.

Reporting

Reporting is not just about sharing values with the carriers; it's about communication with the carrier's policy owners. The safe harbor here, as defined by IRS Revenue Ruling 2003-91, is to have no communication. This is often not practical and probably not required for compliance. But any time the manager veers from the safe harbor as defined by the IRS, there is some compliance risk so it's worth spending time and energy with experienced counsel to understand the communication protocol guidelines. The guidelines should be in writing, and internal personnel should commit to them. As with many tax issues, the actual outcome will depend on facts and circumstances and the manager will want to ensure that a good-faith effort to comply with the rules was made. At the very least, the manager is expected to communicate with the carrier and, in addition to the monthly value reports, an investment narrative is customary quarterly, semiannually, or annually. The carrier may pass this along to its policy owners to keep them informed.

Underwriting and Policy Issuance

Before a new policy owner can make an allocation to the IDF, a new life insurance or annuity policy is required. To avoid frustration down the road, the manager needs to understand this process and its complexity. Unlike marketing outside of the insurance domain, the work is not entirely over once an investor commits to invest. The investor must then get a policy in force and properly instruct the carrier to allocate the premium. The main decision points a policy owner will need to make during the underwriting process break down as follows:

- ❑ Choose an agent.
- ❑ Choose a carrier.
- ❑ Choose a life insurance or annuity policy.
- ❑ Determine the appropriate ownership structure for the policy.
- ❑ Understand and finalize the pricing of the insurance program.
- ❑ Define the funding strategy (single pay versus multipay).
- ❑ Define the policy structure (MEC versus nonMEC).
- ❑ If using life insurance, the insured on the policy will need to complete underwriting, and the carrier will need to assemble the required amount of insurance through its own risk capacity and from reinsurance carriers.
- ❑ The policy will need to be issued and funded.
- ❑ Any free-look period required by state regulators will need to be either waived or satisfied. (Note that most insurance and annuity policies have a free-look period that lasts between 10 and 30 days. During the free-look period, policy owners can review their policies and ask for the return of 100 percent of the premiums if they're dissatisfied. Given the obligation this puts on the carrier, the policy owner's premiums are allocated to a money market fund during this time. Certain carriers give their policy owners the option to waive their rights under the free-look provision and, as a result, get their cash value allocated to an IDF sooner.)
- ❑ The policy owner needs to formally instruct the carrier to allocate the premium to the manager's IDF using the carrier's forms.

When all these steps are completed, the investing can truly begin. Part of the marketing strategy should include gaining a clear understanding of the responsibilities for managing the underwriting and issuance process. A PPLI transaction may never close if it's not actively and properly managed by a competent insurance professional.

Marketing

An IDF can't be built without a well-defined and realistic marketing strategy. Creating and managing an IDF is clearly not without its cost and complexity. If the manager is not rewarded with meaningful assets, it will be a disheartening, dead-end experience. But why doesn't money just rain down on the IDFs? Is it because the life insurance or annuity policies are too expensive? They're not. Or because the existing IDFs lack quality? They don't. Do the funds lack competitive return histories? No. The IRS is likewise blameless, having blessed this structure. As for investors, the benefits are obvious. The value proposition is as powerful as any investment vehicle available.

The reason money is not pouring into most IDFs is that the right marketing strategy is not in place. For starters, finding the right strategy means tapping into the same distribution channels managers use to raise assets for noninsurance funds. But these traditional distribution channels by themselves are unlikely to provide the desired boost for setting up an IDF. It's highly uncommon for traditional hedge fund distributors to feel comfortable with the intricacies of life insurance or annuities. Most managers and their typical distribution channels are hesitant to bring forward any products, services, or ideas that might chip away at their expert reputation.

So does this mean that a manager should turn to the traditional insurance distributors who serve the segment of the market that could allocate meaningful capital to its IDF? This option has been tried and for the most part has been unsuccessful. Insurance professionals who serve this segment of the market are typically highly specialized, and clients do not view them as having the expertise required to suggest hedge fund managers. In fact, many professionals are reluctant to even bring up the subject for fear that it might signal to the client that their focus is drifting away from insurance.

The answer lies in orchestrating a partnership between the hedge fund distributors and quality life insurance agents. To have confidence in a distribution strategy, the manager will need to have investment advisers who've proved they're capable of raising assets and insurance experts who've proved they're capable of closing, implementing, and servicing these PPLI and annuity transactions. Creating a distribution partnership between these two groups that's focused on a manager's IDF is the single most effective way to maximize the chances of successfully attracting new assets to an IDF.

There is a material difference in complexity between life insurance and annuities. A manager's traditional distribution relationships may feel far more comfortable bringing the annuity product attached to its IDF to their client base. Private placement annuities are generally very efficiently priced and require no underwriting. Although they initially offer the tax-deferral advantages of life insurance, a key difference emerges in terms of the policy owner's access to the money in the future. Policy owners who access their cash value in an annuity before age 59½ generally pay a penalty tax on the gain. Even after age 59½, they pay ordinary income tax on a part of the distributions they receive. Life insurance, on the other hand, offers much more tax-efficient access to the cash value at any age. So annuities are not right for everyone, but they've proved to be a tremendously popular product with certain distributors in private banks, brokerage firms, broker-dealers, and other investment-advisory firms. This strategy may not be right for every manager, but a detailed marketing plan that lays out the responsibility for attracting assets to an IDF is essential.

Many IDFs have begun offering financial incentives to their distribution partners. This typically is achieved by offering some form of a fee-sharing arrangement and is often funneled through the insurance carrier. Before offering these types of incentives, the manager must make certain that the compliance and disclosure considerations ensure that the money flows to the right parties without violating any securities or insurance regulations.

Certain tools have become standard in helping to attract policy owner allocations to IDFs:

❑ *The offering memorandum.* This memorandum is a requirement and gives prospective policy owners and their advisers a technical understanding of the IDF.

❑ *Fact sheet.* This standard one-page, front-and-back piece highlights the IDF's return history, other performance measurements, and general terms. Many fact sheets in the IDF market are based on pro forma returns, given that most IDFs are newly funded entities.

❑ *Fund brochure.* This piece, typically a multipage overview and more reader friendly than the offering memorandum, contains all the data in the fact sheet and gives the prospective policy owner a clear idea of how the IDF creates value and is different from other IDFs.

A manager can set up an IDF to include many of the bells and whistles that noninsurance funds are using to differentiate themselves from the competition, including leverage, principal-protection programs, and stable-value programs. Implementing these programs is considerably more complex because they generally involve an outside banking relationship and require approval from the carrier. But this complexity is not insurmountable and should be considered under the right circumstances.

The Outsource Alternative

Administration platforms run by third parties are designed to help hedge fund and fund-of-hedge-fund managers more efficiently create IDFs. They create the insurance-dedicated fund vehicle, set up the relationships with the carriers as well as all of the required administrative infrastructure, and hire the manager to do the one thing the administrator can't do—manage the IDF's investment strategy. In terms of time and money, this may be a more effective and efficient way for a manager to create an IDF. If the PPLI market proves to be a highly successful strategy, the process can be done in house at a later date.

OVER THE YEARS, many traditional investment-management firms have attracted significant assets under management by managing money for the policy owners of insurance carriers. The Internal Revenue Service rulings of 2003 gave substantial clarity on how nontraditional investment-management firms can accomplish the same result. In fact, the benefits of combining tax-inefficient hedge fund returns with insurance and annuity policies are most advantageous. A properly structured insurance-dedicated fund, thoughtfully implemented and combined with a realistic, proactive marketing strategy, can help nontraditional investment-management firms capture a meaningful piece of this emerging market.

CHAPTER 15

Underwriting the Policy

MIKE CHONG AND ANNE MELISSA DOWLING

The charges associated with providing a death benefit under a private placement life insurance (PPLI) policy are the most significant costs a policyholder will incur. Underwriting determines the exact price an individual will pay for this coverage. Although some advisers emphasize the separate account in PPLI, the policy is basically designed to provide a death benefit to the policy beneficiaries. A PPLI policy's net amount at risk, or term insurance, is a significant product benefit and constitutes a significant portion of the product's overall cost. Even if the policyholder wishes to minimize the net amount at risk as much as possible, section 7702 of the Internal Revenue Code (IRC) requires a minimum net amount at risk under the policy based on the age, sex, and underwriting classification of the insured. For example, if the insured is age 40 or younger, the IRC requires the net amount at risk to be at least 250 percent of the policy's surrender value. Stated another way, the net amount at risk is a minimum of two and one-half times the policy's separate-account value. Many policyholders establish an insurance plan (such as a nonmodified endowment contract) that calls for much higher levels of risk.

What Is Underwriting?

Underwriting determines the mortality risk charges assessed under each individual's PPLI policy. The underwriting process for life insurance is similar to the underwriting that occurs for auto insurance. For example, auto insurance premiums are set according to an individual's driving history and safety record. Drivers with safe driving records pay lower premiums. Drivers with multiple speeding tickets or auto accidents are considered risky and are charged higher premiums because there is a higher risk that those drivers will require policy benefits from the insurance company in the near future. A PPLI policy's mortality risk charges are calculated much the same way. The mortality risk charges are based on the degree of risk (life expectancy) the insured presents to the insurance carrier. The shorter the insured's life expectancy, the greater the risk and the higher the mortality risk charges will be. The longer the insured's life expectancy, the smaller the risk and the lower the mortality risk charges will be. Underwriting is simply the insurance carrier's process of accurately assessing the medical and financial risk presented by the proposed insured.

Underwriting Rate Classifications

Most PPLI policies are sold on a full underwriting basis. Full underwriting means that the insurer will conduct thorough research to determine the appropriate risk category for the proposed insured. The means and methods of full underwriting will be discussed later in this chapter.

Through the underwriting process, the insurance company determines whether the proposed insured can be offered preferred, standard, or substandard (rated) mortality risk rates under the PPLI policy or whether the risk is uninsurable. Although this example assumes three rate classes under the policy (that is, preferred, standard, and substandard), in reality an insurance company may offer a single rate class or a large number of rate classes under a single PPLI product.

The method and type of underwriting an insurer uses for a life insurance policy is related to the number of rate classes maintained for that particular policy. If a single rate class is used, the insurer may use a simple series of questions. If multiple rate classes are used, then the insurer may use a more comprehensive set of underwriting tools to facilitate meaningful distinctions in the current and prospective health of the proposed insured.

Insurance companies generally use three underwriting methods: guaranteed-issue underwriting, simplified-issue underwriting, and full underwriting. Guaranteed-issue underwriting is usually associated with policies using a single rate class. Simplified-issue underwriting is normally associated with policies using two rate classes. Full underwriting is usually associated with policies using multiple rate classes.

A guaranteed-issue policy should not be confused with a policy sold on a guaranteed-to-issue basis. Under a guaranteed-to-issue policy, the insurer guarantees to provide insurance to all applicants. Under a guaranteed-issue policy, a potential customer is still subject to some underwriting. A guaranteed-issue policy may use underwriting in the form of certain questions related to the insured's employment and disability. This is the simplest form of underwriting. Based on the answers provided by the proposed insured, the insurer may refuse to accept the risk or ask the applicant to submit simplified-issue or full underwriting information.

Under a simplified-issue policy, a potential insured will be asked to answer some very specific health-related questions. After reviewing the answers to these underwriting questions, the insurance company may offer a higher mortality risk rate structure, offer a limited amount of death benefit, or decline to offer insurance. With full underwriting, an insurer will use substantial resources to determine the appropriate risk category for the proposed insured. As a result of that analysis, the insurance company may offer a specific mortality risk rate structure, offer a limited amount of death benefit, or decline to offer insurance.

Single and Multiple Rate Classes

Potential policy owners may wonder what's more advantageous—a life insurance policy offering a single rate class, very few rate classes, or multiple rate classes. The answer depends on the client's needs.

Insurance is the equitable spreading of risk among similarly situated individuals. The purpose of underwriting is to determine the individuals who are similarly situated and assign them to the appropriate risk pool. If individuals in poor health are put in the same class as individuals in excellent health and both sets of individuals pay the same mortality risk rates, then the individuals in excellent health will be subsidizing the rates paid by the individuals in poor health. This can be one of the consequences of having very few rate classes under a life insurance policy, although this is not always the case because an insurer can offer a single rate class under a policy, offer the policy only to individuals in excellent health, and decline all individuals in poor health. Generally speaking, however, having a greater number of rate classes allows the insurer to fine tune the rates for the individuals assigned to each particular risk pool. A potential customer in excellent health would generally find a life insurance policy offering multiple rate classes very attractive.

Proprietary Mortality Risk Rates

Some prospective insureds believe that the mortality risk rates for a preferred risk class are the same throughout the insurance industry, but that isn't true. All insurance companies consider their rate structures, the way they establish the rates, and the way they underwrite prospective insureds to be proprietary information.

Regardless of the number of rate classes an insurance company establishes, insurance rates under every life insurance policy are essentially separated into current rates and guaranteed rates. The guaranteed rates are usually the same for every insurer's individual life insurance policies issued in the same state during the same period. This is because state insurance regulations require insurance companies to set maximum mortality risk rates under the policy. Most states require the maximum or guaranteed rates to be equal to the insurance commissioner's 1980 standard ordinary mortality table. The commissioner's 2001 standard ordinary mortality table is being adopted by many states and will likely become the maximum or guaranteed rates for newly issued individual life insurance policies in most states by 2010. Although the guaranteed rates are usually the same for all insurance companies issuing life insurance policies in a particular state, the prevailing current rates charged by each insurance company may differ widely.

Each company competes in the life insurance industry based on its current rates. Most insurers hope they will never need to charge the guaranteed rates specified under the policies (see chapter 16). Most state insurance regulators would not expect most insurers to charge their guaranteed rates in most instances. After all, state insurance regulation is designed to protect the consumer *and* to promote the solvency of the insurer. By putting a price ceiling on the mortality risk charges an insurer can assess under a policy (that is, the guaranteed rates), the state insurance regulators indirectly convey the message that the guaranteed rates are sufficient compensation for the risks an insurer is proposing to accept. It's also an indirect message that an insurer should not become insolvent simply because state regulation imposes a ceiling on the insurer's mortality risk rates. Since the guaranteed rates under the PPLI policies issued in the same state are similar, the differentiation between insurance companies lies in their current rates established for each policy. Based on this differentiator, each insurance company competes in the marketplace.

Reinsurance and Retention

PPLI generally requires minimum premium payments of $250,000 or more. As a result, the death-benefit levels under a PPLI policy can be much greater than those of other life insurance products. It's not unusual for a PPLI policy to have a death benefit greater than $30 million. In such cases, an insurance company may elect to reinsure a portion of the risk. Under a reinsurance arrangement, the company issuing the PPLI policy (the primary insurer) maintains primary responsibility to pay claims under the policy. The reinsurance company is responsible for paying the primary insurer a portion of the death benefit in the event of a death claim.

Insurance companies will reinsure portions of the net amount at risk for a variety of reasons, but mainly to allow the primary insurer to stabilize its death claim outflows and to make its mortality experience more predictable. By reinsuring some or all of the risk, an insurer can ensure that a relatively small number of individual risks are pooled with hundreds of thousands of other similar risks, thereby creating a more predictable mortality experience. Because the number of companies offering large amounts of reinsurance in the life insurance marketplace is quite small, many advisers believe that the selection of the primary insurer for policies involving significant risk amounts is not as critical as it may otherwise be, because all the primary insurers will reinsure the risk with the same reinsurance companies. But this belief is based on the false assumption that reinsurers structure their reinsurance arrangements (treaties) with all primary insurers in the same way. They don't.

Reinsurance companies do not charge the same reinsurance rates to all primary insurers. Many factors influence the exact rates primary insurers receive from a reinsurer, including the quality of the primary insurer's underwriting (results of audits) and the amount of business the primary insurer provides to the reinsurer.

If a primary insurer reinsures a portion of the risk, it may do so in different ways. For example, it may reinsure the risk in excess of a threshold amount, such as all risk in excess of $1 million. In such cases, the primary insurer's retention is $1 million and it will reinsure the risk exceeding that amount. A primary insurer may also reinsure a percentage, such as 80 percent, of the entire risk. The difference between these two types of arrangements is important to understand because the risk under a PPLI policy normally fluctuates because of the variable nature of the policy. The practical effect is that under a percentage arrangement, reinsurance will always come into play. Under the excess arrangement, the reinsurance comes into play only when the primary insurer exceeds its retention amount.

In terms of pricing, the key question is how much of the risk the primary insurance company retains and how much it reinsures. Obviously, if an insurer wishes to compete based on its current rates, those rates will compare more favorably to its competitors' if it uses less reinsurance than they do. Therefore, an adviser needs to understand a primary insurer's retention when shopping for a policy involving significant risk amounts.

Reinsurance and Underwriting

Another aspect of reinsurance that varies in the primary insurance marketplace is the transparency of the reinsurance underwriting process to the insured. A reinsurance company is not inclined to accept any portion of a risk underwritten by a primary insurer unless the reinsurer is confident of the primary insurer's underwriting skills. Many reinsurers will allow some of their primary insurers to automatically bind them for coverage at the same rating classification determined by the primary insurer. This is known as *automatic reinsurance.*

Automatic reinsurance is limited in amount depending on the arrangement between the primary insurer and the reinsurer. For example, let's assume that the reinsurer provides an automatic binding limit of $30 million to a primary insurer. Let's also assume that the primary insurer's retention limit is $15 million and that it will reinsure all risk in excess of this limit. In this situation, if the primary insurer's underwriter determines that the proposed risk is eligible for preferred rates under the policy, then the policy can be issued for up to $45 million of risk—all at preferred rates—without input from the reinsurer regarding the risk.

On the other hand, if the primary insurer does not have the option to automatically bind the reinsurer or if the risk will exceed the reinsurer's automatic binding limit, then many different things can occur, all of which affect the policy's mortality risk rates. For example, let's assume the proposed risk under the policy is $45 million and the primary insurer's retention limit is $15 million. Let's also assume that the primary insurer's underwriter determines the proposed risk is eligible for preferred rates and that there is no automatic reinsurance. In this situation, the reinsurer will perform its own underwriting examination of the proposed insured. This is known as *facultative reinsurance*—the reinsurer performs its own underwriting on the proposed risk.

The reinsurer's underwriting on the proposed risk can have several consequences: (1) the reinsurer may determine that the risk is not eligible for preferred mortality risk rates; (2) it may reinsure only the portion of the proposed risk that exceeds the primary insurer's retention; (3) it may decline to reinsure the proposed risk; or (4) it may choose a combination of results one and two. It's not unusual for a reinsurer's underwriters to disagree with a primary insurer's underwriters regarding a proposed risk. When that happens, the policy may be issued with a different combination of mortality risk rates. Using the previous example, the policy could be issued with preferred rates on the first $15 million of risk and standard rates on the next $30 million, or the primary insurer may opt to offer its retention at the rating class determined by the reinsurer, in which case the entire $45 million would be issued at standard rates. The possibility of additional rate combinations increases with policies involving significant risk amounts. For example, an individual life insurance policy with $100 million of risk may involve as many as 10 reinsurers, most of whom will conduct their own underwriting and may well come to different conclusions as to the rate classification that should be granted to the proposed insured. Therefore, it's advantageous for applicants to seek out an insurer that maintains high retention limits, high automatic binding limits, and good underwriting relationships with its reinsurers.

Underwriting Considerations

When examining the potential risks presented by a proposed insured, the insurance underwriter needs to understand the proposed amount of insurance, the reason the insurance is being purchased, the financial need for the insurance, and the insurable interest the owner and beneficiaries have in the insured. Only after this information is obtained will the underwriter investigate an applicant's medical history, lifestyle, and financial risks.

Understanding the proposed amount of insurance is important because it may trigger facultative reinsurance and thus the reinsurer's own underwriting of the proposed risk. In this situation, the primary insurer will immediately alert the reinsurer and work with the reinsurer's underwriters to properly evaluate the policy's entire risk amount.

The underwriter must find out whether the insurance is being purchased by the owner to hedge against a risk or for speculative purposes. It goes without saying that the owner and beneficiary of a life insurance policy should have a greater stake in the insured's living a long life than in the insured's premature death. Insurance policies that are speculative in nature promote the latter rather than the former. That's why the underwriter needs to understand the purpose, financial need, and insurable interest of the proposed policy.

Underwriting Risk Factors

When determining the degree of risk (life expectancy) the proposed insured presents to the insurance carrier, an underwriter will look at certain risk factors in making its determination. Some of these risk factors include the proposed insured's:

- ❑ Age
- ❑ Occupation
- ❑ Residence
- ❑ Avocation(s) (activities, hobbies, etc.)
- ❑ Current health and physical condition
- ❑ Personal medical history and family medical history
- ❑ Smoking history (cigarettes, cigars, chewing tobacco, pipes, etc.)
- ❑ Finances
- ❑ Driving record
- ❑ Foreign travel history and prospective travel plans

Underwriting Tools

When an insurance underwriter examines the risk factors presented by a proposed insured, a number of tools are frequently used to determine the level of the various risk factors. These tools include:

- ❑ A review of the health questions on the insurance application
- ❑ A review of the medical history of the proposed insured
- ❑ A review of the attending physician's statement (APS)—including records from the proposed insured's personal physician(s) or other health-care provider
- ❑ A review of the owner and/or proposed insured's financial situation
- ❑ Interviews with the proposed insured—usually conducted to verify or clarify information contained in the insurance application, to discuss risk factors, or to request personal references
- ❑ Written inspection reports—third-party reports of public records checks, financial reports, and interviews with the proposed insured, and possibly his/her friends, neighbors, and associates
- ❑ Motor vehicle reports
- ❑ A review of information contained in the Medical Information Bureau (MIB)—the MIB is a nonprofit membership organization that operates an information exchange service to assist member organizations in deterring and detecting fraud. The information provided by the MIB is somewhat limited and is used as a starting point from which an insurer begins to conduct its assessment of potential risk factors.
- ❑ A paramedical or MD examination of the proposed insured, which may include:
  - —Height/weight
  - —Blood pressure and pulse
  - —Examination of the heart and other systems
  - —Resting and/or treadmill EKG (electrocardiogram)
  - —Blood profile and urinalysis (including HIV, cholesterol, blood sugar, liver and kidney function, drug and nicotine screening and other studies)

Confidentiality and Privacy

Many of the tools used by an insurance underwriter to examine the risk factors presented by proposed insureds cannot be used without obtaining their consent. For example, the applicant's consent is required if the underwriter wishes to share the information with the applicant's personal physician, a reinsurer, or the MIB. Some potential insureds may have privacy concerns regarding this practice. But privacy laws in the United States require the insurance company to keep personal underwriting information confidential and prevent it from being accessed by insurance company personnel who do not have a business need to review the information or by any of the insurance company's affiliates. It's always in the proposed insured's best interest to provide all of the information requested by the underwriter. The absence of certain information could cause an applicant to be offered less favorable rates than those for which he or she is eligible.

Residency and Travel

Residency and travel to certain countries may cause a proposed insured to be considered a substandard risk or even uninsurable. Whether any particular country causes this type of underwriting concern is necessarily fluid because of the constantly changing civil and political climate throughout the world. But underwriters generally put countries into A, B, C, and D classifications. In 2004, the United States would be an example of an A class country; Iraq would be a D class.

Many primary insurers will underwrite only limited amounts of risk, if any, when the proposed insured resides in or frequently travels to a class C or D country. In addition, most reinsurers will not provide automatic reinsurance in these situations. Instead, the reinsurer will require facultative underwriting on the proposed risk. Like the primary insurer, the reinsurer in these situations could offer to reinsure the policy at substandard rates or for a reduced level of risk or decline to reinsure any of the risk.

Insurance Policy Risk Riders

As mentioned, certain risk factors may cause an insurance underwriter to believe a proposed insured presents an increased risk compared to others. Some common increased risk factors include aviation or auto racing as an avocation or frequent travel to countries experiencing political or civil unrest. If the underwriter encounters these increased risks, the normal options are to offer insurance at substandard rates, cap the amount of risk offered under the policy, decline to insure the proposed risk, or a combination of choices one and two.

But if the policy is to be issued by an offshore insurer or in certain selected jurisdictions in the United States, the insurer may offer to issue the life insurance policy with a policy risk exclusion rider. The rider would essentially state that no death benefit would be payable if the insured were to die while in the performance of the prohibited activity specified in the rider. Some state insurance regulators prohibit the use of these types of riders. The regulators that do permit them will restrict the type of activities that can be proscribed to aviation, certain avocations, travel to certain countries, and military service. Most offshore jurisdictions do not place restrictions on the use of these riders. Naturally, when comparing insurance products, it's important for a prospective customer to understand whether one insurance carrier is offering standard rates with a risk exclusion rider if another carrier is offering standard rates without such a rider.

Select and Ultimate Periods

A frequently misunderstood life insurance pricing characteristic that may inadvertently cause many policyholders to wonder whether their life insurance policy has suddenly become more expensive is the use of select and ultimate periods applied to the mortality risk rates. Their use is common throughout the insurance industry and simply reflects the aging and resulting unreliability of the underwriting that has been performed on the insured.

It's safe to say that most fully underwritten insureds will not die within a year after they've been approved for preferred rates. That's because the information used in making the underwriting determination was current. The period for which the information is deemed reliable is considered the select period. As the information ages, it becomes less reliable. The period in which the information is deemed unreliable is called the ultimate period. The select period is usually the first seven to ten years after the policy has been issued. Thereafter, the policy is considered to have entered its ultimate period. All rate classes have select and ultimate periods, and the rates during these periods are slightly different. A preferred rate during the policy's select period is generally lower than a preferred rate during the policy's ultimate period.

For example, let's assume that Bill, age 45, purchased a fully underwritten policy 10 years ago (at age 35) and was allocated into the preferred rate pool. Now it's 2004, and Bill still owns the policy. During the 2004 calendar year, the risk under the policy is a constant $1 million. Let's also assume that Dave, age 45, purchased the same fully underwritten policy on January 1, 2004, and was also allocated into the preferred rate pool. During the 2004 calendar year, the risk under Dave's policy is also a constant $1 million.

Many individuals would believe that both Bill and Dave will pay the same dollar amount of insurance rate charges during the 2004 calendar year because they have the same policy, are the same age and sex, have the same underwriting classification (preferred), and have the same constant net amount at risk. The reality, however, is that Bill will be paying a higher dollar amount for his net amount at risk than Dave because Bill's policy has entered its ultimate period whereas Dave's policy is still in its select period.

Even though the use of select and ultimate periods is common in the life insurance industry, it confuses some policyholders and may sometimes cause those with older policies to believe that newer life insurance policies are cheaper than the ones they own. But an exchange from an older policy to a new policy should not be pursued simply because the older policy has entered its ultimate period.

A new life insurance policy will be issued only if new underwriting is performed. As a result of the new underwriting, the insured may not be eligible for the same rate classification. A new policy will also require the policyholder to incur new acquisition expenses. In addition, the new policy will also eventually enter its ultimate period in which the rates increase.

Once a policy is issued, an insurer cannot change the rate classification of the insured without the policy owner's consent, even if the insured has experienced a negative change in his or her risk factors or health, provided the policy remains in force. But if an insured has had a significantly favorable change in health following the underwriter's original underwriting decision, the insurer may be willing to reconsider the insured for a better risk class after a period of time has elapsed from the original underwriting decision.

The Insurance Adviser

A successful placement of a PPLI product requires an insurance adviser's assistance in coordinating the underwriting process between the proposed insured and the insurance underwriter. Almost all potential insureds are unfamiliar with the underwriting process. To ensure a successful placement, the adviser should educate the applicant regarding the underwriting process and what the insured should expect.

Some potential PPLI customers view the purchase of a PPLI policy as any other securities transaction. They would like to believe that they can send a premium to the life insurer and have a life insurance policy issued to them the next day. But a potential insured should not attempt to sidestep the underwriting process for a life insurance policy with a significant proposed risk amount. Providing the appropriate information to the underwriter will increase the applicant's chances of obtaining the most favorable risk class.

The underwriting process is normally completed within 90 days. But that's assuming the insurance adviser has assisted the underwriter in obtaining and assembling the necessary paperwork, such as consent paperwork, attending physician's statements, and inspection reports. If the insurance adviser does not assist the underwriter in obtaining the necessary information, the underwriting process can take up to six months. It is vital for an insurance adviser to fully inform a potential insured as to what will be required during the underwriting process. In addition, the adviser should act as a liaison between the underwriter and the proposed insured to obtain and assemble the information necessary for the underwriter to properly assess the risk factors presented by the applicant.

Mortality Risk Charge versus Mortality and Expense Risk Charge

Many advisers and clients tend to focus on the PPLI policy's asset-based charges when comparing costs among insurance carriers. That's because it's easier to compare each insurer's asset-based charges, such as the mortality and expense risk charge (M&E) commonly assessed against the insurance company's separate account underlying the PPLI policy. But it's a mistake to isolate a single PPLI cost element as a basis for carrier selection. When a carrier creates a new product, it anticipates the overall cost it will incur and recovers the overall cost through all the various charges assessed under the policy. Some carriers may decrease their M&E charges under a product and make up the revenue shortfall by increasing their mortality risk charges for the same product. Therefore, when comparing products, advisers and clients should focus on the total charges assessed during the lifetime of the policy rather than on any particular charge.

The most significant expense of a life insurance policy is the cost attributable to the mortality risk of the insured. The underwriting process determines the rate classification that will be offered to an applicant and therefore the mortality risk charges that will be assessed under that individual's life insurance policy. Since most PPLI policies involve significant amounts of risk to the insurer, the underwriting process will be more extensive than it is for other policies. The insurance adviser and the proposed insured must understand the risk factors that the underwriter needs to examine before issuing the policy, and they must be prepared to provide the necessary information. In the end, such preparation will benefit the proposed insured by ensuring that the underwriter can make a timely determination as to the applicant's proper risk classification.

CHAPTER 16

Understanding and Comparing Costs

SUSAN BRUNO

O ne of the most compelling benefits of private placement life insurance (PPLI) is the full disclosure of all expense elements to the buyer and the adviser team. This transparency—not typical of insurance transactions—allows for a detailed evaluation and is refreshing for all parties involved.

With the advent of retail universal life insurance in the 1970s, some light began to penetrate the black box of pricing as insurance companies responded to what had become a frustrating purchasing process (see chapter 11). Now, PPLI has cracked the black box wide open, resulting in full transparency in every element of the policy. Wealthy individuals and experienced advisers demand such disclosure, and PPLI has proved over and over again that it's a straightforward purchase. As the transaction moves through execution, the different expenses are determined. This chapter looks at the evaluation process and the facets that should be in place to secure the best possible contract.

Charges: Current versus Guaranteed

Essential to understanding the various expense elements of a PPLI contract is knowing the difference between current charges and guaranteed charges. There is often a significant difference between the two (see chapter 11). Current charges are applied today and are based on the company's expected experience levels. Guaranteed, or maximum charges, are the highest charges that the company can apply if experience mandates them or if the insurance company wants to change its profitability on a single policy or block of policies.

The buyer is at greater risk from unilateral policy changes than from changes permitted within the parameters disclosed in the policy. An individual PPLI policy does not have the same regulatory protection as a registered retail policy and the potential exists for the carrier to take more aggressive approaches than would be otherwise allowed. Fortunately, elements of the policy can be altered to protect the client. Successful negotiation of even one element in the contract that is otherwise subject to change can save the policy owner thousands of dollars. Such negotiation is one of the most valuable services a knowledgeable insurance adviser can offer the PPLI purchaser.

A carrier illustration that reflects current charges is generally the focus of attention during the purchase process. It reflects what the carrier is currently charging for all elements in the contract but does not necessarily show the maximum amount the carrier may charge. Although it's clearly disclosed that some of the charges are subject to change, the carrier also provides an illustration based on the worst-case scenario: guaranteed (maximum) charges. In reality, if the illustration were based solely on the maximum guaranteed charges—which effectively undermine much of PPLI's economic benefit—a PPLI evaluation would come to a screeching halt. Since elements of the policy are negotiated in confidence between the insurance adviser and the insurance company, there is no widely accepted barometer for what constitutes appropriate limits and the insurance companies have no interest in sharing such details. In the end, achieving a policy in which the costs of the carrier and the policy owner are in balance is the chief role of the insurance adviser.

Key Expense Categories

A PPLI insurance contract has five major expense categories:
1 Federal deferred acquisition cost (DAC)
2 State premium tax
3 Cost of insurance (COI)
4 Mortality and expense (M&E)
5 Structuring/consulting fee

The first four categories are found in nearly all insurance contracts, but the fifth category may or may not be, depending on how and from whom the contract is purchased.

FIGURE 16.1 lists these expense categories and whether they are typically charged as the premium is paid or monthly throughout the life of the contract.

FIGURE **16.1** *Expenses in a PPLI Contract*

MAJOR EXPENSE CATEGORY	PAID AS A PERCENTAGE OF PREMIUM	PAID FOR THE LIFE OF THE POLICY
DAC	X	
State premium	X	
COI		X
M&E		X
Structuring fee	X	

Although figure 16.1 indicates when the charges are assessed, the five major expense categories are more effectively evaluated as premium-based fees, risk-based fees, and asset-based fees.

Premium-Based Fees

Federal DAC tax. Taxes are premium-based fees. Taxes, you say? Yes, a federal tax as well as a separate state tax is imposed on PPLI. These taxes are more akin to sales taxes and are clearly separate from PPLI's main economic engine, the tax deferral of income, capital gains, and estate taxes. The DAC tax is applied indirectly, taking the form of a corporate federal tax imposed on the insurance company itself. Although this tax is commonly referred to as a federal premium tax, that's a misnomer. DAC collection is an insurance company's way of nullifying the effect of a corporate tax law enacted several years ago. The law once allowed insurance companies to expense all costs related to business acquisitions (mainly commissions) in the first year of the policy. Obviously, this practice reduced corporate taxable income and, therefore, corporate tax. Under current tax law, insurance companies must capitalize and amortize their acquisition costs over a longer period of time, which results in greater corporate taxable income in the year the policy is sold. This translates into an indirect tax, and to no one's surprise, the carrier passes it on to the buyer as the DAC charge. The DAC tax is typically deducted as premiums are paid into an insurance contract. The rate charged depends on the carrier selected, but it typically ranges from 70 to 150 basis points on all premiums paid to fund the policy.

State premium tax. The state imposes a direct premium tax. Every state has one, and the insurance company remits to the state 100 percent of the tax charged. Considering the size of PPLI premiums, this can be a significant source of revenue for states where policies are sold. The state premium tax can range from as low as 10 basis points to as high as 500 basis points, with an average around 200 basis points (see chapter 6). In some cases, the rate paid may depend on the carrier, but it's primarily driven by the laws in the state where the contract is sold. For example, a $25 million premium might be assessed as follows:

❑ A low state premium tax would cost the buyer $37,500.
❑ An average state premium tax would cost the buyer $500,000.
❑ A high state premium tax would cost the buyer $1 million.

The premium tax can be the most significant upfront cost of a PPLI policy; therefore, it should not be surprising that sophisticated insurance advisers attempt to minimize it. They may do so by changing the jurisdiction governing the policy either by using a state with low taxes such as Alaska or South Dakota (see chapter 6) or by executing the policy offshore (see chapter 17). Think of it this way: a $500,000 savings in state premium taxes compounds within the policy, making the long-term economic impact much greater than it appears.

Each state has the right to challenge the jurisdiction if one of its residents has gone to another state to enter into an insurance transaction. And how can one state know what insurance transactions occur in another? A unique reporting system tracks insurance transactions, broken down by carrier, state, and annual premiums, and it's readily available to all states. Clearly, a qualified insurance adviser and attorney are important in implementing an effective and efficient PPLI transaction established in the preferred state with minimal aggravation. The challenge would be based on what actually did or did not occur in the given state. Questions such as the location of the underwriting process, medical exam, and related paperwork serve as evidence for or against a state's petition. No matter how ironclad the contract's legal structure may be, the insurance company typically reserves the right to pay a state premium tax out of the policy's cash value if a legitimate challenge is made. Given the leverage the state has over the carrier—it can issue a cease-and-desist order in that state until the matter is resolved—the carrier most likely will remit the additional tax without a substantial fight. This translates into a direct policy withdrawal to pay the higher tax.

Structuring/consulting fee. The structuring fee is paid upfront to the intermediary or adviser who is helping the buyer complete the transaction. A typical structuring fee is 1 percent of premiums paid. The fee is normally calculated based on premium amount but can generally be paid from cash value or paid directly to the adviser outside of the insurance contract.

It should be looked at as value paid for value created. The out-of-pocket and ongoing expenses saved by an effective policy implementation can far surpass the structuring fee. And this fee is paid only after the policy has been structured and funded according to the client's specification.

Risk-Based Fees

Cost of insurance. The risk to a life insurance company in a PPLI transaction is equal to the amount of money the company will have to pay from surplus in the event of death. This policy risk element is called the net amount at risk (NAR). For example, if a policy with a death benefit (DB) of $50 million has a cash value (CV) of $5 million, then the NAR would be $45 million ($50 million DB minus $5 million CV equals $45 million NAR).

A common goal in PPLI transactions is to close the NAR gap as soon as possible, within IRS guidelines, so that the NAR is minimized in future years. This reduction lowers the cost-of-insurance charge applied against the NAR. Of course, closing the NAR brings a commensurate reduction in the death benefit, but this is less material for most wealthy families that have a well-constructed trust program.

COI represents the individual's mortality risk as determined by the underwriting results (see chapter 15) applied against the insurance industry's mortality tables. The COI varies from carrier to carrier and should be carefully reviewed, but three factors affect COI rates:

❑ *Cost of retention:* the carrier's internal cost to retain all or a portion of the risk in an insurance contract
❑ *Cost of reinsurance:* the carrier's cost to acquire additional insurance from other carriers in the reinsurance market if the coverage exceeds the carrier's internal retention capacity
❑ *Profit margin:* the profit element, if any, added to the first two costs

Some carriers retain a good portion of the risk; others depend solely on the reinsurance market. Some carriers simply pass through the cost of the reinsurance with no markup for margin; others mark up to add an element of profit. **FIGURE 16.2** illustrates a sample PPLI policy and the cost per $1,000 at various ages.

It's commonly assumed that insurance is not cost effective for a person over the age of 65, but that's not true with PPLI. Because PPLI contracts are generally purchased to obtain the income tax benefits, the funding is structured based on a minimum death benefit relative to the premium to be paid. This may seem counterintuitive to a typical insurance transaction, but much about PPLI is counterintuitive. As the insured

FIGURE **16.2** *Sample Annual Cost of Insurance per $1,000 of Net Amount at Risk for Male Age 40, Preferred Nonsmoker*

AGE	DEATH BENEFIT	CASH VALUE	NET AMOUNT AT RISK	COST OF INSURANCE PER $1,000	COST OF INSURANCE
40	109,511,824	5,291,824	104,220,000	0.55	57,529
45	136,317,634	32,097,634	104,220,000	0.86	89,921
50	95,012,602	49,744,818	45,267,784	1.73	78,507
55	121,709,822	77,522,180	44,187,642	3.38	149,325
60	162,157,418	121,012,999	41,144,419	4.85	199,661
65	232,909,024	190,909,036	41,999,988	7.07	296,839
70	349,099,058	300,947,464	48,151,594	11.45	551,401
75	507,811,373	474,590,068	33,221,305	18.17	603,646
80	787,565,606	750,062,482	37,503,124	28.80	1,080,165
85	1,240,259,165	1,181,199,205	59,059,960	44.48	2,626,827

person ages, the relative death benefit can be reduced so that the insurance company's NAR is proportionally reduced. Age, NAR, and the death benefit—and the relationship among them—are important variables that the insurance adviser needs to monitor in order to make economically sound changes in the contract. Because an adviser's compensation is based on the policy's cash value, it's in the best interest of all parties to keep policy expenses to a minimum.

Asset-Based Fees

Mortality and expense. Calling this fee "mortality and expense" is the worst insurance misnomer of all time. This expense category has nothing to do with the insured's mortality; it's simply the profit element for the carrier and/or the adviser. Although this charge represents the policy's profit margin, it should be neither too high nor too low. Obviously, the policy owner wants the costs in the contract to be as low as possible, but if the charge is too low, the business line will not be sustainable for the carrier and will not support the adviser's ongoing service requirements. M&E charges for PPLI range from 30 to 100 basis points and often come with price breaks at different cash values and the number of years the policy has been in force. A carrier with a low M&E charge relative to that of the competition may have higher COI charges. That's why M&E and COI charges need to be evaluated in tandem before a price is settled.

Bringing It All Together

FIGURE 16.3 on the following page illustrates how the premium-based, risk-based, and asset-based charges interact when measured by the number of basis points to the policy's cash value. (Because the ongoing expenses of COI and M&E are charged against the policy monthly based on carrier-specific formulas, the figures are estimates.) By the fifth year, the total cost to this policyholder is less than 100 basis points; by the tenth year, expenses decrease to 68 basis points.

PPLI's Real Power

FIGURE 16.4 illustrates the key to PPLI's power. Those who look at the cost of purchasing a PPLI policy without considering the income tax cost of owning the same or similar investments in a taxable portfolio are missing the point. What is mistakenly assumed to be extra drag is actually an enabling device for vastly higher wealth creation. Figure 16.4 is based on a 40-year-old male, paying a $5 million premium for five years and earning a 10 percent rate of return. The death benefit is managed in order to maximize the cash value within the policy.

The thick, horizontal line in figure 16.4 represents the current maximum federal marginal tax rate (35 percent) and, for illustration purposes, excludes any state income tax. But additional state taxes raise an individual's total tax exposure, thereby creating even greater economic benefit for the PPLI policy, represented by the larger gray area. The lower, darker gray area represents all five of the expense elements in the contract: DAC, state premium tax, COI, M&E, and a 1 percent structuring fee (capped at $50,000). Expenses related to cash value drop dramatically after the premiums have been paid, because the upfront premium-based charges (DAC, state premium, and structuring fee) are not paid throughout the life of the contract. The remaining fees (COI and M&E) continue for the life of the contract, but for M&E, there is a breakpoint reduction. The COI charges never become cost prohibitive as a percentage of cash value, even as the insured reaches age 90. The NAR and, therefore, the COI charges depend on the rate of return in the policy. Like any investment portfolio, PPLI contracts must be monitored periodically to prevent

FIGURE **16.3** *Sample Expense Detail of PPLI Contract in Basis Points Relative to Cash Value, Male Age 40, Preferred Nonsmoker*

AGE	OUTLAY PREMIUM	STRUCTURING FEE OF PREM.	STRUCTURING FEE OF CV	FEDERAL DAC TAX OF PREM.	FEDERAL DAC TAX OF CV	STATE PREM. TAX OF PREM	STATE PREM. TAX OF CV
40	5,000,000	100	94	100	94.49	15	14.10
41	5,000,000			100	44.91	15	6.70
42	5,000,000			100	28.55	15	4.26
43	5,000,000			100	20.42	15	3.05
44	5,000,000			100	15.58	15	2.32
45							
46							
47							
48							
49							
50							
51							
52							
53							
54							
55							
60							
65							
70							
75							
80							

COST OF INSURANCE OF CV	M&E CHARGES	TOTAL CHARGES OF CV	CASH VALUE EOY	DEATH BENEFIT
108.71	47.93	365	5,291,824	109,511,824
53.92	47.78	158	11,132,965	115,352,965
40.64	47.75	126	17,511,275	121,731,275
30.80	47.72	107	24,484,457	128,704,457
28.01	47.72	98	32,097,634	136,317,634
28.40	47.72	81	35,009,211	136,317,634
30.52	47.72	83	38,176,405	136,317,634
14.80	47.68	67	41,698,802	87,000,000
14.55	47.68	67	45,547,380	89,728,339
15.78	47.68	68	49,744,818	95,012,602
17.70	38.13	61	54,372,476	100,589,080
19.63	38.14	63	59,418,587	105,765,085
21.77	38.14	65	64,918,458	111,010,564
20.63	38.14	64	70,935,864	116,334,817
19.26	38.13	62	77,522,180	121,709,822
17.22	38.13	60	84,738,165	127,107,247
15.08	19.04	39	132,571,720	172,343,236
15.56	19.04	39	209,133,330	250,959,996
18.90	19.05	43	329,560,598	378,994,687
9.95	19.04	34	520,201,018	546,211,069
15.77	19.04	40	821,646,306	862,728,621

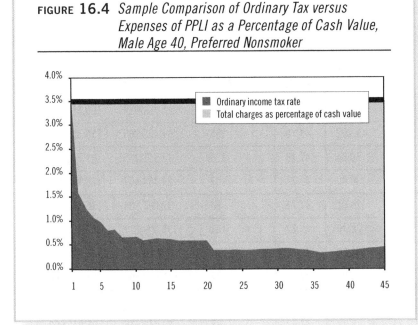

FIGURE **16.4** *Sample Comparison of Ordinary Tax versus Expenses of PPLI as a Percentage of Cash Value, Male Age 40, Preferred Nonsmoker*

Source: ©Beacon Wealth Consulting, LLC

unnecessary inefficiencies from creeping in. This is typically the task of the insurance adviser. For those without capable advisory support, a policy in which the fees are a factor of the cash value (see chapter 11) may be more appropriate. In any case, PPLI's huge economic incentive is clear.

For individuals who own hedge fund or private-equity investments that are not insurance dedicated (see chapter 8) and therefore ineligible for a policy, an evaluation into the investment may be necessary to make clear what the opportunity cost of not executing a PPLI policy may in fact be. For example, assume a hedge fund manager earns a 10 percent ROR (net of management fees) and the return is made up of 100 percent ordinary income. At a 35 percent income tax rate, **FIGURE 16.5** on pages 280–281 shows how much additional wealth is created in a PPLI contract simply from annually compounding PPLI's tax savings. After just 10 years, the same investment earns $10 million more in PPLI than outside of it ($54,372,476 versus $44,239,207).

But it's incorrect to think that only grossly tax-inefficient investments do well in PPLI. Both the return *and* the tax rate must be considered to make an appropriate evaluation. For example, venture capital, which is taxed at a 15 percent capital gains rate, historically has a high rate of return (see chapter 8). In a PPLI policy, venture capital not only has a percentage

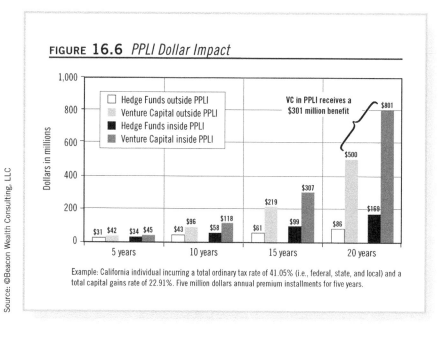

FIGURE 16.6 *PPLI Dollar Impact*

Legend:
- ☐ Hedge Funds outside PPLI
- ▨ Venture Capital outside PPLI
- ■ Hedge Funds inside PPLI
- ▨ Venture Capital inside PPLI

VC in PPLI receives a $301 million benefit

Y-axis: Dollars in millions (0 to 1,000)

5 years: $31, $42, $34, $45
10 years: $43, $96, $58, $118
15 years: $61, $219, $99, $307
20 years: $86, $500, $169, $801

Example: California individual incurring a total ordinary tax rate of 41.05% (i.e., federal, state, and local) and a total capital gains rate of 22.91%. Five million dollars annual premium installments for five years.

Source: ©Beacon Wealth Consulting, LLC

increase in after-tax return comparable to a hedge fund's, but the wealth effect can be enormous because of a much higher after-tax compounded growth rate.

To illustrate this, **FIGURE 16.6** assumes a California resident taxed at a combined federal and state capital gains rate of 22.91 percent making five, $5 million annual premiums with total annual policy charges of 1 percent. The assumed hedge fund and venture capital returns are based on asset-class benchmarks. To make the venture capital analysis comparable, the capital gains rate for the non-PPLI investment is taken every five years.

In all periods, venture capital's PPLI benefit outpaces a hedge fund's but at an increasing rate. The exponential increase results from venture capital's compounding at a higher *after-tax* return, even though the casual observer would classify venture capital as "tax efficient" (see chapter 8).

Both examples illustrate one key point: a PPLI policy's charges pale in comparison to the policy's economic benefit. Clients and advisers must take care not to miss the forest for the trees.

Cash Value and Associated Costs

An attractive feature of a non-MEC policy is the insured's access to the cash value through loans and withdrawals. However, there is a cost to execute a loan as well as a reduction (cost) to the policy's economic benefit. Assume, for example, that a policy owner who has paid premiums of $25 million

FIGURE **16.5** *Sample Taxed Investment versus Private Placement Life Insurance, Male Age 40, Preferred Nonsmoker*

AGE	ANNUAL ADDITIONS	LONG-TERM CAPITAL GAINS	ORDINARY INCOME	CAPITAL GAIN TAXES	ORDINARY INCOME TAXES	VALUE NET OF CURRENT TAXES	IRR
			HYPOTHETICAL 10% NET TAXED INVESTMENT				
40	5,000,000	0	500,000	0	(175,000)	5,325,000	6.50%
41	5,000,000	0	1,032,500	0	(361,375)	10,996,125	6.50%
42	5,000,000	0	1,599,613	0	(559,864)	17,035,873	6.50%
43	5,000,000	0	2,203,587	0	(771,256)	23,468,205	6.50%
44	5,000,000	0	2,846,821	0	(996,387)	30,318,638	6.50%
45	0	0	3,031,864	0	(1,061,152)	32,289,350	6.50%
46	0	0	3,228,935	0	(1,130,127)	34,388,157	6.50%
47	0	0	3,438,816	0	(1,203,586)	36,623,388	6.50%
48	0	0	3,662,339	0	(1,281,819)	39,003,908	6.50%
49	0	0	3,900,391	0	(1,365,137)	41,539,162	6.50%
50	0	0	4,153,916	0	(1,453,871)	44,239,207	6.50%
51	0	0	4,423,921	0	(1,548,372)	47,114,756	6.50%
52	0	0	4,711,476	0	(1,649,017)	50,177,215	6.50%
53	0	0	5,017,722	0	(1,756,203)	53,438,734	6.50%
54	0	0	5,343,873	0	(1,870,356)	56,912,252	6.50%
59	0	0	7,321,570	0	(2,562,549)	77,974,717	6.50%
64	0	0	10,031,185	0	(3,510,915)	106,832,120	6.50%
69	0	0	13,743,593	0	(4,810,258)	146,369,263	6.50%
74	0	0	18,829,913	0	(6,590,470)	200,538,575	6.50%
79	0	0	25,798,613	0	(9,029,515)	274,755,227	6.50%
84	0	0	35,346,335	0	(12,371,217)	376,438,472	6.50%
	25,000,000	0	661,105,709	0	(231,386,998)		

1. Earnings rates (net of management and custody): Taxed Currently 10.00%; Appreciation 0.00%.
2. Tax Rates: Ordinary Income 35.00%.

PRIVATE PLACEMENT POLICY 10% NET

CASH VALUE		DEATH BENEFIT	
AMOUNT	IRR	AMOUNT	IRR
5,291,824	5.84%	109,511,824	2090.24%
11,132,965	7.37%	115,352,965	332.91%
17,511,275	7.94%	121,731,275	149.88%
24,484,457	8.26%	128,704,457	90.79%
32,097,634	8.45%	136,317,634	63.12%
35,009,211	8.60%	136,317,634	47.35%
38,176,405	8.69%	136,317,634	37.61%
41,698,802	8.77%	87,000,000	22.28%
45,547,380	8.84%	89,728,339	19.49%
49,744,818	8.88%	95,012,602	17.77%
54,372,476	8.93%	100,589,080	16.43%
59,418,587	8.96%	105,765,085	15.28%
64,918,458	8.99%	111,010,564	14.33%
70,935,864	9.01%	116,334,817	13.52%
77,522,180	9.03%	121,709,822	12.82%
121,012,999	9.11%	162,157,418	10.88%
190,909,036	9.20%	232,909,024	10.15%
300,947,464	9.26%	349,099,058	9.84%
474,590,068	9.30%	507,811,373	9.53%
750,062,482	9.34%	787,565,606	9.48%
1,181,199,205	9.36%	1,240,259,165	9.48%

1. Policy values reflect ownership in the state of Alaska.

has a cash value now worth $50 million. He or she can withdraw the $25 million in premiums tax-free as a return of basis. Should the policy owner wish to access additional funds, it could be done in the form of a policy loan of up to 85–90 percent of the policy's cash value. Again, this loan distribution is tax-free. (The proceeds of the loan are not taxable as long as the contract has not lapsed. When a policy has lapsed, it means that it does not have sufficient cash to maintain the death benefit and related charges until the insured dies. It also means that coverage ceases, the contract is void, and taxes must be paid on 100 percent of the gain borrowed from the policy. This obviously must be avoided and further demonstrates the importance of having quality advice during the execution and ongoing monitoring phases.)

The key element to understand about loans is the policy's loan spread. The loan spread is the insurance company's charge, which represents the difference between the interest credited to the policy owner's account (that is, borrowing one's own funds) and the interest rate charged against the policy. In a well-priced PPLI contract, this spread is nominal in the first 10 years and possibly reduced to zero thereafter. A high loan spread can be one of those overlooked cost elements that doesn't become clear until it's too late. The adviser must be mindful of this during the policy's negotiation, not when a loan is executed.

Tax-free access to the policy's cash value represents a valuable resource to the policy owner. The drawback, of course, is that the amount of cash withdrawn or borrowed loses the economic benefit of tax-free compounding at the potential rates earned by hedge funds and private equity. The earlier investment examples showed that there is potentially more than enough wealth created to justify the policy's costs, but the policy's ultimate value will be diminished because of the reduced return. This return reduction must be monitored by the adviser to ensure that the death benefit is adjusted to avoid higher than expected COI charges.

Exiting the Policy

Unlike retail variable universal life policies, PPLI does not typically have surrender charges. Carriers generally compensate the adviser of retail policies with an upfront commission that needs to be returned if the buyer surrenders (that is, exits) the policy. Because carriers do not pay advisers of PPLI policies upfront commissions, no surrender charge is imposed.

Accountants and attorneys are big fans of such efficient exit strategies. Although a retail policy rarely would be surrendered in the early years, when a surrender charge is imposed, a PPLI policy owner incurs only the soft costs of losing the upfront charges of executing the policy, such as state premium taxes, DAC taxes, and the structuring fee. Although these

PPLI charges are sunk costs, a policy owner should consider the financial impact if a policy surrender is a possibility. Practically speaking, though, a well-structured policy executed under the guidance of an experienced insurance adviser should not lapse unless the client's circumstances have changed drastically. Short of that, PPLI's economic benefits are too impressive to lose.

MARKET COMPETITION over the past five years has produced PPLI policies that are priced fairly for the carrier, the adviser, and the policy owner. For the individual or family contemplating a PPLI solution, a decision to forego PPLI is not likely to have anything to do with pricing, provided that expert support is at hand to negotiate and ensure an optimal contract.

CHAPTER 17

Jurisdiction
Home or Away?

PETER M. WILLIAMS

Aprivate placement life insurance (PPLI) policy can be executed either in the United States or offshore, and that choice should be made early in the evaluation process. The best option for the client depends on the reasons for purchasing PPLI, but the policies can help high-net-worth individuals meet three objectives. Most often, the client desires an investment-accumulation product for tax-inefficient investments. This policy is called a *nonmodified endowment contract* (non-MEC), and it provides the smallest possible death benefit but offers the insured access to the cash value on a tax-favored basis through loans or withdrawals. The client determines an annual premium commitment for a fixed number of years. The importance of the death benefit is secondary to the purchase and is often thought of as a necessary cost to gain PPLI's economic benefits.

Many clients simply want a product with maximum potential for cash accumulation and do not foresee the need to use the cash values during the insured's lifetime. This product, which may be funded with a single-premium payment, is referred to as a *modified endowment contract* (MEC). Cash values are not available through loans or withdrawals on a tax-favored basis during the insured's lifetime, but the structure allows for the greatest cash accumulation with the least cost. Clients who wish to fund a charitable bequest or a dynasty trust whose beneficiaries will not need access to the cash values for one or two generations often use a MEC.

Other clients desire a very large death benefit and wish to pay the least amount of premium required to fund the death benefit over the insured's lifetime. This is commonly referred to as a *death-benefit purchase.*

Determining Jurisdiction

Determining the client's PPLI objective is critical in narrowing down the most appropriate choices for the insurance company, product, product design, and policy owner jurisdiction. The choice of jurisdiction can change how one thinks about the other items, so it's critical to the PPLI implementation process that the client's insurance adviser get answers early on to key questions that will help determine the optimum jurisdiction.

How important is it for the transaction to be simple? Offshore PPLI requires the establishment of an offshore trust or company to serve as owner. An offshore bank account and an offshore address are also necessary for implementing and maintaining the offshore policy. If the client is adverse to complexity and is unwilling to travel offshore to execute a PPLI purchase, onshore PPLI is the only alternative. Chances are that the client will be happier purchasing PPLI in the state of residency rather than considering another onshore jurisdiction that may offer other advantages.

Is asset protection a major priority? Almost every client who considers asset protection as a top priority in PPLI will choose an offshore jurisdiction. An exception to this rule would be a client residing in a state where cash values are wholly exempt from creditors (see chapter 4). In that case, the client may be willing to pay the state premium tax to capture the cash value credit protection.

What is the primary objective? To accumulate investments on a tax-favored basis? Or to provide a low-cost death benefit for the heirs? If the objective is to achieve tax-favored accumulation, the client may be a more likely candidate for an offshore transaction. But other factors must be considered. The client who is using PPLI to maintain a low-cost death benefit will do better onshore.

Is a survivorship PPLI policy being considered? Offshore survivorship PPLI products are not yet available. Survivorship PPLI is offered only onshore.

How large a premium is the client willing to commit to PPLI? Typically, the greater the premium commitment, the more likely the client will choose to purchase PPLI offshore. For example, a client recently committed $25 million to PPLI over a five-year premium-payment period. The client and his advisers debated whether to purchase PPLI in Bermuda or in South Dakota. They calculated the premium tax savings for purchasing in Bermuda would total $107,100, so they bought the PPLI in Bermuda.

Is the client planning to make an in-kind premium payment? Since the PPLI revenue rulings issued in July 2003, very few carriers have been interested in accepting in-kind premium payments (that is, accepting noncash assets such as securities as the premium payment). The only insurance companies known to consider such an arrangement are located offshore.

How are the cash values to be invested? All PPLI companies keep a current list of approved funds including insurance-dedicated funds (see chapter 14), and a policy owner may choose one or more of the available options. If a client wants to use an unapproved investment adviser or insurance-dedicated fund, the insurance company must complete a due diligence process. Most often, an offshore company will agree to consider a new investment adviser for a premium commitment of $5 million. However, an onshore PPLI carrier will require a minimum commitment of $8 million and potentially as much as $20 million.

Does the client desire to own assets offshore? A client recently completed an offshore PPLI transaction using a British Virgin Islands company as the ownership entity. His main purpose for purchasing PPLI offshore was to own assets that could be denominated in a currency other than U.S. dollars. He happens to be a very astute investor and businessman and never strongly considered purchasing PPLI onshore.

Is it important that the client interface with the insurance adviser during the PPLI analysis? PPLI obtained offshore may not be solicited in the United States. All onshore communication should be strictly between the client and the other advisers, *excluding the insurance adviser.* The insurance adviser may provide generic offshore PPLI information to advisers in the United States, but this material must not be specific to any client.

How important is the choice of insurance company? Most offshore insurance companies are small and have relatively shallow amounts of capital and surplus. A client who is willing to use only a large, highly rated insurance company will have but a few offshore choices, most of whom are offshore subsidiaries of large U.S. insurance companies.

Summarizing the Differences

FIGURE 17.1 compares client PPLI preferences and offers an assessment of client suitability for an offshore jurisdiction. Provided the client's preferences don't preclude either an onshore or offshore policy, an analysis of the choices is the next step. The adviser can now take the answers to the questions and begin the filtering process that will identify the direction to follow. Having an adviser to conduct this analysis is a major benefit to the individual or family in reducing PPLI's complexity and moving toward a solution.

FIGURE 17.1 *Offshore and Onshore Suitability Rating*

PPLI ELEMENTS	OFFSHORE VERSUS ONSHORE*	
1. Product design	0	0
2. U.S. tax-compliant	0	0
3. Underwriting standards	0	0
4. Product pricing	+	−
5. In-kind premium	+	−
6. Managed account minimum premium threshold	+	−
7. Investment-management flexibility	+	−
8. Access to offshore investments	+	−
9. Asset-protection planning	+	−
10. SEC regulation	+	−
11. State approval	+	−
12. Legal documentation and costs	−	+
13. IRS reporting requirements	−	+

* + (Better);   − (Worse);   0 (Neutral)

The Pros and Cons

Both offshore and onshore PPLI products are designed to adhere to U.S. tax laws—IRC §§ 101(a), 7702, and 7702(a). Conforming to these laws provides the benefits of tax-deferred accumulation, tax-free loans/withdrawals, and tax-free death benefits. Most product design alternatives may be achieved both offshore and onshore with the exception of designs using a survivorship product. Employing a highly skilled PPLI insurance adviser is instrumental in accomplishing the client's objectives and using the most cost-efficient design. Certain designs put a greater emphasis on a particular cost factor. For example, a death-benefit purchase will place more emphasis on the cost-of-insurance charges than on other pricing factors. A cash value accumulation purchase will place more importance on product design, which minimizes the death benefit and has a low mortality and expense charge.

Clients who want to incorporate gift, estate, and generation-skipping planning with PPLI will be subject to the same U.S. tax laws whether they purchase PPLI offshore or onshore. Also, there is very little difference in medical and financial underwriting requirements when applying for a policy in either jurisdiction. But there are more highly rated insurance companies underwriting PPLI onshore than offshore. If underwriting is of concern, the client is more likely to receive a better underwriting offer onshore.

Offshore Advantages

Product pricing. PPLI product pricing may vary significantly from company to company. Insurance advisers also have some pricing flexibility in terms of the sales load and the ongoing account-management fees built into the product. For example, one insurance adviser may charge a 3 percent sales load per premium payment and another insurance broker may sell the same product and charge a 1 percent sales load.

A West Coast lawyer/adviser asked me to submit a sales illustration for a hypothetical offshore PPLI policy assuming an annual premium payment of $2.5 million payable for four years. She also requested the same illustration from two other insurance advisers who happened to use two different offshore insurance products. She calculated the total expense charges for the first 15 policy years for all three sales illustrations. These charges included sales loads, DAC taxes, account-management fees, mortality and expense charges, and cost-of-insurance charges. In reporting her findings, she determined that one product had total charges of $1 million less than the other two proposals. Clearly, product pricing in the PPLI market varies significantly. An expert insurance adviser is critical in shopping the market and pricing the PPLI product competitively.

Offshore PPLI has several pricing advantages over similar products issued onshore. Offshore PPLI does not require a state premium tax deduction. As noted in chapter 6, this may result in a savings of 2–3 percent on each premium payment.

If the insurance company is a U.S. taxpayer (a 953(d) company), the offshore premium payments are reduced by a DAC tax. For example, one major PPLI carrier's offshore product carries a DAC tax of 0.7 percent per premium; its onshore product has a 1 percent DAC charge. A non-953(d) insurance company requires the client to pay a 1 percent excise tax per premium payment. Therefore, the client may enjoy a 0.3 percent advantage per premium by using a 953(d) company for the purchase.

In-kind premium. Some offshore insurance companies and jurisdictions will allow the policy owner to make premium payments in kind. This enables the client to avoid liquidating assets and having them become a portion of the cash value. This transfer of assets may trigger a taxable capital-gains event because technically there is a transfer of control from the client to the insurance company. However, the policy will require liquid assets to pay all loads and ongoing charges. The policy must meet the diversification requirements outlined in IRC § 817(h), which will prevent the transferred asset from representing more than 55 percent of the assets in the policy's separate account.

Managed-account minimum-premium threshold. Onshore, if a potential PPLI policy owner wishes to use a specific investment manager in an insurance company's policy, the client will have to commit approximately $8–$20 million to seed the separate account. This amount may be funded with premium payments over a three- to four-year period. Insurance companies are reluctant to acquiesce on the commitment amount because of the initial costs of establishing a separate account and the ongoing administrative expenses. This, of course, assumes that the insurance company is first willing to take on the due diligence and approve the investment option (see chapter 13).

Some offshore insurance companies will consider setting up a separate account for a substantially smaller premium commitment, but may charge a fee for establishing a new investment-adviser relationship.

The approval process for establishing a offshore separate account typically requires less time than its onshore counterpart. The offshore due diligence process should take no more than 60 days to complete, whereas the onshore approval may take three to six months.

Investment-management flexibility and access to offshore investments. All PPLI contracts, whether they're executed offshore or onshore, must adhere to U.S. tax laws, the investor-control doctrine, and the IRC § 817(h) diversification requirements (see chapter 12). A violation of these laws will result in the separate account's losing its tax-favored status, and the insurance contract will be lost, thereby subjecting the investment gain to ordinary income taxes.

Since the issuance of the two rulings released in July 2003 (Revenue Rulings 2003-91 and 2003-92), clients are somewhat reluctant to have PPLI cash values invested in anything other than insurance-dedicated funds. But some clients may choose to be aggressive and use alternative investments and managed accounts that are not insurance-dedicated.

Before these rulings were issued, clients were attracted to offshore PPLI primarily for its flexible investment management. Most offshore clients were choosing an investment adviser to manage the assets of the separate account. Some clients' investment advisers would allocate among several different hedge funds and fund managers. Others managed cash values that were invested in private-equity and publicly traded stock, which may have been contributed to the PPLI as an in-kind premium payment.

Some offshore companies still allow the use of such a managed account, but most onshore companies will not. One offshore company, for example, accepted private equity as a portion of the cash value on a client's 1035 exchange of another offshore policy, but this is unheard of in the onshore market.

Investment-management flexibility does have limits:

❏ The investment adviser must have sole and absolute investment discretion over the portfolio and exercise this discretion independently of the policy owner.

❏ There should be no prearrangement between the investment adviser and the policy owner regarding investment decisions to be made within the PPLI.

❏ The insurance company must have the final word in hiring or terminating investment advisers.

Non–U.S.-taxpaying, offshore insurance companies (that is, non-953(d) companies) often allow investment of PPLI cash values in passive foreign-investment companies (PCIF). PCIFs are not accessible through onshore PPLI.

Many hedge funds and fund of funds have been formed offshore to circumvent the problem of unrelated business taxable income (UBTI) for qualified plan assets. These funds are also typically available only through offshore PPLI.

Asset-protection planning. High-net-worth U.S. investors are well aware of how highly litigious our society is. Many of these individuals are fearful of losing assets in lawsuits pertaining to malpractice, accidents, homeowner's liability, director and officer liability.

Several asset-protection ownership entities are available for PPLI (see chapter 4). These include irrevocable trusts, limited liability companies, and family limited partnerships. These entities offer varying degrees of protection if established before an actual claim, so as not to be considered a fraudulent transfer. These entities tend to simply slow the creditor but not fully protect the assets.

In 1997, Alaska and Delaware passed legislation that allows a settlor to create an asset-protection trust for which the settlor is a beneficiary. This type of trust is commonly referred to as a *self-settled spendthrift trust* (see chapter 6). Both state statutes require the following:

❏ The trust must be irrevocable.

❑ A trustee in that state must administer the trust. Administration should include custody of assets and maintenance of records.

❑ The trust must contain a spendthrift provision.

❑ The trust must prohibit fraudulent conveyances for child support and tort claims occurring before the date of the trust transfer.

❑ The settlor is permitted to retain powers to veto a distribution from the trust, to have a testamentary special power of appointment, and to receive a discretionary distribution from the trustee.

The Alaska and Delaware self-settled trusts afford greater onshore asset protection than had been available under onshore trust law. However, it's still not known whether Alaska and Delaware may be required to accept adverse judgments in other states. Also, fraudulent transfers have a four-year statute of limitations in Alaska and Delaware. This means that fraudulent transfers that have been contested within four years of the date of transfer may be available to creditor judgments.

Onshore PPLI cash values are protected from creditors to varying degrees, depending on the laws of each state, situs of policy owner, and the designated beneficiaries. Some states, such as Arizona, Connecticut, Nevada, South Carolina, Wisconsin, Florida, Michigan, New Mexico, and Oklahoma, protect the entire cash value, provided there was no fraudulent intent in establishing the policy.

Offshore PPLI provides a U.S. investor additional asset protection from creditor claims not available with onshore policies (see chapter 4). The offshore jurisdictions of Bermuda and the Cayman Islands, for example, limit the risk of liability through the establishment of a PPLI ownership entity such as an asset-protection trust, international business corporation, limited liability company, or a family limited partnership.

Generally, offshore insurance products provide exceptional asset protection because a garnishment order or order of attachment issued by a U.S. court will have no legal consequences in various offshore jurisdictions. Therefore, if the PPLI policy is owned by a foreign entity, which is not subject to the jurisdiction of the U.S. court, an attachment order will have no effect on the cash value or death proceeds within that foreign jurisdiction. Keep in mind that the policies all comply with U.S. insurance law so the policy owner maintains regulatory protection.

Foreign asset-protection trusts are a valuable asset-protection device when established in a jurisdiction with laws that severely restrict the rights of creditors. The following are the most important factors in analyzing a foreign jurisdiction's asset-protection laws:

❑ Will the jurisdiction recognize U.S. claims?

❑ Will it require the suit to be brought within the foreign jurisdiction?

❏ Does it have a more lenient fraudulent-conveyance law than the U.S. does?

Other factors must be considered when selecting foreign trust situs:

❏ The situs should be in a nation that bases its trust law on the British common law system. These jurisdictions will have similar trust principles and a longstanding history of trust law.

❏ It's important that there are no adverse trust tax consequences.

❏ Trustee fees are generally high, so it's important to find the lowest available.

❏ Some foreign jurisdictions require disclosure of the beneficiaries of a trust, but most do not.

❏ It may be important to change the trust's situs; therefore, finding a jurisdiction that will allow you to quickly change is imperative.

When offshore PPLI is chosen as the more attractive situs, strong consideration should be given to the jurisdictional laws that control the PPLI policy and the insuring company. Insurance companies domiciled in Bermuda, the Cayman Islands, the Bahamas, and Guernsey have separate account legislation that protects PPLI assets from the general creditors of the insurance company. Also, death benefits payable at the death of the insured are distributed directly to the separate account and do not pass through the general account of the company.

Clearly, clients who rank asset protection as a high priority will want to purchase the PPLI policy offshore in a jurisdiction with the most favorable asset-protection laws. Keep in mind that the foreign jurisdiction of choice will not honor a U.S. court judgment, which necessitates litigation of the claim in the offshore jurisdiction. Litigation offshore may be very time consuming and is extremely expensive. Foreign jurisdictions have shorter statutes of limitations for fraudulent conveyances, typically two years or less; Delaware and Alaska have a four-year statute of limitations.

SEC regulation. The SEC does not regulate the sale and maintenance of offshore PPLI policies. But some offshore companies still require a signed disclosure agreement and a qualified-purchaser questionnaire.

Onshore PPLI is sold as a nonregistered security through a regulation D offering memorandum. A qualified-purchaser questionnaire must be completed and signed. Securities regulations generate company costs, which are passed through to the policy owner.

State approvals. Each state must preapprove the PPLI contract before the product may be marketed and sold in that state. Every state has its own nuances in the contractual language of the PPLI contract, requiring significant costs to gain the desired state approvals.

Offshore PPLI has no product-approval guidelines required by any regulatory body. The offshore company and the insurance adviser simply verify that the PPLI policy complies with U.S. tax law.

Offshore Disadvantages

Legal documentation. Purchasing PPLI offshore is nearly always more complex than purchasing it onshore. For example, an onshore product may be owned by the insured, much like any life insurance product. In that case, the insured names, say, a spouse, a child (or children), or the estate as beneficiary. Other than the insurance application and securities documentation provided by the insurance company, no other legal documents or fees are required to execute the policy.

An offshore PPLI transaction requires the selection of a jurisdiction and the formation of a trust or a company to be the policy owner in that jurisdiction. The desired level of asset-protection planning will dramatically affect the legal documentation and costs associated with the planning.

One client who completed an offshore transaction wanted to keep the legal documentation to a minimum and keep the annual maintenance costs as low as possible. The client established a British Virgin Island company to own the offshore PPLI. A Bermuda-based life insurance company with a U.S. parent issued the PPLI policy. The client was required to hire an offshore trust company to establish a mailing address and to file the forms necessary to maintain the BVI company's status. The client also had to open a foreign bank account to wire premium payments to the offshore insurance company. Although these steps may seem complex, the initial costs and the annual maintenance of the ownership structure are minimal.

IRS reporting requirements. Offshore insurance premiums must be paid from an offshore bank account. U.S. investors must report their ownership of the account and any offshore financial accounts using IRS Form TDF 90-22.1. PPLI is not within the offshore financial account or bank account classification domain and therefore is not subject to the offshore account-reporting requirements. The PPLI policy will not be identified on the policy owner's income tax return because the policy earnings are not subject to income tax reporting. If the offshore PPLI owner is an offshore company, IRS Form 5471 must also be filed.

The Adviser's Role in Offshore Transactions

Any individual or adviser can purchase a PPLI policy directly provided that a licensed insurance agent is available to issue the policy. Some advisers may be appropriately licensed; if not, the insurance company can stand in as the agent of record. The investor's or adviser's goal should not be to merely purchase a PPLI policy but rather to do so at the lowest cost with the best available investment options from the most able carrier and with the least amount of difficulty.

PPLI is not a solution that will be used repeatedly, so it's generally not efficient for an investor to acquire the knowledge to make the purchase on his own. Most people have better uses for their time. The efficient and effective deployment of PPLI requires the capabilities of a knowledgeable, experienced, and trusted insurance adviser. A lot can be gained by working with an adviser who has the requisite information, background, contacts, and creativity to get PPLI in place with as little effort as possible.

A high-net-worth investor's insurance adviser will perform the following services either during the execution phase or as part of ongoing monitoring:

❑ Insurance company due care with regard to capital issues, credit risk, reinsurance capacity, and commitment to the PPLI marketplace

❑ Marketing services including product analysis, pricing, and solicitation compliance

❑ Ongoing services including annual policy review, review of reinsurance treaties, and insurance company due care updates

Insurance Company Due Care

Capital issues. The regulatory capital requirements for an offshore insurance company are less onerous than for onshore insurance carriers. This is an advantage because the offshore carrier may have slightly better pricing, but it's also a disadvantage because the company has less capital to handle adverse circumstances and prevent insolvency. The insurance adviser should be thoroughly familiar with the amount and quality of the company's capital and surplus positions. The adviser must also evaluate whether the insurance company has ready access to capital via the equity markets, parent company infusions, and/or debt capacity.

Credit risk. An offshore company may have a parent company with good ratings, and the parent guarantees the contracts issued by its offshore subsidiary. The parent company's guarantee is often referred to as a cut-through agreement and is included in the policy contract.

Others will be rated by one or more of the major U.S. rating services. If the company does not have a rating, the role of the insurance adviser in the due care process becomes much more vital as a fill-in analyst to determine the capabilities of the carrier.

Even though the separate-account legislation protects the offshore

PPLI's cash values from the insurance company's creditors, the death benefit in excess of the cash value (net amount at risk) is subject to the claims of the general creditors of the insurance company. Therefore, the solvency of the insurance company is important in eventually receiving all the benefits due the policy owner.

Reinsurance. The worldwide reinsurance market for life insurance is shrinking because of consolidation and the impact of a few large death claims. Reinsurance capacity is paramount in the jumbo death-benefit transactions common in the high-net-worth market. The insurance adviser should be knowledgeable of the offshore companies and their respective reinsurance treaties and capacity limits. Going through the entire transaction only to find that the insurance company is unable to support the desired policy value would be a deep disappointment to everyone involved (see chapter 1).

Company commitment to PPLI. A good indicator of the depth and breadth of a company's commitment to this market is how much PPLI business the carrier has on its books. A way to test both past and present commitment is to ask these questions:

❑ What are the premium goals for the current year?
❑ What distribution system is in place to achieve the premium goals?

Unless the company provides precise answers to these questions, the insurance adviser should move on to another carrier.

Marketing Services

Product analysis and pricing. Offshore PPLI purchased by U.S. citizens must comply with U.S. tax law, namely, IRC §§ 7702 and 817(h) (see chapter 12). It's critical for the insurance adviser to test the proposed product for tax compliance with the expectation that the product has sufficient design flexibility to match the clients' objectives in these areas:

❑ Access to the cash values via policy loans
❑ Loan provisions permitting loans in the early policy years
❑ Contractual loan interest rates and interest crediting rates on the loan clearly identified to calculate the loan net cost to the policy owner. (Some products have a higher loan net cost during the first 10 policy years than they have after the first 10 years.)

Solicitation compliance. Typically, an insurance adviser purchases onshore life insurance as a result of a direct solicitation by an insurance company in the client's state of residency. What makes the offshore PPLI purchase cumbersome is that under state law, the insurance adviser may not solicit offshore products onshore. Therefore, after offshore suitability is determined, the client essentially makes a commitment to meet the insurance adviser offshore to formally begin the execution phase.

The legal adviser may give a client generic information concerning offshore PPLI, but actual sales illustration presentations and client education may take place only in the offshore jurisdiction. All of the steps that are part of the execution phase must occur offshore:

- ❑ Physical exams
- ❑ Completion and signing of an offshore trust or company to purchase and own the policy
- ❑ Establishment of an offshore account to hold funds for premium payments and other ongoing maintenance costs

These steps may be streamlined and can even be quite enjoyable for the client when properly orchestrated by an experienced offshore insurance adviser. For example, I recently met a prospective offshore PPLI client in Bermuda. A driver met him and his wife at the airport and drove them to their hotel in Hamilton, Bermuda. That evening we met and had dinner at a highly rated restaurant on the island. It gave us a chance for a social visit before getting business under way the next day.

The driver met us at the hotel at 8:45 a.m. the next morning and drove us to the doctor's office a few minutes away. The doctor ushered the client into the examination room immediately, and by 9:45 a.m. we had left the doctor's office and were on our way to the cardiologist's office for a stress test. En route the driver provided Danish and coffee for the client, who was hungry because he had to skip breakfast as a part of his medical exam regimen. By 11:00 a.m. we were sitting in the insurance company's conference room discussing offshore PPLI and reviewing specific sales illustrations. The insurance company provided a catered lunch. At 12:30 p.m., a representative of the insurance company called the client into the conference room and completed the inspection report. The rest of the early afternoon was spent making final decisions and completing the paperwork. We were finished by 2:30 p.m., and the client and his wife were off to explore the island.

Ongoing Services

Annual policy review. The offshore insurance adviser should provide in-force PPLI sales illustrations annually (see chapter 11). These illustrations should be based on the current cash value, with future values projected based on the client's anticipated investment rate and current policy charges.

Tax compliance must be reviewed for each premium payment to make sure the contract still meets the definition of life insurance. If the policy were designed as a non-MEC, it must be tested to verify that it's still in compliance (see chapter 11). Furthermore, some policy designs anticipate a death-benefit change in a particular year. The insurance adviser must be aware when these changes occur and communicate them to the client, when a change is desirable.

Review of reinsurance treaties and COI charges. Exceptional investment performance may increase the amount of death benefit, thereby increasing the need for additional reinsurance. The insurance adviser should periodically review the insurance company's reinsurance treaties to ensure that there is adequate insurance available to maintain the policy's favorable tax benefits. Also, these treaties determine the cost of insurance charges (see chapter 16), which are deducted monthly from the cash values. The lower the reinsurance cost, the lower the cost of insurance charges.

Insurance company due care update. Some offshore jurisdictions have minimal regulatory oversight. Therefore, the insurance adviser must continually update the due care analysis of the insurance company. The insurance company's ratings may have dropped because of poor investment performance or other factors. In other instances, a carrier's parent company may have sold its ownership stake, which may, in turn, affect the carrier's credit rating. Other considerations are changes in tax laws, which may cause the policy's current jurisdiction to be less favorable than others.

The Best Fit

Clients with following objectives and desires are favorable prospects for offshore PPLI:

- ❑ Asset-protection planning is of the utmost importance, and the client wishes to hold assets in a jurisdiction that provides the ultimate in creditor protection.
- ❑ The client is willing to make a minimum premium commitment of $5 million.
- ❑ The client wishes to choose an investment adviser to manage a separate account or the assets to be managed necessitate investment flexibility.
- ❑ The client is willing to make a substantial premium commitment and does not want to pay state premium tax or a higher DAC tax.
- ❑ The client wishes to pay a portion of the premiums in-kind.
- ❑ The client demands ultimate privacy.
- ❑ The client wishes to own assets offshore.
- ❑ The client wishes to have access to offshore investments.

The following client objectives and characteristics may lead a client to purchase onshore PPLI:

- ❏ The client is willing to allocate cash values in already approved and available investment choices, including insurance-dedicated hedge funds, fund of funds, and private equity.
- ❏ The client is uncomfortable with offshore jurisdictions.
- ❏ The client is willing to create an ownership entity in a state with a very low state premium tax.
- ❏ The client wishes to make a very large premium commitment and wants the cash values managed by the client's preferred investment adviser.
- ❏ The client wishes to purchase survivorship PPLI.
- ❏ The client is uncomfortable with the solicitation issues of an offshore policy and needs to fully analyze the transaction with the insurance adviser before making a commitment.
- ❏ The client does not want to incur additional legal fees and ongoing trustee fees.
- ❏ The client resides in a state that exempts all cash values from creditors and is willing to pay the state premium tax.

DECIDING BETWEEN offshore and onshore PPLI can be complicated, depending on the client's needs and preferences. Nonetheless, a well-executed policy is possible no matter what the circumstances. The complexity can be dramatically reduced by using legal and insurance advisers expert in both onshore and offshore jurisdictions, knowing that whichever path is chosen, a highly effective solution will be in place to meet the individual's or family's investment needs.

PART FOUR

SETTING UP SHOP

The hallmark of success for any new investment product is to move from a cottage industry to broad-based acceptance. In the affluent marketplace—which PPLI best serves—this hinges on the use of the product by large wealth-management organizations and highly influential investors, who operate as opinion makers to other investors. But the use of PPLI by such firms carries with it a unique set of challenges.

A wealth-management firm takes on increased exposure when its use of a new solution moves from a sampling of clients to a core strategy for all. For such an expansion to succeed, funda-mental activities must take place within the firm, such as aligning the organization, setting principles and policies for best practices, establishing educational programs, and conducting ongoing oversight.

Family offices represent not only a primary target market for PPLI but also an important proving ground for its effectiveness as a wealth-management tool. The family-office manager and the advisory team often move cautiously with new initiatives because of the complexities inherent in the family's structure, but also because the manager has a professional objective to introduce only the best, most fruitful solutions.

This section describes the challenges these organizations face in joining PPLI's vanguard and offers practical solutions for meeting those challenges.

CHAPTER 18

Making a Place in Private Banking

RICHARD BRINDISI

As a planning tool for private wealth management, private placement life insurance (PPLI) is becoming mainstream. The benefits of an institutional PPLI program can be enormous. PPLI can allow a private bank to strengthen its platform of asset-management and planning services, thereby attracting new, very sticky assets. And it will inoculate a private-banking client's assets against a competitive overture from a rival private bank, wirehouse, or insurance group. But the education, compliance, and execution challenges for a large-scale rollout of PPLI and annuities in a private-banking institution are quite different from those faced by a single investment-advisory firm or a specialized wealth-management operation—and more formidable.

A Natural Fit

When the phrase "PPLI program" is used, it almost always refers to an alternative investment portfolio (for example, hedge funds and private equity) and a PPLI policy. Insurance carriers are now providing investment platforms with up to 20 different fund of funds—a nice selection as long as the client likes one of the 20. To put this in perspective, there are more than 5,000 different hedge fund options in the marketplace. A choice of 20 funds may or may not suit the client's investment objective; and the client may not be able to discern the optimal choice of funds or fund mix (see chapters 8 and 9).

Often an asset allocator is added to the mix to avoid running afoul of the investor-control doctrine that was clarified by the IRS in Revenue Rulings 2003-91 and 2003-92 (see chapter 12). An asset allocator in this context is akin to the person unlucky enough to be first on the scene of an accident where someone needs medical help. It's likely that the Good Samaritan isn't a doctor, but under the circumstances, he will have to do. Asset allocators—attorneys, accountants, and insurance professionals are typically enlisted for the job—often are not technically competent to make investment and allocation decisions, but they're the only ones around when the client wants to execute the policy. Clearly, not enough thought is put into the asset allocator's qualifications. The occasion calls for sound investment analysis and the kind of advice a private banker, family-office investment manager, or other investment professional can provide. Going forward, the optimal plan for PPLI execution will include a large private bank or family office.

The idea of an institutional PPLI program is not new in the marketplace. But the actual execution of a fully integrated private placement program, where all relevant departments are aware of the program and its opportunities, is rare. It's common for a client to inquire whether PPLI is available from the institution and be told both yes and no, depending on which department receives the inquiry. When the client does obtain a PPLI policy, most of the time it's the result of a transaction that is outside the scope of the private banking or institutional relationship. These nonrecurring transactions are commonly referred to as "one-off transactions." One-off transactions involving PPLI are usually in conjunction with a third-party insurance group or insurer involved with an outside asset manager. Successfully completing a one-off transaction shouldn't be mistaken for the competency of delivering PPLI and annuities on a mass scale to the firm's suitable clients. Mistaking institutional one-off private placement transactions for an institutional rollout can lead to a number of consequences. The best are embarrassing; the worst can cause the loss of the client.

Telling a client the organization does not provide PPLI is at least an accurate answer—although one that reflects a lack of institutional integration and coordination of relevant departments for the delivery of PPLI and annuities. But is that answer ideal for the client's needs?

Getting an Act Together

Several institutions have considered the idea of a PPLI program sponsored by an internal department, such as the alternative investment arm or retail insurance division. The idea usually spawns further discussion within the department and, in many cases, across departments. The negative end results have been remarkably similar, though the causes may have differed widely. What are some of the reasons for this failure?

❑ Recognition that creating the program is a far larger task than the department's resources can support.

❑ Several competing departments are unwilling to share revenues for the greater benefit of the firm.

❑ A project manager is assigned who lacks the organizational authority and influence to champion the cause effectively.

How does this last scenario typically play out for a large private wealth manager? The executive committee will give the project manager the go-ahead to build the PPLI program. From there, the project manager has to:

❑ Negotiate with the various departments within the firm to coordinate roles

❑ Interface, negotiate, and integrate third-party insurance vendors

❑ Create marketing strategies

❑ Educate the sales force

❑ Provide support for private bankers at client meetings (these meetings will often include the client's counsel, accountant, and any other professional advisers)

❑ Design policy specifications including the private placement memorandum

❑ Coordinate jurisdiction selection

❑ Coordinate policy execution and underwriting

❑ Provide in-force policy support, which may include policy investment diversification monitoring

Almost invariably, the project manager ends up having to propose that the project become his or her full-time job. But the project manager's functional manager is usually unwilling to spare the person. Furthermore, the program will likely require additional resources to grow, which, by the way, is the most common of the reasons mentioned above for PPLI's failure to become a mainstream private-banking tool. Whatever new resources may be forthcoming, the business plan will inevitably end up as a political, territorial football that never gets anywhere near a goal line.

Can PPLI be delivered short of a chief executive mandate? Definitely. Is it worth undertaking? Absolutely. The tangible and intangible benefits of having a well-coordinated PPLI program far outweigh the time and expense of setting up the program.

PPLI's Role in the Institution

One of the most important steps in creating a PPLI program is to determine what the institution wants to accomplish by having one. PPLI and annuities can be used in a number of ways and benefit several departments within the institution. Of course, applications that will be very useful to one department may be wholly irrelevant to another. For instance, the financial-planning arm may see PPLI as a wonderful estate-planning integration tool, whereas an alternative-investment department may see PPLI as an opportunity to gain tax-deferred growth for the department's hedge fund, private-equity, and venture capital offerings. A solid private placement program will be able to serve both goals, as well as others, in a fashion that leads the public to view the institution as a well-organized service provider capable of handling every facet of a client relationship.

Many departments within a private-banking institution can benefit from a PPLI program—the traditional asset-management department, alternative investments, structured products, financial planning, trust, lending, broker-dealer, investment banking, marketing, and the department responsible for handling retail insurance products. Here's how.

Traditional asset management. This department is responsible for in-house asset management as well as for conducting due diligence on traditional, long-only investment managers in various asset categories such as equities (growth, value, equity income, etc.) and fixed-income securities (government bonds, high-quality and high-yield bonds, preferred stock, REITs, etc.). PPLI's benefits to this department are fairly obvious since PPLI and annuities are designed to use these asset-management services within the insurance carrier's separate account. To determine whether an investment's tax efficiency is suitable for PPLI, both the investment's return and its resulting tax rate must be calculated together. An asset with high returns at a 15 percent tax rate benefits greatly from PPLI's tax deferral. That's because many of these asset managers manage qualified plan assets and do so in a way that results in far greater turnover of portfolio assets because there are no tax consequences. When designing a private placement policy, the planning team should be careful to use the asset managers whose investments result in the greatest tax burden on the client—based on both the historical return achieved by the manager and the mix of ordinary and capital gains taxes.

Alternative investments. This department is responsible for conducting due diligence on numerous private investments (hedge funds, hedge funds of funds, private equity, and venture capital) that are hard to understand, hard to obtain quality due diligence information on, sometimes hard to value, and which create an unusually large tax burden (compared with traditional long-only investments). What's more, the spectacular failures of a handful of hedge funds and the SEC Regulation D solicitation restrictions (see chapter 13) make alternative investments hard to market. PPLI and annuities offer both quantitative and qualitative reasons for investing in alternative assets. First, they mitigate the tax burden on the growth of these investments. An owner of a properly structured PPLI policy may never pay taxes on the growth of the investments within the policy. Furthermore, most insurers that offer PPLI and annuities put either the funds themselves or the alternative-investment department conducting institutional due diligence under their own due-diligence microscope. The insurance company's scrutiny—an added layer of due diligence—can aid marketing efforts by offering a greater sense of security to potential clients and their personal advisers.

Structured products. The structured-product department handles exotic investments that are built contractually. Examples of these products are prepaid variable forwards, SWAPs, collars, private note structures.. What's exciting about this department is that it can turn ideas into reality in the sense that, assuming the numbers work out, an investment can be built with identified characteristics that specifically suit a selected client's needs. Since this department exists within a private bank, the private banker (who usually becomes the asset allocator for a private placement policy) can design a structured product to accomplish a specific goal in the overall investment portfolio of the policy. The structured product department can also provide funding for private placement policies by providing products that convert an otherwise illiquid position into investment cash.

Financial planning. The financial-planning department is arguably the most important department within a private bank in terms of how to get the largest "share of wallet" for each client. A solid financial-planning department can mean the difference between whether the private banker pushes products or develops a plan that's fulfilled by the bank's product line. Surprisingly, financial-planning departments are underfunded within most private-banking institutions because they're generally not profit centers, serving instead a vital support role, with revenues coming into the firm from the various product centers. This lack of revenue makes it difficult for the heads of financial-planning departments to make a case for certain needed resources unless there is an internal crediting system in place that can allow the department to track how many assets have been acquired as a result of their efforts.

Financial-planning departments can be constructed to cover a wide range of topics. In the United States, the driving issue on which a financial plan is built is the estate- and gift-tax objectives of the clients. Try comparing the difference in wealth lost from the failure to properly manage taxes on investment income to the amounts lost because of failure to properly manage estate-tax liability at the most punitive estate- and gift-tax rates (55 percent). In many cases, greater wealth is lost from the failure to manage income taxes than from poorly managed estate taxes. But let's assume an equal amount of wealth is lost from both. That means that most of the spending on financial-planning resources is devoted to fixing 50 percent of the client's tax problem. To see why such shortsightedness rules, examine the cause. Estate- and gift-tax planning is done through the use of legal constructs such as trusts, partnerships, sales, private notes, life insurance, and other tools that must be put together like building blocks to achieve the appropriate outcome for a particular client. It's the province of attorneys. Income tax planning is generally accomplished through accounting techniques such as increasing deductions and credits and/or reducing taxable income. It is the province of accountants.

The financial-planning industry, and by extension the investment community, have built their businesses on the ability to use the various available legal tools to mitigate the estate tax. This makes sense because, with the exception of municipal bonds and certain index-linked notes, which don't offer much in the way of investment flexibility, there are no tools available to help investors manage the income taxes created by the growth of their investments.

PPLI and annuities have now come on the scene as tools that provide investment flexibility while managing the income tax burden created by the growth of the investments. They present an enormous opportunity for financial-planning departments (and by extension the entire institution) that are willing to make the investment to build the capabilities to properly integrate this income tax management tool into estate and gift-tax planning.

Trust departments. Trusts are separate, tax-paying, legal entities. Several different types of trusts can accomplish many different functions (see chapter 6). Private placement life insurance and annuities can turbo-charge the growth of a trust in several ways. Trust departments that incorporate PPLI planning can recognize significant benefits in the form of reducing taxes on distributions to beneficiaries, enlarging distributions to charitable beneficiaries, increasing control over income distributions, and extending the length of a trust's existence. The ultimate result will be more satisfied clients and the chance to attract additional trust assets. Significant benefits also follow from combining trusts and insurance for international clients.

Lending department. Many private banks have lending capabilities. PPLI can create significant lending opportunities for this department because many policies are funded using premium financing. Premium-financing opportunities are numerous because assets that are otherwise illiquid can be collateralized in exchange for cash that would fund a policy, thereby diversifying the client's assets without having to sell and realize a taxable event. In some cases, a lender will collateralize the policy, which requires far less additional collateral. The exciting aspect of this type of business is that loan programs of this sort typically involve a minimum of $5 million, with several in the $30–50 million range.

Broker-dealer. Part of the attractiveness of PPLI and annuities is the cost efficiencies involved in the implementation and ongoing administration of the policies. But even though there are low margins in private placement policies, the size of the policies creates considerable revenues that pass through the various broker-dealers of the parties involved.

Investment banking. Investment banks use PPLI to transfer wealth to business owners while lowering the selling price of the business to a buyer. PPLI techniques are also particularly useful when the purchasing company retains the seller for a time in a consulting position to ensure continuity. The challenge for the institution is to get the investment bankers to realize PPLI opportunities as a part of their normal course of business. Anything that detracts attention from the transaction at hand tends to be very unpopular, but investment bankers are some of the most intelligent and creative minds in the financial world. Once PPLI's advantages are grasped, the potential for new applications is very high.

Marketing. Marketing in this context refers to the sales force that interfaces with the clients of the firm. Every new technique that involves the use of PPLI and annuities provides a new market for the sales force and a new opportunity for them to contact their existing clients. PPLI policies have not yet substantially penetrated the private-banking community, so the first movers among private bankers can capture significant new assets by marketing the firm's private placement capabilities.

Retail insurance department. Many times during an analysis of whether a PPLI policy is suitable for a particular client, the client's situation makes it clear that a retail insurance policy is a better fit. The reasons for this can vary. A client may want certain guarantees from a policy, such as guaranteed crediting rates from the policy investments, which are common with a general-account insurance product but do not exist in PPLI. Or the amount of premium desired may not reach the minimum levels necessary for PPLI. In any event, these circumstances can result in significant retail insurance sales. The PPLI and annuity market is quite different from the retail life insurance and annuity market, so the two not only can coexist but they can also mutually benefit each other.

Private bankers that have clients with a net worth exceeding $10 million should consider analyzing PPLI's benefits, if for no other reason than to protect the client relationship from competitors' broaching. Financial institutions that serve clients with more than $10 million in net worth should have the ability to do a PPLI analysis as part of the comprehensive planning package. The competency to deliver product goes hand-in-hand with the PPLI analysis, clearly showing a private banker's ability to meet client needs.

Execution Considerations

Any institution launching a PPLI program has to take into consideration compliance, tax, and legal support, and insurance licensing. The solicitation of PPLI is governed under SEC Regulation D, which prohibits solicitation to anyone who is not an accredited investor (having $1 million in net worth or "a natural person with income exceeding $200,000 in each of the two most recent years or joint income with a spouse exceeding $300,000 for those years and a reasonable expectation of the same income level in the current year"). The regulation also prohibits mass advertising, among other forms of solicitation. That makes a private banker a natural conduit to introduce PPLI to suitable clients.

Most financial institutions, while offering tax and financial planning advice, make it a point not to practice law. Therefore, PPLI clients are encouraged to consult with their own legal counsel regarding the tax aspects of their overall plan. That does not mean that the financial institution's representatives should passively stand by while this occurs. They should obtain the client's permission to speak with the attorney and provide a clear picture of why PPLI was recommended. This can be enormously helpful to legal counsel and will greatly reduce the completion time.

A PPLI program within a financial institution requires both initial and ongoing educational support for its private bankers and financial-planning professionals. PPLI is an odd duck; its broad application concepts are fairly simple, but the details of execution are complex. A practitioner needs to understand how much information to convey to identify the proper clients without presenting so much detail that PPLI seems daunting. As potential clients are identified, ongoing education, usually on a case-by-case basis, will crystallize the issues. The goal is to give practitioners the tools to move cases forward themselves before calling in the advanced-planning team. The advanced-planning team, or the person responsible for the PPLI program, will be needed to make sure the case is complete for presentation to the insurance company. Every insurance carrier has its own special rules and requirements for PPLI. Presenting the case properly can save significant time getting it completed and may, in some cases, be the difference between success and failure.

Unlike other, one-size-fits-all estate-planning tools that can be provided turnkey by law firms, PPLI can take many forms and involves input from several parties with different areas of expertise. This is a key difficulty for many institutions that would like to provide a PPLI option. An institution that wants the capability to provide this type of service will need to hire at least one full-time employee to handle the case flow. This employee will need to have knowledge of (1) advanced tax-planning techniques used by wealthy clients, (2) financial institutions and the various departments that are critical to a well-functioning PPLI program, and (3) how insurance companies run their PPLI departments.

Insurance company PPLI departments are diverse and continually evolving. Knowing a particular insurer's stance on an issue is critical to delivering the proper PPLI policy to the client. Given the scarcity of employees this knowledgeable, an institution may be inclined to outsource the position. If outsourcing is chosen, there are several issues that must be resolved to ensure that the private-banking relationships are protected. A thorough due diligence analysis would consider the following:

Several PPLI providers also have asset-management capabilities or relationships. This may or may not be obvious. Some insurance providers readily admit that they provide wealth-management services; others may have ownership interests in an asset manager that bears another name or have a concealed revenue-sharing agreement with an asset manager. This creates a conflict of interest that cannot be ignored. Even if this conflict is candidly addressed in the contract, the fact that it even exists will not sit well with the bankers who will be bringing their clients to the table. The program could suffer greatly as a result.

The ideal partner would be an entity that derives zero compensation from asset management and will share revenues in such a fashion as to align the financial interests of the outsourcing partner and the financial institution. These entities may exist as a division of another financial institution that's willing to put in the requisite firewalls and other confidentiality provisions to deliver service to the institutional marketplace. This will give the private banker the comfort of knowing that his or her asset-management relationship is safe.

Most private banks have clients outside the United States. A PPLI outsourcing partner should be able to plan and execute both domestic and international policies. This is easier said than done. The insurance regulators within the United States are extremely sensitive about a licensed domestic insurance provider soliciting nondomestic business to clients within the United States. Therefore, the outsourcing partner needs to be able to provide the name of a separate international entity for client referrals, such as an offshore subsidiary, if an offshore policy may be desirable (see chapter 17). One preliminary question that will indicate whether an outsourcing partner has a separate offshore entity is to ask where international payments are sent. Most international insurers will not send funds into the United States for business produced internationally. To get around this, some producers will simply set up a bank account rather than set up a legitimate business entity. If a legitimate business entity exists, ask whether it has a representative other than the person doing business in the United States. This should shed some light on the legitimacy of the operation.

A good outsourcing partner will have experience working through the issues that arise from the compartmentalization of a large private bank. Having done one-off transactions within private banks does not come close to what's required to set up a program within an institution. The last thing an institution wants is to have an outsourcing partner abandon the program because it can't navigate the institutional bureaucracy that will inevitably arise. Quality outsourcing partners exist in the PPLI marketplace. The key is to ask the right questions to separate the legitimate contenders from those that, despite a lot of rhetoric, haven't produced any business.

PPLI OFFERS A PLATFORM that enables a private-banking organization to not only offer broader solutions to a client's investment, tax, and planning needs but also to deepen the client relationship. The long-term nature of PPLI assets lends itself to multigenerational planning and relationships. Consequently, a private bank needs to recognize that PPLI is one of the few investment solutions that links generations. The long-term value of the policy may far exceed that of any other existing investment product.

CHAPTER 19

The Family Office
A Perfect Fit

KIRK LOURY AND MARK WATSON

T he most attractive market for private placement life insurance (PPLI) is the family office. These businesses are established by families with a net worth of $100 million or more to direct investments and monitor a wide range of financial and personal needs. Although setting up a family office may displace the fees and expenses associated with managing a large asset base, a family office's most important functions are to preserve wealth for younger generations and to make certain that decisions made in the family's name uphold the first generation's beliefs and principles.

To those ends, a family office's primary purpose is investment planning and wealth management. This may include managing the family's various portfolios, providing financial and tax-planning services for each family member, executing and maintaining the array of family trusts, and screening and managing service providers. Other family offices extend their services to include management of lifestyle needs (concierge services), financial education, and philanthropic endeavors. Essentially, a family office is a customized entity devoted to providing whatever services the founding family deems appropriate.

Since the mid-1990s, firms called multifamily office (MFO) organizations have formed to deliver family-office services to multiple families, each with a minimum of $20 million in net worth. Often, an MFO originates as a single-family office that chooses to expand by bringing in other families with similar wealth, objectives, and interests. Other firms have been established to offer family-office services in order to gain an edge in the extremely competitive wealth-management industry. For the superaffluent market in general, the opportunity to acquire services of all types through what is essentially a buying cooperative is very cost-effective and practical. Even in the economic stratosphere, much is gained by sharing burdens.

Serving the Family: The PPLI Evaluation

PPLI essentially is made up of a portfolio of alternative investments (see chapter 8) and an insurance policy. The death benefit, while a critical wealth-preservation asset, is generally minimized to the extent the applicable law allows. On the one hand, the selected mix of hedge funds and venture capital investments used to construct the PPLI portfolio represents an area in which a family office often has extensive experience. On the other hand, navigating the nuances of insurance companies, applications, and underwriting is beyond the typical family office's expertise or interest. Consequently, executing a successful PPLI evaluation hinges much more on the office's gaining critical insurance knowledge. Then, the in-force policy or policies are married to the family office's investment expertise to enable PPLI's wealth-creating engine.

A PPLI evaluation has five stages:
- ❑ Initial assessment
- ❑ Adding PPLI expertise to the advisory team
- ❑ Adviser integration
- ❑ Planning integration
- ❑ Monitoring and reporting

Stage One: Initial Assessment

Other chapters have provided details on PPLI's use in tax management, asset protection, trust administration, estate planning, and executive benefits. Every family office the world over has a need for services in most of these areas. The challenge for the family-office manager rests not in PPLI's applicability but in introducing an unfamiliar investment vehicle, much less an insurance product, in the face of day-to-day inertia. Understandably, the troubling past experiences with insurance companies cause many family offices and their advisers to turn and run when presented with the notion of "the greatest insurance program around" (see chapter 1). PPLI requires the manager to take leadership of the new product and definitively match the family's needs to PPLI's structural advantages. Indeed, other chapters in this book provide the context necessary to make this objective assessment without any sales pressure from PPLI's various constituencies (for example, insurance advisers, insurance companies, or investment managers).

Assuming that PPLI offers one or several solutions to some of the family's needs, the best way to move forward from the generic evaluation is to identify the key components that require family-specific answers. For example, at Asset Management Advisers, a multifamily office affiliate of SunTrust Banks, these variables include:

- ❏ Income tax planning
- ❏ Investment time horizon
- ❏ Investment options
- ❏ Investment risk
- ❏ Minimum premium requirement
- ❏ Policy charges
- ❏ The insured's life
- ❏ Policy ownership/estate planning
- ❏ Domestic versus foreign insurance policy
- ❏ Carrier ratings and qualifications

For many of these components, the answers appropriate to a specific family's situation can be easily determined from the existing trust, estate, tax, and investment plans. The most efficient process will be for the family-office manager to assemble a bid sheet that includes the family's profile; a needs inventory applicable to PPLI; summaries of existing tax, trust, and estate structures; and expectations regarding the evaluation process such as the decision time frame, confidentiality requirements, communication forms, communication frequency, and compensation parameters.

Stage Two: Adding PPLI Expertise to the Advisory Team

PPLI is a powerful and flexible investment tool, but it does not typically warrant the addition of in-house expertise except in the case of large MFOs. For most single-family offices, this would be a little-used resource once the policy was executed. As with trusts and estate plans, once the front-end work has been done, the task moves to maintenance, with periodic evaluations. These check-ups would address revisions to the family's mission statement and attendant objectives; new or revised laws and regulations; and changing needs as a result of marriage, divorce, births, and/or changes in physical health. Family offices that pride themselves on complete self-sufficiency would do best to assign the in-house trust or tax counsel the task of gaining comprehensive PPLI expertise. Most family offices, though, will supplement the advisory team by engaging an external insurance adviser.

With the bid sheet completed, the family-office manager can determine the appropriate PPLI expert to hire. Assembling a list of suitable candidates is a two-pronged process. First, the family-office manager can have the family's accounting and trust/estate advisers engage their respective networks for referrals. This is obviously the best resource because of its built-in filtering. Few advisers would risk their professional reputations by offering less than top-caliber candidates.

The second source for gathering adviser candidates is from PPLI insurance companies. Any insurance company will gladly provide a list of insurance advisers offering the carrier's PPLI policy. Keep in mind that it's best to go to the top three or four insurance companies to get the largest possible list. Culling this list is no different from selecting any adviser—with one caveat. The family-office manager must make an effort not to be too impressed with insurance advisers who are able to tout intricate details about insurance companies and their policy features. Expertise is obviously a precondition to being hired, but it's not something that should carry too much weight. Any PPLI insurance adviser with references and a client base will be knowledgeable in these areas:

- ❑ PPLI tax, asset protection, trust, and estate applications
- ❑ Investment relationships
- ❑ Portfolio construction
- ❑ Insurance company choices
- ❑ Underwriting guidelines
- ❑ Policy execution

If PPLI expertise is a given among advisers, then what are the definitive criteria that the family-office manager can use to separate the good advisers from the best? The following three criteria will winnow the list:

Fee-based revenue stream. A successful PPLI execution is not an off-the-shelf project but one that is shaped to an individual's or family's particular circumstances. Not surprisingly, the candidates best able to customize PPLI solutions are those that have significant experience. The best indicator of that experience is the percentage of revenue the candidate receives from fees versus commissions. Traditional, commission-focused agents who occasionally sell PPLI will not have a significant fee-based revenue component, whereas those that have built substantive PPLI businesses will have significant fee-based revenues. Buyers are attracted to the fee-based model for financial products because the seller's reward is tied to the success of the solution. In other words, there is an alignment of interests.

Broad geographic presence. Insurance companies have long made the agent–policy owner relationship a local one, yet proximity is largely irrelevant for PPLI. Again, the burst of activity that accompanies the initiation and execution of a policy wanes dramatically once the policy is in force. Ongoing communication and reporting is done electronically, largely eliminating the need for face-to-face meetings other than for periodic reevaluations. In any case, an insurance adviser committed to PPLI and the family-office market must have a national focus simply because of the relatively small number of family offices nationwide. "Have PPLI expertise, will travel" is the way it works.

Education and communication. Added value comes when the PPLI adviser's leadership saves time, effort, money, and aggravation as he or she filters the variables to fit the family's unique circumstances. This value shows itself through the clear and precise information provided as well as through the creative thinking and problem-solving skills that come from experience. Unfortunately, this screening is largely subjective in that the family-office manager must assess an adviser candidate's ability to be an effective PPLI educator/communicator for this particular family's decision makers and advisers.

Ultimately, selecting a PPLI adviser means being able to identify a solid mix of competence, chemistry, and communication. These three Cs apply to all adviser relationships, but for PPLI, the educational intensity and high customization required call for a professional who can perform his or her duties immediately, without the customary warm-up phase typical of more traditional relationships.

Stage Three: Adviser Integration

A competent PPLI adviser has the knowledge and skills necessary to demonstrate PPLI's importance to family decision makers and their advisory team. Given the negative perceptions that many people have of insurance solutions, a kick-off meeting is suggested that will allow the PPLI adviser to demonstrate how PPLI will support and not supplant the other advisers' efforts. The insurance adviser can get the entire team and family's attention merely by illustrating how quickly PPLI's portfolio can grow to become a sizable component of the family's wealth. Given this platform, emphasis should quickly shift to a presentation of the implementation plan. An effective implementation plan will demonstrate that PPLI's complexity largely dissipates once key variables are identified, such as an offshore/onshore policy, the carrier, and the trust/estate role.

Once the preamble to the process is completed, the family-office manager must determine whether PPLI fits best in the domain of the investment team or the trust and estate team. Traditionally, the trust/estate attorney would take the lead. These days, the investment team is best suited to comprehend the alternative investments in the PPLI portfolio as well as how PPLI's wealth accumulation affects the family's overall investment program.

Stage Four: Planning Integration

PPLI's role as a vital tool supporting the family's long-term wealth planning typically moves through four application levels, ranging from the customary to the unusual.

- ❑ *Level one.* PPLI is integrated into the tax-management program to generate high tax efficiency for investments generating ordinary income, such as hedge funds, or producing high returns but at low relative tax rates, such as venture capital (see chapter 8).
- ❑ *Level two.* PPLI provides an income tax–free death benefit as part of an irrevocable trust (see chapter 5 and 6).
- ❑ *Level three.* PPLI provides efficient mechanisms for the family office's deferred compensation, employee benefits, and key man insurance planning (see chapter 7).
- ❑ *Level four.* PPLI supports more unique family needs such as prenuptial arrangements and immigration planning.

Of course, the manner in which these levels are incorporated is a wholly customized process. The family-office manager must emphasize to the advisory team that PPLI is a tool, and for the vast majority of family offices, it will be unnecessary to uproot pre-existing plans to accommodate PPLI. In other words, it should be viewed as a round peg to fit into the round holes in the tax-management, trust, estate, and executive benefit plans.

The implementation horizon can be fairly short as long as the manager establishes the momentum to promote sufficient understanding of PPLI among the family members and the advisory team. Having a common understanding and language provides a platform for the advisory team to revisit the various wealth plans and evaluate whether PPLI is a more effective tool, in whole or in part, than other techniques.

For family offices where the management team is on an incentive plan, a lever that the manager can pull to generate the motivation for an evaluation is to illustrate the economic advantages PPLI achieves through its tax-management applications (level one). The manager would do well to point out that PPLI's economic benefits accrue to the family's wealth plan (and the management team's personal incentive) almost immediately. PPLI structured as a non-MEC (see chapter 11) gives the concept of insurance a new face. The financial benefits of insurance no longer need to be inextricably linked with the death of a family member. In fact, the compounding of the tax savings from high-return asset classes such as hedge funds and venture capital has the potential to generate wealth at a rate far faster than any other investment vehicle. And this wealth is accessible through loans and withdrawals, making the increase in wealth a tangible benefit for the living. For the vast majority of family offices, this single benefit makes PPLI an essential wealth-planning tool.

Once this implementation momentum is established, the manager can task the advisory team with a general assessment of PPLI's use for other needs that fall within the other application levels. The number of application levels that PPLI penetrates is not the main point. First and foremost, the manager puts in place an educational platform and the incentive to revisit existing planning structures. More often than not, these structures become stale as the family's needs evolve. PPLI gives the manager the economic incentive to take the time and energy to update the wealth-planning process and to report to the family that the most effective wealth-building tools and techniques have been evaluated and appropriately deployed.

Stage Five: Monitoring and Reporting

Unlike most other life insurance products, whose economic benefit lies dormant until the policy owner dies, PPLI is an active investment tool. Because of this, there are three key areas that the family-office manager should review periodically.

Portfolio construction. The investment team can review the PPLI investment options as frequently as the family's other portfolio investments. The first review stage assesses the relative performance of the investment selections in relation to their respective objectives. The portfolio underlying the PPLI policy should not be treated any differently than the overall portfolio. At the second review stage, the insurance adviser reports to the family-office manager on the new insurance-dedicated funds (see chapter 14) that have been added to the insurance company's roster as well as those that have been added across all insurance companies in the PPLI segment. Any new investment option on the insurance company's platform that will add incremental value compared to an existing choice can be substituted as a tax-free transaction.

If a desired investment option is not offered as part of the insurance company's platform, the adviser can request that the company conduct a due diligence review (see chapter 13) as a precursor to adding the option for an allocation within the policy. Insurance companies have minimum investment levels that the policy owner must meet before the company undertakes the due diligence process and lays in the administrative overhead, and the insurance adviser will consider two factors before agreeing to such a request. The first question is whether the family's policy is large enough by itself to generate the required critical mass to establish a fund on a carrier's platform. The second question is whether the adviser has other families that own the insurance company's policies, and if so, can these other policies also reallocate a portion of the cash value to achieve the minimum investment necessary.

Portfolio integration. As discussed in chapter 8, the tax-free compounding of high-return asset classes such as hedge funds and venture capital has the potential of producing wealth that outstrips conventional portfolios. The PPLI portfolio is a key component of the family's overall investment program, and its potential as a single source for fulfilling the family's wealth creation investment objective may allow the family's investment team to reduce the risk exposure of the overall portfolio. In effect, the larger that PPLI's cash value becomes relative to the family's wealth, the more flexibility is gained in allocating the assets of the overall portfolio.

Policy cost effectiveness. An annual policy review must be added to the monitoring schedule when traditional PPLI policies are used. Although PPLI requires little maintenance, this review will serve the family well in keeping the policy's costs in line with its economic and death benefits (see chapter 11). If portfolio performance necessitates an increase in the insurance charges, the family's insurance adviser may determine that it's worthwhile to rebid the policy with various insurance carriers for a possible Rule 1035 exchange. The main stipulations of such an exchange are that the person insured and the amount of insurance must stay the same and a new underwriting must be done. Also any outstanding loans must be replicated in the new policy or the amount reduced by an unduplicated loan will be taxable.

PPLI IS A TOOL that effectively addresses many key needs of a wealthy family and the needs of younger generations. Moreover, the nature of a family office easily accommodates PPLI's premium requirements. But there are two caveats. First, PPLI requires a burst of activity leading up to and including its execution, although maintenance thereafter is relatively modest. Second, particularly in the family-office market, PPLI is a customized solution that requires a licensed insurance adviser with highly specialized knowledge.

These two requirements make it more cost-effective for a single-family office to retain the services of an outside insurance adviser, since ongoing maintenance of a PPLI program is periodic and not rigorous. For an MFO, it does make sense to hire and/or retain dedicated PPLI expertise, because of its built-in market for PPLI solutions.

Overall, PPLI's distinct advantages should compel virtually every family office to take a receptive look at the solutions PPLI can offer for a family's mid- and long-term investment, trust, and estate-planning needs.

Continuing Education Exam

EARN TWELVE HOURS of continuing-education credit by passing the following exam at www.bloomberg.com/ce, and entering code **17P33LKL**. All the material covered has been previewed by the CFP Board of Standards.

ONE: An Introduction to PPLI
1. Which of the following is *not* a characteristic of permanent life insurance?
a.   Tax-free access of the underlying portfolio
b.   Protection from creditors in all 50 states
c.   Income tax–free death benefits
d.   The ability to have more than one life represented in the policy

TWO: Risk Management: Redefining Safe Harbors
2.   **Personal risk management focuses on minimizing controllable risks through prevention programs, insurance products, and self-insurance.**
a.   True
b.   False

THREE: Tax Management: Building Wealth, Reducing Taxes
3. **Tax-efficient investing considers each of these taxes *except:***
a.   Income taxes
b.   Capital gains taxes
c.   Property taxes
d.   Estate taxes

FOUR: Asset Protection: Riches Out of Reach
4.   **The public policy reasoning behind asset protection through life insurance is that:**
a.   It keeps the family of a deceased person from being a societal burden
b.   The assets are actually owned by the insurance company
c.   It's a competitive response to offshore investing
d.   All of the above

FIVE: Estate Planning: When Insurance Tames Taxes

5. PPLI can be used for the following estate-planning applications:
a. Replace wealth lost through premature death
b. Accumulate wealth tax deferred
c. Transfer wealth without estate taxes
d. Pay estate settlement costs
e. All of the above

SIX: Trust Administration: The Domestic Advantage

6. A dynasty trust includes both the present and future beneficiaries of an estate.
a. True
b. False

SEVEN: Executive Benefits: The Plan That Pays Its Way

7. Which of the following statements are true of a nonqualified deferred compensation plan?
a. Assets belong to the employee
b. The employer does not receive an immediate tax deduction for contributions
c. Benefits paid to the employee are taxable
d. a and c
e. b and c

EIGHT: Toward a More Powerful Portfolio

8. The formula used to determine the actual tax efficiency of an investment includes all of the following *except:*
a. Federal income taxes
b. State income taxes
c. Estate taxes
d. Dividend taxes
e. Rate of return

9. Which is *not* a key factor in selecting investments for the PPLI portfolio?
a. Historical returns
b. Standard deviation
c. Tax exposure
d. Low correlations
e. Competitive fees

NINE: Who's Afraid of Hedge Funds?

10. Since 1998, hedge fund managers have added value while mutual fund managers have subtracted value.

a. True

b. False

11. A potential hedge fund investor can detect overuse of leverage by:

a. Comparing average inflows of assets into the portfolio to peak inflows

b. Comparing quarterly returns for the past 12 months to those of the previous 24 months

c. Comparing the fund's historical volatility to the strategy's benchmark

d. Looking at the size of the fund's assets for the past 12 months

TEN: In Search of Skilled Investment Managers

12. Which of the following is *not* a component of manager attribution for hedge fund of fund managers?

a. Relative performance ranking to a broad market index

b. Allocation to hedge fund strategies

c. Selection of specific managers

d. Persistence of returns over time

13. The ability to judge a manager's relative performance to a benchmark is only possible over a long period of time.

a. True

b. False

ELEVEN: Policy Structure: The Good, the Bad, the Ugly

14. Which of the following characteristics do PPLI and retail VUL *not* share?

a. Mortality expectations

b. A medical underwriting exam must be passed

c. Sales materials must be approved by the NASD

d. The death benefit is a function of financial and medical underwriting

e. Premiums must be paid in cash

15. The two tests for determining the proper ratio of premium to death benefit are:

a. PDB and DBA

b. GPT and CVAT

c. CVDB and PTC

d. PPDB and PCV

TWELVE: Getting It Right: A Regulatory Overview

16. To qualify as life insurance, section 7702 requires that a policy comply with which of the following?
a. Be approved by appropriate state laws
b. Meet minimum death-benefit standards
c. Satisfy the cash value or the guideline premium test
d. a and c
e. b and c

17. Which of the following requirements are part of the investor-control provision?
a. The policyholder cannot tell the investment manager how to invest
b. The policyholder is able to select which investments to include
c. The insurance company retains control over the investments offered
d. The insurance company determines which investment firms manage the investment options
e. All of the above

18. The prudent man rule is the reason insurance companies usually require independent asset managers to represent that their funds or partnerships will be adequately diversified.
a. True
b. False

THIRTEEN: Investment Due Diligence: Beyond the Questionnaire

19. The greatest concern faced by insurance companies conducting due diligence on managers is:
a. How interesting the fund will be to potential policyholders
b. The uniqueness of the fund's strategy compared to other insurance companies' options
c. The difficulty of operating, monitoring, and reporting for the fund
d. The likelihood that a fund manager will fail

FOURTEEN: Creating and Administering an Insurance-Dedicated Fund

20. Which of the following should not be a concern for an investment manager who's considering setting up an insurance-dedicated fund (IDF)?
a. Restrictive nature of the IRS guidelines
b. Time and cost to put a plan together
c. Challenges in marketing to high-net-worth investors
d. Forming the fund to comply with insurance regulators

21. Which of the following is *not* one of the legal documents needed for an insurance-dedicated fund?
a. The private placement memorandum
b. The subscription documents
c. The insurance policy's investment addendum
d. The limited partnership agreement

22. Which statement about the 817(h) diversification rules is false?
a. No more than 60 percent of the assets can be in any one security
b. No more than 70 percent can be in any two securities
c. No more than 80 percent can be in any three securities
d. No more than 90 percent can be in any four securities

FIFTEEN: Underwriting the Policy

23. Which of the following statements about underwriting is false?
a. Underwriting standards vary from one insurance company to another
b. Simplified issue policies are lower in cost
c. Underwriting results are a major factor in the policy's cost
d. Mortality risk rates can vary from company to company

24. Which of the following is *not* true of the "select period" of an underwriting?
a. It's the period with the most current medical information
b. It lasts up to 10 years
c. It's the period in which the policyholder can select the policy before execution
d. It's the time wherein the policies' rates are least costly

SIXTEEN: Understanding and Comparing Costs

25. Which of the categories below is *not* associated with a PPLI policy's costs?
a. Federal deferred acquisition cost
b. State trust administration tax
c. State premium tax
d. Cost of insurance
e. Consulting fees

26. A PPLI policy's loan spread is the net interest charged by the insurance company to the policyholder.
a. True
b. False

SEVENTEEN: Jurisdiction: Home or Away?

27. An advantage of onshore PPLI compared to offshore PPLI is:
a. Costs are lower
b. Assets are more easily protected
c. Legal hurdles are fewer
d. Regulatory approval is less difficult

28. One advantage of offshore policies is that the need for the insurance company to secure reinsurance is eliminated.
a. True
b. False

EIGHTEEN: Making a Place in Private Banking

29. A wealth-management firm planning to introduce PPLI to its client base must consider which of the following items:
a. Compliance to regulations
b. Tax and legal support
c. Licensing for relationship managers
d. a and b
e. b and c
f. All of the above

NINETEEN: The Family Office: A Perfect Fit

30. The three factors to consider in selecting an insurance adviser to support a PPLI initiative are:
a. Percent of revenues from fees, broker-dealer affiliation, and local proximity
b. Percent of revenues from fees, broker-dealer affiliation, and client list
c. Percent of revenues from fees, educational expertise, and geographical coverage
d. Percent of revenues from fees, educational expertise, and offshore expertise

INDEX

ABOUT BLOOMBERG

Bloomberg L.P., founded in 1981, is a global information services, news, and media company. Headquartered in New York, the company has sales and news operations worldwide.

Bloomberg, serving customers on six continents, holds a unique position within the financial services industry by providing an unparalleled range of features in a single package known as the BLOOMBERG PROFESSIONAL® service. By addressing the demand for investment performance and efficiency through an exceptional combination of information, analytic, electronic trading, and Straight Through Processing tools, Bloomberg has built a worldwide customer base of corporations, issuers, financial intermediaries, and institutional investors.

BLOOMBERG NEWS®, founded in 1990, provides stories and columns on business, general news, politics, and sports to leading newspapers and magazines throughout the world. BLOOMBERG TELEVISION®, a 24-hour business and financial news network, is produced and distributed globally in seven different languages. BLOOMBERG RADIO℠ is an international radio network anchored by flagship station BLOOMBERG® 1130 (WBBR-AM) in New York.

In addition to the BLOOMBERG PRESS® line of books, Bloomberg publishes *BLOOMBERG MARKETS®* and *BLOOMBERG WEALTH MANAGER®*. To learn more about Bloomberg, call a sales representative at:

London:	+44-20-7330-7500
New York:	+1-212-318-2000
Tokyo:	+81-3-3201-8900

FOR IN-DEPTH MARKET INFORMATION and news, visit the Bloomberg website at **www.bloomberg.com,** which draws from the news and power of the BLOOMBERG PROFESSIONAL® service and Bloomberg's host of media products to provide high-quality news and information in multiple languages on stocks, bonds, currencies, and commodities.

Printed and bound by CPI Group (UK) Ltd, Croydon, CR0 4YY

16/04/2025

14658446-0005